D1005942

Viereck: Varieties of English in GB and Ireland

Between sending the manuscript to the publisher in mid-October 1983 and the publication of the bibliography in March 1984 the following additions/changes came to my notice:

Item No.

98 Bertz, Siegfried, "Der Dubliner Stadtdialekt. Eine synchronische Beschreibung der Struktur und Variabilität des heutigen Dubliner Englischen. Teil I: Phonologie." Diss. (= German Ph.D.) Freiburg 1975. Delete asterisk.

259a Fisiak, Jacek, "Middle English *-ong* > *-ung* revisited", *Studia Anglica Posnaniensia* 14 (1982):17-27.

259b ---, "Some problems in historical dialectology", *Studia Anglica Posnaniensia* 16 (1983):5-14. This is a revised version of "Isophones or isographs: a problem in historical dialectology", in John M. Anderson, ed., *Language Form and Language Variation. Papers dedicated to Angus McIntosh.* Amsterdam: Benjamins 1982:117-28.

259c ---, "English dialects in the fifteenth century: some observations concerning the shift of isoglosses", *Folia Linguistica Historica* 5,1 (1984).

259d ---, "Some remarks concerning the distribution of *(n)either* in Middle English in the 15th century", *Festschrift for A. Heinz.* Cracow 1984 [In Polish].

377a Hickey, Raymond, "The phonology of English loan-words in Inis Meáin Irish", *Ériu* 33 (1982):137-56.

418, 419 Titles of these two items to be reversed.

486 Leitner, Gerhard, *BBC English und der BBC. Geschichte und soziolinguistische Interpretation des Sprachgebrauchs in einem Massenmedium.* Linguistische Berichte. Papier Nr. 60. Wiesbaden 1979.

487a ---, "The social background of the language of radio", in Howard Davis and Paul Walton, eds., *Language, Image, Media.* Oxford: Blackwell 1983: 50-74.

504a Lorimer, W.L. (transl.), *The New Testament in Scots.* Edinburgh: Southside Publ. (distributor Canongate Publ.) 1983.

514 John Benjamins 1983.

571a ---, "Scottis, Inglis, Suddroun: Language labels and language attitudes", in R. Lyall and F. Riddy, eds., *Proceedings of the Third International Conference on Scottish Language and Literature.* Stirling: U. of Stirling Press 1981:52-70.*

625 Milroy, Lesley, "The effect of two interacting extra-linguistic variables on patterns of variation in urban vernacular speech", in David Sankoff and Henrietta Cedergren, eds., *Variation Omnibus.* Carbondale and Edmonton: Linguistic Research Inc. 1981:161-8. Delete asterisk.

671a ---, *Studies in Anglo-Cornish Phonology. Aspects of the History and Geography of English Pronunciation in Cornwall.* Redruth: Institute of Cornish Studies 1983.

676 The Mercier Press 1980, repr. 1983. Delete asterisk.

707 rev. and publ. under the title "On linguistic attitudes in a northern English village", *Vetenskap och Företagsledning. Essays in Economics and Management in Honour of Lars Wahlbeck.* Publications of the Swedish School of Economics and Business Administration 31 (1982), 381-406.

743a ---, "Fieldwork for the *Survey of Anglo-Welsh Dialects:* North Wales 1980-81", in Viereck 1984.

752a ---, "Who is really doing dialectology?", in David Crystal, ed., *Linguistic Controversies: Essays in Linguistic Theory and Practice in Honour of F.R. Palmer* . London: Edward Arnold 1982:192-208.

835a ---, "A short report on the Linguistic Minorities Project". London: Institute of Education 1983.

838a ---, "The English Dialect Survey's dictionary project", in Karl Hyldgaard-Jensen and Arne Zettersten, eds., *Proceedings of the Symposium on Lexicography September 1-2, 1982, at the University of Copenhagen. Germanistische Linguistik* 5-6/82 (1983): 73-85.

847 ---, *Good or Bad Scots? Attitudes to Optional Lexical and Grammatical Usages in Edinburgh.* Acta Universitatis Upsaliensis. Studia Anglistica Upsaliensia 48. Uppsala 1983.

853 in Hans Goebl, ed., *Dialectology.* Quantitative Linguistics 21. Bochum: N. Brockmeyer 1984:15-60.

931a Thomas, Alan R., "The English language in Wales", in Y. Matsumara, ed., *English around the World.* Tokyo: Kenkyusha 1983:137-93 [In Japanese].

933 ---, "Welsh English: a grammatical conspectus", in Viereck 1984.

964 The correct pagination is: 172-91.

1007 ---, "The data of the *Survey of English Dialects* computerised: Key and conventions", in Viereck 1984.

1058 *English World-Wide* (forthcoming).

Index (Additions)

A BIBLIOGRAPHY, 1965-1983

Varieties of English Around the World

General Editor:

Manfred Görlach
Anglistisches Seminar der Universität
Kettengasse 12
D-6900 HEIDELBERG
Germany

GENERAL SERIES
Volume 3

Wolfgang Viereck, Edgar Schneider and Manfred Görlach (comps.)
A Bibliography of Writings on Varieties of English, 1965-1983

A BIBLIOGRAPHY OF WRITINGS ON VARIETIES OF ENGLISH, 1965-1983

compiled by

Wolfgang Viereck, Edgar W. Schneider and Manfred Görlach

JOHN BENJAMINS PUBLISHING COMPANY
AMSTERDAM/PHILADELPHIA

1984

CIP-Data:

Viereck, Wolfgang

A bibliography of writings on varieties of English, 1965-1983 / comp. by Wolfgang Viereck, Edgar W. Schneider and Manfred Görlach. -
Amsterdam [etc.]: Benjamins. -
(Varieties of English around the world. General series; vol. 3)
With bibliogr., index.
ISBN 90-272-4861-3
SISO enge 837 UDC 802.0(01)
Subject headings: English linguistics; bibliographies.

Table of Contents

Prefatory Note

After the growth of English and American dialectology since the 1930's and the expansion of sociolinguistics since the 1960's, the study of 'world English' has emerged in recent years to join these other disciplines - a field to which the present series and the journal English World-Wide are devoted. This bibliography is intended to reflect what has been achieved in this area and to serve as a research tool for further investigations.

Much shorter versions of its three parts were pre-published as articles between 1979 and 1982, and they have now been revised, expanded, updated and combined in book form. Work on the bibliography was completed in September 1983, when the manuscript was sent to the publisher. We have of course attempted to achieve a certain degree of homogeneity with respect to the topics covered and the bibliographical conventions used, yet different subject matters quite naturally entail differences in the selection of items. Thus, each of the three parts is preceded by a preface which explains the procedures followed, and each of the authors is solely responsible for his part. Each of the sections is followed by an index which we consider an essential part of the whole. It classifies the relevant items according to specific areas, ethnic groups, or similar topics, and should thus make the bibliography much easier to handle for the user.

Bamberg and Heidelberg

W.V.
E.W.S.
M.G.

A bibliography of writings on varieties of English spoken in England, Wales, Scotland and Ireland and on attitudes towards them (1965 - mid-1983)

Wolfgang Viereck

What appears below is a supplemented and updated version that was published under the same title in *English World-Wide* 2 (1981): 184-224.

Great care was taken in the compilation of this bibliography. Whenever possible, I checked the primary sources themselves. The great help provided by the staff of the national and international library loan services is gratefully acknowledged here. But in a number of cases I had to rely on information provided in other bibliographies, in footnotes in books and articles etc. This naturally increases inaccuracies. A comparison of the same items in several sources not infrequently revealed discrepancies in almost every respect (authors' first names, mention/non-mention of additional authors, titles of contributions, journal volumes, publication dates and pagination). The number of working papers that are being published at British universities or similar institutions is constantly growing: The *British Linguistic Newsletter* recently listed as many as 18. Some of these appear and disappear; most of them contain(ed) material relevant to my purpose. But repeatedly my attempts to have access to them failed. This is also true of publications such as *The Journal of the Lakeland Dialect Society*, which contains relevant contributions in Nos. 29, 30 (by Peter Wright) and 37 (by J.T. Relph), or the *Transactions of the Cumberland and Westmorland Antiquarian Society* with a relevant item by R.S. Dilley in vol. 70 (1970). Coverage of these regional journals must necessarily remain unsystematic. Every pre-mid-1983 item that I could not personally view is marked with an asterisk.

The following sources were checked systematically:

Bibliographie Linguistique for the years 1965-1980 (1983); *Publications of the Modern Language Association of America* 1965-1980 (1981); *Current Contents Linguistik*, vols. 1-11/2 (1983), *Nichtkonventionelle Literatur Linguistik*, Nos. 1 for 1974 (1975) - 8 for 1981 (1982); *Bibliographie Linguistischer Literatur*, vols. 1, 1971/1975 - 6, 1980 (1981); *English and American Studies in German* 1968-1981 (1982); *Language and Language Behavior Abstracts*, incl. vol. 17,1 (1983); *Index to Theses Accepted for Higher Degrees by the Universities of Great Britain and Ireland*, incl. vol. 31,1 (1982), *Computers and the Human-*

ities, incl. vol. 14 (1980), the Newsletter of the American Dialect Society, incl. No. 15,2 (1983), Internationale Bibliographie der Zeitschriftenliteratur aus allen Gebieten des Wissens, incl. vol. 18,2 (1982) and Research in Progress. Augsburger I-& I-Schriften 6 (1979) and later issues of the twice-yearly publication Augsburger Informationen, incl. no. 36 (1983).

The kind help of the following is gratefully acknowledged: Stanley Ellis, Klaus Forster, Manfred Görlach, John M. Kirk, Sebastian Köppl, Oleg Mutt, David North, Valerie Sargent, Edgar Schneider and Charles Thomas.

The bibliography attempts as complete a listing as possible of contributions on regional, social and occupational varieties of English, on English varieties spoken by minorities in Britain and on attitudes towards these varieties. It lists both scholarly and popular publications as well as reprints of works published earlier - all this testifies to the increasing interest in varieties research. The starting point is arbitrary. Although 1965 was the general cut-off date, a few important 1964 contributions have been included, together with as many titles as possible from 1983 and 1984 (noted, where no precise information was available, as forthcoming). I am quite aware that the inclusion of forthcoming titles may increase inaccuracies.

The bibliography illustrates clearly the different methodological approaches - traditional and innovative ones - as well as the many objectives in the fields included. For reasons of space the following aspects have been excluded: onomastic studies, including English influence on place-names in such areas as Wales; exclusively diachronic studies (e.g., Alan Bliss, Spoken English in Ireland 1600-1740: Representative Texts Assembled and Analysed. Dublin: Dolmen Press 1979); studies narrowly restricted to slang, jargon and cant (e.g. Partridge's dictionaries); studies of literary dialect lacking a linguistic interest; etymological studies; exclusive treatment of Survey of English Usage and Survey of Spoken English material, i.e. variation in educated English (except variation in RP); documents on bilingualism, work on language planning and language policy, e.g., in Wales and Ireland, with no discussion of English; Bernstein and his school and, last but not least, reviews. No systematic survey of scholarly evaluation, important though it would be, can be achieved. Review articles have, however, been included. Whenever the information was available, authors' first names have been written out. Since the places where journals are published may change they remained unmentioned.

1 **Aarts, Flor G.A.M.,** "Varieties of English", in J. Van Haver, Handelingen van het XXXe Vlaams Filologencongres: Gent 1 - 3 april 1975. Zellik: Secretariaat van de Vlaamse Filologencongressen 1975: 149-52.

2 ---, "The description of linguistic variation in English: from Firth till the present day", English Studies 57 (1976): 239-51.

3 ---, Describing Linguistic Variation: Towards a 'Variety Grammar' of English? Linguistic Agency University of Trier. Series A. No. 43 (1977).

4 **Abercrombie, David,** "A Scottish vowel" [1954], in David Abercrombie, Studies in Phonetics and Linguistics. Language and Language Learning 10 (1965): 137-8.

5 ---, "The accents of Standard English in Scotland", Work in Progress. University of Edinburgh. Department of Linguistics 10 (1977): 21-32.

6 ---, "The accents of Standard English in Scotland", in Aitken/McArthur 1979: 68-84.

7 --- and **Dennis B. Fry,** eds., In Honour of Daniel Jones. London: Longmans 1964.

8 **Acton, Thomas** and **Gerwyn Davies,** "Educational policy and language use among English Romanies and Irish travellers (tinkers) in England and Wales", International Journal of the Sociology of Language 19 (1979): 91-110.

9 **Adams, G. Brendan,** ed., Ulster Dialects: An Introductory Symposium. Holywood: Ulster Folk Museum 1964.

10 ---, "Ulster dialects", in Adams 1964: 1-4.

11 ---, "A register of phonological research on Ulster dialects", in Adams 1964: 193-201.

12 ---, "The Ulster advanced /ü/ phoneme", Ulster Dialect Archive Bulletin 3 (1965): 3-28 [Ms.].

13 ---, "Counting-rhymes and systems of numeration", Ulster Folklife 11 (1965): 87-97.

14 ---, "The work and words of haymaking", Ulster Folklife 12 (1966): 66-91 and 13 (1967): 29-53.

15 ---, "Phonemic systems in collision in Ulster English", Verhandlungen des Zweiten Internationalen Dialektologenkongresses, I. Zeitschrift für Mundartforschung, Beihefte N.F. 3 (1967): 1-6.

16 ---, "A note on the term Thawluck", *Ulster Folklife* 13 (1967): 68.

17 ---, "Northern England as a source of Ulster dialects", *Ulster Folklife* 13 (1967): 69-74.

18 ---, "Ulster dialect origins", *Ulster Folklife* 17 (1971): 99-102.

19 ---, "The dialects of Ulster", in Ó Muirithe 1978: 56-70.

20 ---, "Belfast middle-class speech - a personal view", *Belfast Working Papers in Language and Linguistics* 3 (1978): 59-69.

21 ---, "Common features in Ulster Irish and Ulster English", *Linguistic Studies in Honour of Paul Christophersen. Occasional Papers in Linguistics and Language Learning* 7 (1980): 85-104.

22 ---, "Dialect work in Ulster: an historical account of research in the area", in Barry 1981: 5-17.

23 ---, "The voiceless velar fricative in northern Hiberno English", in Barry 1981: 106-17.

24 ---, "Letter from G.B. Adams in reply to M.V. Barry's article 'Towards a description of a regional standard pronunciation of English in Ulster", *NISLF Journal. Northern Ireland Speech Language Forum* 7 (1981): 70-77.

25 ---, "Report on dialect work in Ulster", *Scottish Language* 1 (1982): 6-12.

26 ---, **Michael V. Barry** and **Philip M. Tilling,** "A tape-recorded survey of Hiberno-English dialects: preliminary report", *Ulster Folklife* 19 (1973): 75-77.

27 ---, **Michael V. Barry** and **Philip M. Tilling,** *A Tape-Recorded Survey of Hiberno-English. Questionnaire*. Belfast: Queen's University 1976 [privately published].

28 **Agnihotri, Rama Kant,** "Processes of assimilation: a sociolinguistic study of Sikh children in Leeds." D.Phil. York 1980.*

29 **Agutter, Alexandra J.L.,** "The linguistic significance of current British slang." Ph.D. Edinburgh 1979.

30 --- and **Leslie N. Cowan,** "Changes in the vocabulary of Lowland Scots dialects", *Scottish Literary Journal Supplement* 14 (1981): 49-62.

31 **Aitken, Adam Jack,** "The present state of Scottish language studies", *Scottish Literary News*, March 1972: 34-44.

32 ---, "Gaelic, Scots and Gullane", Scottish Literary News, March 1972: 45-46.

33 ---, ed., Lowland Scots. Papers presented to an Edinburgh conference. The Association for Scottish Literary Studies. Occasional paper No. 2. Edinburgh 1973; repr. 1975 and 1978.

34 ---, "The Scots language and the teacher of English in Scotland". Department of English Language. University of Edinburgh 1974 /¯Ms._7.*

35 ---, "The Scottish National Dictionary", The Scottish Review 1 (1975): 17-19.*

36 ---, "The Scottish vowel-length rule". University of Edinburgh 1975 /¯Ms._7.*

37 ---, "The Scots language and the teacher of English in Scotland", Scottish Literature in the Secondary School. Edinburgh: Scottish Education Department HMSO 1976: 48-55.

38 ---, "Scottish speech: a historical view, with special reference to the Standard English of Scotland", in Aitken/McArthur 1979: 85-118.

39 ---, "Studies on Scots and Scottish Standard English today", in Aitken/McArthur 1979: 137-49.

40 ---, "New Scots: the problems", in McClure/Aitken/Low 1980: 45-63.

41 ---, "The Scottish vowel-length rule", in Benskin/Samuels 1981: 131-57.

42 ---, "The good old Scots tongue: Does Scots have an identity?" in Haugen/McClure/Thomson 1981: 72-90.

43 ---, "Bad Scots: some superstitions about Scots speech", Scottish Language 1 (1982): 30-44.

44 ---, "Scots and English in Scotland", in Trudgill 1984.

45 ---, "Scots dialects and accents", in Trudgill 1984.

46 --- and **Tom McArthur,** eds., Languages of Scotland. The Association for Scottish Literary Studies. Occasional Paper No. 4. Edinburgh: Chambers 1979.

47 ---, **Angus McIntosh** and **Hermann Pálsson,** eds., Edinburgh Studies in English and Scots. London: Longmans 1971.

48 **Ajulo, E.B.,** "Survey of modern English lexical choice-function and social stratification among certain sociolinguistic groups based in Sheffield City." Ph.D. Sheffield 1980.*

49 **Al-Azzawi, Mary Lee,** "An analytical and comparative integration of the Lowman and Ellis transcriptional practices for some southern English dialects." Ph.D. Illinois Institute of Technology, Chicago 1975.

50 **Alderson, J.C.,** "A study of the cloze procedure with native and non-native speakers of English." Ph.D. Edinburgh 1978.*

51 **Aldus, Judith Butler,** "Anglo-Irish dialects: a bibliography", Regional Language Studies 2 (1969): 1-17.

52 ---, "Anglo-Irish dialects: a bibliography", Regional Language Studies 7 (1976): 7-28.

53 **Allen, Harold B.** and **Gary N. Underwood,** eds., Readings in American Dialectology. New York: Appleton Century Crofts 1971.

54 **Ambler, Pamela J.,** "The terminology of the beer barrel at Queensbury in the West Riding" [1954]; repr. in Peter M. Anderson 1980: 30-35.

55 **Anderson, E.,** "The reading behaviour of a group of children of families of West Indian origin." M.Phil. Nottingham 1979.*

56 **Anderson, John M.** and **Charles Jones,** eds., Historical Linguistics II. Theory and Description in Phonology. Amsterdam: North-Holland Publishing Company 1974.

57 **Anderson, Peter M.,** "The dialect of Eaton-by-Tarporley (Cheshire): a descriptive and historical grammar." 2 vols. Ph.D. Leeds 1977.

58 ---, "A new light on Early English Pronunciation", Transactions of the Yorkshire Dialect Society 14, LXXVII (1977): 32-41.

59 ---, "The development of ME oi/ui in the dialects of the north-west Midlands", The Journal of the Lancashire Dialect Society 27 (1978): 18-23.

60 ---, Yorkshire at Work. In Memory of Harold Orton. The Yorkshire Dialect Society 1980.

61 **Arnold, Roland,** "On the social variability of English: Problems of investigating substandard English", in Roland Arnold and Albrecht Neubert, eds., Englisch heute. Vorträge der sprachwissenschaftlichen Arbeitstagung anläßlich des 100. Jahrestags der Anglistik in Greifs-

wald am 4. und 5. Mai 1981. Linguistische Studien. Reihe A. Arbeitsberichte 100. 1982: 2-22.

62 **Ashley, Leonard,** "Rhyme and reason: the methods and meanings of Cockney rhyming slang, illustrated with some proper names and some improper phrases", Names 25 (1977): 124-54.

63 **Association of Teachers of English to Pupils from Overseas** (Birmingham Branch), Work Group of West Indian Pupils Report (1970).*

64 **Axeby, S.,** "West Indian English in London: syntactic and morphological features." M.A. Reading 1977.*

65 **Aylwin, Bob,** A Load of Cockney Cobblers. With a Foreword by Leslie Crowther and Cartoons by Tony Holland. Edinburgh and London: Johnston and Bacon 1973.*

66 **Bähr, Dieter,** "Gibt es einen standardisierten Haupttonvokalismus im schottischen Englisch?" Zeitschrift für Dialektologie und Linguistik 37 (1970): 337-41.

67 ---, "Phonische Interferenzen beim gälisch-englischen Sprachwechsel", Zeitschrift für Dialektologie und Linguistik 39 (1972): 59-76.

68 ---, Standard English und seine geographischen Varianten. UTB 160. Munich: Fink 1974.

69 **Bagley, Christopher, Martin Bart** and **Joyce Wong,** "Antecedents of scholastic success in West Indian Ten-year-olds in London", in Verma/Bagley 1979: 84-94.

70 ---, **Kanka Mallick** and **Gajendra K. Verma,** "Pupil self-esteem: a study of black and white teenagers in British schools", in Verma/Bagley 1979: 176-91.

71 **Bailey, Charles-James N.,** Variation and Linguistic Theory. Arlington: Center for Applied Linguistics 1973.

72 ---, "Conceptualizing 'dialects' as implicational constellations rather than as entities bounded by isoglossic bundles", Dialekt und Dialektologie. Zeitschrift für Dialektologie und Linguistik, Beiheft N.F. 26 (1980): 234-68.

73 **Bailey, Richard W.** and **Manfred Görlach,** eds., English as a World Language. Ann Arbor: The University of Michigan Press 1982.

74 **Baker, G.W.,** "Creole language features in the speech of West Indian primary school children in Nottingham." M.Phil. Nottingham 1976.*

75 **Barker, D.,** "From free morpheme to bound morpheme? A West Yorkshire example", Lore and Language 3/3, Part A (1980): 28-31.

76 **Barltrop, Robert** and **Jim Wolveridge,** The Muvver Tongue. London and West Nyack: Journeyman Press 1980.

77 **Barnes, William,** A Glossary of the Dorset Dialect with a Grammar of Its Word Shapening and Wording. Dorchester: M. & E. Case and London: Trübner 1886; St. Peter Port, Guernsey: Toucan Press, 2nd ed. 1970.

78 **Barnickel, Klaus-Dieter,** Sprachliche Varianten des Englischen - nationale, regionale und soziale Varianten. Hueber Hochschulreihe 45. Vol. I. Munich 1980. Chapters 3.7, 3.8, 3.9, 4 and 5.2, 5.3.

79 ---, Sprachliche Varianten des Englischen - Register und Stile. Hueber Hochschulreihe 45. Vol. II. Munich 1980.

80 **Barry, Michael V.,** "Yorkshire sheep-scoring numerals", Transactions of the Yorkshire Dialect Society 12, LXVII (1967): 21-31.

81 ---, "Traditional enumeration in the North Country", Folk Life 7 (1969): 75-91.

82 ---, "The morphemic distribution of the definite article in contemporary regional English", in Wakelin 1972: 164-81.

83 ---, "Phonemic analysis", Computers and the Humanities 8 (1974): 44.

84 ---, "The southern boundaries of northern Hiberno-English speech", Linguistic Studies in Honour of Paul Christophersen. Occasional Papers in Linguistics and Language Learning 7 (1980): 105-52; prepublished in The Tape-Recorded Survey of Hiberno-English Speech, Working Papers I. Institute of Irish Studies. Queen's University of Belfast and repr. in Barry 1981: 52-95.

85 ---, "Towards a description of a regional standard pronunciation of English in Ulster", NISLF Journal. Northern Ireland Speech Language Forum 6 (1980): 43-47; repr. in Barry 1981: 47-51.

86 ---, "The methodology of the tape-recorded survey of Hiberno-English speech", in Barry 1981: 18-46.

87 ---, ed., Aspects of English Dialects in Ireland. Vol. I: Papers arising from the Tape-recorded Survey of Hiberno-English Speech. Belfast: Queen's University, Institute of Irish Studies 1981.

88 ---, "Handling three age groups in a large regional dialect survey in Ireland", in H.J. Warkentyne [1982]: 113-25.

89 ---, "The English language in Ireland", in Bailey/Görlach 1982: 84-133.

90 ---, "Rural dialects in England. Appendix 2: Manx English", in Trudgill 1984.

91 **Barth, Ernst,** *The Dialect of Naunton (Gloucestershire)*. Zürich: P.G. Keller 1968.

92 **Beaken, M.A.,** "A study of the phonological development in a primary school population of East London." Ph.D. London 1971.*

93 **Bellin, Wynford,** "Welsh and English in Wales", in Trudgill 1984.

94 **Benskin, Michael** and **M.L. Samuels,** eds., *So Meny People Longages and Tonges: Philological Essays in Scots and Medieval English Presented to Angus McIntosh*. Edinburgh: Middle English Dialect Project 1981.

95 **Berger, Joerg,** "The present-day dialect of the Holy Island of Lindisfarne", *Computers and the Humanities* 8 (1974): 44.

96 ---, "Computing and phonology", *Association for Literary and Linguistic Computing Bulletin* 2,1 (1974): 4-6.

97 ---, *The Dialect of Holy Island. A Phonological Analysis*. European University Studies, Series XIV, Vol. 83. Bern: Peter Lang 1980.

98 **Bertz, Siegfried,** "Der Dubliner Stadtdialekt. Eine synchrone Beschreibung der Struktur und Variabilität des heutigen Dubliner Englisch." Diss. (= German Ph.D.) Freiburg 1975.*

99 **Bhaldraithe, Tomás de** cf. De Bhaldraithe, Tomás; similarly De Fréine, Seán.

100 **Bilton, Linda,** "A note on Hull intonation", *Journal of the International Phonetic Association* 12 (1982): 30-35.

101 **Blake, Norman F.,** *Non-standard Language in English Literature*. The Language Library. London: André Deutsch 1981.*

102 **Bliss, Alan J.,** "Thallage, thawlogue and thawluck", *Ulster Folklife* 14 (1968): 28-33.

103 ---, "The language of Synge", in Maurice Harmon, ed., *J.M.Synge Centenary Papers 1971*. Dublin: Dolmen Press 1972: 35-62.

104 ---, "Languages in contact: Some problems of Hiberno-English", Proceedings of the Royal Irish Academy 72, Section C, No. 3, 1972: 63-82.

105 ---, "The development of the English language in early modern Ireland", in T.W. Moody, F.X. Martin, F.J. Byrne, eds., A New History of Ireland, vol. III. Oxford: The Clarendon Press 1976: 546-60.*

106 ---, "The emergence of modern English dialects in Ireland", in Ó Muirithe 1978: 7-19.

107 ---, "'Bother' and 'Pother'", Notes & Queries N.S. 25, No. 6 (1978): 536-40.

108 ---, "English in the South of Ireland", in Trudgill 1984.

109 ---, "The English language in Ireland." Dublin n.d. [Ms.].*

110 **Bloom, D.,** "Curriculum development in a multicultural classroom: Some factors concerning the use of Jamaican patois." Department of Educational Studies, Manchester Polytechnic (1979) [Ms.].*

111 ---, "The case for patois in schools", Learning 1 (1979): 49-51.*

112 **Bothe, Dieter,** Direkte und indirekte Transkription. Ein Vergleich zwischen dem phonetischen Notationsmaterial des 'Survey of English Dialects (Worcestershire)' und Magnetbandtranskripten. The Cooper Monographs 16. Bern: Francke 1971.

113 **Bourhis, Richard Y.** and **Howard Giles,** "The language of cooperation in Wales: a field study", Language Sciences 42 (1976): 13-16.

114 --- and **Howard Giles,** "The language of intergroup distinctiveness", in Giles 1977: 119-35.

115 --- and **Howard Giles,** "Children's voices and ethnic categorization in Britain", La Monda Lingvo-Problemo 6 (1977): 85-94.

116 ---, **Howard Giles** and **Henri Tajfel,** "Language as a determinant of Welsh identity", European Journal of Social Psychology 3 (1973): 447-60.

117 ---, **Howard Giles, Henri Tajfel** and **D.M. Taylor,** "The determinants of Welsh identity." Paper read at Annual Conference of the British Psychological Society, Bangor 1974 [Ms.].

118 **Bowyer, Robert,** "A study of social accents in a South London suburb." M.Phil. Leeds 1973.

119 **Braidwood, John,** "Ulster and Elizabethan English", in Adams 1964: 5-109.

120 ---, *The Ulster Dialect Lexicon.* New Lecture Series 51. Belfast: Queen's University 1969.

121 ---, "Terms for 'left-handed' in the Ulster dialects", *Ulster Folklife* 18 (1972): 98-110.

122 ---, "Crowls and runts. Ulster dialect terms for 'The weakling of the litter'", *Ulster Folklife* 20 (1974): 71-84.

123 ---, *An Ulster Dialect Dictionary* (forthcoming).

124 **Bratt, M.F.,** "Evaluative reactions to speech varieties in 5 year old children." M.Litt. Edinburgh 1974.*

125 **Bremann, Rolf,** "Exemplarische Darstellung von Unterschieden zwischen Standard English / Received Pronunciation und dem Sheffield-Dialekt anhand von ausgewählten Tonbandaufnahmen." Münster 1977 [Ms.].*

126 ---, "Vergleichende empirische Untersuchungen zur dialektalen Aussprache des Englischen in West- und Ost-Cornwall auf soziolinguistischer Basis." Final state exam. dissertation Münster 1979.*

127 ---, "Soziolinguistische Untersuchungen zum Englisch von Cornwall." Diss. (= German Ph.D.) Münster 1983; to be published as vol. 14 of *Bamberger Beiträge zur Englischen Sprachwissenschaft* 1984.

128 **Brook, George Leslie,** *English Dialects.* The Language Library. London: Deutsch 1963, 2nd ed. 1965, 3rd ed. 1978.

129 ---, "Varieties of English", *Bulletin of the John Rylands Library* 51 (1968-69): 271-91.

130 ---, "The future of English dialect studies", in Ellis 1968 (1969): 15-22.

131 ---, *Varieties of English.* London: Macmillan 1973, 2nd ed. 1979.

132 **Brown, E. Keith,** "Relative clauses in a corpus of spoken Scottish English" (forthcoming).

133 ---, "Double modals in Hawick Scots" (forthcoming).

134 ---, "Relative clauses in Lothian and Edinburgh Scots". Paper read at the 1979 Walsall Sociolinguistics Symposium [Ms.].*

135 --- and **Martin P. Millar,** "Auxiliary verbs in Edinburgh speech", *Work*

in Progress. Edinburgh University. Linguistics Department 11 (1978): 146-84.*

136 --- and **Martin P. Millar,** "Auxiliary verbs in Edinburgh speech", Transactions of the Philological Society 1980 (1980): 81-133.

137 --- and **J. Miller,** "Modal verbs in Scottish English", Work in Progress. University of Edinburgh. Department of Linguistics 8 (1975): 99-114.

138 **Brown, Gillian, Karen L. Currie** and **Joanne Kenworthy,** Questions of Intonation. London: Croom Helm 1980.

139 **Brown, Robin,** "A grammar of the dialect of Great Hale, Lincolnshire." 2 vols. M.Phil. Leeds 1969.

140 **Bubennikova, O.A.,** "Lexical peculiarities of the written language of Scotland." Candidate thesis. Moscow 1980 /̄ in Russian_7.*

141 ---, "Concerning the sociolinguistic aspect of analysis of Scottish lexical dialectisms in English fiction" /̄ in Russian_7, Vestnik Moskovskogo Universiteta, Filologiya 35 (1980): 63-68.*

142 **Buckle, Richard,** ed., U and Non-U Revisited. London: Debrett's Peerage and New York: Viking 1978.

143 **Bundy, W.M.S.,** "Studies in the conservative dialect of Carmarthenshire, Dyfed." M.A. Wales, Swansea 1975.*

144 **Burchfield, Robert W.,** The Spoken Word: a BBC Guide. London: British Broadcasting Corporation 1981; repr. 1982.

145 ---, **Denis Donoghue** and **Andrew Timothy,** The Quality of Spoken English on BBC Radio. London: British Broadcasting Corporation 1979.

146 **Burghardt, Lorraine H.,** ed., Dialectology: Problems and Perspectives. Knoxville: University of Tennessee 1971.

147 **Burgschmidt, Ernst,** Koexistenz, Distribution, Äquivalenz, Synonymie. Studien zur Beschreibung der mittelenglischen Lokal- und Temporalpräpositionen. Nürnberg: Verlag E. Burgschmidt 1976.

148 **Butcher, Andrew** and **Claus Gnutzmann,** "Cockney rhyming slang", Linguistische Berichte 50/1977: 1-10.

149 **Cairns, E.** and **B. Duriez,** "The influence of speaker's accent on recall by Catholic and Protestant school children in Northern Ireland", British Journal of Social and Clinical Psychology 15 (1976): 441-2.*

150 **Cairns, Robert,** "The languages of Scotland", Scotia Review 6 (1974): 20-26.

151 **Campbell-Platt, Kiran,** Linguistic Minorities in Britain. Rev. by Shan Nicholas. London: The Runnymede Trust 1978.

152 **Campion, G. Edward,** Lincolnshire Dialects. With a Foreword by John D.A. Widdowson. Boston, Lincs.: Richard Kay 1976; repr. 1979.

153 **Cashmore, Ernest,** Rastaman. The Rastafarian Movement in England. London: Allen and Unwin 1979; 2nd impr. 1981; 3rd impr. 1982.

154 **Chambers, J.K.** and **Peter Trudgill,** Dialectology. Cambridge Textbooks in Linguistics. Cambridge: UP 1980 / with accompanying cassette /.

155 **Chapman, Anthony J., Jean R. Smith** and **Hugh C. Foot,** "Language, humour and intergroup relations", in Giles 1977: 137-69.

156 **Cheshire, Jenny L.,** "Present tense verbs in Reading English", in Trudgill 1978: 52-68.

157 ---, "Grammatical variation in the English spoken in Reading, Berkshire." Ph.D. Reading 1979.*

158 ---, "Syntactic and semantic constraints on ain't", The Nottingham Linguistic Circular 9 (1980): 1-17.

159 ---, "British nonstandard never and the problem of where grammars stop." School of Modern Languages. University of Bath 1981 / Ms. /.*

160 ---, "Variation in the use of ain't in an urban British English dialect", Language in Society 10 (1981): 365-81.

161 ---, "Linguistic variation and social function", in Romaine 1982: 153-66.

162 ---, "Dialect features and linguistic conflict in schools", Educational Review 34 (1982): 53-67.

163 ---, Variation in an English Dialect: A Sociolinguistic Study. Cambridge Studies in Linguistics 37. Cambridge: UP 1982.

164 ---, "Standard and non-standard dialects and accents of English", in Trudgill 1984.

165 **Chesters, V.A.,** "Studies in the linguistic geography of the vale of Glamorgan, the Swansea valley and the Breconshire hinterland." M.A. Wales, Swansea 1971.*

166 **Cheyne, William M.,** "Stereotyped reactions to speakers with Scottish and English regional accents", The British Journal of Social and Clinical Psychology 9 (1970): 77-79.

167 ---, **G. Jahoda** and **T. Veness,** "Regional accents as cues in the perception of speakers." Paper read at the Annual Conference of the B.P.S. (1968).*

168 **Clark, James M.,** The Vocabulary of Anglo-Irish. St. Gall: Zollikofer 1917; repr. Folcroft, Pa.: Folcroft Library Editions 1974 and Richard West 1977.

169 **Claxton, A.O.D.,** The Suffolk Dialect of the 20th Century. Ipswich, Suffolk: 1954, 2nd ed. 1960, 3rd ed. 1968; repr. Woodbridge, Suffolk: Boydell Press 1973, 1981.

170 **Clay, Marie M.,** "The effect of two educated dialects on sentence repetition scores of five year old Scottish children", Language and Speech 19 (1976): 244-50.

171 **Clement, R.D.,** "Highland English", Scottish Literary Journal Supplement 12 (1980): 13-18.

172 **Collins, Henry Eaton,** "A phonology of the dialect of Southern Warwickshire." Ph.D. Yale 1964.*

173 **Collins English Dictionary.** London: Wm. Collins and Sons 1979. [Introductory articles on the pronunciation of British English, on regional dialects of England, on the English of Scotland and on Irish English: XIX - XXV].

174 **Connolly, John H.,** "On the segmental phonology of a South Welsh accent of English", Journal of the International Phonetic Association 11 (1981): 51-61.

175 **Coupland, Nikolas,** "Style-shifting in a Cardiff work-setting", Language in Society 9 (1980): 1-12.

176 ---, "The social differentiation of functional language use: a sociolinguistic investigation of travel agency talk." Ph.D., Wales, Institute of Science and Technology 1981.

177 ---, "Sociolinguistic aspects of place-names: Ethnic affiliation and the pronunciation of Welsh in the Welsh capital", in Viereck 1984.

178 **Criper, C.** and **A. Davies,** Research on Spoken Language in the Primary School. Report to the Scottish Education Department (1974).*

179 **Crump, S.,** "The language of West Indian children and its relevance for schools." M.A. London Institute of Education 1979.*

180 **Currie, Karen L.,** "Contour systems of one variety of Scottish English", Language and Speech 22 (1979): 1-20.

181 ---, "Intonation systems in Scottish English." Ph.D. Edinburgh 1979.*

182 **Davenport, Michael, Erik Hansen** and **Hans Frede Nielsen,** eds., Current Topics in English Historical Linguistics: Proceedings of the Second International Conference on English Historical Linguistics held at Odense University 13 - 15 April, 1981. Odense University Studies in English 4. Odense:UP 1983.

183 **Davies, Gerwyn,** "Investigation of egocentric language behaviour in traveller children." B.Phil. Birmingham 1976.*

184 **Davis, Alva L.** and **Lawrence M. Davis,** "Recordings of Standard English questionnaire", Orbis 18 (1969): 385-404.

185 **Davis, Lawrence M.,** ed., Studies in Linguistics in Honor of Raven I. McDavid, Jr. University, Ala.: University of Alabama Press 1972.

186 ---, English Dialectology: An Introduction. University, Ala.: University of Alabama Press 1983.

187 **Day, Richard R.,** "Children's attitudes toward language", in Ryan/Giles 1982: 116- 31.

188 **De Bhaldraithe, Tomás,** "Report on dialect study in Ireland", Communications et Rapports du Premier Congrès International de Dialectologie Générale (Louvain du 21 au 25 août, Bruxelles les 26 et 27 août 1960). Quatrième Partie. Louvain: Centre International de Dialectologie Générale 1965: 90-95.

189 **De Fréine, Seán,** "The dominance of the English language in the 19th century", in Ó Muirithe 1978: 71-87.

190 **Dean, Christopher,** "Some consonantal elements in Northern English dialects", The Canadian Journal of Linguistics 12 (1966): 9-23.

191 **Delahunty, Gerald P.,** "Dialect and local accent", in Ó Muirithe 1978: 127-49.

192 **Dickinson, L., A. Hobbs, S.M. Kleinberg** and **P.J. Martin,** A Sociolinguistic Study of the Immigrant School Learner in Glasgow. Glasgow: Jordanhill College of Education 1974.*

193 **Dobson, Scott,** Larn Yersel' Geordie. Newcastle-upon-Tyne: Frank Graham 1969, amended 1976.

194 ---, Hist'ry o' the Geordies. Book one. Newcastle-upon-Tyne: Frank Graham 1970.

195 ---, Advanced Geordie Palaver. Newcastle-upon-Tyne: Frank Graham 1970, repr. 1977.

196 ---, The Geordie Dictionary. Newcastle-upon-Tyne: Frank Graham 1974.*

197 **Dodson, M.** and **R. Sacsek,** A Dictionary of Cockney Slang and Rhyming Slang. London: Hedgehog Enterprises 1972.*

198 **Douglas, Ellen,** "Sociolinguistic variation in a rural community in Northern Ireland", in Reid 1976: 8-9.

199 **Douglas-Cowie, Ellen,** "Linguistic code-switching in a Northern Irish village: social interaction and social ambition", in Trudgill 1978: 37-51.

200 ---, "The sociolinguistic situation in N. Ireland", in Trudgill 1984.

201 **Duncan, Pauline,** "Forms of the feminine pronoun in modern English dialects", in Wakelin 1972: 182-200.

202 **Dyson, B.R.,** "Glossary of Sheffield cutlering terms" /1932/, repr. in Peter M. Anderson 1980: 47-55.

203 **Edel, Anna,** Hochsprache und Mundart in Nordengland: Der hochsprachliche Einfluß auf den Wortschatz der Mundart in Northumberland und Cumberland. Zürich: Juris 1973.

204 **Edwards, John R.,** "Ethnic identity and bilingual education", in Giles 1977: 253-82.

205 ---, "The speech of disadvantaged Dublin children", La Monda Lingvo-Problemo 7 (= Language Problems and Language Planning 1) (1977): 65-72.

206 ---, "Students' reactions to Irish regional accents", Language and Speech 20 (1977): 280-6.

207 ---, "Social class differences and the identification of sex in children's speech", Journal of Child Language 6 (1979): 121-27.

208 ---, "Judgements and confidence in reactions to disadvantaged speech", in Howard Giles and Robert St. Clair, eds., Language and Social Psychology. Language in Society 1. Oxford: Blackwell 1979: 22-44.

209 ---, Language and Disadvantage. Studies in language disability and remediation 5. London: Edward Arnold 1979.

210 ---, "Language attitudes and their implications among English speakers", in Ryan/Giles 1982: 20-33.

211 ---, "Irish and English in Ireland", in Trudgill 1984.

212 **Edwards, Viv K.,** "Can dialect cause comprehension problems for West Indian children?" Multiracial School 4 (1975): 1-6.

213 ---, "Effects of dialect on the comprehension of West Indian children", Educational Research 18 (1976): 83-95.

214 ---, "Language and comprehension in West Indian children." Ph.D. Reading 1976.*

215 ---, "Dialect interference in West Indian children", Language and Speech 21,1 (1978): 76-86.

216 ---, "Language attitudes and underperformance in West Indian children", Educational Review 30 (1978): 51-58.

217 ---, The West Indian Language Issue in British Schools: Challenges and Responses. London: Routledge and Kegan Paul 1979.

218 ---, "Black British English: a bibliographical essay on the language of children of West Indian origin", SAGE. Race Relations Abstracts 5, Nos. 3-4 (1980): 1-25.

219 ---, West Indian Verbal Skills. London: Commission for Racial Equality and Routledge & Kegan Paul 1980.*

220 ---, "Dialect and reading: a case study of West Indian children in Britain", in John Edwards, ed., The Social Psychology of Reading. Vol. 1. Silver Spring, Md.: Institute of Modern Languages 1981: 207-16.

221 ---, "Patterns of language use in the Black British community", English World-Wide 2 (1981): 154-64.

222 ---, "Research priorities in the sociolinguistic description of British Black English", Language and Ethnicity. A Report of a Seminar

jointly organized by the Linguistic Minorities Project and the British Association of Applied Linguistics at the University of London Institute of Education, January 1982.*

223 ---, Language Variation in the Multicultural Classroom. Reading: Centre for the Teaching of Reading /¯1982_7.

224 ---, Language in Multicultural Classrooms. London: Batsford 1983.

225 ---, "British Black English and education", in Trudgill 1984.

226 --- and **David Sutcliffe,** "When creole can be king", The Times Educational Supplement, March 18, 1977.

227 --- and **Bert Weltens,** "Research on non-standard dialects of British English - progress and prospects", in Viereck 1984.

228 **Ellis, Alexander John,** The Existing Phonology of English Dialects Compared with that of West Saxon Speech. Early English Text Society. Extra Series 56. Part V of On Early English Pronunciation. London 1889; repr. New York: Greenwood Press 1968.

229 **Ellis, Stanley,** "Dialects", Leeds and its Region. Leeds: Arnold 1967: 109-15.

230 ---, "Lancashire dialect and its Yorkshire subsidiary", The Journal of the Lancashire Dialect Society 17 (1968): 18-21.

231 ---, ed., Studies in Honour of Harold Orton on the Occasion of his Seventieth Birthday. Leeds Studies in English N.S. 2, 1968 (1969).

232 ---, "The assessment of linguistic boundaries by local dialect speakers", The Journal of the Lancashire Dialect Society 18 (1969): 5-8; also in Actes du Xe Congrès International des Linguistes 1967. II. Bucarest 1970: 109-12.

233 ---, "Regional, social and economic influences on speech: Leeds University Studies", in Viereck 1976: 93-103, 357.

234 ---, "A note on the vocabulary of the Lathe or barn in upper Wharfedale in the West Riding" /¯1952_7, repr. in Peter M. Anderson 1980: 9-14.

235 ---, "On unstressed /ə/ vs. /ɪ/ in dialectal British English", Leeds Studies in English. Festschrift A.C. Cawley (forthcoming).

236 ---, 24 Dialect Recordings and Transcripts /¯1 LP_7 (forthcoming).

237 **Elmer, Willy,** The Terminology of Fishing. A Survey of English and

Welsh Inshore-Fishing. Things and Words. The Cooper Monographs. English Dialect Series 19. Bern: Francke 1973.

238 **Elworthy, Frederic T.,** The Grammar of the Dialect of West Somerset. Transactions of the Philological Society 1877, 1878, 1879. London: Trübner & Co.; repr. Vaduz: Kraus Reprint 1965.*

239 **Elyan, Olwen, Philip Smith, Howard Giles** and **Richard Bourhis,** "RP-accented female speech: the voice of perceived androgyny?" in Trudgill 1978: 122-31.

240 **English Dialect Society Publications** Nos. 1-80. 1873-1876; repr. New York: Kraus 1974.

241 **Esling, John H.,** "Sociolinguistic preliminaries to an experimental phonetic study of voice features", Work in Progress. Edinburgh University. Linguistics Department 8 (1975): 126-7.*

242 ---, "Articulatory setting in the community", in Reid 1976: 19-20.

243 ---, "Voice quality in Edinburgh: a sociolinguistic and phonetic study." Ph.D. Edinburgh 1978.

244 ---, "The identification of features of voice quality in social groups", Journal of the International Phonetic Association 8 (1978): 18-23.

245 ---, "Methods in voice quality research in dialect surveys", in H.J. Warkentyne [1982]: 126-38.

246 **Eustace, Sinclair S.,** "Present changes in English pronunciation", Proceedings of the Sixth International Congress of Phonetic Sciences. Held at Prague 7 - 13 September 1967. Prague: Academia Publishing House 1970: 303-6.

247 **Evans, William,** "'You' and 'thou' in Northern England", South Atlantic Bulletin 34 (1969): 17-21; repr. in Shores/Hines 1977: 93-102.

248 ---, "The survival of the second-person singular in the southern counties of England", The South Central Bulletin 30 (1970): 182-6; repr. in Transactions of the Yorkshire Dialect Society 14, LXXVI (1976): 17-29.

249 **Ewen, Colin J.,** "Aitken's law and the phonatory gesture in dependency phonology", Lingua 41 (1977): 307-29.

250 **Fagan, S.F.W.,** "Analysis of the written English of some Jamaican city children." M.A. London 1967.*

251 **Fashola, J.B.,** "The influence of received pronunciation on a West-Cumbrian speaker of English provincial standard." M.Phil. London, School of Oriental and African Studies 1970.*

252 ---, "Structural and non-structural factors in linguistic interference. A study of the influence of received pronunciation on a speaker of English provincial standard from Workington, Cumberland", Zeitschrift für Dialektologie und Linguistik 38 (1971): 296-312.

253 **Fawcett, Robin P.** and **Michael R. Perkins,** "Child language transcripts 6 - 12 with a preface." 4 vols. Department of Behavioural and Communication Studies, Polytechnic of Wales, Pontypridd, Mid Glamorgan 1980.*

254 **Fennel, D.,** "Can a shrinking linguistic minority be saved? Lessons from the Irish experience", in Haugen/McClure/Thomson 1981: 32-39.

255 **Fenton, Alexander,** "The tabu language of the fishermen of Orkney and Shetland", Ethnologia Europaea 2-3 (1968-69): 118-22.

256 ---, The Northern Isles: Orkney and Shetland. Edinburgh: John Donald 1978. [Scots lexicographic material passim and, in particular, Terminology of the one-stilted plough (304-306), List of sheep marks, 1934 (473-474), Terminology of sheep marks (484-490) and The sea language of fishermen and the end of Norn (616-622)].

257 **Filppula, Markku,** "VSO and SVO languages in contact: Sentence-thematic peculiarities of Hiberno-English", in Thorstein Fretheim and Lars Hellan, eds., Papers from the Sixth Scandinavian Conference of Linguistics. Røros, June 19 - 21, 1981. Dragvoll: Tapir 1982: 50-59.

258 **Fischer, Andreas,** Dialects in the South-West of England: A Lexical Investigation. Cooper Monographs. English Dialect Series 25. Bern: Francke 1976.

259 **Fisiak, Jacek,** "Was there a kl-, gl- > tl-, dl- change in early Modern English?" Lingua Posnaniensia 23 (1980): 87-90.*

260 ---, "The voicing of initial fricatives in Middle English", in Viereck 1984.

261 **Flanagan, James G.,** "Kinship, locality and language usage", in Anthony E.C.W. Spencer and H. Tovey, eds., Proceedings of First and Fourth Annual Conferences of the Sociological Association of Ireland. Belfast 1978: 8-12.

262 **Flynn, K.,** "A grammar of the dialect of Moulton (Cheshire): descriptive and historical." 2 vols. M.Phil. Leeds 1975.

263 **Forby, Robert,** The Vocabulary of East Anglia. 2 vols. London 1830. Facsim. repr. Newton Abbot: David and Charles 1970.

264 **Ford, Ernest,** "Westhoughton terms and the phonological puzzles they bring", The Journal of the Lancashire Dialect Society 24 (1974): 27-30.

265 **Forster, Klaus,** "Studien zur Syntax der nordenglischen Mundarten." Habilitationsschrift Erlangen 1984.

266 **Foster, Brian,** The Changing English Language. London: Macmillan 1968; repr. in Papermacs 1981; esp. Chapter 6.

267 **Fox, Anthony T.C.,** "Systemic variation in north Staffordshire speech", Work in Progress. Department of Phonetics. University of Edinburgh 1 (1967): 8-18.

268 **Francis, W. Nelson,** The English Language: An Introduction. New York 1963; revised British edition London: Hodder and Stoughton 1967; esp. Chap. 6.

269 ---, "Modal daren't and durstn't in dialectal English", in Ellis 1968 (1969): 145-63.

270 ---, "Computer production of dialect maps", Computers and the Humanities 3 (1969): 290.

271 ---, "English dialectology", Computers and the Humanities 4 (1970): 332-3.

272 ---, "Some dialect isoglosses in England" [1959], repr. in Allen/Underwood 1971: 245-54.

273 ---, "Some dialectal verb forms in England" [1961], repr. in Williamson/Burke 1971: 108-20, and in Allen/Underwood 1971: 255-64.

274 ---, "Word geography of England", American Speech 53 (1978): 221-31 [rev. art.].

275 ---, Dialectology. An Introduction. London: Longmans 1983.

276 ---, "Amn't I, or the hole in the pattern", in Viereck 1984.

277 ---, **Jan Svartvik** and **Gerald M. Rubin,** Computer-Produced Representation of Dialectal Variation: Initial Fricatives in Southern British

English. COLING. International Conference on Computational Linguistics. Preprint No. 52. Stockholm 1969.

278 **Fraser, Kenneth C.,** "The rebirth of Scots", Scotia Review 6 (1974): 32-35.

279 **Fudge, Erik,** "Long and short /æ/ in one southern British speaker's English", Journal of the International Phonetic Association 7 (1977): 55-65.

280 **Gailey, Alan,** "Kitchen furniture (with a glossary of household terms compiled by G. Brendan Adams)", Ulster Folklife 12 (1966): 18-34.

281 ---, "The Scots element in north Irish popular culture", Ethnologia Europaea 8,1 (1975): 2-22.

282 --- and **Caoimhin O Danachair,** "Ethnological mapping in Ireland with a linguistic contribution by G.B.Adams", Ethnologia Europaea 9,1 (1976): 14-34.

283 **Gallagher, Catherine,** "Aspects of bilingualism in North West Donegal", in Barry 1981: 142-70.

284 **Ganguly, S.R.** and **M.B. Ormerod,** "The structure and correlates of attitudes to English among pupils of Asian origins", Journal of Multilingual and Multicultural Development 1 (1980): 57-70.*

285 **Gatherer, W.A.,** "Scots language in education", Edinburgh Association for Scottish Literary Studies Language Committee 1975 [Ms.].*

286 **Gatilova, V.K.,** "The expression of the perfective aspect in Irish English." Candidate thesis, Moscow 1980 [in Russian].*

287 **Geeson, Cecil,** A Northumberland and Durham Word Book. The Living Dialect. Including a Glossary, with Etymologies and Illustrative Quotations, of Living Dialect Words. Newcastle-upon-Tyne: Harold Hill 1969.

288 **Gepp, Edward,** An Essex Dialect Dictionary. London 1920, 2nd ed. 1923; republished with an Addendum and Bibliography by John S. Appleby. East Ardsley: S.R. Publ. 1969.

289 **Germer, Rudolf,** "Wesen und Wandlung der 'Received Pronunciation' seit Jones", Neusprachliche Mitteilungen aus Wissenschaft und Praxis 1 (1967): 10-18.

290 **Giffhorn, Barbara,** Untersuchungen zu den englischen Dialekten: Der me. Typus "waishen". Diss. (= German Ph.D.) Bonn 1978.

291 **Giffhorn, Jürgen,** Studien am Survey of English Dialects: Wörter des Typus know und grow mit den Reflexen der me. Phoneme /au/und /ū/. Munich: Fink 1979.

292 **Giles, Howard,** "Evaluative reactions to accents", Educational Review 22 (1970): 211-27.

293 ---, "A study of speech patterns in social interaction: accent evaluation and accent change." Ph.D. Bristol 1971.*

294 ---, "Ethnocentrism and the evaluation of accented speech", The British Journal of Social and Clinical Psychology 10 (1971): 187-88.

295 ---, "Patterns of evaluation to R.P., South Welsh and Somerset accented speech", The British Journal of Social and Clinical Psychology 10 (1971): 280-1.

296 ---, "Our reactions to accent", New Society, 14 October 1971: 713-5; repr. in Pugh/Lee/Swann 1980: 27-34.

297 ---, "The effect of stimulus mildness-broadness in the evaluation of accents", Language and Speech 15 (1972): 262-69.

298 ---, "Evaluation of personality content from accented speech as a function of listeners' social attitudes", Perceptual and Motor Skills 34 (1972): 168-70.

299 ---, "Accent mobility: a model and some data", Anthropological Linguistics 15 (1973): 87-105.

300 ---, "Communicative effectiveness as a function of accented speech", Speech Monographs 40 (1973): 330-1.

301 ---, ed., Language, Ethnicity and Intergroup Relations. European Monographs in Social Psychology 13. London: Academic Press 1977.

302 --- and **Richard Y. Bourhis,** "Dialect perception revisited", The Quarterly Journal of Speech 59 (1973): 337-42.

303 --- and **Richard Y. Bourhis,** "Linguistic assimilation: West Indians in Cardiff", Language Sciences 38 (1975): 9-12.

304 --- and **Richard Y. Bourhis,** "Racial identification of British blacks from speech", Language Sciences (forthcoming).

305 ---, **Richard Y. Bourhis, Peter Trudgill** and **Alan Lewis,** "The imposed norm hypothesis: a validation", The Quarterly Journal of Speech 60 (1974): 405-10.

306 ---, **C. Harrison, P.M. Smith** and **N. Freeman,** "A developmental study

of language attitudes: A British case." University of Bristol 1981 / Ms. /.*

307 --- and **Patricia Marsh,** "Perceived masculinity, androgyny and accented speech", Language Sciences 1/1979: 301-15.*

308 --- and **Peter F. Powesland,** Speech Style and Social Evaluation. European Monographs in Social Psychology 7. London, New York and San Francisco: Academic Press 1975.

309 --- and **Bernard Saint-Jacques,** eds., Language and Ethnic Relations. Oxford: Pergamon Press 1979.

310 ---, **D.M. Taylor** and **Richard Y. Bourhis,** "Dimensions of Welsh identity", European Journal of Social Psychology 7 (1977): 29-39.

311 **Giles, Raymond H.,** The West Indian Experience in British Schools. London: Heinemann 1977.*

312 **Gillies, W.,** "English influences on contemporary Scottish Gaelic", Scottish Literary Journal Supplement 12 (1980): 1-12.

313 **Gimson, Alfred C.,** An Introduction to the Pronunciation of English. London: Edward Arnold 1962; 2nd ed. 1970; 3rd ed. 1980; repr. with corrections 1981.

314 ---, "English RP: Ancient or modern?" Praxis des Neusprachlichen Unterrichts 26 (1979): 149-56.

315 ---, "The R.P. accent", in Trudgill 1984.

316 **Gladwell, Anne C.,** "Patterns in distribution: an intensive study of dialect and tradition in rural and industrial Monmouthshire." Ph.D. Wales, Swansea 1973.*

317 **Glauser, Robert Beat,** The Scottish-English Linguistic Border: Lexical Aspects. The Cooper Monographs on English: English Dialect Series 20. Bern: Francke 1974.

318 ---, "Synchronic vowel shift in the present-day speech of Grassington in North Yorkshire (England)", in Wolfgang U. Dressler and Oskar E. Pfeiffer, eds., Phonologica 1976: Akten der dritten Internationalen Phonologie-Tagung Wien, 1. - 4. September 1976. Innsbrucker Beiträge zur Sprachwissenschaft 19 (1977): 149-51.

319 ---, "The phonology of present-day Grassington speech (North Yorkshire)." Habilitationsschrift Basle 1980.

320 ---, "The linguistic atlas and generative phonology", in Kirk/ Sanderson/Widdowson 1984.

321 **Glen, Duncan,** "The spelling of Scots", *Scotia Review* 3 (1970): 1-4.*

322 **Godber, Chris,** *Ey up! It's the Death Knocker. The recollections of a door-to-door insurance man in the Meadows District of Nottingham.* Ilkeston, Derbys.: Scollins & Titford 1979.

323 **Görlach, Manfred,** ed., *Focus on: Scotland.* Varieties of English around the World. General Series. Amsterdam: John Benjamins 1984.

324 **Graddol, David** and **Course Team,** *Language Variation and Diversity.* Language in Use (E 263) Block 1. Milton Keynes: Open UP 1981.

325 **Graham, John J.,** *The Shetland Dictionary.* Stornoway: Thule Press 1979.

326 **Graham, William,** "Teach yourself Scots", *Lallans* 7 (1976): 27-29; 8 (1977): 28-30; 9 (1978): 25-27.*

327 ---, *The Scots Word Book.* Edinburgh: Ramsay Head 1977, 2nd ed. 1978, 3rd ed. 1980.

328 **Grant, William,** *The Pronunciation of English in Scotland* [Original Preface dated Dec. 1912]. Repr. College Park, Maryland: McGrath Publ. Comp. 1970.

329 --- and **David D. Murison,** *The Scottish National Dictionary.* Vols. I-X. Edinburgh: The Scottish National Dictionary Association 1929-76.

330 **Gregersen, Edgar,** "Dialect variation within RP", *Le Maître Phonétique* 124/1965: 20-22.

331 **Gregg, Robert J.,** "The boundaries of the Scottish-Irish dialects in Ulster." Ph.D. Edinburgh 1964.*

332 ---, "Scotch-Irish urban speech in Ulster. A phonological study of the regional Standard English of Larne, County Antrim", in Adams 1964: 163-92.

333 ---, "Linguistic change observed: three types of phonological change in the Scotch-Irish dialects", in André Rigault and René Charbonneau, eds., *Proceedings of the Seventh International Congress of Phonetic Sciences.* Janua Linguarum, Series Maior 57. The Hague: Mouton 1972: 722-24.

334 ---, "The Scotch-Irish dialect boundaries in Ulster", in Wakelin 1972: 109-39.

335 ---, "The diphthongs [əɪ] and [ɑɪ] in Scottish, Scotch-Irish and Canadian English", *Canadian Journal of Linguistics* 18 (1973): 136-45.

336 ---, "The distribution of raised and lowered diphthongs as reflexes of M.E. ī in two Scotch-Irish dialects", in Wolfgang U. Dressler and F.V. Mareš, eds., Phonologica 1972. Akten der zweiten Internationalen Phonologie-Tagung Wien, 5. - 8. September 1972. Munich: Fink 1975: 101-5.

337 ---, "The feature 'dentality' as a sociolinguistic marker in Anglo-Irish dialects", Abstracts of Papers. Eighth International Congress of Phonetic Sciences. Leeds 1975, No. 109. /‾A volume with the full Congress papers was never published._/

338 ---, The Scotch-Irish Dialects of Ulster: Their Distribution and Their Boundaries (forthcoming).

339 **Griffin, C.,** "Dialect in practice", Issues in Race and Education, March 1977.*

340 **Griffiths, Dennis,** Talk of my Town. Buckley: Young People's Cultural Association 1969.

341 **Gumperz, John J., Tom C. Jupp** and **Celia Roberts,** Crosstalk: A Study of Cross-Cultural Communication. Background material and notes to accompany the B.B.C. film. London: The National Centre for Industrial Language Training 1979; repr. 1979, 1980, 1981 (with corrections).

342 **Gussenhoven, C.** and **A. Broeders,** "Scots English", in The Pronunciation of English. A Course for Dutch Learners. Groningen: Wolters-Noordhoff-Longmans 1976: 201-11.

343 **Hadi, S.,** "Some language issues." Paper based on a Survey undertaken as Part of the Schools Council/NFER Education for a Multiracial Society Project 1976 /‾Ms._/.*

344 **Haggard, Andrew,** Dialect and Local Usages of Herefordshire. London: Grower Books 1972.

345 **Hancock, Ian F.,** "Shelta, a problem of classification", in David DeCamp and Ian F. Hancock, eds., Pidgins and Creoles: Current Trends and Prospects. Washington, D.C.: Georgetown UP 1974: 130-7.

346 ---, The Social and Linguistic Development of Angloromani. Working Papers in Sociolinguistics 38. Austin 1977.

347 ---, "Pidginization and the development of Anglo-Romani", Journal of the Gypsy Lore Society 4 (1979): 1/3.*

348 ---, "Palari and Shelta", in Trudgill 1984.

349 ---, "Romani and Anglo-Romani", in Trudgill 1984.

350 *Handlist of Work in Progress and Work Completed on Anglo-Irish Dialect Studies*. The Royal Irish Academy, Dublin: Committee for the Study of Anglo-Irish Language and Literature. Nov. 1972 [Ms.].*

351 *Handlist of Work in Progress: Committee for the Study of Anglo-Irish Language and Literature. Royal Irish Academy*. Dublin: Royal Irish Academy 1973 [Ms.].*

352 *Handlist of Work in Progress: Committee for the Study of Anglo-Irish Language and Literature. Royal Irish Academy*. Dublin: Royal Irish Academy 1974 [Ms.].*

353 **Harman, H.,** *Buckinghamshire Dialect*. [1929]. With a new Preface by Stewart F. Sanderson. Republished East Ardsley: S.R. Publ. 1970.

354 **Harris, John,** "The underlying non-identity of English dialects: a look at the Hiberno-English verb phrase", *Belfast Working Papers in Language and Linguistics* 6 (1982): 1-36.

355 ---, "The Hiberno-English 'I've it eaten' construction: What is it and where does it come from?" *Teanga. Journal of the Linguistic Institute of Ireland* 3 (1982).*

356 ---, "English in the north of Ireland", in Trudgill 1984.

357 --- and **James Milroy,** "Variation in 'the short /ɔ/' system in Belfast." Report to Social Science Research Council 1982.*

358 **Harris, Martin,** "The phonology and grammar of the dialect of South Zeal, Devonshire." 2 vols. Ph.D. London 1967.

359 ---, "Demonstrative adjectives and pronouns in a Devonshire dialect", *Transactions of the Philological Society 1968* (1969): 1-11.

360 ---, "Relationships of place in a Devonshire dialect", *Archivum Linguisticum* N.S. 1 (1970): 43-48.

361 **Harris, P. Valentine,** *Pembrokeshire Place-Names and Dialect* [1960]. Revised ed. Tenby: H.G. Walters 1974 [Title on book cover reads: *Guide to Place Names and Dialects of Pembrokeshire*].

362 **Harrison, Godfrey, Wynford Bellin, Brec'hed Piette,** *Bilingual Mothers in Wales and the Language of their Children*. Social Science Monographs 6. Cardiff: University of Wales Press 1981.

363 **Haugen, Einar, J. Derrick McClure** and **Derrick S. Thomson,** eds., *Minority Languages Today*. Edinburgh: UP 1981.

364 **Heath, Christopher D.,** "A study of speech patterns in the urban district of Cannock, Staffordshire." Ph.D. Leeds 1971.

365 ---, The Pronunciation of English in Cannock, Staffordshire. A Socio-Linguistic Survey of an Urban Speech-Community. Publications of the Philological Society XXVIV [sic]. Oxford: Blackwell 1980.

366 **Heaton, Susan,** "The occupational dialect of a Blackhall coal-miner", The Journal of the Lancashire Dialect Society 21 (1972): 19-21.

367 **Hedberg, Johannes,** "Some notes on language and atmosphere in Dubliners", Moderna Språk 75 (1981): 113-32.

368 **Hedevind, Bertil,** The Dialect of Dentdale in the West Riding of Yorkshire. Studia Anglistica Upsaliensia 5 (1967).

369 **Henry, Patrick L.,** "Anglo-Irish word-charts", in Adams 1964: 147-61.

370 ---, "English and its varieties", Encyclopaedia of Ireland. Dublin: A. Figgis 1968: 118-9.

371 ---, "Anglo-Irish and its Irish background", in Ó Muirithe 1978: 20-36.

372 ---, "The linguistic atlas and lexis", in Kirk/Sanderson/Widdowson 1984.

373 **Herdman, John,** "The progress of Scots", Akros 7,20 (1972): 31-42.

374 **Hettinga, J.,** "Standard and dialect in Anstruther and Cellardyke", Scottish Literary Journal Supplement 14 (1981): 37-48.

375 **Hewson, Michael,** "A word-list from South-West Clare", North Munster Antiquarian Journal 9 (1962-65): 182-6.*

376 **Hickey, Raymond,** "Syntactic ambiguity in Hiberno-English", Studia Anglica Posnaniensia 15 (1982): 39-45.

377 ---, "Remarks on pronominal usage in Hiberno-English", Studia Anglica Posnaniensia 15 (1982): 47-53.

378 **Hill, Archibald A.,** "The habituative aspect of verbs in Black English, Irish English, and Standard English", American Speech 50 (1975): 323-4.

379 **Hirooka, Hideo,** "Verbal and pronominal forms in English dialects", Studies in English Literature 45 (1969): 181-92.

380 ---, Thomas Hardy's Use of Dialect. Tokyo: Shinozaki Shorin [1983].

381 **Hockey, Susan,** A Guide to Computer Applications in the Humanities. Baltimore and London: John Hopkins UP 1980; Chapter 4: "Vocabulary Studies, Collocations and Dialectology".

382 **Hogan, Jeremiah Joseph,** The English Language in Ireland. Dublin: The Educational Co. of Ireland 1927; repr. College Park, Maryland: McGrath Publ. Comp. 1970.

383 **Homan, R.,** "A sociological analysis of the language behaviour of old-time Pentecostals." Ph.D. Lancaster 1978.*

384 **Houck, Charles L.,** "Methodology of an urban speech survey", in Ellis 1968 (1969): 115-28.

385 **Hubmayer, Karl,** Lautveränderungen im gegenwärtigen Englisch. Eine experimental-phonetische Studie zur lautlichen Performanz der 'Received Pronunciation'. /_ Diss. (= Austrian Ph.D.) Salzburg 1978_/ Wien: VWGÖ 1980.

386 ---, "Die 'Received Pronunciation' - Norm und Variabilität", Arbeiten aus Anglistik und Amerikanistik 4 (1979): 37-51.

387 **Hudson, Richard A.,** Sociolinguistics. Cambridge: UP 1980; esp. Chapters 2 and 5.

388 --- and **A.F. Holloway,** "Variation in London English." Final Report to the Social Science Research Council of Great Britain on Grant 4595. 1977. (Department of Phonetics and Linguistics, University College London) /_ Ms._/.*

389 **Hughes, Arthur** and **Peter Trudgill,** English Accents and Dialects: An Introduction to Social and Regional Varieties of British English. London: Edward Arnold 1979 /_ with accompanying tape or cassette resp._/.

390 **Hughes, John P.,** "The Irish language and the 'brogue': a study in substratum", Word 22, 1966 (1973): 259-75.

391 **Hurford, J.R.,** "The speech of one family: a phonetic comparison of the speech of three generations in a family of East Londoners." Ph.D. London, University College 1967.*

392 ---, "The range of contoidal articulations in a dialect", Orbis 17 (1968): 389-95.

393 ---, "English: Cockney", Le Maître Phonétique 130/1968: 32-34; 132/1969: 41-43; 134/1970: 38-39.

394 **Hutterer, Claus Jürgen,** Die Germanischen Sprachen. Ihre Geschichte in Grundzügen. Budapest: Akadémiai Kiadó 1975; Chapter IV.5.

395 **Ihalainen, Ossi,** "Periphrastic do in affirmative sentences in the dialect of East Somerset", Neuphilologische Mitteilungen 77 (1976): 608-22.

396 ---, "Relative clauses in the dialect of Somerset", Neuphilologische Mitteilungen 81 (1980): 187-96.

397 ---, "A note on eliciting data in dialectology. The case of periphrastic 'do'", Neuphilologische Mitteilungen 82 (1981): 25-27.

398 ---, "He took the bottle and put'n in his pocket: The object pronoun it in present-day Somerset", in Viereck 1984.

399 ---, A Study of Folk Speech in Somerset (forthcoming).

400 **ILEA English Centre,** Dialect and Language Variety. London: Ebury Teachers' Centre 1979.*

401 **Jacks, D.S.M.,** "The living dialect of Stokesay, Shropshire. The Mercian defensive earthworks on the Kerry Hill ridgeway (Shropshire and Montgomeryshire) to the west of Offa's Dyke." M.Phil. Leeds 1967-68.

402 **Jacobson, Joanne,** "The dialect of Golcar." M.A. Leeds 1974.

403 **James, G.,** "Variables in relative clause structure in a dialect of English." M.Phil. Reading 1978.*

404 **Jamieson, John,** An Etymological Dictionary of the Scottish Language. A new edition by John Longmuir and David Donaldson. 4 vols. and supplement. Paisley: Alexander Gardner 1879-87; repr. New York: AMS Press 1966.

405 **Jamieson, Peter,** "Sea-speech and beliefs of Shetland fishermen", The New Shetlander 110 (1974): 30-32.*

406 **Jarman, Eric** and **Alan Cruttenden,** "Belfast intonation and the myth of the fall", Journal of the International Phonetic Association 6 (1976): 4-12.

407 **Jassem, Wiktor,** The Phonology of Modern English. Warszawa: Państwowe Wydawnictwo Naukowe 1983; Chapter 3.4.2: "The main phonological features of Regional British English".

408 **John, Brian S.,** "The linguistic significance of the Pembrokeshire Landsker", The Pembrokeshire Historian 4 (1972): 7-29.*

409 **Johnston, Paul A.,** "A synchronic and historical view of border area bimoric vowel systems." Ph.D. Edinburgh 1980.

410 ---, "Variation in the Standard Scottish English of Morningside", English World-Wide 4,2 (1983).

411 ---, "The linguistic atlas and sociolinguistics", in Kirk/ Sanderson/Widdowson 1984.

412 ---, "Sociolinguistic investigation of Edinburgh speech" (continuation of a project begun by Suzanne Romaine). SSRC Project No. HR4765/1.*

413 **Johnston, Rhona Poole,** "Social class and grammatical development: a comparison of the speech of five year olds from middle and working class backgrounds", Language and Speech 20 (1977): 317-24.

414 **Jones, B. Lewis,** "Welsh: Linguistic conservation and shifting bilingualism", in Haugen/McClure/Thomson 1981: 40-52.

415 **Jones, Jack,** Rhyming Cockney Slang. Bristol: Abson Books 1971; sixth impr. 1976.

416 **Jones, Valerie,** "The Tyneside Linguistic Survey - an approach to data processing in sociolinguistics", Statistical Methods in Linguistics Quarterly Journal 2 (1978): 5-23.

417 ---, "Some problems in the computation of sociolinguistic data." Ph.D. Newcastle-upon-Tyne 1979.

418 **Jones-Sargent, Valerie,** Tyne Bytes. A Computerised Sociolinguistic Study of Tyneside. Bamberger Beiträge zur englischen Sprachwissenschaft 11 (1983).

419 ---, "Tyneside syntax: a presentation of some data from the Tyneside Linguistic Survey", in Viereck 1984.

420 **Joyce, Patrick W.,** English as we Speak it in Ireland. London and Dublin: Longman 1910; repr. with an Introduction by Terence Dolan. Portmarnock, Co. Dublin: Wolfhound Press 1979.

421 **Kean, Mary,** Scottish-English, English-Scottish. Bristol: Abson Books 1972; ninth impr. 1981.

422 **Keil, Gerald C.,** "IMPAC (indexing, map plotting, and analysis by computer)", Computers and the Humanities 7 (1972): 116.

423 ---, "Narrow phonetic transcription on the computer: taking the phone off the hook", Computers and the Humanities 8 (1974): 217-29.

424 **Kelly, J.,** "On the phonology of an English urban accent", Le Maître Phonétique 127/1967: 2-5.

425 **Kendall, Sydney T.,** Up the Frog. The Road to Cockney Rhyming Slang. London: Wolfe 1969.

426 **Kenrick, Donald,** "Anglo-Romani today", in Thomas A. Acton, ed., Current Changes amongst British Gypsies and their Place in International Patterns of Development. Oxford: National Gypsy Education Council 1971: 5-14.

427 ---, "Romani English", International Journal of the Sociology of Language 19 (1979): 111-20.

428 **Kenworthy, Joanne,** "The intonation of questions in one variety of Scottish English", Work in Progress. Edinburgh University. Linguistics Department 10 (1977): 70-81.

429 ---, "The intonation of questions in one variety of Scottish English", Lingua 44 (1978): 267-82.

430 **Kerr, R.D.,** A Glossary of Mining Terms used in Fife. Kirkcaldy: College of Technology 1980.*

431 **Khleif, Bud B.,** "Language as an ethnic boundary in Welsh-English relations", International Journal of the Sociology of Language 20 (1979): 59-74.

432 ---, Language, Ethnicity, and Education in Wales. Contributions to the Sociology of Language 28. The Hague, Paris: Mouton 1980.

433 **Kiberd, Declan,** Synge and the Irish Language. London: Macmillan 1979; esp. Chapters 3 and 8.

434 **Kilford, Valerie,** Shropshire Words and Dialect. Church Stretton: Bielby's Printpress n.d.

435 **Kirk, John M.,** "Prolegomena to a survey of modern Scottish usage." Sheffield 1980 /_ Ms._/.

436 ---, "Vernacular restructuring in twentieth-century Scottish speech." Paper to the First International Conference on Minority Languages. Glasgow 1980. /_ Ms._/.

437 ---, "On Scottish Non-Standard English", The Nottingham Linguistic Circular 10 (1981): 155-78.

438 ---, "The linguistic atlas and grammar", in Kirk/Sanderson/Widdowson 1984.

439 ---, **Stewart F. Sanderson** and **John D.A. Widdowson,** eds., Studies in Linguistic Geography. London: Croom Helm 1984.

440 **Kloss, Heinz,** Die Entwicklung neuer germanischer Kultursprachen seit 1800. [1952] Düsseldorf: Schwann, 2nd ed. 1978: "Niederschottisch (Lallans)", 256-64; "Angelirisch", 267-8.

441 **Knapp, Karlfried** and **Annelie Knapp-Potthoff,** "Farbige Immigranten in Großbritannien - Linguistische und soziale Aspekte einer multiethnischen Gesellschaft", Studium Linguistik 8/9 (1980): 144-62.

442 **Kniezsa, Veronika,** "To the phonetical aspects of the development of the Standard Scots vowel system", Acta Linguistica Academiae Scientiarum Hungaricae 26 (1976): 457-66.

443 ---, "The problem of the merger of Middle English /a:/ and /ai/ in Northern English", in Davenport/Hansen/Nielsen 1983: 95-102.

444 **Knowles, Gerald,** "A discussion of Houck's dialectology." Leeds 1968 [Ms.].*

445 ---, "Scouse: the urban dialect of Liverpool." Ph.D. Leeds 1974.

446 ---, "Identifying phonological variables in Scouse", in Reid 1976: 17-18.

447 ---, "The nature of phonological variables in Scouse", York Papers in Linguistics 7 (1977): 129-49.*

448 ---, "The nature of phonological variables in Scouse", in Trudgill 1978: 80-90.

449 **Kökeritz, Helge,** The Phonology of the Suffolk Dialect: Descriptive and Historical. Uppsala: Lundequistska Bokhandeln 1932; repr. University Microfilms International L2G-OP42636 'Books on Demand' (n.d.).

450 **Kohler, Klaus J.,** "Aspects of the history of English pronunciation in Scotland." Ph.D. Edinburgh 1964.*

451 **Kolb, Eduard,** "Skandinavisches in den nordenglischen Dialekten", Anglia 83 (1965): 127-53.

452 ---, "An exercise in dialect detection", Transactions of the Yorkshire Dialect Society, Vol. XI, Pt. LXV (1965): 11-17.

453 ---, Phonological Atlas of the Northern Region. The Six Northern Counties, North Lincolnshire and the Isle of Man. Bern: Francke 1966.

454 ---, "Die Infiltration der Hochsprache in die nordenglischen Dialekte", Anglia 86 (1968): 1-13.

455 ---, "Ein skandinavisches Wort an der englischen Küste", Anglia 91 (1973): 241-4.

456 ---, "'Elmet'. A dialect region in northern England", Anglia 91 (1973): 285-313.

457 ---, "Sun and son in England", English Studies 60 (1979): 498-504.

458 --- and **Willy Elmer,** "Field recordings from Chirnside, Greenlaw, Lanton, Newcastleton, Langholm, Ecclefechan." Basle 1969 [Ms.].*

459 ---, **Beat Glauser, Willy Elmer** and **Renate Stamm,** Atlas of English Sounds. Bern: Francke 1979.

460 **Kramarae, Cheris,** "Gender: How she speaks", in Ryan/Giles 1982: 84-98.

461 **Kristensson, Gillis,** "A piece of Middle English word geography", English Studies 60 (1979): 254-60.

462 ---, "Dialectology and historical linguistics", in Davenport/ Hansen/Nielsen 1983: 29-35.

463 **Kurath, Hans,** A Phonology and Prosody of Modern English. Heidelberg: Carl Winter 1964.

464 ---, "British sources of selected features of American pronunciation: problems and methods", in Abercrombie/Fry 1964: 146-55; repr. in Allen/Underwood 1971: 265-72.

465 ---, "Contributions of British folk speech to American pronunciation", in Ellis 1968 (1969): 129-34.

466 ---, "English sources of some American regional words and verb forms", American Speech 45 (1970): 60-68.

467 ---, "Some aspects of Atlantic seaboard English considered in their connections with British English" [1960/1965]; repr. in Williamson/ Burke 1971: 101-7.

468 ---, "The origin of the dialectal differences in spoken American English" [1928]; repr. in Williamson/Burke 1971: 12-21.

469 ---, Studies in Area Linguistics. Bloomington and London: Indiana UP 1972; Chapters 5 and 6.

470 ---, "Relics of English folk speech in American English", in Davis 1972: 367-75.

471 --- and † **Guy S. Lowman, Jr.,** The Dialectal Structure of Southern England: Phonological Evidence: Publication of the American Dialect Society 54. 1970 (1974).

472 **Lander, Steve,** "Morpho-syntactic features in the writing of second-generation West Indians." M.A. Sheffield 1979.*

473 ---, "On southern /a:/", Lore and Language 3/3, Part A (1980): 24-27.

474 ---, "Creole and non-creole influences on the English of the British-born children of Caribbean immigrants", The Nottingham Linguistic Circular 10 (1981): 179-85.*

475 ---, "The written English of second generation West Indians", First Language (forthcoming).

476 **Lass, Roger,** "Linguistic orthogenesis? Scots vowel quantity and the English length conspiracy", York Papers in Linguistics 4 (1973); repr. in Anderson/Jones 1974: 311-52.

477 **Lauder, Afferbeck,** Fraffly well spoken. How to speak the language of London's West End. Sydney: Ure Smith and London: Wolfe Publ. 1968.

478 **Lediard, James,** "The sounds of the dialect of Canton, a suburb of Cardiff." Appendix A in Parry 1977: 261-70.

479 **Leeds, Winifred,** Herefordshire Speech. The South-West Midland Dialect as Spoken in Herefordshire and Its Environs. Ross-on-Wye: M. Spurway [1974].

480 **Lehnert, Martin,** Substandard English (Vulgärenglisch). Sitzungsberichte der Akademie der Wissenschaften der DDR. Gesellschaftswissenschaften. Jg. 1980. Nr. 11G. Berlin: Akademie-Verlag 1981.

481 **Leigh, Egerton,** A Glossary of Words used in the Dialect of Cheshire. [1877]. New Introduction by Stewart F. Sanderson. Republished East Ardsley: E.P. Publ. 1973.

482 **Leisi, Ernst,** Das heutige Englisch: Wesenszüge und Probleme. Heidelberg: Carl Winter 1955; 6th ed. 1974; esp. Chapter V.

483 **Leith, Richard,** "Dialectology in London." M.A. Leeds 1971.

484 ---, "The traditional phonology of north London speech." M.Phil. Leeds 1973.

485 ---, A Social History of English. London: Routledge and Kegan Paul 1983 (Language and Society Series); esp. Chapters 5 'Pronunciation' and 6 'The imposition of English in the British Isles'.

486 **Leitner, Gerhard,** Geschichte und soziolinguistische Interpretation des Sprachgebrauchs in einem Massenmedium. Linguistische Berichte - Papier Nr. 60. Wiesbaden 1979 [Short description of contents in Linguistische Berichte 62/1979: 107].

487 ---, "The consolidation of 'educated southern English' as a model in the early 20th century", International Review of Applied Linguistics in Language Teaching 20 (1982): 91-107.

488 **Le Page, Robert B.,** Caribbean Connections in the Classroom. A pamphlet of guidance for teachers concerned with the language problems of children of Afro-Caribbean descent. London: The Mary Glasgow Language Trust 1981.

489 **Levitt, John H.,** "Some aspects of north Staffordshire vocabulary", The Journal of the Lancashire Dialect Society 19 (1970): 8-19.

490 ---, "Further notes on north Staffordshire vocabulary", The Journal of the Lancashire Dialect Society 20 (1971): 8-15.

491 ---, "A further note on 'Chonnock'", The Journal of the Lancashire Dialect Society 29 (1980): 31-32.

492 **Lewis, E. Glyn,** "Attitude to language among bilingual children and adults in Wales", International Journal of the Sociology of Language 4 (1975): 103-25.

493 ---, "Bilingualism in education in Wales", in Bernard Spolsky and Robert L. Cooper, eds., Case Studies in Bilingual Education. Rowley, Mass.: Newbury House Publ. 1978: 249-90.

494 **Linguistic Minorities Project**: "First progress report." London 1980. "Second progress report." London 1981 [Mss.].

495 **Little, Alan,** "The educational achievement of ethnic minority children in London schools", in Gajendra K. Verma and Christopher Bagley, eds., Race and Education across Cultures. London: Heinemann 1975: 48-69.

496 **Local, John,** "The Tyneside urban dialect survey." Newcastle-upon-Tyne 1975 /_ Ms._7.*

497 ---, "Studies towards a description of the development and functioning of children's awareness of linguistic variability." Ph.D. Newcastle-upon-Tyne 1978.*

498 ---, "Modelling intonational variability in children's speech", in Romaine 1982: 85-103.

499 ---, "On the interpretation of linguistic variability in children", (forthcoming).

500 **Lodge, Ken R.,** "The Stockport dialect", Le Maître Phonétique 126/1966: 26-30.

501 ---, "Stockport revisited", Journal of the International Phonetic Association 3 (1973): 81-87.

502 ---, "A Stockport teenager", Journal of the International Phonetic Association 8 (1978): 56-71.

503 ---, "A three-dimensional analysis of non-standard English", Journal of Pragmatics 3 (1979): 169-95.

504 **Long, W.H.,** A Dictionary of the Isle of Wight Dialect /¯etc._7. /_ London 1886_7; repr. Norwood, Pa.: Norwood Editions 1975.

505 **Low, John Thomas,** "The Scots language: The contemporary situation", in McClure /¯1975_7: 17-27.

506 ---, "A Scots language policy for education", in McClure/Aitken/Low 1980: 67-95.

507 ---, "Mid twentieth century drama in Lowland Scots", in McClure 1983: 170-94.

508 **Lunny, P.A.,** "Linguistic interaction: English and Irish in Ballyvourney, West Cork", in Barry 1981: 118-41.

509 ---, "Studies in the modern English dialect of Ballyvourney, West Cork." Ph.D. Belfast 1981.*

510 **Lyne, A.A.,** "How broad was my 'u'", Lore and Language 1,9 (1973): 3-6.

511 **Macafee, Caroline,** "Characteristics of non-standard grammar in Scotland." 1980 /¯Ms._7.*

512 ---, "Nationalism and the Scots Renaissance now", English World-Wide 2 (1981): 29-38; repr. in Görlach 1984.

513 ---, "Glasgow dialect in literature", Scottish Language 1 (1982): 45-53.

514 ---, Glasgow. Varieties of English around the World. Text Series Vol. 3. Amsterdam: John Benjamins 1984.

515 **Macaulay, Donald,** "Borrow, calque and switch: The law of the English frontier", in John Anderson, ed., Language Form and Linguistic Variation. Papers dedicated to Angus McIntosh. Amsterdam Studies in the Theory and History of Linguistic Science IV. Current Issues in Linguistic Theory 15. Amsterdam: John Benjamins B.V. 1982: 203-37.

516 **Macaulay, Ronald K.S.,** "Double standards", American Anthropologist 75 (1973): 1324-37.

517 ---, "I don't really believe in that middle class, you know, myself to be honest: social class and language in Glasgow." 1975 [Ms.].*

518 ---, "Linguistic insecurity", in McClure [1975]: 35-43.

519 ---, "Negative prestige, linguistic insecurity, and linguistic self-hatred", Lingua 36 (1975): 147-61.

520 ---, "Tongue-tied in the Scottish classroom", Education in the North 13 (1976): 13-16.

521 ---, "Social class and language in Glasgow", Language in Society 5 (1976): 173-88.

522 ---, "Variation and consistency in Glaswegian English", in Trudgill 1978: 132-43.

523 ---, "The narrative skills of a Scottish coal miner", in Görlach 1984.

524 ---, "Dialect maps: visual aid or abstract art?" in Kirk/Sanderson/Widdowson 1984.

525 ---, "A comparative study of urban speech in Scotland" (forthcoming).

526 --- and **G.D. Trevelyan,** "Language education and employment in Glasgow." Edinburgh: The Scottish Council for Research in Education 1973 (2 vols.).

527 --- (with the assistance of **G.D. Trevelyan**), Language, Social Class, and Education: A Glasgow Study. Edinburgh: UP 1977.

528 **MacDonald, Christine,** "Variation in the use of modal verbs with

special reference to Tyneside English." Ph.D. Newcastle-upon-Tyne 1981.*

529 **Mac Einrí, Fidélis,** "An Irish English vowel system", *Abstracts of Papers. Eighth International Congress of Phonetic Sciences.* Leeds 1975, No. 181. [A volume with the full Congress papers was never published.]

530 **Mac Eoin, Gearóid,** "Linguistic contacts in Ireland", in Ureland 1982: 227-35.

531 **Mackay, Charles,** *A Dictionary of Lowland Scotch, with an Introductory Chapter on the Poetry, Humour, and Literary History of the Scottish Language and an Appendix of Scottish Proverbs.* London: Whittaker 1888; republ. Detroit: Gale 1968.

532 **Mackie, Albert,** *Talking Glasgow.* Belfast: Blackstaff 1978.

533 ---, *Speak Scotch or Whistle.* Belfast: Blackstaff 1979.

534 **Mackinnon, D.,** *Language and Social Class.* Milton Keynes: Open UP 1977.

535 **Mackinnon, Iain,** *Lowland Scots Glossary.* Stirling: A. Learmonth & Son 1966.

536 **MacKinnon, Kenneth M.,** "Language shift and education: conservation of ethnolinguistic culture amongst schoolchildren of a Gaelic community", *Linguistics* 198/1977: 31-55.

537 **Maclaran, R.,** "The variable (ʌ), a relic form with social correlates", *Belfast Working Papers in Language and Linguistics* 1 (1976): 45-68.

538 **MacMahon, M.,** "A phonetic and phonemic study of the East Holderness dialect." Diploma in Linguistics Reading 1966.*

539 **Makovskij, M.M.,** *English Dialectology. Present-day English Territorial Dialects of Great Britain.* Moscow: Vysšaja škola 1980 [in Russian].*

540 **Manley, Sandra,** "The Black Country dialect in the Cradley Heath area." M.A. Leeds 1971.

541 **Manners, Penny,** "The teaching of English to immigrants", *The Incorporated Linguist* 16 (1977): 12-14.

542 **Mardle, Jonathan [Eric Fowler],** *Broad Norfolk.* Norwich: Wensum Books 1973.

543 **Martin-Jones, Marilyn,** "The newer minority languages: written languages - form and status", in Trudgill 1984.

544 **Mather, James Y.,** "Dialect research in Orkney and Shetland after Jakobsen", Froðskaparrit 13 (1964): 33-43.

545 ---, "Aspects of the linguistic geography of Scotland: I", Scottish Studies 9 (1965): 129-44.

546 ---, "Aspects of the linguistic geography of Scotland. II: East coast fishing", Scottish Studies 10 (1966): 129-53.

547 ---, "Aspects of the linguistic geography of Scotland. III: Fishing communities of the east coast (Part 1)", Scottish Studies 13 (1969): 1-16.

548 ---, "Linguistic geography and the traditional drift-net fishery of the Scottish east coast", in Wakelin 1972: 7-31.

549 ---, "The Scots we speak today", in Aitken 1978: 56-68.

550 ---, "Social variation in present-day Scots speech", in McClure [1975]: 44-53.

551 ---, "The dialect of Caithness", Scottish Literary Journal Supplement 6 (1978): 1-16.

552 ---, "The dialect of the eastern borders", Scottish Literary Journal Supplement 12 (1980): 30-42.

553 --- and **Hans-Henning Speitel,** eds., The Linguistic Atlas of Scotland. Scots Section. London: Croom Helm. Vol. 1 (1975), Vol. 2 (1977), Vol. 3 (forthcoming).

554 **Mathias, Roland,** "The Welsh language and the English language", in Meic Stephens, ed., The Welsh Language Today. Llandysul: Gomer Press 1973: 32-63.

555 **Matthews, William,** Cockney Past and Present: A Short History of the Dialect of London. London: Routledge and Kegan Paul 1938; repr. with additional Preface. London and Boston: Routledge and Kegan Paul 1972.

556 **Maxim, J.,** "A grammatical analysis of language in the elderly." Ph.D. Reading (forthcoming).

557 **McArthur, Tom,** "The status of English in and furth of Scotland", in Aitken/McArthur 1979: 50-67.

558 **McCaughan, Michael,** "Flax scutching in Ulster: Techniques and terminology", Ulster Folklife 14 (1968): 6-13.

559 **McClure, J. Derrick R.,** "Some features of Standard English as spoken in south-west Scotland." M.Litt. Edinburgh 1970.*

560 ---, ed., The Scots Language in Education. Aberdeen College of Education and the Association for Scottish Literary Studies. Occasional Papers No. 3. Aberdeen n.d. [1975].

561 ---, "Two sociolinguistic variables in the English of Scotland". Abstracts of Papers. Eighth International Congress of Phonetic Sciences. Leeds 1975, No. 179. [A volume with the full Congress papers was never published.]

562 ---, "A historical phonology for the dialects of Scots". Abstracts of Papers. Eighth International Congress of Phonetic Sciences. Leeds 1975, No. 180. [A volume with the full Congress papers was never published.]

563 ---, "The English speech of Scotland", The Aberdeen University Review 46 (1975): 173-89.

564 ---, "The Linguistic Atlas of Scotland", American Speech 51 (1976): 223- 34 [review art.].

565 ---, "Vowel duration in a Scottish accent", Journal of the International Phonetic Association 7 (1977): 10-16.

566 ---, "Scots: its range of uses", in Aitken/McArthur 1979: 26-48.

567 ---, "Developing Scots as a national language", in McClure/Aitken/Low 1980: 11-41.

568 ---, "Western Scottish intonation: a preliminary study", in Linda R. Waugh and C.H. van Schooneveld, eds., The Melody of Language. Baltimore: University Park Press 1980: 201-17.

569 ---, "The spelling of Scots: a phoneme-based system", Scottish Literary Journal Supplement 12 (1980): 25-29.

570 ---, "The synthetisers of Scots", in Haugen/McClure/Thomson 1981: 91-99.

571 ---, "Urban Scots", Teaching English 15 (1981): 35-40.*

572 ---, ed., Scotland and the Lowland Tongue. Studies in the Language and Literature of Lowland Scotland in Honour of David D. Murison. Aberdeen: UP 1983.

573 ---, ed., *Minority Languages in Central Scotland*. Aberdeen: Association for Scottish Literary Studies. Occasional Paper No. 5 (1983a).

574 ---, "Scots in Dialogue: some uses and implications", in McClure 1983: 129-48.

575 ---, "Two sociolinguistic variables in Scottish English." n.d. /¯Ms._7.*

576 ---, **Adam J. Aitken** and **John Thomas Low,** *The Scots Language. Planning for Modern Usage*. Edinburgh: The Ramsay Head Press 1980.

577 ---, **John Thomas Low, J.K. Annand, A.D. Mackie** and **J.J. Graham,** "Our ain leid? The predicament of a Scots writer", *English World-Wide* 2 (1981): 3-28; repr. in Görlach 1984.

578 **McDavid, Raven I., Jr.,** "Two studies of dialects of English", in Ellis 1968 (1969): 23-48; repr. in Anwar S. Dil, ed., *Varieties of American English. Essays by Raven I. McDavid, Jr.* Stanford: UP 1980: 206-33.

579 ---, "Dialects: British and American standard and nonstandard", in Archibald A. Hill, ed., *Linguistics Today*. New York: Basic Books 1969: 79-88.

580 ---, "The sound system of a West Midland dialect: Kniveton, Derbyshire", in Viereck 1984.

581 **Mees, I.,** "Language and social class in Cardiff: a survey of the speech habits of schoolchildren." Thesis, Leiden 1977.*

582 **Meier, Hans H.,** "Scots is not alone: The Swiss and Low German analogues", in Adam J. Aitken, Matthew P. McDiarmid and Derick S. Thomson, eds., *Bards and Makars: Scottish Language and Literature, Medieval and Renaissance*. Glasgow: UP 1977: 201-13.

583 **Melchers, Gunnel,** *Studies in Yorkshire Dialects. Based on Recordings of 13 Dialect Speakers in the West Riding. I; II: Transcriptions.* Stockholm Theses in English 9 (1972).

584 ---, "Modal auxiliaries in regional dialects", in Sven Jacobson, ed., *Papers from the Scandinavian Symposium on Syntactic Variation. Stockholm, May 18 - 19, 1979*. Acta Universitatis Stockholmiensis. Stockholm Studies in English 52. Stockholm: Almquist & Wiksell 1980: 113-23.

585 ---, "The Norn element in Shetland dialect today - a case of never-accepted language death", in Eva Ejerhed and Inger Henrysson, eds., *Nordisk Tvåsprakighet: Föredrag från Tredje Nordiska Tvåsprakighetssymposiet 4 - 5 Juni 1980, Umeå Universitet*. Umeå Studies in the Humanities 36. Umeå: Univ.-bibl. 1981: 254-61.*

586 ---, "The Scandinavian element in Shetland dialect." Report No. 1: A Presentation of the Project. Stockholm/Sweden and Dragvoll/Norway 1983.

587 ---, "Knappin - proper English - modified Scottish - language attitudes in the Shetland Isles", in Görlach 1984.

588 **Mercer, Liz,** "Ethnicity and the supplementary school", in Neil Mercer 1981: 147-57.

589 **Mercer, Neil,** ed., Language in School and Community. London: Edward Arnold 1981.

590 --- and **Janet Maybin,** "Community language and education", in Neil Mercer 1981: 77-95.

591 ---, **Elizabeth Mercer** and **Robert Mears,** "Linguistic and cultural affiliation amongst young Asian people in Leicester", in Giles/Saint-Jacques 1979: 15-26.

592 **Millar, Martin P.** and **E. Keith Brown,** "Tag questions in Edinburgh speech", Linguistische Berichte 60/1979: 24-45.

593 **Miller, Jim E.,** "Get in a corpus of Scottish English" [Ms.].*

594 ---, "Reference to future time in a corpus of Scottish English" [Ms.].*

595 ---, "Negatives in Scottish English" [Ms.].*

596 ---, "The expression of necessity and obligation in Scottish English." Part of Final Report to SSRC on Grant HR 5152 (1980).*

597 ---, "The expression of possibility and permission in Scottish English." Part of Final Report to SSRC on Grant HR 5152 (1980).*

598 ---, "Syntax and discourse in a corpus of spoken Scottish English" [Ms.].*

599 --- and **E. Keith Brown,** Syntax of Scottish English. Social Science Research Council. Final Report 1980.*

600 --- and **E. Keith Brown,** "Aspects of Scottish English syntax", English World-Wide 3 (1982): 3-17; repr. in Görlach 1984.

601 **Miller, Stephen,** Specimen of Shetland Words from Vocabulary compiled by W.A. Grant, from the Bonaparte Collection in the Biblioteca Provincial de Vizcaya, Bilbao, Pais Vascos. Papers in Folklife Studies 3. The School of English, The University of Leeds 1982.

602 **Milroy, James,** "Length and height variations in the vowels of Belfast vernacular", Belfast Working Papers in Language and Linguistics 1 (1976): 69-110.

603 ---, "Synopsis of Belfast vowels", Belfast Working Papers on Language and Linguistics 1 (1976): 111-16.*

604 ---, "Stability and change in non-standard English in Belfast", Bulletin of the Northern Ireland Speech and Language Forum (1978).*

605 ---, "Lexical alternation and diffusion in vernacular speech", Belfast Working Papers in Language and Linguistics 3 (1978): 100-14.

606 ---, "Lexical alternation and the history of English: evidence from an urban vernacular", in Elizabeth C. Traugott, Rebecca Labrum and Susan Shepherd, eds., Papers from the 4th International Conference on Historical Linguistics. Amsterdam 1980: 355-62.

607 ---, The Pronunciation of English in Belfast. Belfast: Blackstaff 1981.

608 ---, Regional Accents of English: Belfast. Belfast: Blackstaff 1981.

609 ---, "Probing under the tip of the iceberg: phonological 'normalization' and the shape of speech communities", in Romaine 1982: 35-47.

610 ---, "Some connections between Galloway and Ulster speech", Scottish Language 1 (1982): 23-29.

611 ---, "On the sociolinguistic history of /h/-dropping in English", in Davenport/Hansen/Nielsen 1983: 37-53.

612 --- and **John Harris,** "When is a merger not a merger? The MEAT/MATE problem in Belfast vernacular", Belfast Working Papers in Language and Linguistics 4 (1980): 30-40.

613 --- and **John Harris,** "When is a merger not a merger? The MEAT/MATE problem in a present-day English vernacular", English World-Wide 1 (1980): 199-210.

614 --- and **Lesley Milroy,** "A sociolinguistic project in Belfast: Preliminary statement of aims", Sociolinguistics Newsletter 6,1 (1975): 18-20.

615 --- and **Lesley Milroy,** "Speech community and phonological variation in Belfast", in Reid 1976: 6-7.

616 --- and **Lesley Milroy,** "Speech community and language variety in Belfast." Report to the Social Science Research Council 1977 /_End-of-grant Report HR 3771. 1979_7.*

617 --- and **Lesley Milroy,** "Belfast: change and variation in an urban vernacular", in Trudgill 1978: 19-36.

618 --- and **Lesley Milroy,** "Sociolinguistic variation and linguistic change in Belfast." New Social Science Research Council Grant. *SSRC Newsletter* 39, April 1979: 39.

619 **Milroy, Lesley,** "Phonological correlates to community structure in Belfast", *Belfast Working Papers on Language and Linguistics* 1 (1976): 1-44.*

620 ---, "Investigating linguistic variation in three Belfast working class communities", *Sociological Association of Ireland. Proceedings of Third Annual Conference, Dublin, 23 - 24 April, 1976*. Belfast 1976: 18-26.

621 ---, "Guide to phonemic transcription of educated Ulster speech." Northern Ireland Polytechnic 1977 /̄ Ms. _7.*

622 ---, "Stylistic variation in urban vernacular speech", *Bulletin of the Northern Ireland Speech and Language Forum* (1978).*

623 ---, "Social networks and language maintenance", in Pugh/Lee/Swann 1980: 35-45.

624 ---, *Language and Social Networks*. Language in Society 2. Oxford: Blackwell 1980.

625 ---, "The effect of two interacting extralinguistic variables on urban vernacular speech", in D. Sankoff and H. Cedergren, eds., *Variation Omnibus*. Edmonton: Linguistic Research Inc. 1981.*

626 ---, "Social network and linguistic focusing", in Romaine 1982: 141-52.

627 ---, "Language and group identity", *Journal of Multilingual and Multicultural Development* 3 (1982).*

628 ---, "Urban dialects in the British Isles", in Trudgill 1984.

629 --- and **Sue Margrain,** "Vernacular language loyalty and social network", *Belfast Working Papers in Language and Linguistics* 3 (1978): 1-58.*

630 --- and **Sue Margrain,** "Vernacular language loyalty and social network", *Language in Society* 9 (1980): 43-70.

631 --- and **P. McClenaghan,** "Stereotyped reactions to four educated accents in Ulster", *Belfast Working Papers in Language and Linguistics* 2 (1977), No. 4: 1-10.*

632 --- and **James Milroy,** "Speech and context in an urban setting", Belfast Working Papers in Language and Linguistics 2 (1977): 1-85.*

633 **Mitchell, Austin** and **Sid Waddell,** Teach Thissen Tyke. Yorksher speyks No. 2. Newcastle-upon-Tyne: Frank Graham 1971.

634 **Mitchell, J. Lawrence,** "'Sliding' in English dialects", Canadian Journal of Linguistics 24,1 (1979): 7-24.

635 **Moody, F.W.,** "The nail and clog-iron industries of Silsden in the West Riding" [1951], repr. in Peter M. Anderson 1980: 36-45.

636 **Moor, Edward,** Suffolk Words and Phrases [1823]. New Introduction by Stanley Ellis. Newton Abbot: David and Charles 1970.

637 **Mordecai, J.,** "West Indian children's language study." Ph.D. Birmingham 1966.*

638 **Morgan, Byron J.T.** and **David J. Shaw,** "Graphical methods for illustrating data in The Survey of English Dialects", Lore and Language 3/7, 1982 (1983): 14-29.

639 **Morgan, Edwin,** "Glasgow speech in recent Scottish literature", in McClure 1983: 195-208.

640 **Muir, James,** "Some observations on the Scots language", Zielsprache Englisch 4/1978: 22-28.

641 **Mulder, Jan W.F.,** "Descriptive adequacy in phonology and the vowel phonemes of the Scottish dialects of Angus and Perthshire compared with the southern English system", La Linguistique 10,1 (1974): 71-91.

642 **Mulvenna, M.,** "A study of the dialect of Staveley in Westmorland." Sheffield 1966 [Ms.].*

643 **Mungo, C.J.,** "The use of a dialect of West Indian origin in British schools", Education Journal April - May (1979).*

644 **Murison, David D.,** "A survey of Scottish language studies", Forum for Modern Language Studies 3 (1967): 276-85.

645 ---, "The future of Scots", in Duncan Glen, ed., Whither Scotland? London: Gollancz 1971: 171-86.

646 ---, "The Dutch element in the vocabulary of Scots", in Aitken/McIntosh/Pálsson 1971: 159-76.

647 ---, "The Scottish National Dictionary", University of Edinburgh Journal 25 (1972): 305-9.*

648 ---, "The vocabulary of the Kirk" (Part I), Liturgical Review 4,2 (1974): 45-49.

649 ---, "The vocabulary of the Kirk" (Part II), Liturgical Review 5,1 (1975): 53-55.

650 ---, "The speech of Moray", in Donald Omand, ed., The Moray Book. Edinburgh: Paul Harris 1976: 275-82.*

651 ---, The Guid Scots Tongue. Edinburgh: Blackwood 1977; 2nd ed. 1978.

652 ---, "The historical background", in Aitken/McArthur 1979: 2-13.

653 **Mutt, Oleg,** "Some notes on recent and current research into English and the teaching of English (2): Sociolinguistic studies", Linguistica 4. Tartu 1972: 53-67.

654 ---, Social and Regional Varieties of Present-day English. Tartu: Tartu State University, Department of English Studies 1977; 2nd ed. 1981.

655 ---, "Some notes on recent and current research into English and the teaching of English (4): Regional and socioregional dialects", Linguistica 11 (Acta et Commentationes Universitatis Tartuensis 502). Tartu 1979: 70-79.

656 **Nally, E.V.,** "Notes on a Westmeath dialect", Journal of the International Phonetic Association 1 (1971): 31-38.

657 **Neill, William,** "Language and Scotland", Catalyst 3, Spring 1970: 10-11.*

658 **Newbrook, Mark,** "Scot or Scouser? An anomalous informant in outer Merseyside", English World-Wide 3 (1982): 77-86.

659 ---, "Sociolinguistic reflexes of dialect interference in West Wirral." Ph.D. Reading 1982.*

660 **Newton, G.,** "South-west Lancashire: The decay of an older vowel pattern?" The Journal of the Lancashire Dialect Society 20 (1971): 19-21.

661 **Ní Chasaide, A.,** "Laterals in Gaoth-Dobhair Irish and Hiberno-English", Occasional Papers in Linguistics and Language Learning. The New University of Ulster 6 (1979): 54-78.

662 **Nida, Eugene A.,** ed., The Book of a Thousand Tongues [1939]. London: United Bible Societies, 2nd ed. 1972: 123-27, containing

excerpts from the Scriptures in the following English dialects: Cornwall, Cumberland, Devonshire, Dorset, Durham, Lancashire, Northumberland, Norfolk, Lowland Scottish, Somerset, Sussex, Westmorland, Wiltshire and Yorkshire.

663 **Ní Ghallchóir, Caitríona,** "Aspects of bilingualism in NW Donegal", in Barry 1981: 142-70.

664 **Nitschke, Wolfhard,** "Einige charakteristische Merkmale des schottischen Englisch", Lebende Sprachen 26 (1981): 104-6.

665 **Nixon, Graham,** "Aims and methodology of the British urban linguistic survey", in Reid 1976: 33-34.

666 ---, "'Fall-back' varieties", Lore and Language 3/3, Part A (1980): 17-23.

667 **North, David J.,** "Some linguistic and cultural boundaries in south-east England", Transactions of the Yorkshire Dialect Society 14, LXXIX (1979): 8-37.

668 ---, "Two west Kent dialects: a comparative phonological study of the dialects of Hever and Chiddingstone, Kent." M.A. Leeds 1979.

669 ---, "Some lexical distribution patterns in the dialects of Cornwall", Transactions of the Yorkshire Dialect Society 15, LXXXII (1982): 14-28.

670 ---, The Importance of Local Systems in Dialectology. Papers in Folk Life Studies 2. The School of English, The University of Leeds 1982.

671 ---, "Aspects of the phonology and agricultural terminology of the rural dialects of Surrey, Kent and Sussex." Ph.D. Leeds 1982.*

672 ---, "Spatial aspects of linguistic change in Surrey, Kent and Sussex", in Viereck 1984.

673 --- and **Adam Sharpe,** A Word-Geography of Cornwall. Redruth: Institute of Cornish Studies 1980.

674 **O'Connor, J.D.,** Phonetics. Harmondsworth: Penguin 1973; Chapters 5 and 6.

675 **O'Donnell, W.R.** and **Loreto Todd,** Variety in Contemporary English. London: Allen and Unwin 1980; Chapter 2.

676 **O'Farrell, Padraic,** How the Irish speak English. Dublin and Cork: The Mercier Press 1980.*

677 **O'Flaherty, Bernard,** "Choice of post-primary school and Dublin working-class speech", in Anthony E.C.W. Spencer and H. Tovey, eds., Proceedings of First and Fourth Annual Conferences of the Sociological Association of Ireland. Belfast 1978: 14-20.

678 **Ojanen, Anna-Liisa,** "A syntax of the Cambridgeshire dialect." Licentiate Thesis. Helsinki 1982.*

679 ---, "Use and non-use of prepositions in spatial expressions in the dialect of Cambridgeshire", in Viereck 1984.

680 **O'Kane, Domini,** "Overt and covert prestige in Belfast vernacular speakers: the results of self-report tests", Belfast Working Papers in Language and Linguistics 2 (1977): 54-77.

681 **Ó Maoláin, Séamus,** "An Anglo-Irish lexicon of County Kilkenny." Ph.D. Galway, University College 1973.*

682 **Ó Muirithe, Diarmaid,** ed., The English Language in Ireland. Dublin and Cork: The Mercier Press 1977; repr. 1978.

683 ---, "The Anglo-Normans and their English dialect of south-east Wexford", in Ó Muirithe 1978: 37-55.

684 **Onoe, Masaji,** "The preposition on in Anglo-Irish", Anglica 5,5 (1965): 1-25.*

685 **Opie, Iona** and **Peter Opie,** The Lore and Language of Schoolchildren. Oxford and London: Oxford UP 1959; repr. repeatedly, e.g., in 1960, 1967 and 1973; London: Paladin 1977 (Paperback edition).

686 --- and **Peter Opie,** Children's Games in Street and Playground. Oxford: Clarendon Press 1969.

687 **O'Prey, H.,** "Long versus short /e/ in the area of Newry: a sonographic approach", The Northern Ireland Speech and Language Forum Journal 2 (1976): 38-48.

688 **Orton, Harold,** Survey of English Dialects (A): Introduction. Leeds: E.J. Arnold 1962; 2nd ed. 1964.

689 ---, "A linguistic atlas of England", The Advancement of Science 27 (1970): 80-96.

690 ---, "An English dialect survey: Linguistic atlas of England" [1960], repr. in Allen/Underwood 1971: 230-44.

691 ---, "L[inguistic] A[tlas of] N[ew] E[ngland] and L[inguistic] A[tlas of] E[ngland]: lexical links", in Burghardt 1971: 3-37.

692 ---, "Editorial problems of an English linguistic atlas", in Burghardt 1971: 79-115.

693 --- and **Michael V. Barry,** eds., Survey of English Dialects (B): The Basic Material. Vol. II: The West Midland Counties. Leeds: E.J. Arnold 1969-1971 (three parts).

694 --- and **Wilfrid J. Halliday,** eds., Survey of English Dialects (B): The Basic Material. Vol. I: The Six Northern Counties and the Isle of Man. Leeds: E.J. Arnold 1962-1963 (three parts).

695 --- and **Philip M. Tilling,** eds., Survey of English Dialects (B): The Basic Material. Vol. III: The East Midland Counties and East Anglia. Leeds: E.J. Arnold 1969-1971 (three parts).

696 --- and **Martyn F. Wakelin,** eds., Survey of English Dialects (B): The Basic Material. Vol. IV: The Southern Counties. Leeds: E.J. Arnold 1967-1968 (three parts).

697 --- and **Nathalia Wright,** A Word Geography of England. London and New York: Seminar Press 1975 /_The book erroneously bears the publication date 1974_/.

698 ---, **Stewart F. Sanderson** and **John Widdowson,** The Linguistic Atlas of England. London: Croom Helm 1978.

699 **O'Shaughnessy, Patrick,** "A glossary of market-traders' argot with supplement", Lore and Language 2,3 (1975): 24-30.

700 ---, "A glossary of market-traders' argot. Corrections and second supplement", Lore and Language 2,8 (1978): 20-23.

701 **Ostapenko, I.A.,** "Some aspects of the linguistic situation and peculiarities of English in Scotland." Candidate thesis. Moscow 1979 /_in Russian_/.*

702 **Page, Norman,** "Convention and consistency in Dickens's Cockney dialect", English Studies 51 (1970): 339-44.

703 **Påhlsson, Christer,** "A sociolinguistic questionnaire for English dialectology", Zeitschrift für Dialektologie und Linguistik 38 (1971): 257-71.

704 ---, The Northumbrian Burr. A Sociolinguistic Study. Lund Studies in English 41 (1972).

705 ---, "A study of the burr in its linguistic contexts. Introductory

report." Helsinki/Helsingfors: Swedish School of Economics 1973 /̲ Ms._7.*

706 ---, "Some notes on the origin of the Northumbrian burr." Helsinki/Helsingfors: Swedish School of Economics 1973 /̲ Ms._7.*

707 ---, "A sociolinguistic study on linguistic attitudes. A background report." Helsinki/Helsingfors: Swedish School of Economics 1973 /̲ Ms._7.*

708 ---, "Some notes on the origin of the Northumbrian burr", Transactions of the Yorkshire Dialect Society Pt. LXXIV, Vol. XIII (1974): 12-15.

709 ---, "A sociolinguistic study on linguistic attitudes." Report No. 2: "The social position of eight English accents." Helsinki/Helsingfors: Swedish School of Economics 1974 /̲ Ms._7.*

710 ---, "The dog's letter and its rambles through a village: some aspects of the methods used in a study of the Northumbrian burr", in Viereck 1976: 171-92, 362-4.

711 **Painting, V.W.,** "The lore and language of schoolchildren of south Cheshire." M.A. Wales, Swansea 1976.*

712 **Parish, W.D.,** A Dictionary of the Sussex Dialect and Collection of Provincialisms in Use in the County of Sussex. Lewes: Farncombe 1875. New ed. expanded, augmented and illustrated by Helena Hall, together with some Sussex Sayings and Crafts. Bexhill (Sx): Gardners 1967.

713 **Parkinson, Joy,** "English language problems of overseas doctors working in the UK", English Language Teaching Journal 34 (1980): 151-56.

714 **Parry, David R.,** "Studies in the linguistic geography of Radnorshire, Breconshire, Monmouthshire and Glamorganshire." M.A. Leeds 1964.

715 ---, "Newport English", The Anglo-Welsh Review 19 (1971): 228-33.

716 ---, "Anglo-Welsh dialects in south-east Wales", in Wakelin 1972: 140-63.

717 ---, The Survey of Anglo-Welsh Dialects: Vol. I: The South-East. Swansea: David Parry, University College 1977; Vol.II: The South-West. Swansea: David Parry, University College 1979; Vol. III: The North-East; Vol. IV: The North-West; Vol. V: An Anglo-Welsh Linguistic Atlas /̲ vols. III - V are in the planning stage_7.

718 ---, Notes on the Dialects of Gwent. University College, Swansea 1978.

719 ---, Notes on the Glamorgan Dialects. University College, Swansea 1979.

720 ---, "The survey of Anglo-Welsh dialects", Lore and Language 3,1 (1979): 9-14.

721 ---, "On producing a linguistic atlas: the survey of Anglo-Welsh dialects", in Kirk/Sanderson/Widdowson 1984.

722 ---, "The Anglo-Welsh dialects of south-west Wales", English World-Wide (forthcoming).

723 **Patchett, John H.,** "A phonological study of the dialects of Hebden Bridge, Lumbutts and Todmorden in upper Calderdale." M.A. Leeds 1980 / handwritten /.

724 ---, "The dialect of Upper Calderdale", Transactions of the Yorkshire Dialect Society. Part LXXXI, Vol. XV (1981): 24-37.

725 **Pellowe, John N.H.,** "Studies towards a classification of varieties of spoken English, based on specimens collected in Jesmond." M.Litt. Newcastle-upon-Tyne 1967.*

726 ---, "Establishing some prosodic criteria for a classification of speech varieties." Newcastle University English Department 1970 / Ms. /.*

727 ---, "Establishing speech varieties of conurbations." I, II, III. Newcastle University English Department 1970 / Ms. /.*

728 ---, "A problem of diagnostic relativity in the Tyneside Linguistic Survey", Classification Society Bulletin 3,1 (1973): 2-8.

729 ---, "The Tyneside Linguistic Survey." Mimeo distributed at "Colloquium on Empirical Work in Sociolinguistics". London School of Economics, 27 April 1974.*

730 ---, "The Tyneside Linguistic Survey: aspects of a developing methodology", in Viereck 1976: 203-17, 365-7.

731 --- and **Valerie M. Jones,** "Structures in phonological variety". Abstracts of Papers. Eighth International Congress of Phonetic Sciences. Leeds 1975, No. 227. / A volume with the full Congress papers was never published. /.

732 --- and **Valerie Jones,** "On intonational variability in Tyneside speech." Newcastle University English Department 1977 / Ms. /.*

733 --- and **Valerie Jones,** "On intonational variability in Tyneside speech", in Trudgill 1978: 101-21.

734 --- and **Valerie Jones,** "Representing and interpreting the structure of linguistic variation", Proceedings of the Vth International Symposium on Computers in Literary and Linguistic Research. Aston University, Birmingham 1978.*

735 --- and **Valerie Jones,** "Establishing intonationally variable systems in a multidimensional linguistic space", Language and Speech 22 (1979): 97-116.

736 --- and **Valerie Jones,** "Tyneside Linguistic Survey", Computers and the Humanities 13,1 (1979), 54-55.

737 ---, **Graham Nixon** and **Vincent McNeany,** "Defining the dimensionality of a linguistic variety space." Newcastle University English Department 1972 [Ms.]. (Preliminary draft prepared for Colloquium on "Urban Speech Surveying", Newcastle 22 April 1972).*

738 ---, **Graham Nixon** and **Vincent McNeany,** "Some sociolinguistic characteristics of phonetic analysis", in A. Rigault and R. Charbonneau, eds., Proceedings of the Seventh International Congress of Phonetic Sciences, Montreal 22-28 August 1971. The Hague 1972: 1172-8.

739 ---, **Graham Nixon, Barbara Strang** and **Vincent McNeany,** "A dynamic modelling of linguistic variation: the Tyneside Linguistic Survey." Newcastle University English Department 1971 [Ms.].*

740 ---, **Graham Nixon, Barbara Strang** and **Vincent McNeany,** "A dynamic modelling of linguistic variation: the urban (Tyneside) Linguistic Survey", Lingua 30 (1972): 1-30.

741 **Pemberton, A.C.,** "The dialect of Pennington." M.A. Leeds 1978 [handwritten].

742 **Penhallurick, Robert J.,** "Two dialects of the Gower Peninsula: a phonological comparison of Penclawdd and Reynoldston." M.A. Leeds 1980 [handwritten].

743 ---, "Two Gower accents: a phonological comparison of Penclawdd and Reynoldston", Transactions of the Yorkshire Dialect Society Pt. LXXXII. Vol. XV (1982): 29-41.

744 ---, "The Anglo-Welsh dialects of North Wales." Ph.D. Swansea 1984.

745 **Pepper, John,** A Quare Geg. Belfast: Blackstaff Press 1979.

746 ---, Ulster-English Dictionary. Belfast: Appletree Press 1981.

747 ---, Ulster Phrasebook. Belfast: Appletree Press 1982.

748 **Petrie, P.E.,** "West Indian syntax appearing in the speech of children

of West Indian parentage, in the infant school." M.A. London Institute of Education 1972.*

749 **Petyt, K. Malcolm,** Emily Brontë and the Haworth Dialect. A Study of the Dialect Speech in 'Wuthering Heights'. The Yorkshire Dialect Society. Menston, Yorks. 1970.

750 ---, "'Dialect' and 'accent' in the industrial West Riding: a study of the changing speech of an urban area." Ph.D. Reading 1977.*

751 ---, "Secondary contractions in West Yorkshire negatives", in Trudgill 1978: 91-100.

752 ---, The Study of Dialect. An Introduction to Dialectology. The Language Library. London: Deutsch 1980.

753 **Phillips, Dianne,** "Linguistic skill and ethnic group", Research in Education 19 (1978): 25-37.

754 **Phillipps, Kenneth C.,** Westcountry Words and Ways. Newton Abbot: David and Charles 1976.

755 **Pinsker, Hans,** "Neuenglisch ain't", Festschrift Prof. Dr. Herbert Koziol zum siebzigsten Geburtstag. Wiener Beiträge zur Englischen Philologie 75 (1973): 238-54.

756 **Pitts, Ann Hollingsworth,** "Urban influence in northern Irish English: a comparison of variation in two communities." Ph.D. Michigan 1982.*

757 ---, "The elusive vernacular: an account of fieldwork techniques in urban sociolinguistic studies in Northern Ireland", Belfast Working Papers in Language and Linguistics 6 (1982): 104-22.

758 **Policansky, Linda,** "Grammatical variation in Belfast English", Belfast Working Papers in Language and Linguistics 6 (1982): 37-66.

759 ---, "Verb concord variation in Belfast vernacular". Paper delivered to the Sociolinguistics Symposium, Walsall 1980 (to be published in Belfast Working Papers in Language and Linguistics).*

760 **Pollner, Clausdirk,** "English in a Scottish New Town: Livingston, West Lothian (A phonological analysis)." Habilitationsschrift Aachen 1983.*

761 ---, "Linguistic fieldwork in a Scottish New Town", in Görlach 1984.

762 **Poole's Glossary,** with some Pieces of Verse of the Old Dialect of the English Colony in the Baronies of Forth and Bargy, County of Wexford, newly ed. by T.P. Dolan and Diarmaid Ó Muirithe. Wexford: The Ui Cinsealaigh Historical Society 1979.

763 **Portz, Renate,** Sprachliche Variation und Spracheinstellungen bei Schulkindern und Jugendlichen. Eine empirische Untersuchung in Norwich/England (Diss. (= German Ph.D.) Berlin FU 1981). Tübinger Beiträge zur Linguistik 184. Tübingen: Narr 1982.

764 ---, "Geschlechtsspezifik in Sprachgebrauch und Spracherwerb im Englischen. Ein Forschungsüberblick", Arbeiten aus Anglistik und Amerikanistik 7 (1982): 77-90.

765 **Price, Susan, Michael Fluck** and **Howard Giles,** "The effects of language of testing in bilingual pre-adolescents' attitudes towards Welsh and varieties of English", Journal of Multilingual and Multicultural Development 4 (1983).*

766 **Proud, D.,** "North Lancashire speech in the nineteen sixties." Ph.D. Lancaster 1968-69.*

767 **Pugh, A.K., V.J. Lee** and **J. Swann,** eds., Language and Language Use. London: Heinemann and Open University 1980.

768 **Purushothaman, M.,** The Education of Children of Caribbean Origin: Select Research Bibliography. Centre for Information and Advice on Educational Disadvantage (1978).*

769 **Purves, David,** "The spelling of Scots", Lallans 4 (1975): 26-28.

770 ---, "A Scots orthography", Scottish Literary Journal Supplement 9 (1979): 62-76.

771 **Quin, E.G.,** "The collectors of Irish dialect material", in Ó Muirithe 1978: 115-26.

772 **Quiñones, A. Leitty,** "Varieties of British pronunciation", Revista de la Universidad de Costa Rica 41 (1975): 233-5.

773 **Quirk, Randolph,** The English Language and Images of Matter. Language and Language Learning 34. London: Oxford UP 1972.

774 ---, The Linguist and the English Language. London: Edward Arnold 1974; esp. Chapter 1.

775 --- and **Sidney Greenbaum,** A University Grammar of English. London: Longmans 1973; esp. Chapter 1.

776 ---, **Sidney Greenbaum, Geoffrey Leech, Jan Svartvik,** A Grammar of Contemporary English. London: Longmans 1972; esp. Chapter 1.15 - 37.

777 The **Reader's Digest** Complete Atlas of the British Isles. London: The Reader's Digest Association 1965: "Language and Dialects" 122-3.

778 **Reah, K.,** "Some aspects of linguistic variation in Blyth." M.A. Sheffield 1978.*

779 **Reid, Euan,** "Social and stylistic variation in the speech of some eleven-year-old Edinburgh boys", Work in Progress. Edinburgh University. Linguistics Department 8 (1975): 124-6.*

780 ---, "Social and stylistic variation in the speech of some Edinburgh schoolchildren." M.Litt. Edinburgh 1976.

781 ---, ed., Abstracts of 1976 Research Seminar on Sociolinguistic Variation. Walsall: West Midlands College, Communications Research Unit 1976.

782 ---, "Social and stylistic variation in the speech of some Edinburgh school children", in Reid 1976: 16.

783 ---, "Social and stylistic variation in the speech of children: some evidence from Edinburgh", in Trudgill 1978: 158-73.

784 ---, "The newer minority languages: spoken languages and varieties", in Trudgill 1984.

785 **Riach, W.A.D.,** "A dialect study of comparative areas in Galloway, with particular reference to the Irish connection." Ph.D. Edinburgh 1978.*

786 ---, "A dialect study of comparative areas in Galloway", Scottish Literary Journal Supplement 9 (1979): 1-16.

787 ---, "A dialect study of comparative areas in Galloway (2nd report)", Scottish Literary Journal Supplement 12 (1980): 43-60.

788 ---, "A dialect study of comparative areas in Galloway (3rd and last report)", Scottish Language 1 (1982): 13-22.

789 **Richmond, John,** "Dialect features in mainstream school writing", New Approaches to Multiracial Education 8 (1979): 9-15.

790 ---, "Jennifer and 'Brixton Blues': language alive in school", in Supplementary Reading for Block 5, PE 232 Language Development. Milton Keynes: Open UP 1979 and in Stephen Eyers and John Richmond, eds., Becoming our own Experts: Studies in language and learning made by the Talk Workshop Group at Vauxhall Manor School 1974-79. London: ILEA English Centre 1982: 60-98.

791 ---, "Dialect as part of the work of the English classroom", in Sutcliffe 1982: 81-91.

792 **Robertson, T.,** "Extracts from a Shetland dictionary under preparation", The New Shetlander 92 (1970): 35-36 and 93 (1970): 28.

793 ---, "Shetland dialect", The New Shetlander 107 (1974): 8-10.*

794 **Robson, Dirk,** Krek Waiter's Peak Bristle (Correct Way to speak Bristol): A Guide to What the Natives Say and Mean in the Heart of the Wess Vinglun. Bristol: Abson Press 1970; 3rd impr. 1971.

795 ---, Son of Bristle: A Second Guide to What the Natives Say and Mean in the Heart of Wess Vinglun. Bristol: Abson Books 1971.

796 **Rock, Margaret,** "A dialect study of Quarry Bank near Dudley, Worcestershire", The Journal of the Lancashire Dialect Society 23 (1974): 5-20.

797 **Rodrigues, Raymond J.,** "Bilingual and monolingual English syntax on the Isle of Lewis, Scotland", Research in the Teaching of English 14 (1980): 139-46.*

798 **Rogers, Norman,** Wessex Dialect. Bradford-on-Avon: Moonraker Press 1979.

799 **Roider, Ulrike,** "Der Sprachwechsel bei den keltischen Völkern", Zeitschrift für Dialektologie und Linguistik. Beihefte 32 (1980): 421-24.

800 ---, "Zweisprachigkeit und grammatische Inter- und Transferenz im Keltischen der Britischen Inseln", in Wolfgang Meid and Karin Heller, eds., Sprachkontakt als Ursache von Veränderungen der Sprach- und Bewußtseinsstruktur. Eine Sammlung von Studien zur sprachlichen Interferenz. Innsbrucker Beiträge zur Sprachwissenschaft 34. Innsbruck: Institut für Sprachwissenschaft 1981: 195-201.

801 **Romaine, Suzanne,** "Linguistic variability in the speech of some Edinburgh schoolchildren." M.Litt. Edinburgh 1975.

802 ---, "Approaches to the description of Scots English", Work in Progress. Edinburgh University. Linguistics Department 8 (1975): 121-4.*

803 ---, "Problems in the investigation of linguistic attitudes in Scotland", Work in Progress. Edinburgh University. Linguistics Department 11 (1978): 11-29.*

804 ---, "Postvocalic /r/ in Scottish English: sound change in progress?" in Trudgill 1978: 144-57.

805 ---, "A sociolinguistic investigation of Edinburgh speech." Social Science Research Council Interim Report 1978.*

806 ---, "The language of Edinburgh schoolchildren: the acquisition of sociolinguistic competence", Scottish Literary Journal Supplement 9 (1979): 55-61.

807 ---, "The social reality of phonetic descriptions", NISLF Journal. Northern Ireland Speech Language Forum 5 (1979): 21-36.*

808 ---, "Stylistic variation and evaluative reactions to speech: problems in the investigation of linguistic attitudes in Scotland", Language and Speech 23 (1980): 213-32.

809 ---, "A critical overview of the methodology of urban British sociolinguistics", English World-Wide 1 (1980): 163-98.

810 ---, "The relative clause marker in Scots English: Diffusion, complexity, and style as dimensions of syntactic change", Language in Society 9 (1980): 221-47.

811 ---, Socio-Historical Linguistics. Its Status and Methodology. Cambridge Studies in Linguistics 34. Cambridge: UP 1982.

812 ---, ed., Sociolinguistic Variation in Speech Communities. London: Edward Arnold 1982.

813 ---, "The English language in Scotland", in Bailey/Görlach 1982: 56-83.

814 ---, "The problem of short /a/ in Scotland", in Görlach 1984.

815 --- and **Euan Reid,** "Glottal sloppiness? A sociolinguistic view of urban speech in Scotland", Teaching English. The Journal of Teachers of English in Scotland 9,3 (1976): 12-18.*

816 --- and **Nancy C. Dorian,** "Scotland as a linguistic area", Scottish Literary Journal Supplement 14 (1981): 1-24.

817 **Rosen, Harold,** "Linguistic diversity in London schools", in Pugh/ Lee/Swann 1980: 46-75.

818 --- and **Tony Burgess,** Languages and Dialects of London School Children. An Investigation. London: Ward Lock Educational 1980.

819 **Rosen, M.,** "In their own voice", Issues in Race and Education 16 (1978).*

820 **Ross, Alan S.C.,** "'You' in the north", Notes and Queries N.S. 15 (1968): 323-4.

821 ---, How to pronounce it. London: Hamilton 1970.

822 --- and **Robin Brackenbury,** "U and non-U today: language", in Alan S.C. Ross, ed., What are U? London: André Deutsch 1969: 11-17.

823 **Ross, J.,** "A selection of Caithness dialect words", in Donald Omand, ed., The Caithness Book. Inverness: Highland Printers 1972: 241-60.*

824 **Rubin, Gerald M.,** "Computer-produced mapping of dialectal variation", Computers and the Humanities 4/4 (1970): 241-6.

825 **Russ, Charles V.J.,** "The geographical and social variation of English in England and Wales", in Bailey/Görlach 1982: 11-55.

826 **Russell, Ralph,** Ethnic Minority Languages and the Schools. London: The Runnymede Trust 1980.

827 **Ryan, Ellen Bouchard** and **Howard Giles,** eds., Attitudes towards Language Variation. Social and Applied Contexts. The Social Psychology of Language 1. London: Edward Arnold 1982.

828 **Rydland, Kurt,** "Structural phonology and the Survey of English Dialects. A critical evaluation of the material", Zeitschrift für Dialektologie und Linguistik 39 (1972): 309-26.

829 ---, "Vowel systems and lexical-phonemic patterns in south-east Cumbria. A study in structural dialectology", 2 vols. Doctoral thesis. Bergen 1978.

830 ---, "Vowel differences and accent areas in Westmorland and North Lonsdale", The Journal of the Lakeland Dialect Society 40 (1979): 15-27.*

831 ---, Vowel Systems and Lexical-Phonemic Patterns in South-East Cumbria. A Study in Structural Dialectology. Studia Anglistica Norvegica 1. Bergen 1982.

832 **Sabban, Annette,** Gälisch-englischer Sprachkontakt. Zur Variabilität des Englischen im gälischsprachigen Gebiet Schottlands. Eine empirische Studie (Diss. (= German Ph.D.) Saarbrücken 1980). Sammlung Groos 11. Heidelberg: Groos 1982.

833 ---, "On the variability of Hebridean English syntax: the verbal group", in Görlach 1984.

834 **Saifullah Khan, Verity,** Bilingualism and Linguistic Minorities in Britain. Developments, Perspectives. London: The Runnymede Trust 1977.*

835 ---, "The Linguistic Minorities Project", English World-Wide 2 (1981): 227- 8.

836 **Samuels, M.L.,** Linguistic Evolution with special reference to English. Cambridge Studies in Linguistics 5. Cambridge: UP 1972.

837 **Sanders, Robert A.,** "Alexander John Ellis. A study of a Victorian philologist." Ph.D. Memorial University of Newfoundland, St. John's 1977.*

838 **Sanderson, Stewart F.,** "Language on the map", The University of Leeds Review 20 (1977): 160-71.

839 --- and **John D.A. Widdowson,** "The aims, directives and prospects of linguistic geography", in Kirk/Sanderson/Widdowson 1984.

840 **Sandi, Gabor,** "The phonology of the dialects of England." M.A. University of British Columbia 1977.*

841 **Sandred, Karl Inge,** "On the terminology of the plough in England", Studia Neophilologica 38 (1966): 323-38.

842 ---, "Notes on the distribution of some plough terms in modern English dialects", Studia Neophilologica 40 (1968): 80-93.

843 ---, "Two dialect words in the Fenland: ModE haff and stow", in Nordiska Namn. Festskrift till Lennart Moberg 13 December 1974. Uppsala: Lundequistska Bokhandeln 1974: 82-91.

844 ---, "A modern poem in Lowland Scots", Moderna Språk 75 (1981): 27-32.

845 ---, "Linguistic taboo in the speech of Scottish fishermen. A few observations in the light of recent research", Scottish Language 1 (1982): 1-5.

846 ---, "Overt and covert prestige: the evaluative boundaries of the speech community", in Görlach 1984.

847 ---, Attitudes Towards Optional Lexical and Grammatical Usages in Edinburgh (forthcoming).

848 **Sargent, Valerie,** "Cycles and the equal society", Classification Society Bulletin 4,3 (1979): 31-45.

849 ---, "The Tyneside Linguistic Survey: Phase 4." Final Report, SSRC Research Grant No. HR 5490/1 (1980).*

850 **Scherer, Klaus R.** and **Howard Giles,** eds., Social Markers in Speech. Cambridge: UP and Paris: Maison des Sciences de l'Homme 1979.

851 **Schmidt, Christa M.,** "Das kymrische Substrat im Englischen in Südost-Wales: Eine phonologische Untersuchung." Diss. (= German Ph.D.) Freiburg (forthcoming).

852 **Schmitt, Ludwig Erich,** ed., *Germanische Dialektologie. Festschrift für Walther Mitzka zum 80. Geburtstag.* II. Zeitschrift für Mundartforschung. Beihefte N.F. 6 (1968).

853 **Schneider, Edgar W.** and **Wolfgang Viereck,** "The use of the computer in American, Canadian and British English dialectology and sociolinguistics", in Hans Goebl, ed., *Quantitative Dialektologie*. Bochum: Brockmeyer 1983.

854 **Scollins, Richard** and **John Titford,** *Ey up mi Duck! An Effectionate Look at the Speech, History and Folklore of Ilkeston and the Erewash Valley*. Part I. Ilkeston: Scollins & Titford 1976, repr. 1977; Part II. Ilkeston: Scollins & Titford 1976; Part III. Ilkeston: Scollins & Titford 1977.

855 **Ščur, Georgij S.,** "On the non-finite forms of the verb *can* in Scottish", *Acta Linguistica Hafniensia* 11 (1968): 211-8.

856 **Sharp, D.** *et al.*, *Attitudes to Welsh and English: An Interim Report.* Schools Council Research and Development Project. University College of Swansea, Wales 1970.*

857 --- *et al.*, *Attitudes to Welsh and English. Report of Research Project*. Schools Council for England and Wales. London 1973.*

858 --- *et al.*, *Some Aspects of Welsh and English: A Survey in the Schools of Wales*. Schools Council Research Studies. London: Macmillan 1973.*

859 **Sharpe, Adam,** "The Institute of Cornish Studies survey of Cornish dialect: a progress report", *Cornish Studies* 6 (1978): 9-13.

860 --- and **Charles Thomas,** *Cornish Dialect - a Progress Report.* Redruth: Institute of Cornish Studies 1979.

861 **Shaw, David,** *Statistical Analysis of Dialectal Distribution: Preliminary Report*. Internal Document: University of Kent, Canterbury (1972).*

862 ---, "Statistical analysis of dialectal boundaries", *Computers and the Humanities* 8,3 (1974): 173-7.

863 **Shaw, D.H.,** "A comparative study (descriptive and historical) of the dialect of Bedfordshire, based upon a survey conducted in five widely spread areas of the county." Ph.D. London, King's College 1967-68.*

864 **Shaw, Frank, Fritz Spiegl** and **Stan Kelly,** Lern Yerself SCOUSE: How to Talk Proper in Liverpool. Liverpool: Scouse Press 1966.

865 **Shepherd, R.G., G. Shorrocks** and **R. Watson,** "A glossary of the dialects of Pilling and Preesall", The Journal of the Lancashire Dialect Society 28 (1979): 22-29.

866 **Shields, Mike,** "Dialects of north-eastern England", Lore and Language 1,10 (1974): 3-9.

867 **Shores, David L.** and **Carole P. Hines,** eds., Papers in Language Variation. University Ala.: The University of Alabama Press 1977.

868 **Shorrocks, Graham,** "A linguistic bibliography of Lancashire dialects. Part I", The Journal of the Lancashire Dialect Society 25 (1976): 6-14.

869 ---, "A linguistic bibliography of Lancashire dialects. Part II", The Journal of the Lancashire Dialect Society 26 (1977): 6-9.

870 ---, "Aspects of two Lancashire phonemes: /a/ and /ɛɪ/", The Journal of the Lancashire Dialect Society 26 (1977); 20-26.

871 ---, "Linguistic bibliography of the Lancashire dialects, first supplement", The Journal of the Lancashire Dialect Society 27 (1978): 8-12.

872 ---, "'Yes' and 'No' in a Lancashire dialect", Regional Bulletin (Centre for North West Regional Studies, University of Lancaster) 7, No. 22 (1978): 12-13.*

873 ---, "The phonetic realisation of the definite article in Lancashire dialect, and its representation in dialect writing", The Record (Journal of the Lancashire Authors' Association) No. 256 (September 1978): 13-14.*

874 ---, "A phonemic and phonetic key to the orthography of the Lancashire dialect writer Teddy Ashton", The Journal of the Lancashire Dialect Society 27 (1978): 45-59.

875 ---, "Local traditions - things to collect", The Journal of the Lancashire Dialect Society 28 (1979): 11-15.

876 ---, "A brief glossary of east Yorkshire dialect", Lore and Language 3/3, Part A (1980): 1-16.

877 ---, "A grammar of the dialect of Farnworth and district (Greater Manchester County, formerly Lancashire)." Ph.D. Sheffield 1980. Published by University Microfilms International, ref. no. A81-70, 023. 1981.

878 ---, "A note on dialect orthographies", The Journal of the Lancashire Dialect Society 30 (1981): 12-15.

879 ---, "Relative pronouns and relative clauses in the dialect of Farnworth and District (Greater Manchester County, formerly Lancashire)", Zeitschrift für Dialektologie und Linguistik 49 (1982): 334-43.

880 ---, "The /'tɑmɪ nɛ:(r)/ stories: An example of twentieth century urban folktale", Lore and Language 3/7, 1982 (1983): 68-81.

881 **Shuken, Cynthia R.,** "Vowel length in Lewis English", Work in Progress. Department of Linguistics. University of Edinburgh 12 (1979): 54-57.*

882 ---, "English in a bilingual community: Hebridean English." Second Year Progress Report to the Social Science Research Council. September 1980 /⁻Ms._7.*

883 ---, "On Hebridean English phonology", in Görlach 1984.

884 ---, "Highland and Island English", in Trudgill 1984.

885 ---, "Gaelic influence on the English of Lewis and Skye." A Paper presented to the Universities' Forum on Scots Language Research, Nov. 5, 1979, University of Edinburgh (forthcoming).

886 **Skea, M.,** "Change and variation in a non-standard dialect: a sociolinguistic study of dialect lexicon in North Down." Ph.D. Ulster Polytechnic (forthcoming).

887 **Skeat, Walter A.,** English Dialects from the Eighth Century to the Present Day. Cambridge: UP 1912. New York: Kraus Reprint Co. 1968.

888 **Skelton, Michael G.,** "A phonological study of two Newcastle idiolects." M.A. Leeds 1976.

889 **Sledd, James,** "A note on buckra philology", American Speech 48, 1973 (1975): 144-6.

890 **Smith, G.,** "Attitudes to language in a multilingual community in east London." Ph.D. London 1979.*

891 **Smith, John B.,** "Tradition and language in an urban community", Lore and Language 2,2 (1975): 5-8.

892 ---, "A reflex of Middle English ich", Somerset and Dorset Notes and Queries 30, 302 (1975): 122- 4.

893 ---, "Linguistic variation in some dialects of Wessex", Quinquereme. New Studies in Modern Languages 1 (1978): 121-30.

894 ---, "Proverbial sayings from the north Midlands and south-west of England", The Journal of the Lancashire Dialect Society 29 (1980): 14-22.

895 **Smolins, G.,** "Reading and comprehension: a comparative study of some 8 - 9 year-old children of English and West Indian origin." M.A. London, Birkbeck College 1974.*

896 **Speitel, Hans Henning,** "Some studies in the dialect of Midlothian." 2 vols. Ph.D. Edinburgh 1969.*

897 ---, "An early specimen of Edinburgh speech", Work in Progress. Department of Phonetics and Linguistics. University of Edinburgh 3 (1969): 26-36.*

898 ---, "An areal typology of isoglosses: isoglosses near the Scottish-English border", Zeitschrift für Dialektologie und Linguistik 36 (1969): 49-66.

899 ---, "The stressed vowels in Standard Scottish English. A reply to D. Bähr", Zeitschrift für Dialektologie und Linguistik 39 (1972): 215-6.

900 ---, "Dialect" (Paper presented to the Social Science Research Council Seminar on Language and Learning 1973), in Alan Davies, ed., Problems of Language and Learning. London: Heinemann 1975: 34-60.

901 ---, "'Caller ou!': An Edinburgh fishwives' cry and an old Scottish sound change", Scottish Studies 19 (1975): 69-73.

902 ---, "The word geography of the borders", Scottish Literary Journal Supplement 6 (1978): 17-38.

903 ---, "The geographical position of the Scots dialect in relation to the highlands of Scotland", in Benskin/Samuels 1981: 107-29.

904 --- and **James Y. Mather,** "Schottische Dialektologie", in Schmitt 1968: 520-41.

905 --- and **Cynthia R. Shuken,** "English in a bilingual community. Aspects of Hebridean English /HR 5794/2/." New Social Science Research Council Grant. SSRC Newsletter 39, April 1979: 39.

906 **Spiegl, Fritz,** Lern Yerself SCOUSE, or - The ABZ of Scouse, vol. 2. Liverpool: Scouse Press 1966; repr. 1970 and 1979.

907 **Stern, Janet,** "The English and Welsh dialects of Pumpsaint, Carmarthenshire." M.A. Leeds 1973.

908 **Sternberg, Thomas,** The Dialect and Folk-Lore of Northamptonshire [1851]. With a New Foreword by A.E. Green. East Ardsley: S.R. Publ. 1971 and London: British Bk. Ctr. 1974.

909 **Storr, J.G.,** "Survey of the dialect of Selston in the Erewash valley." M.A. Sheffield 1977.

910 **Strang, Barbara M.H.,** "The Tyneside Linguistic Survey", Verhandlungen des Zweiten Internationalen Dialektologenkongresses [1965] II. Zeitschrift für Mundartforschung. Beihefte N.F. 4 (1968): 788-94.

911 **Strauss, Dietrich,** "Scots is not alone - Further comparative considerations", in Jean-Jacques Blanchot and Claude Graf, eds., Actes du 2e Colloque de Langue et de Litérature Écossaises - Moyen Age et Renaissance. Strasbourg: Institut d'Etudes Anglaises de L'Université de Strasbourg 1978: 80-97.

912 ---, "Schottland - einsprachig oder dreisprachig? Beobachtungen und Überlegungen aus nichtschottischer Sicht", in Ureland 1982: 297-306.

913 **Strevens, Peter D.,** "Varieties of English" [1964], in Peter D. Strevens, Papers in Language and Language Teaching. Language and Language Learning 9 (1965): 74-86.

914 **Stringer, David** for the Course Team, Language Variation and English. Language and Learning Block 1. Milton Keynes: Open UP 1973; repr. 1975 and 1977.

915 **Strongman, Kenneth T.** and **Janet Woosley,** "Stereotyped reactions to regional accents", The British Journal of Social and Clinical Psychology 6 (1967): 164-7.

916 **Stuart, Douglas Kent,** "Craven Yorkshire dialect." Ph.D. Illinois Institute of Technology, Chicago 1976.

917 **Stursberg, Mario,** The Stressed Vowels in the Dialects of Longtown, Abbey Town, and Husonby (Cumberland): A Structural Approach. [Diss. (= Swiss Ph.D.)] Basle: Econom-Druck 1970.

918 **Sullivan, James P.,** "The genesis of Hiberno-English: a socio-historical account." Ph.D. Yeshiva University New York 1976.*

919 ---, "The validity of literary dialect: Evidence from the theatrical portrayal of Hiberno-English forms", Language in Society 9 (1980): 195-219.

920 **Sutcliffe, David,** "The study of dialect selection in the young Bedford black community", in Reid 1976: 21.

921 ---, "Hou dem taak in Bedford, sa", Journal of the Multiracial School 5 (1976): 19-24.*

922 ---, "The language of first and second generation West Indian children in Bedfordshire." M.Ed. Leicester 1978.*

923 ---, "British Black English in British schools", in Neil Mercer 1981: 115-46.

924 ---, British Black English. Oxford: Blackwell 1982.

925 ---, "British Black English and West Indian Creoles", in Trudgill 1984.

926 **Takahashi, Kiyoshi,** "English in London today", Area and Culture Studies 29 (1979): 55-73 / in Japanese with English summary /.*

927 **Taniguchi, Jiro,** A Grammatical Analysis of Artistic Representations of Irish English with a brief discussion of sounds and spelling. Tokyo: Shinozaki Shorin 1972.

928 **Tattersall, Gay,** "Expressions from north Nottinghamshire", The Journal of the Lancashire Dialect Society 25 (1976): 16-17.

929 **Taylor, Mary Vaiana,** "The great southern Scots conspiracy: pattern in the development of northern English", in Anderson/Jones 1974: 403-26.

930 **Taylor, R.C.,** "A descriptive and historical study of the phonology of the dialect of Lumb-in-Rossendale." M.A. Manchester 1975.*

931 **Templeton, Janet M.,** "Scots: an outline history", in Aitken 1973; repr. 1978: 4-19.

932 **Thomas, Alan R.,** "Welsh English", in Trudgill 1984.

933 ---, "Aspects of Welsh English syntax", in Viereck 1984.

934 **Thomas, Charles,** "Dialect Studies, I: The Rablen Collection, and the establishment of an isogloss", Cornish Studies 2 (1974): 65-74.

935 ---, "Dialect Studies, II: Cornish dialect derivatives of Middle English stoc 'stump', stikien 'to stick'", Cornish Studies 6 (1978): 14-19.

936 ---, "A glossary of spoken English in the Isles of Scilly", Journal of the Royal Institution of Cornwall. N.S. 8, Pt. 2 (1979): 109-47.

937 ---, "Dialect Studies, III: Arthur Rablen's 1937 Essay", Cornish Studies 8 (1980): 37-47.

938 **Thomas, R.M.,** "The linguistic geography of Carmarthenshire, Glamorganshire and Pembrokeshire from 1750 to the present day." M.A. Wales, Aberystwyth 1966-67.*

939 **Thomas, R.,** "Vindication and infringement: towards an ethnographic analysis of classroom interaction." M.A. London Institute of Education 1979.*

940 **Thomson, Derick,** "Gaelic in Scotland: Assessment and prognosis", in Haugen/McClure/Thomson 1981: 10-20.

941 **Tidholm, Hans,** The Dialect of Egton in North Yorkshire. Göteborg: Bokmaskinen 1979.

942 **Tilling, Philip M.,** "Local dialect and the poet: A comparison of the findings in the Survey of English Dialects with dialect in Tennyson's Lincolnshire poems", in Wakelin 1972: 88-108.

943 ---, "Age-group variation in the speech of Kinlough, Co. Leitrim", in Barry 1981: 96-105.

944 ---, "The Tape-recorded Survey of Hiberno-English", in Kirk/Sanderson/Widdowson 1984.

945 **Tindall, Mabel S.,** "Crab and lobster fishing at Staithes in the North Riding" /‾1950_7, repr. in Peter M. Anderson 1980: 23-29.

946 **Todd,** Loreto, "Tyrone English", Transactions of the Yorkshire Dialect Society 13, LXXI (1971): 29-40.

947 **Tooth, E.E.,** "A comparative phonology between Tunstall and Longton." M.A. Leeds 1970.

948 **Trudgill, Peter J.,** "The social differentiation of English in Norwich." Ph.D. Edinburgh 1971.

949 ---, "Sex, covert prestige and linguistic change in the urban British English of Norwich", Language and Society 1 (1972): 179-95; repr. in B. Thorne and N. Henley, eds., Language and Sex: Difference and Dominance. Rowley, Mass.: Newbury House 1975; 3rd print. 1978: 88-104 and in Trudgill 1983: 169-185.

950 ---, "Phonological rules and sociolinguistic variation in Norwich English", in C.-J.N. Bailey and R.W. Shuy, eds., New Ways of Analysing Variation in English. Washington: Georgetown UP 1973: 149-63.

951 ---, The Social Differentiation of English in Norwich. Cambridge Studies in Linguistics 13. Cambridge: UP 1974. Paperback edition 1979.

952 ---, Sociolinguistics: An Introduction. Harmondsworth: Penguin Books 1974; repr. every year.

953 ---, "Linguistic change and diffusion: description and explanation in sociolinguistic dialect geography", Language in Society 3 (1974): 215-46; rev. in Trudgill 1983: 52-87 as "Linguistic change and diffusion: Description and explanation in geolinguistics".

954 ---, "Sociolinguistics and Scots dialects", in McClure [1975]: 28-34.

955 ---, Accent, Dialect and the School. London: Edward Arnold 1975.

956 ---, "Linguistic geography and geographical linguistics", in C. Board, R.J. Chorley, P. Haggett, D.R. Stoddart, eds., Progress in Geography 7 (1975): 227-52.

957 ---, "On the empirical study of grammatical change", in Reid 1976: 4-5.

958 ---, "Sociolinguistics in Scotland: a brief comment", Sociolinguistics Newsletter 8,3 (1977): 27.

959 ---, ed., Sociolinguistic Patterns in British English. London: Edward Arnold 1978.

960 ---, "Standard and non-standard dialects of English in the United Kingdom: problems and policies", International Journal of the Sociology of Language 21 (1979): 9-24; repr. in Trudgill 1983: 186-200 as "Standard and non-standard dialects of English in the United Kingdom: Attitudes and Policies".

961 ---, "Sociolinguistic influence on the nature of linguistic change." New Social Science Research Council Grant. SSRC Newsletter 40, October 1979: 26.

962 ---, "A sociolinguistic study of linguistic change in urban East Anglia." End-of-Grant Report HR 2672 to the Social Science Research Council n.d. [1980].*

963 ---, "Linguistic accommodation: sociolinguistic observations on a sociopsychological theory", Papers from the Parasessions. Chicago Linguistic Society 1981: 218-37.*

964 ---, "On the limits of passive 'competence': sociolinguistics and the polylectal grammar controversy", in David Crystal, ed., Linguistic Controversies: Essays in Linguistic Theory and Practice in Honour of F.R. Palmer. London: Edward Arnold 1982: 172-81.

965 ---, On Dialect. Social and Geographical Perspectives. Oxford: Blackwell 1983.

966 ---, "The contribution of sociolinguistics to dialectology", International Conference on Sociolinguistics. International Christian University, Tokyo 1981; rev. as "Sociolinguistics and dialectology: Geolinguistics and English rural dialects", in Trudgill 1983: 31-51.

967 ---, "British Standard English", in Trudgill 1984.

968 ---, ed., Language in the British Isles. Cambridge: UP 1984.

969 --- and **Tina Foxcroft,** "On the sociolinguistics of vocalic mergers: transfer and approximation in East Anglia", in Trudgill 1978: 69-79; repr. in Trudgill 1983: 88-101 as "The sociolinguistics and geolinguistics of vowel mergers: Dialect contact in East Anglia".

970 --- and **Howard Giles,** "Sociolinguistics and linguistic value judgements: correctness, adequacy and aesthetics", Linguistic Agency University of Trier. Series B, No. 10 (1976); repr. in F. Coppieters and D.L. Goyvaerts, eds., Functional Studies in Language and Literature. Ghent: E. Story-Scientia 1978: 167-90 and in Trudgill 1983: 201- 25.

971 --- and **Jean Hannah,** International English. A Guide to Varieties of Standard English. London: Edward Arnold 1982 [with accompanying cassette]; Chapters 2.1 The RP Accent, 2.3 Welsh English and 5 Scottish and Irish English.

972 **Trumper, John,** "A contribution to the history of the English vowel system: some problems regarding the linguistic correlates of social stratification in Anglo-Welsh", Quaderni Patavini di Linguistica 1 (1979-80): 77-179.*

973 **Tulloch, Graham,** The Language of Walter Scott: A Study of his Scottish and Period Language. London: André Deutsch 1980.

974 **Turner, Violet M.,** "The tongue that Shakespeare spake", The Journal of the Lancashire Dialect Society 22 (1973): 20-23.

975 ---, "Stranger beware", The Journal of the Lancashire Dialect Society 23 (1974): 23-27.

976 ---, "Further findings of Shakespearian usage at Mow Cop on the Cheshire-Staffordshire borders", The Journal of the Lancashire Dialect Society 24 (1974): 20-22.

977 **Upton, Clive S.,** "Studies in the linguistic geography of Pembrokeshire and the Gower Peninsula." M.A. Wales, Swansea 1970.*

978 ---, "Language butchered: back-slang in the Birmingham meat trade", Lore and Language 2,1 (1974): 31-35.

979 ---, "The language of the meat trade: a survey of terms used by a selected sample of butchers in the United Kingdom." Ph.D. Leeds 1977.

980 ---, "Meat-cut terms: a check-list", *Lore and Language* 2,10 (1979): 25-32.

981 ---, *Popular Linguistic Atlas of England* (forthcoming).

982 **Ureland, P. Sture,** ed., *Die Leistung der Strataforschung und der Kreolistik. Typologische Aspekte der Sprachkontakte. Akten des 5. Symposions über Sprachkontakt in Europa, Mannheim 1982*. Linguistische Arbeiten 125. Tübingen: Niemeyer 1982.

983 **Vaiana /Taylor/, Mary Estelle,** "A study in the dialect of the southern counties of Scotland." Ph.D. Indiana University 1972.*

984 **Verma, Gajendra K.** and **Christopher Bagley,** eds., *Race, Education and Identity*. New York: St. Martin's Press 1979.

985 **Viereck, Wolfgang,** "Der 'English Dialect Survey' und der 'Linguistic Survey of Scotland' - Arbeitsmethoden und bisherige Ergebnisse", *Zeitschrift für Mundartforschung* 31 (1964): 333-55.

986 ---, "Zur Entstehung und Wertung des uvularen r unter besonderer Berücksichtigung der Situation in England", *Phonetica* 13 (1965): 189-200. A longer version appeared in *Jahrbuch des Marburger Universitätsbundes* 4 (1965): 125-34.

987 ---, "Specimen passages of the speech of Gateshead-upon-Tyne", *Le Maître Phonétique* 123/1965: 6-7.

988 ---, *Phonematische Analyse des Dialekts von Gateshead-upon-Tyne, Co. Durham*. Britannica et Americana 14. Hamburg: Cram, de Gruyter 1966.

989 ---, "Guy S. Lowman's contribution to British English dialectology", *Transactions of the Yorkshire Dialect Society* 12, LXVIII (1968): 32-39.

990 ---, "Englische Dialektologie", in Schmitt 1968: 542-64.

991 ---, "A diachronic-structural analysis of a northern English urban dialect", in Ellis 1968 (1969): 65-79.

992 ---, "Britische und amerikanische Sprachatlanten", *Zeitschrift für Dialektologie und Linguistik* 38 (1971): 167-205.

993 ---, "Regional verb forms in southern England", in Davis 1972: 185-205.

994 ---, "A critical appraisal of the 'Survey of English Dialects'", Orbis 22 (1973): 72-84.

995 ---, Lexikalische und grammatische Ergebnisse des Lowman-Survey von Mittel- und Südengland, 2 vols. Munich: Fink 1975.

996 ---, Regionale und soziale Erscheinungsformen des britischen und amerikanischen Englisch. Anglistische Arbeitshefte 4. Tübingen: Niemeyer 1975 [with accompanying tape].

997 ---, ed., Sprachliches Handeln - Soziales Verhalten. Ein Reader zur Pragmalinguistik und Soziolinguistik. Kritische Information 52. Munich: Fink 1976.

998 ---, "Sprachliche Variation im Englischen und ihre Erforschung", Zeitschrift für Dialektologie und Linguistik 45 (1978): 161-74.

999 ---, "Social dialectology: a plea for more data", Studia Anglica Posnaniensia 11, 1979 (1980): 15-25.

1000 ---, "Dialektometrie und englische Dialektologie", Grazer Linguistische Studien 11/12 (1980): 335-56.

1001 ---, "The dialectal structure of British English: Lowman's evidence", English World-Wide 1 (1980): 25-44. For an earlier version of this article cf. Hungarian Studies in English 12, 1979 (1980): 203-31.

1002 ---, "A bibliography of writings on varieties of English spoken in England, Wales, Scotland and Ireland and on attitudes towards them (1965-1980)", English World-Wide 2 (1981): 181-224.

1003 ---, "Englisch auf den britischen Inseln", Englisch - Formen und Funktionen einer Weltsprache. Ausstellung des Lehrstuhls für Englische Sprachwissenschaft und Mediävistik und der Universitätsbibliothek. Bamberg 1983: 27-49.

1004 ---, "The presentation and interpretation of English dialects: computer-assisted projects", in Proceedings of the XIIIth International Congress of Linguists, Tokyo, Aug. 29 - Sept. 4, 1982. Tokyo 1983.

1005 ---, "Der Einsatz des Computers in der amerikanisch-englischen und britisch-englischen Dialektologie und Soziolinguistik", Zeitschrift für Dialektologie und Linguistik 51 (1984).

1006 ---, ed., Focus on: England and Wales. Varieties of English around the World. General Series. Amsterdam: John Benjamins 1984.

1007 ---, "The dialectal structure of British English: the evidence of the Survey of English Dialects", in Viereck 1984.

1008 ---, "On the interrelationship of British and American English: morphological evidence", in Viereck 1984.

1009 ---, "The linguistic atlas and dialectometry", in Kirk/Sanderson/Widdowson 1984.

1010 ---, "Computerization of the lexical, morphological and syntactic data of the Survey of English Dialects" (forthcoming).

1011 **Wächtler, Kurt,** Geographie und Stratifikation der englischen Sprache. Studienreihe Englisch 16. Düsseldorf/Bern 1977; Chapters 2.8 - 2.10 and 3.2.

1012 ---, "Sociolinguistic aspects of a phonetic change in the RP-model of British English", Linguistische Berichte 53/1978: 21-28.

1013 **Waddington-Feather, John,** Yorkshire Dialect. Clapham: Dalesman 1970; 2nd ed. 1977; repr. 1980.

1014 **Wakefield, Gay,** "Vocabulary and idiom peculiar to the Ashton in Makerfield area", The Journal of the Lancashire Dialect Society 21 (1972): 27-28.

1015 **Wakelin, Martyn F.,** "Names for the cow-house in Devon and Cornwall", Devon and Cornwall Notes and Queries, April - July 1968: 52-56; repr. in Studia Neophilologica 42 (1970): 348-52.

1016 ---, "Studies in the linguistic geography of Cornwall." Ph.D. Leeds 1969.

1017 ---, "Crew, cree and crow: Celtic words in English dialect", Anglia 87 (1969): 273-81.

1018 ---, "A dialect note: south-western breakfast in the 'Survey of English Dialects'", Orbis 19 (1970): 47-48.

1019 ---, "Welsh influence in the west of England: dialectal TALLET", Folk Life 8 (1970): 72-80.

1020 ---, English Dialects: An Introduction. London: Athlone Press 1972; 2nd ed. 1977; repr. 1981.

1021 ---, ed., Patterns in the Folk Speech of the British Isles. With a Foreword by Harold Orton. London: Athlone Press 1972.

1022 ---, "Dialect and place-names: the distribution of kirk", in Wakelin 1972: 73-87.

1023 ---, "Dialectal 'Skippet': Consonant mutations in Cornwall", Devon and Cornwall Notes and Queries 1972: 152-3.

1024 ---, Language and History in Cornwall. Leicester: UP 1975.

1025 ---, "Norse influence in Cornwall: A Survey of the evidence", Cornish Studies 4/5 (1976-77): 41-49.

1026 ---, Discovering English Dialects. Aylesbury: Shire Publications 1978, 2nd ed. 1979.

1027 ---, "Evidence for spoken regional English in the sixteenth century", Revista Canaria de Estudios Ingleses 5 (1982): 1-25.*

1028 ---, "The stability of English dialect boundaries", English World-Wide 4 (1983): 1-15.

1029 ---, "Rural dialects in England", in Trudgill 1984.

1030 ---, "Rural dialects in England. Appendix 1: Cornish English", in Trudgill 1984.

1031 --- and **Michael V. Barry,** "The voicing of initial fricative consonants in present-day dialectal English", in Ellis 1968 (1969): 47-64.

1032 **Walkerdine, V.,** West Indian Children in Schools. Research Report. University of Bristol: School of Education Research Unit 1974.*

1033 **Walsh, Brian,** "Studying local speech", Use of English 25 (1973): 36-41.

1034 **Warkentyne, H.J.,** "The phonology of the dialect of Hexham in Northumberland." M.Phil. London, University College 1965.*

1035 ---, ed., Papers from the Fourth International Conference on Methods in Dialectology. University of Vancouver, B.C. [July 21 - 24] 1981 [1982].

1036 **Warrack, Alexander,** Chambers Scots Dictionary (with an introduction and dialect map by William Grant). Edinburgh: W. & R. Chambers 1911; latest repr. 1977.

1037 **Waterhouse, Keith,** Daily Mirror Style: Mirror's Way with Words. London: Mirror Books 1981.

1038 **Weijnen, Antonius A.,** Atlas Linguarum Europae. Introduction. Assen: Van Gorcum 1975.

1039 ---, Atlas Linguarum Europae. Premier Questionnaire: Onomasiologie, Vocabulaire Fondamental, préparé par Joep Kruijsen. Assen: Van Gorcum 1976.

1040 ---, Outlines for an Interlingual European Dialectology. Assen: Van Gorcum 1978.

1041 ---, Atlas Linguarum Europae. Second Questionnaire: I Syntaxe, II Morphologie, III Phonologie, IV Lexicologie. Texte établi par A. Weijnen et J. Kruijsen. Assen: Van Gorcum 1979.

1042 --- and **Mario Alinei,** The Wheel in the Atlas Linguarum Europae. Bijdragen en Mededelingen der Dialectencommissie van de K.N. Akad. van Wetenschappen te Amsterdam 1974.

1043 **Weissmann, Erich,** "Phonematische Analyse des Stadtdialekts von Bristol I, II", Phonetica 21 (1970): 151-81, 211-40.

1044 **Wells, John C.,** "Local accents in England and Wales", Journal of Linguistics 6 (1970): 231-52.

1045 ---, "Phonological adaptation in the speech of Jamaicans in the London area." Ph.D. London 1971.*

1046 ---, "A Scots diphthong and the feature /̄continuant_7", Journal of the International Phonetic Association 1 (1971): 29-32.

1047 ---, Jamaican Pronunciation in London. Publications of the Philological Society 25. Oxford: Blackwell 1973.

1048 ---, "The brogue that isn't", Journal of the International Phonetic Association 10 (1980): 74-79.

1049 ---, Accents of English. Vol. 1: An Introduction, Vol. 2: The British Isles. Cambridge: UP 1982 /̄ with accompanying tape In a manner of speaking. London: BBC and Cambridge: UP 1982_7.

1050 ---, "English accents in England", in Trudgill 1984.

1051 **Weltens, Bert,** "Non-standard periphrastic do in the dialects of south west Britain", Lore and Language 3,8 (1983): 56-64.

1052 **Wickens, Beatrice,** "Caithness speech: Studying the dialect with the help of school children", Scottish Literary Journal Supplement 12 (1980): 61-76.

1053 ---, "Caithness Speech: Studying the dialect with the help of school children (Part II)", Scottish Literary Journal Supplement 14 (1981): 25-36.

1054 **Widdowson, John D.A.,** "A pronouncing glossary of the dialect of Filey in the East Riding of Yorkshire." M.A. Leeds 1966. Published in microfilm/microfiche by E.P. Publishers, Wakefield 1972.

1055 ---, "The dialect of Filey: a selection of terms concerning fishing and the sea", Transactions of the Yorkshire Dialect Society 12, LXVI (1966): 28-41.

1056 ---, "The dialect of Filey (Yorkshire, East Riding): the vowels of stressed syllables", in Ellis 1968 (1969): 81-95.

1057 ---, "Proverbs and sayings from Filey", in Wakelin 1972: 50-72.

1058 ---, "Lexical erosion in English regional dialects", English World-Wide 4,2 (1983).

1059 **Wight, Jim,** "West Indian linguistics intelligibility Project: reports I and II." University of Birmingham 1967 / Ms. /.*

1060 ---, "Teaching English to West Indian children", English for Immigrants 2 (1969), No. 2 and Association of Teachers of English to Pupils from Overseas, Birmingham Branch 1970: 58-60.*

1061 ---, "Dialect in school", Educational Review 24 (1971): 47-58.

1062 ---, "How much interference?" Times Educational Supplement, 14 May 1976.*

1063 --- and **R.A. Norris,** Teaching English to West Indian Children: The Research Stage of the Project. Schools Council Working Paper 29. London: Evans/Methuen Educational 1970.

1064 **Wiles, Silvaine,** "Language issues in the multi-cultural classroom", in Neil Mercer 1981: 51-76.

1065 **Williams, Colin H.,** "Linguistic decline and nationalist resurgence in Wales." Ph.D. University of Wales 1978.*

1066 ---, "An ecological and behavioural analysis of ethnolinguistic change in Wales", in Giles/Saint-Jacques 1979: 27-55.

1067 **Williams, Dick** and **Frank Shaw,** The Gospels in Scouse. With an Introduction by David Sheppard, Bishop of Liverpool. London, Sydney and Toronto: White Lion Publ. 1967; rev. ed. 1977.

1068 **Williams, S.S.,** "A sociolinguistic analysis of the general practice interview." M.A. Birmingham 1974-75.*

1069 **Williamson, Juanita V.** and **Virginia M. Burke,** eds., A Various Language: Perspectives on American Dialects. New York: Holt, Rinehart and Winston 1971.

1070 **Williamson, Keith,** "Lowland Scots in education. An historical survey. Part I", Scottish Language 1 (1982): 54-77.

1071 **Willsher, S., B. Callaghan** et al., "A multiracial high school speaks", Journal of the Multiracial School 6 (1977), Spring issue.*

1072 **Wilson, David,** "The phonology and accidence of the dialect of the north Staffordshire potteries, and a glossary of Staffordshire dialect words." M.A. Birmingham 1970.*

1073 ---, Staffordshire Dialect Words: A Historical Survey. Buxton: Moorland Publishing Co. 1974.

1074 **Winston, Millicent,** "Some aspects of the pronunciation of educated Scots." M.Litt. Edinburgh 1971.*

1075 **Withrington, Donald J.,** "Scots in education: a historical retrospect", in McClure [1975]: 9-16.

1076 **Wölck, Wolfgang,** Phonematische Analyse der Sprache von Buchan. Frankfurter Arbeiten aus dem Gebiete der Anglistik und der Amerika-Studien 10 (1965).

1077 **Wood, Richard E.,** "Potential issues for language planning in Scotland", Language Planning Newsletter. Honolulu: East-West Culture Learning Institute 3 (1977): 1-6.

1078 ---, "Sociolinguistics in Scotland", Sociolinguistics Newsletter 8,1 (1977): 3-9.

1079 ---, "Bilingual education in Scotland", in Hernan LaFontaine, Barry Persky and Leonard H. Golubchick, eds., Bilingual Education. Wayne, N.J.: Avery Publ. Comp. 1978: 241-7.

1080 ---, "Scotland: The unfinished quest for linguistic identity", Word 30, 1979 (1980): 186-202.

1081 **Wright, Joseph,** The English Dialect Dictionary, 6 vols. Oxford 1898-1905, and The English Dialect Grammar. Oxford 1905; repr. Norwich: Fletcher 1970.

1082 **Wright, John T.,** "Urban dialects: a consideration of method", Zeitschrift für Mundartforschung 33 (1966): 232-46.

1083 **Wright, Peter,** "A proposal for a short questionnaire for use in fishing communities", Transactions of the Yorkshire Dialect Society 11, Pt. LXIV (1964): 27-32.

1084 ---, "Yorkshire steel terms today", Transactions of the Yorkshire Dialect Society 12, LXVI (1966): 41-47; repr. in Peter M. Anderson 1980: 56-62.

1085 ---, "A Lancashire fishing survey", The Journal of the Lancashire Dialect Society 16 (1967): 2-8.

1086 ---, Language at Work. An English Textbook for the Non-Specialist. London: Heinemann 1968; Chapter 6 Spoken English.

1087 ---, "Fishing language around England and Wales", The Journal of the Lancashire Dialect Society 17 (1968): 2-14.

1088 ---, "Coal-mining language: a recent investigation", in Wakelin 1972: 32-49.

1089 ---, The Lanky Twang: How it is spoke. Clapham: Dalesman 1972; repr. 1973, 1975.

1090 ---, The Yorkshire Yammer: How it is spoke. Clapham: Dalesman 1973.

1091 ---, The Cheshire Chatter: How it is spoke. Clapham: Dalesman 1974.

1092 ---, The Language of British Industry. London: Macmillan 1974.

1093 ---, The Derbyshire Drawl: How it is spoke. Clapham: Dalesman 1975.

1094 ---, Lancashire Dialect. Clapham: Dalesman 1976; 2nd ed. 1980.

1095 ---, "Sociolinguistic material from British industries and city dialects", in Reid 1976: 23.

1096 ---, "Fair play for British cities", The Journal of the Lancashire Dialect Society 27 (1978): 14-17.

1097 ---, Cumbrian Chat. How it is spoke. Clapham: Dalesman 1978.

1098 ---, The Notts Natter. How it is spoke. Clapham: Dalesman 1979.

1099 ---, Cumbrian Dialect. Clapham: Dalesman 1979.

1100 ---, The Yorkshireman's Dictionary. Clapham: Dalesman 1980; repr. 1981.

1101 ---, Cockney Dialect and Slang. London: B.T. Batsford 1981.

1102 ---, "Collecting dialect data in London, England", in H.J. Warkentyne [1982]: 29-40.

1103 --- and **Fritz Rohrer,** "Early work for the 'Survey of English Dialects': the academic and human sides", in Ellis 1968 (1969): 7-13.

1104 --- and **G.B. Smith,** "A Lancashire fishing survey", *The Journal of the Lancashire Dialect Society* 16 (1967): 2-8.

1105 **Wünschmann, Dieter,** "Zweisprachigkeit in Wales", *Zeitschrift für Mundartforschung* 34 (1967): 13-30.

1106 **Yule, George,** "The intonational correlates of givenness in spoken discourse", *Work in Progress.* Edinburgh University. Linguistics Department 12 (1979).*

1107 ---, "Speakers' topics and major paratones", *Lingua* 52 (1980): 33-47.

1108 ---, "The functions of phonological prominence in one variety of Scottish English", *Archivum Linguisticum* N.S. 11 (1980): 31-46.

Addenda:

258a **Fishlock, T.,** *Wales and the Welsh*. London: Cassell 1972; esp. Chapters 4 and 5.*

374a **Hewitt, R.,** "White adolescent creole users and the politics of friendship", *Journal of Multilingual and Multicultural Development* 3 (1982): 217-32.*

408a **Johnson, P.** and **Howard Giles,** "Values, language and inter-cultural differentiation: the Welsh-English context", *Journal of Multilingual and Multicultural Development* 3 (1982): 103-16.*

776a **Rampton, M.B.H.,** "Some flaws in educational discussion of the English of Asian schoolchildren in Britain", *Journal of Multilingual and Multicultural Development* 4 (1983): 15-28.*

Index

There are, of course, various ways to group the items. The system adopted here is self-explanatory. To reduce the length of the index, publications are indexed only according to their main emphasis. Thus, Cheshire's book of 1982 also has a chapter on sex differentiation in language. Since this is not its main concern, the item number does not appear under "Sex" in the index. Collections of papers are only indexed when the majority of the papers are relevant for the bibliography. Also for reasons of length, items are grouped under such headings as "Rural" and "Urban" within certain areas without specifying counties and cities investigated. These can easily be traced by working from the item numbers to the respective titles in the bibliography. The division of England follows that of the Survey of English Dialects. The numbering of sections is identical for all countries.

1.2.2. Urban
48, 100, 125, 202, 232, 384, 416-9, 424, 445-8, 496-9, 528, 658-9, 666, 725-40, 750, 778, 849, 864, 888, 906, 910, 987-8, 991, 1067, 1096.

1.3. West Midlands

1.3.1. Rural
57, 59, 91, 112, 172, 262, 267, 316, 344, 401, 434, 479, 481, 489-91, 540, 580, 711, 754, 796, 854, 947, 974-6, 1019, 1051, 1072-3, 1091, 1093.

1.3.2. Urban
364-5, 500-2, 794-5, 1043.

1.4. East Midlands and East Anglia

1.4.1. Rural
139, 152, 169, 263, 288, 322, 353, 449, 542, 678-9, 843, 863, 908-9, 928, 969, 1098.

1.4.2. Urban
763, 948-52, 961-3, 969.

1.5. The South

1.5.1. Rural
77, 126-7, 238, 248, 258, 279, 358-60, 395-9, 457, 504, 636, 667-73, 712, 798, 859-60, 892-4, 934-7, 993, 995, 1001, 1008, 1015-8, 1023-5, 1030-1, 1051.

1.5.2. Urban
65, 76, 92, 118, 148, 156-8, 160-3, 197, 388, 391-3, 415, 425, 473, 477, 483-4, 555, 817-8, 891, 926, 1096, 1101-2.

1.6. Occupational

366, 699-700, 978-80, 1037, 1092, 1095.

1.7. Sex

239, 307, 460, 764, 949.

1.8. Minorities/Bilingualism/Educational

8, 28, 55, 63-64, 69, 74, 110-1, 115, 151, 153, 162, 179, 183, 212-26, 250, 304, 311, 341, 343, 345-9, 374a, 383, 400, 426-7, 441, 472, 474-5, 488, 494-5,

541, 543, 556, 588-91, 637, 643, 713, 748, 753, 768, 776a, 784, 789-91, 817-9, 826, 834-5, 895, 920-5, 939, 955, 1032, 1045, 1047, 1059-64, 1071.

1.9. Attitudes/Reactions/Values

70, 166-7, 187, 210, 284, 292-302, 305-6, 308-9, 707, 709, 763, 827, 890, 915, 970.

1.10. Dialect and Literature

101, 141, 380, 452, 702, 749, 774, 874, 880, 942.

2.0. Wales

2.1. General (linguistic and methodological)

68, 78-79, 93, 237, 253, 324, 389, 394, 439, 482, 685-6, 799-800, 825, 932-3, 971-2, 1002-3, 1006, 1019, 1021, 1044, 1049, 1051, 1065-6, 1081, 1087.

2.1.1. Rural
143, 165, 174, 361, 408, 714, 716-22, 742-4, 851, 907, 938, 977.

2.1.2. Urban
175, 340, 478, 581, 715.

2.6. Occupational

176.

2.8. Minorities/Bilingualism/Educational (cf. also 2.9)

8, 204, 258a, 303, 362, 414, 432, 493, 554, 858, 1105.

2.9. Attitudes/Reactions/Values (cf. also 2.8)

113-4, 116-7, 155, 177, 299, 306, 310, 408a, 431, 492, 765, 856-7.

3.0. Scotland

3.1. General (linguistic and methodological)

4-6, 29, 35, 66, 68, 78-79, 132, 137, 140, 150, 154, 170, 173, 178, 180-1, 186, 228, 249, 278, 285, 321, 323-4, 326-9, 335, 342, 373, 394, 404, 411, 421, 428-9, 435-7, 439, 440, 442, 450, 476, 482, 505-6, 511-2, 516, 520, 524-5, 531, 533, 535, 545-50, 553, 557, 559-73, 575-7, 582, 593-600, 628, 640, 644-9, 651-2, 654, 657, 664, 685-6, 701, 761, 769-70, 777, 781, 799-800, 802, 804, 810-4, 816, 845, 853, 855, 899-900, 903-4, 911-2, 929, 931, 954, 958-9, 971, 984, 996, 1002-3, 1011, 1021, 1036, 1046, 1049, 1070, 1074-5, 1077-8, 1080-1.

3.2. North and West of the Celtic Border

3.2.1. Rural
67, 171, 312, 515, 536, 551, 797, 832-3, 881-5, 905, 940.

3.3. South and East of the Celtic Border

3.3.1. Rural
30-34, 36-46, 133-4, 255-6, 317, 325, 374, 405, 409, 430, 458, 544, 551-2, 585-7, 601, 610, 641, 650, 662, 785-8, 792-3, 823, 896, 898, 902, 983, 1052-3, 1076.

3.3.2. Urban
134-6, 138, 241-5, 389, 410, 412, 514, 517-8, 521-2, 526-7, 532, 592, 760-1, 779-80, 782-3, 801, 805-6, 815, 847, 897, 901, 1096, 1106-8.

3.8. Minorities/Bilingualism/Educational

151, 192, 955, 1079.

3.9. Attitudes/Reactions/Values

124, 166, 519, 803, 808, 846.

3.10. Dialect and Literature

507, 513, 523, 574, 577, 639, 844, 973.

4.0. Ireland

4.1. General and rural (linguistic and methodological)

9-19, 21-27, 51-52, 68, 78-79, 83-89, 102, 104-9, 119-23, 168, 173, 188-9, 191, 198-200, 211, 257, 261, 280-2, 286, 324, 331-8, 350-2, 354-6, 369-72, 375-8, 382, 390, 394, 420, 439, 440, 482, 508-9, 529-30, 537, 558, 610, 621, 654, 656, 661, 676, 681-4, 687, 745-7, 757, 762, 771, 781, 799-800, 886, 889, 918, 927, 943-4, 946, 959, 971, 1002-3, 1011, 1021, 1048-9, 1081.

4.2.2. Urban
20, 98, 205, 207, 357, 389, 406, 602-9, 612-20, 622-30, 632, 677, 680, 756-9.

4.8. Minorities/Bilingualism/Educational

254, 261, 283, 663.

4.9. Attitudes/Reactions/Values

149, 206, 208, 631.

4.10. Dialect and Literature

103, 367, 433, 919, 927.

5.0. Channel Islands

5.1. General

1003.

A Bibliography of Writings on American and Canadian English (1965 - 1983)

Edgar W. Schneider

This bibliography lists writings on American English (AmE) and Canadian English (CanE) published between 1965 and the summer of 1983. A few forthcoming items likely to appear in the near future have also been included. It is based on a search of a variety of sources: the standard bibliographies, such as the MLA Bibliography and the Bibliographie Linguistique; Bibliographie Linguistischer Literatur; more up-to-date collections like Current Contents Linguistics; Language and Language Behavior Abstracts; Dissertation Abstracts International (DAI); the "Publications received"-sections of Language and other journals; the Newsletter of the American Dialect Society; relevant journals and books; library catalogues; other bibliographies; publishers' catalogues; etc. I have tried to check as many items as possible in order to verify the bibliographic data and to obtain information relevant for the index, yet, as is to be expected, these attempts have regrettably not been successful in all cases. Thanks are due to Lee Pederson (Atlanta, Ga.) and Michael Montgomery (Columbia, S.C.), who commented on an earlier and much shorter version of this bibliography published in English World-Wide 3:2 (1982).

Considering the subject, there is certainly a need for a bibliography of AmE. Raven McDavid's 1979 "bibliographic essay" is a most useful guide to the most important literature on the subject, including older books and publications, and in relatively recent years two important surveys of research (Allen 1977 [1981] and Pederson 1977 [1981]) and a number of special bibliographies (the most important ones being McMillan 1971 on Southern AmE, Brasch/Brasch 1974 on Black English, and Bähr 1977 and Avis/Kinloch 1978 on CanE) have been published, yet there has been no bibliography covering the whole of the United States, not to speak of North America, since Vito Joseph Brenni's American English: A Bibliography (Pennsylvania: UP 1964). Considerable problems are involved in compiling such a list, however, for the field is wide and diffuse and the number of pertinent publications is high, yet every bibliographer has to draw a line somewhere. In order to fulfill my duty as a bibliographer, I will state my aims and the principles of selection applied.

Relevant work in the disciplines of dialectology and sociolinguistics certainly constitutes the core of the bibliography, so I have attempted to be as comprehensive as possible with respect to descriptive accounts of regionally and socially varying linguistic forms and features. Within the present framework of world-wide variation of English, it has been decided to include also publications on (Standard) "AmE" as a national variety if they contain some relevant information on distictively American linguistic forms (e.g. as opposed to British English), but not if they are concerned exclusively with some structural property of English and just happen to have been based on American English data. Of course, the latter distinction can be to a certain extent arbitrary and subjective, but it seems necessary in order not to expand the list unduly and at the same time reduce its usefulness as a bibliography on varieties proper. Also included are writings on bilingualism, language contact, and language interference, unless they deal mainly with the non-English language involved; on attitudes towards varieties of English; on theory and methodology of sociolinguistics or dialectology, if they provide a certain amount of American English data for illustration; and on the development and state of these two disciplines in North America. Publications on literary dialect, on bilingual education and the language education of minority children, on modern or historical lexicography (e.g. on the origin and etymology of Americanisms) and on slang and argot as well as reprints of books have been included selectively. Excluded are reviews; reprints of articles; articles in non-scholarly publications, such as newspapers; unpublished manuscripts and papers read at conferences; and onomastic studies. Hawaii is covered not here but in Manfred Görlach's section of the book. The main body of the bibliography is followed by an index, which indirectly often provides information additional to the title of an item, especially with respect to the area a publication deals with.

Abbreviations used

U.	University
AS	American Speech
FFLR	The Florida Foreign Language Reporter
JEngL	Journal of English Linguistics
PADS	Publication of the American Dialect Society
RLS	Regional Language Studies - Newfoundland
WPLUH	Working Papers in Linguistics, University of Hawaii

1 **Abrahams, Roger D.**, "'Talking my talk': Black English and social segmentation in black American communities", African Language Review 9 (1970-71 /¯1973_7): 227-54.

2 ---, Toward a Black Rhetoric: Being a Survey of Afro-American Communication Styles and Role Relationships. Austin: U. of Texas 1972.

3 ---, "Black talking on the streets", in Richard Baumann and Joel Sherzer, eds., Explorations in the Ethnography of Speaking. London: Cambridge UP 1974: 240-62.

4 --- and **John F. Szwed,** "Black English: an essay review", American Anthropologist 77 (1975): 329-35.

5 --- and **Rudolph C. Troike,** eds., Language and Cultural Diversity in American Education. Englewood Cliffs, N.J.: Prentice-Hall 1972.

6 **Adamko, Jerzy,** "Some remarks on tense and aspect in Black English", Lubelskie Materialy Neofilologiczne 1976 (1978): 145-52.

7 **Adams, Charles Clinton,** "Boontling: limited language of Boonville, California, and its environs." Ph.D. U. of Washington 1967. DAI 28: 5, 1804A.

8 ---, Boontling: An American Lingo, with a Dictionary of Boontling. Austin: Texas UP 1971.

9 **Adams, Ramon F.,** Western Words: a Dictionary of the American West. 2nd ed. Norman, Okla.: Oklahoma UP 1968.

10 **Aguirre, Adalberto, Jr.,** An Experimental Sociolinguistic Study of Chicano Bilingualism. San Francisco: R & E Research Associates 1978.

11 **Akers, William G.,** "Black English. An American sociolinguistic problem", in Manfred Mayrhofer et al., eds., Antiquitates Indogermanicae. Studien zur Indogermanischen Altertumskunde und zur Sprach- und Kulturgeschichte der indogermanischen Völker. Gedenkschrift für Hermann Güntert zur 25. Wiederkehr seines Todestages am 23. April 1973. Innsbruck: Institut für Sprachwissenschaft der U. Innsbruck 1974: 505-14.

12 **Akin, Johnnye,** "Intonation contours in American English", in The Study of Sounds. Vol. 12. Papers Delivered at the Second World Congress of Phoneticians, Tokyo, 26 - 31 August 1965. Tokyo: Phonetic Society of Japan 1966: 415-28.

13 **Alatis, James E.,** "The American English pronunciation of Greek

immigrants: a study in language contact with pedagogical implications." Ph.D. Ohio State U. 1966. DAI 27: 9, 3027A.

14 ---, ed., Linguistics and the Teaching of Standard English to Speakers of Other Languages or Dialects. Report of the Twentieth Annual Round Table Meeting on Linguistics and Language Studies. Washington, D.C.: Georgetown UP 1970.

15 ---, ed., International Dimensions of Bilingual Education. Georgetown University Round Table on Languages and Linguistics 1978. Washington, D.C.: Georgetown UP 1978.

16 ---, ed., Current Issues in Bilingual Education. Georgetown University Round Table on Languages and Linguistics 1980. Washington, D.C.: Georgetown UP 1980.

17 **Albin, Alexander,** "A Yugoslav community in San Pedro, California", General Linguistics 16 (1976): 78-94.

18 --- and **Ronelle Alexander,** The Speech of Yugoslav Immigrants in San Pedro, California. The Hague: Vijhoff 1972.

19 **Allen, George D.,** "Two behavioral experiments on the location of the syllable beat in conversational American English." Ph.D. U. of Michigan 1966. DAI 28: 2, 652A.

20 ---, "Transcription of the American /r/", in Harry Hollien and Patricia Hollien, eds., Current Issues in the Phonetic Sciences. Proceedings of the IPS-77 Congress, Miami Beach, 17 - 19 Dec. 1977. Amsterdam: Benjamins 1979: 1019-25.

21 **Allen, Harold B.,** "Some problems in editing the Linguistic Atlas of the Upper Midwest", in Burghardt 1971: 54-78.

22 ---, "Principles of informant selection", AS 46 (1971): 47-51.

23 ---, "Curds and checklists in the Upper Midwest", in L. Davis 1972: 3-7.

24 ---, The Linguistic Atlas of the Upper Midwest, vol. 1: The Project and the Lexicon. Minneapolis: Minnesota UP 1973.

25 ---, "The use of Atlas informants of foreign parentage", in Scholler/Reidy 1973: 17-24.

26 ---, "Two dialects in contact", AS 48 (1973): 54-66.

27 ---, "English as a second language", in Sebeok 1973: 295-320.

28 ---, "Language variation and TESOL", TESOL Quarterly 7 (1973): 13-23.

29 ---, The Linguistic Atlas of the Upper Midwest, vol. 2: The Grammar. Minneapolis: Minnesota UP 1975.

30 ---, The Linguistic Atlas of the Upper Midwest, vol. 3: The Pronunciation. Minneapolis: Minnesota UP 1976.

31 ---, "The Linguistic Atlas of the Upper Midwest as a source of sociolinguistic information", in Raymond/Russell 1977: 3-19.

32 ---, "Regional dialects, 1945-1974", AS 52 (Issue for Fall/Winter 1977; 1981): 163-261.

33 --- and **Gary N. Underwood,** eds., Readings in American Dialectology. New York: Appleton-Century Crofts 1971.

34 **Allen, Irving Lewis,** The Language of Ethnic Conflict: Social Organization and Lexical Culture. New York: Columbia UP 1983.

35 **Alvarez, Ana Isabel,** "Code-switching among bilingual children." Ph.D. U. of Massachusetts 1979. DAI 40, 3899B.

36 **Ammon, Paul R.,** "Syntactic elaboration in the speech of lower-class black and middle-class white preschool children." ERIC, ED 081 493, 1973.

37 **Andersen, Roger W.,** ed., The Aquisition and Use of Spanish and English as First and Second Languages. Washington: TESOL, Georgetown U. 1979.

38 ---, "The relationship between first language transfer and second language overgeneralization: data from the English of Spanish speaking learners", in Anderson 1979: 43-58.

39 **Andersen, Stan,** "The British-American differences. Processes of change", Neuphilologische Mitteilungen 73 (1972): 855-65.

40 **Anderson, Bernadette,** "An analysis of the relationship of age and sex to type and frequency of disfluencies in lower socioeconomic preschool black children." Ph.D. Northwestern U. 1981. DAI 42: 9, 3642A.

41 **Anderson, Edward,** "Dimensions of language and rhetorical styles in Black America." Ph.D. U. of Michigan 1974. DAI 35: 11, 7243A.

42 **Anderson, Frances J.,** "Comparison of the language of white and negro children from low socioeconomic groups." Ph.D. U. of Alabama 1972. DAI 33: 6, 2914A.

43 **Anderson, James,** "GI slang and the Vietnam area", in Cooley/Barnes/Dunn 1979: 488-95.

44 **Andersson, Theodore** and **Mildred Boyer,** eds., Bilingual Schooling in the United States. 2 vols. Washington, D.C.: U.S. Government Printing Office 1970. 2nd ed.: Austin, Texas: National Educational Laboratory Publishers 1978.

45 **Andersson, Thomas,** "'As crazy as two walking mice': About American similes", Moderna Språk 65 (1971): 223-6.

46 **Andreacchi, Joseph,** "Listening comprehension and reading comprehension of negro dialect speakers in negro dialect and in Standard English." Ph.D. Columbia U. 1973. DAI 34: 5, 2417A.

47 **Anisman, Paul H.,** "Some phonological correlates of code switching in the English of Puerto Rican teenagers in New York City." Ph.D. Rochester 1975. DAI 36: 1, 335A.

48 ---, "Some aspects of code switching in New York Puerto Rican English", Bilingual Review 2 (1975): 56-85.

49 **anon.,** "Notes and queries: North Idaho mining vocabulary", Western Folklore 24 (1965): 290.

50 **anon.,** "An Appalachian relic: notes on 'swarp'", Appalachian Journal 8 (1981): 203-5.

51 **Anshen, Frank Stephen,** "Speech variation among negroes in a small southern community." Ph.D. New York U. 1969. DAI 30: 6, 2509A.

52 ---, "A sociolinguistic analysis of a sound change", Language Sciences 9 (1970): 20-21.

53 ---, "Some data which do not fit some models", in Bailey/Shuy 1973: 62-68.

54 --- and **Mark Aronoff,** "'Dragon fly': Lexical change, local scatter, and the national norm", Language in Society 11 (1982): 413-7.

55 **Appleby, Jane,** "Is Southern English good English?" in Shores/Hines 1977: 225-8.

56 **Applegate, Joseph R.,** "Urban speech analysis", in Alatis 1970: 259-61.

57 **Arahili, Edward Joseph, Jr.,** "The effect of differing dialects upon the comprehension and attitude of eighth grade children." Ed.D. U of Florida 1970. DAI 31: 11, 6030A.

58 **Aricò, Danielle,** Dall' inglese d'Inghilterra all' inglese d'America. Bologna: Pàtron 1966.

59 **Armstrong, Bondie Ernest,** "A study of dialect and its interference with learning to write." Ed.D. Memphis 1982. DAI 43: 7, 2335A.

60 **Armstrong, Hollis Marlon,** "Black English and reading." Ph.D. U. of Michigan 1981. DAI 42: 9, 3928A.

61 **Arnold, Marjorie R., John W. Rosado, Jr.,** and **Douglas A. Penfield,** "Language choice by bilingual Puerto Rican children on a picture labeling task", The Modern Language Journal 63 (1979): 349-54.

62 **Arrington, John Nathan,** "A comparison of language, communicative styles and speech patterns of blacks and non-blacks." Ph.D. United States International U. 1977. DAI 39: 11, 6594A.

63 **Arthur, Bradford, Dorothee Farrar** and **George Bradford,** "Evaluation reactions of college students to dialect differences in the English of Mexican-Americans", Language and Speech 17 (1974): 255-70.

64 **Asante, Molefi Kete,** "Television's impact on black children's language: an exploration", in Molefi Kete Asante and Abdulai S.Vandi, eds., Contemporary Black Thought: Alternative Analyses in Social and Behavioral Science. Beverly Hills: Sage 1980: 181-94.

65 **Ash, Sharon,** "The vocalization of /l/ in Philadelphia." Ph.D. U of Pennsylvania 1982. DAI 43: 3, 784A.

66 **Ashley, Leonard R. N.,** "Bilingualism and the clash of cultures in the United States", Geolinguistics 7 (1981): 23-47.

67 ---, "My gimmick: a thingummy on omnibus terms in American slanguage", Comments on Etymology (U. of Missouri, Rolla) 10,15 (1981): 4-8.

68 **Assam, Ann Padmore,** "A comparison of written English of non-West Indian Canadian-born and immigrant West Indian Students in Canada." Ph.D. Buffalo, New York 1981. DAI 42: 4, 1585A.

69 **Atwood, E. Bagby,** A Survey of Verb Forms in the Eastern United States. Ann Arbor: Michigan UP 1953, repr. 1967.

70 ---, "Amerikanische Dialektologie", in Ludwig Erich Schmitt, ed., Germanische Dialektologie. Festschrift für Walther Mitzka zum 80. Geburtstag. Wiesbaden: Steiner 1968: 565-600.

71 ---, The Regional Vocabulary of Texas. Austin: Texas UP 1962, repr. 1980.

72 **Austin, Jessie Gardner,** "Syntactic maturity as an element of clas dialect." Ph.D. U. of Alabama 1969. DAI 30: 8, 3442A.

73 **Austin, William M.,** "Some social aspects of paralanguage", Canadia Journal of Linguistics 11 (1965): 31-39.

74 **Avis, Walter S.,** A Bibliography of Writings on Canadian English (1857 1965). Toronto: Gage 1965.

75 ---, "Problems in the study of Canadian English", Communications e rapports du Premier Congrès International de Dialectologie général (Louvain du 21 au 25 août, Bruxelles les 26 et 27 aout 1960) Troisième Partie. Louvain: Centre international de Dialectologi générale 1965: 183-91.

76 ---, "Canadian spoken here", in M.H. Scargill and P.G. Penner, eds. Looking at Language. Toronto 1966: 17-39.

77 ---, "Linguistica Canadiana", Canadian Journal of Linguistics 1 (1969): 70-73.

78 ---, "The phonemic segments of an Edmonton idiolect", in L. Davi 1972: 239-50.

79 ---, "So eh? Is Canadian, eh?" Canadian Journal of Linguistics 1 (1972): 89-104.

80 ---, "The English language in Canada", in Sebeok 1973: 40-74.

81 ---, "Eskimo words in Canadian English", in Scholler/Reidy 1973 25-36.

82 ---, "Problems in editing a Canadian dictionary: phonology", in McDavid/Duckert 1973: 110-4.

83 ---, "Speech differences along the Ontario-United States border", in Chambers 1975: 67-77.

84 ---, "Canadian English", in W.S. Avis, ed., Funk and Wagnalls Standard College Dictionary: Canadian Edition. Toronto: Fitzhenry and Whiteside 1976: xv-xvi.

85 ---, Essays and Articles. Kingston, Ont.: Royal Military College 1978.

86 ---, "Canadian English in its North American context", in Avis 1978: 35-49.

87 --- and **A.M. Kinloch,** Writings on Canadian English 1792-1975: An Annotated Bibliography. Toronto: Fitzhenry and Whiteside 1978.

88 --- et al., Dictionary of Canadian English. The Senior Dictionary. Toronto: Gage 1967.

89 --- et al., A Dictionary of Canadianisms on Historical Principles. Toronto: Gage 1967.

90 --- et al., A Concise Dictionary of Canadianisms. Toronto: Gage 1973.

91 **Bachmann, James Kevin,** "A comparison of nonstandard grammatical usage in some negro and white working-class families in Alexandria, Virginia." Ph.D. Georgetown U. 1969. DAI 31: 5, 2364A.

92 **Bähr, Dieter,** Standard English und seine geographischen Varianten. München: Fink 1974.

93 ---, "Vorläufige Analyse des 'Survey of Canadian English'", Zeitschrift für Dialektologie und Linguistik 43 (1976): 305-17.

94 ---, A Bibliography of Writings on the English Language in Canada from 1857 to 1976. Heidelberg: Winter 1977.

95 ---, Die englische Sprache in Kanada. Eine Analyse des 'Survey of Canadian English'. Tübingen: Narr 1981.

96 **Bailey, Beryl Loftman,** "Toward a new perspective in negro English dialectology", AS 40 (1965): 171-7.

97 **Bailey, Charles-James N.,** "Dialectal differences in the syllabification of non-nasal sonorants in American English", General Linguistics 8 (1968): 79-91.

98 ---, "Is there a 'Midland' dialect of American English?" ERIC ED 021-240, 1968.

99 ---, "An exploratory investigation of variations in the accented outputs of underlying short vowels in a dialect of Southern States English", WPLUH 1,1 (1969): 57-64.

00 ---, "Introduction to Southern States phonetics", WPLUH 1,4 (1969): 81-144; 1,5 (1969): 107-84; 1,6 (1969): 105-203; 1,7 (1969): 71-95; 1,8 (1969): 139-79; 1,9 (1969): 61-147; 1,10 (1969): 101-23; 1,11 (1969): 143-76.

01 ---, "Black English", WPLUH 2,6 (1970): 1-22.

02 ---, "Southern States phonetics", WPLUH 2,2 (1970): 163-8.

103 ---, "Vowel reduction and syllabic sonorants in English", WPLUH 3,2 (1971): 35-104.

104 ---, "Tempo and phrasing", WPLUH 3,2 (1971): 105-14.

105 ---, "Intonation (Excerpt from revised chapter ten of 'Southern States phonetics')", WPLUH 3,5 (1971): 43-117.

106 ---, "The patterning of language variation", in Bailey/Robinson 1973: 156-86.

107 ---, "Four low-level pronunciation rules of Northern States English", Journal of the International Phonetic Association 8 (1978): 24-33.

108 ---, "Restructuring of nuclear length in 'r-less' Southern States English", Arbeiten aus Anglistik und Amerikanistik 6 (1981): 119-26.

109 ---, "Irish English and Caribbean Black English: another joinder", AS 57 (1982): 237-9.

110 --- and **Roger W. Shuy,** eds., New Ways of Analyzing Variation in English. Washington, D.C.: Georgetown UP 1973.

111 **Bailey, Guy Hubert III.,** "Folk speech on the Cumberland plateau: a phonological analysis." Ph.D. U. of Tennessee 1979. DAI 40: 9, 5031A.

112 **Bailey, Richard W.,** "Haliburton's eye and ear", Canadian Journal of Linguistics 26 (1981): 90-101.

113 ---, "The English language in Canada", in Bailey/Görlach 1982: 134-76.

114 --- and **Manfred Görlach,** eds., English as a World Language. Ann Arbor: Michigan UP 1982.

115 --- and **Jay L. Robinson,** eds., Varieties of Present-Day English. New York: Macmillan 1973.

116 **Baird, Allyne Higgason,** "Rural Southwest Georgia speech: a phonological analysis." Ph.D. Georgia State U. 1982. DAI 43: 6, 1956A.

117 **Baird, Keith E.,** "Guy B. Johnson revisited: another look at Gullah", Journal of Black Studies 10 (1980): 425-35.

118 **Baird, Scott James,** "Employment interview speech: a social dialect study in Austin, Texas." Ph.D. Austin 1969. DAI 30: 4, 1543A.

119 **Baligand, Renée,** "Glide-usage and effects of palatalization", in Leon/Martin 1979: 97-110.

120 **Ball, Donald B.,** "Notes on the slang and folk speech of Knoxville, Knox County, Tennessee", Tennessee Folklore Society Bulletin 44 (1978): 134-42.

121 **Ball, Ian M.,** "Amerenglish", Encounter 43,4 (1974): 56-62.

122 **Barankin, Joseph Paul,** "Selected issues related to the social phenomenon of Black English." Ph.D. United States International U. 1980. DAI 41: 4, 1567A.

123 **Baratz, Joan C.,** "A bi-dialectal task for determining language proficiency in economically disadvantaged negro children", Child Development 40 (1969): 889-901.

124 ---, "'Ain't' ain't no error", FFLR 9 (1971): 39-40, 54.

125 ---, "The language of the ghetto child", in Bentley/Crawford 1973: 77-79.

126 ---, "Language abilities of black Americans", in Kent S. Miller and Ralph Mason Dreger, eds., Comparative Studies of Blacks and Whites in the United States. New York, London: Seminar Press 1973: 125-83.

127 --- and **Roger W. Shuy,** eds., Teaching Black Children to Read. Washington, D.C.: Center for Applied Linguistics 1969.

128 **Baran, Jane** and **Harry N. Seymour,** "The influence of three phonological rules of Black English on the discrimination of minimal word pairs", Journal of Speech and Hearing Research 19 (1976): 467-74.

129 **Barber, Carroll G.,** "Trilingualism in an Arizona Yaqui village", in Turner 1973: 295-318.

130 **Barkin, Florence** and **Elizabeth A. Brandt,** eds., Speaking, Singing and Teaching: A Multidisciplinary Approach to Language Variation. Tempe: Arizona State U. 1980.

131 ---, --- and **Jacob Ornstein-Galicia,** eds., Bilingualism and Language Contact: Spanish, English, and Native American Languages. Hagerstown, Md.: Teachers College Press 1982.

132 **Barnes, Linda S.,** "Rural expressions in Bedford County, Tennessee." M.A. Thesis, Middle Tennessee State U. 1981.

133 **Barnhart, Clarence L.,** "American lexicography, 1945-1973", AS 53 (1978): 83-140.

134 **Barnickel, Klaus-Dieter,** Sprachliche Varianten des Englischen. Teilband I: Nationale, regionale und soziale Varianten. München: Hueber 1982.

135 **Baron, Dennis E.,** Grammar and Good Taste. Reforming the American Language. New Haven: Yale UP 1982.

136 **Bartelt, Hans Guillermo,** "Language transfer of Navajo and Western Apache speakers in writing English." Ph.D. U. of Arizona 1980. DAI 41: 1, 228A.

137 ---, "Semantic overgeneralization in Apachean English interlanguage", JEngL 15 (1981): 10-16.

138 ---, "Some observations on Navaho English", Papers in Linguistics 14 (1981): 377-85.

139 ---, **Susan Penfield Jaspar** and **Bates Hoffer,** eds., Essays in Native American English. San Antonio: Trinity U. 1982.

140 **Baskervill, Robert David, Jr.,** "The assessment of Black English syntactic and phonologic language forms." Ph.D. Buffalo, New York 1979. DAI 39, 5860B.

141 **Bateman, Stanley C.E.,** "Survey of Canadian English: a comparison of the language patterns of English-speaking New Brunswickers at two different levels of education." M.Ed. Thesis, U. of New Brunswick 1975.

142 **Baubkus, Lutz** and **Wolfgang Viereck,** "Recent American studies in sociolinguistics", Archivum Linguisticum N.S. 4 (1973): 103-9.

143 **Bauer, Laurie,** "The feature 'tense/lax' with special reference to the vowel system of (American) English", Zeitschrift für Anglistik und Amerikanistik 28 (1980): 244-53.

144 ---, **John M. Dienhart, Hans H. Hartvigson** and **Leif K. Jakobsen,** American English Pronunciation. Copenhagen: Gyldendal 1980.

145 **Bauerle, Richard F.,** "Salties on the Great Lakes", AS 45 (1970): 156-7.

146 **Baugh, John Gordon, Jr.,** "Linguistic style-shifting in Black English." Ph.D. U. of Pennsylvania 1979. DAI 40: 6, 3269A.

147 ---, "A reexamination of the Black English copula", in Labov 1980: 83-105.

148 **Bauman, Richard** and **Joel Sherzer,** eds., Language and Speech in American Society: A Compilation of Research Papers in Sociolinguistics. Austin: Southwest Educational Development Laboratory 1980.

149 **Beaty, Eartha David, Jr.,** "Black English forms as a function of an

identity transformation process, self-concept, and internal-external control." Ph.D. Columbia U. 1978. DAI 39, 5637B.

150 **Beaudoin, Michael, Jim Cummins, Helen Dunlop, Fred Genesee** and **André Obadia,** "Bilingual education: a comparison of Welsh and Canadian experiences", Canadian Modern Language Review 37 (1981): 498-509.

151 **Beaudry, Mary Carolyn,** "'Or what else you please to call it': folk semantic domains in early Virginia probate inventories." Ph.D. Brown U. 1980. DAI 41: 12, 5153A.

152 **Beck, Kay,** "Speech behavior and social environment: selective interactions in the American South", Discourse Processes 2 (1979): 335-42.

153 **Bell, Afesa M.** and **Charles Turner,** "A social psychological approach to languages of the African diaspora", in Paul F.A. Kotey and Haig Der-Houssikian, eds., Language and Linguistic Problems in Africa. Proceedings of the VII Conference on African Linguistics. Columbia, S.C.: Hornbeam 1977: 479-86.

154 **Bell, Ellen Faye,** "Comparison of features of black and white speech: Bradley, Ga." M.A. Thesis, Chapel Hill, North Carolina 1973.

155 **Ben-Dor, Shmuel,** Makkovik: Eskimos and Settlers in a Labrador Community: A Contrastive Study in Adaptation. St. John's, Nfld.: Memorial U. of Newfoundland 1966.

156 **Benjamin, Steven M.** and **Luanne von Schneidemesser,** "German loanwords in American English, a bibliography of studies", AS 54 (1979): 210-5.

157 **Bennett, Don J.** and **Stanley B. Woll,** "Some social psychological influences on the linguistic performance of black teenagers", Discourse Processes 3 (1980): 73-97.

158 **Bentley, Robert H.** and **Samuel D. Crawford,** eds., Black Language Reader. Glenview, Ill., Brighton: Scott, Foresman and Company 1973.

159 **Berdan, Robert,** Have/got in the Speech of Anglo and Black Children. Los Alamitos, Calif.: Southwest Regional Library for Educational Research and Development 1973.

160 ---, "Polylectal comprehension and the polylectal grammar", in Fasold/Shuy 1977: 12-29.

161 ---, "Sufficiency conditions for a prior creolization of Black English", in Day 1980: 147-62.

162 --- and **Carol W. Pfaff,** *Sociolinguistic Variation in the Speech of Young Children: An Experimental Study.* Los Alamitos, Calif.: Southwest Regional Library for Educational Research and Development 1972.

163 **Berger, Marshall D.,** "The internal dynamics of a metropolitan New York vocalic paradigm", *AS* 43 (1968): 33-39.

164 ---, "Accent, pattern, and dialect in North American English", *Word* 24 (1968): 55-61.

165 ---, "New York City and the ante-bellum South: the maritime connection", *Word* 31 (1980): 47-54.

166 **Bettridge, William Edwin,** "American borrowings of British motoring terms", *AS* 41 (1966): 38-44.

167 **Betts, Leonidas,** "Folk speech from Kipling", *North Carolina Folklore* 14 (1966): 37-40.

168 **Bickerton, Anthea,** *American English, English American: A Two-Way Glossary of Words in Daily Use on Both Sides of the Atlantic.* Bristol: Abson 1971.

169 **Billiard, Charles Edward,** "Dialect features affecting the social mobility and economic opportunities of the disadvantaged in Fort Wayne, Indiana." Ph.D. Purdue U. 1969. DAI 30: 11, 4962B.

170 --- and **Lee Pederson,** "Composition of the LAGS urban complement: Atlanta words", *Orbis* 28 (1979): 223-41.

171 **Bills, Garland,** ed., *Southwest Areal Linguistics.* San Diego, Calif.: Institute for Cultural Pluralism 1974.

172 ---, "Vernacular Chicano English: dialect or interference", *Journal of the Linguistic Association of the Southwest* 2 (1977): 230-6.

173 **Binger, Norman H.,** "German elements in the American vocabulary", *Semasia* 2 (1975): 31-41.

174 **Biondi, Lawrence S.J.,** "The linguistic development and socialization of Italian-American children in Boston's North End." Ph.D. Georgetown U 1975. DAI 36: 1, 336A.

175 ---, *The Italian-American Child: His Sociolinguistic Acculturation.* Washington, D.C.: Georgetown UP 1975.

176 **Birmingham, John C., Jr.,** "Black English near its roots: the transplanted West African creoles", in Dillard 1980: 335-46.

177 **Blansitt, Edward L., Jr.,** and **Richard V. Teschner,** eds., A Festschrift for Jacob Ornstein: Studies in General Linguistics and Sociolinguistics. Rowley, Mass.: Newbury 1980.

178 **Blanton, Linda L.,** "The verb system in Breathitt County, Kentucky: a sociolinguistic analysis." Ph.D. Illinois Institute of Technology 1974. DAI 35: 12, 7888A.

179 **Bloome, David Michael,** "An ethnographic approach to the study of reading activities among black junior high school students: a sociolinguistic ethnography." Ph.D. Kent State U. 1981. DAI 42: 7, 2993A.

180 **Boatner, Maxine Tull** and **John Edward Gates,** A Dictionary of American Idioms. Rev. ed., ed. by Adam Makkai. Woodbury, N.Y.: Barron's 1976.

181 **Bock, E. Hope** and **James H. Pitts,** "The effect of three levels of black dialect on perceived speaker image", Speech Teacher 24 (1975): 218-25.

182 **Boertien, Harmon S.,** "The double modal construction in Texas", Texas Linguistic Forum 13 (1979): 14-33.

183 --- and **Sally Said,** "Syntactic variation in double modal dialects", Journal of the Linguistic Association of the Southwest 3 (1980): 210-22.

184 **Boesen, Mary Lorraine,** "Contextual incidence of verb forms in the speech of selected sixth grade Minneapolis-born children." Ph.D. U. of Minnesota 1968. DAI 29: 7, 2240A.

185 **Boiarsky, Carolyn,** "Consistency of spelling and pronunciation deviations in Appalachian students", Modern Language Journal 53 (1969): 347-50.

186 **Bolinger, Dwight,** "Are you a sincere h-dropper?" AS 50 (1975): 313-5.

187 **Bonnie, Diane Marie,** "The jargon of car salesmen", AS 50 (1975): 311-3.

188 **Boswell, George W.,** "Class competition in Kentucky dialect study", Kentucky Folklore Record 17 (1971): 48-52.

189 ---, "Potpourri of Mississippi dialect", Mississippi Folklore Register 16,2 (1982): 25-32.

190 **Bountress, Nicholas,** "Approximations of selected Standard English sentences by speakers of Black English", Journal of Speech and Hearing Research 20 (1977): 254-62.

191 ---, "Comprehension of pronominal reference by speakers of Black English", *Journal of Speech and Hearing Research* 21 (1978): 96-102.

192 **Bradford, Arthur,** "The interaction of dialect and style in urban American English", *Language Learning* 21 (1971): 161-73.

193 **Bradley, N. Ruth,** "Bilingual education and language maintenance in Acadian Louisiana", in E. Sryder and A. Valdman, eds., *Identité culturelle et francophonie dans les Amériques*. Québec: Les Presses de l'Université Laval 1976.

194 **Bragdon, Ida Brownlee,** "An essay on a linguistic issue: what is Black English?" *Journal of Negro Education* 43 (1974): 265-74.

195 **Bragg, Willie Andrew,** "A study of the early stages of language acquisition and morphological development of black children." Ph.D. Indiana U. 1979. DAI 40: 7, 3997A.

196 **Brandes, Paul D.** and **Jeutonne Brewer,** *Dialect Clash in America: Issues and Answers*. Metuchen, N.J.: The Scarecrow Press Inc. 1977.

197 **Brasch, Ila. Wales** and **Walter Milton Brasch,** *A Comprehensive Annotated Bibliography of American Black English*. Baton Rouge: Louisiana State UP 1974.

198 **Brasch, Walter M.,** *Black English and the Mass Media*. Amherst: Massachusetts UP 1981.

199 **Brazeau, Jacques** and **Edouard Cloutier,** "Interethnic relations and the language issue in contemporary Canada: a general appraisal", in Milton J. Esman, ed., *Ethnic Conflict in the Western World*. Ithaca: Cornell UP 1977: 204-27.

200 **Bream, Carol,** "La nasalisation des voyelles orales suivies de consonnes nasales dans le francais et l'anglais parlés au Canada", in Pierre R. Léon, ed., *Recherches sur la structure phonique du francais canadien*. Montreal: Didier 1969: 100-18.

201 **Brend, Ruth M.,** "Male-female intonation patterns in American English", in André Rigault and René Charbonneau, eds., *Proceedings of the Seventh International Congress of Phonetic Sciences*. The Hague: Mouton 1972: 866-70.

202 **Brennan, Eileen Mary Muench,** "Mexican American accented English: phonological analysis, accent scaling, and evaluative reactions." Ph.D. U. of Notre Dame 1977. DAI 38, 1434B.

203 --- and **John Stephen Brennan,** "Accent scaling and language attitude: reactions to Mexican American speech", *Language and Speech* 24 (1981): 207-21.

204 ---, ---, "Measurements of accent and attitude toward Mexican-American speech", Journal of Psycholinguistic Research 10 (1981): 487-501.

205 ---, **Miguel A. Carranza** and **Ellen B. Ryan,** "Language attitudes of Mexican-American adolescents in two midwestern cities", in Schach 1980: 148-56.

206 **Brewer, Jeutonne Patten,** "Subject concord of be in Early Black English", AS 48 (1973): 5-21.

207 ---, "The verb be in Early Black English: a study based on the WPA ex-slave narratives." Ph.D. Chapel Hill, North Carolina 1974. DAI 36: 1, 337A.

208 ---, "Nonagreeing am and invariant be in Early Black English", The SECOL Bulletin: Southeastern Conference on Linguistics 3,2 (1979): 81-100.

209 ---, "The WPA Slave Narratives as linguistic data", Orbis 29 (1980 [1982]): 30-54.

210 --- and **R.W. Reising,** "Tokens in the Pocosin: Lumbee English in North Carolina", AS 57 (1982): 108-20.

211 **Briggs, Delores Griffin,** "Deviations from Standard English in papers of selected Alabama negro high school students." Ph.D. U. of Alabama 1968. DAI 29: 10, 3595A.

212 **Briggs, Olin Dewitt,** "A study of deviations from Standard English in papers of Negro freshmen at an Alabama college." Ph.D. U. of Alabama 1968. DAI 29: 10, 3596A.

213 **Bright, Elizabeth S.,** "A word geography of California and Nevada." Ph.D. Berkeley, California 1967. DAI 29: 1, 244A. Published: Berkeley: California UP 1971.

214 **Bright, William, ed.,** Sociolinguistics. Proceedings of the UCLA Sociolinguistics Conference, 1964. The Hague, Paris: Mouton 1966.

215 **British Council,** Varieties of English: American, Canadian, Australian, New Zealand. Specialised Bibliography. London: British Council 1973.

216 **Brook, G.L.,** English Dialects. 2nd ed. London: Deutsch 1965.

217 **Brook, Sr., Richard John,** "Computer reduction and retrieval of dialect data: a methodology for cartographic and tabular display of lexical and sociolinguistic variation." Ph.D. U. of Iowa 1970. DAI 31: 6, 2898A.

218 **Brown, Claude,** "The language of soul", in Kochman 1972: 134-9.

219 **Brown, H. Rap,** "Street talk", in Kochman 1972: 205-8.

220 **Broz, James J., Jr.,** "Trends and implications of current research in dialectology." ERIC, ED 010-690, 1965.

221 **Bruckner, D.J.R.,** ed., Politics and Language: Spanish and English in the United States. Chicago: U. of Chicago Center for Policy Study 1980.

222 **Buck, Joyce F.,** "The effects of negro and white dialectal variations upon attitudes of college students", Speech Monographs 35 (1968): 181-6.

223 **Buffington, Albert F.,** "The influence of the Pennsylvania German dialect on the English spoken in the Pennsylvania German area", in Sheema Z. Buehne, James L. Hodge and Lucille B. Pinto, eds., Helen Adolph Festschrift. New York: Ungar 1968: 30-41.

224 **Burghardt, Lorraine H.,** ed., Dialectology: Problems and Perspectives. Knoxville: U. of Tennessee 1971.

225 **Burling, Robbins,** Man's Many Voices. New York: Holt, Rinehart and Winston 1970.

226 ---, English in Black and White. New York: Holt, Rinehart and Winston 1973.

227 **Burnaby, Barbara,** "Second language testing procedures used with native people in Saskatchewan", in Darnell 1973: 157-70.

228 **Burrows, Evelyn Honor,** "Some correlates of speech in Tallahassee, Florida." Ph.D. Ohio State U. 1976. DAI 37, 714B.

229 **Butler, Melvin A.,** "Lexical usage of negroes in northeast Louisiana." Ph.D. U. of Michigan 1968. DAI 29: 3, 888A.

230 **Butters, Ronald R.,** "Black English {-z} - some theoretical implications", AS 48 (1973): 37-45.

231 ---, "Acceptability judgements for double modals in southern dialects", in Bailey/Shuy 1973: 276-86.

232 ---, "Variability in indirect questions", AS 49 (1974): 230-4.

233 ---, "More on indirect questions", AS 51 (1976): 57-62.

234 ---, "Unstressed vowels in Appalachian English", AS 56 (1981): 104-10.

235 ---, "Dialect at work: Eudora Welty's artistic purposes", Mississippi Folklore Register 16,2 (1982): 33-39.

236 **Byrd, Patricia,** "Star trek lives: trekker slang", AS 53 (1978): 52-58.

237 **Byron, Gilbert,** "Eastern shore idiom", Maryland English Journal 4 (1965): 12-16.

238 **Caldwell, G.,** A Demographic Profile of the English-Speaking Population of Quebec 1921-71. Quebec 1974.

239 **Callary, Robert Edward,** "Syntactic correlates of social stratification." Ph.D. Louisiana State U. 1971. DAI 32: 7, 3975A.

240 ---, "Dialectology and linguistic theory", AS 46 (1971): 200-9.

241 ---, "Indications of regular sound shifting in an Appalachian dialect", Appalachian Journal: A Regional Studies Review 1 (1973): 238-40.

242 ---, "Phonological change and the development of an urban dialect in Illinois", Language in Society 4 (1975): 155-69.

243 ---, "Syntax and social class", Linguistics 143 (1975): 5-16.

244 ---, "Aspects of language change in Illinois", in Haller 1980: 242-8.

245 **Camhi, Paul,** "A reevaluation of the 'writer-rule' for American English", CUNY Forum: Papers in Linguistics 5-6 (1978-79): 154-62.

246 **Campbell, A. Luella,** "Vowel shortening and t-voicing in Canadian English", Calgary Working Papers in Linguistics 1,1 (1975): 260-28.

247 **Canfield, Rip,** "A note on Navajo-English code-mixing", Anthropological Linguistics 22 (1980): 218-20.

248 **Caramazza, A., G.H. Yeni-Komshian, E.B. Zurif** and **E. Carbone,** "The acquisition of a new-phonological contrast: the case of stop consonants in French-English bilinguals", Journal of the Acoustical Society 54 (1973): 421-8.

249 **Cárdenas, Daniel,** "Chicano language: what? why? how?", Hispania 58 (1975): 185-8.

250 **Carlock, Elizabeth K.,** "Prosodic analysis of two varieties of Buffalo English", in Wölck/Garvin 1979: 377-82.

251 **Carlson, David R.,** "The common speech of Boston." Ph.D. U. of Massachusetts 1973. DAI 34: 8, 5139A.

252 ---, "Rules, predictions and the Linguistic Atlas", JEngL 16 (1983): 8-12.

253 **Carmony, Marvin D.,** "The speech of Terre Haute: a hoosier dialect study." Ph.D. Indiana U. 1965. DAI 27: 4, 1044A.

254 ---, "Some phonological rules of an Indiana dialect", in Griffith/Miner 1970: 1-16.

255 ---, "Aspects of regional speech in Indiana", in L. Davis 1972: 9-24.

256 ---, Indiana Dialects in their Historical Setting. Terre Haute, Ind.: Indiana Council of Teachers of English 1972.

257 ---, "The regional vocabulary of Terre Haute", Midwestern Journal of Language and Folklore 3 (1977): 3-34.

258 **Carothers, Gibson** and **James Lacey,** Slanguage. America's Second Language. New York: Sterling 1979.

259 **Carpenter, Charles,** "Folk-language of mid-Appalachia", Journal of the Alleghenies 9 (1973): 27-31.

260 **Carr, Donna H.,** "Reflections of Atlantic coast lexical variations in three Mormon communities." Master's thesis, U. of Utah 1966.

261 **Carranza, Michael Anthony,** "Language attitudes and other cultural attitudes of Mexican American adults: some sociolinguistic implications." Ph.D. U. of Notre Dame 1977. DAI 38: 3, 1693A.

262 --- and **Ellen Bouchard Ryan,** "Evaluative reactions of bilingual Anglo and Mexican American adolescents toward speakers of English and Spanish", Linguistics 166 (1975): 83-104.

263 **Carroll, William S.,** "A phonology of Washington negro speech." Ph.D. Georgetown U. 1971. DAI 32: 3, 1494A.

264 **Carstensen, Broder,** "Amerikanisches Englisch", in Paul Hartig, ed., Amerikakunde. Frankfurt: Diesterweg 1966: 546-82.

265 **Cartwright, D.G.** and **H.W. Taylor,** "Bilingual accommodation in language islands: Penetanguishene and Essex County, Ontario", Canadian Ethnic Studies 11,1 (1979): 99-114.

266 **Cascaito, James** and **Douglas Radcliff-Umstead,** "An Italo-English dialect", AS 50 (1975): 5-17.

267 **Cassidy, Frederic G.,** "American regionalism and the harmless drudge", PMLA 82 (1967): 12-19.

268 ---, "Dialectology and the electronic drudge", in Ellis 1968: 135-43.

269 ---, "Collecting the lexicon of American regional English", in The Promise of English. Champaign, Ill.: National Council of Teachers of English 1970: 99-114.

270 ---, "Dialect studies, regional and social", in Sebeok 1973: 75-100.

271 ---, "The Atlas and DARE", in Scholler/Reidy 1973: 91-95.

272 ---, "The meaning of 'regional' in DARE", AS 48 (1973): 282-9.

273 ---, "Lexical elaboration: some examples from the Dictionary of American Regional English", Names 23 (1975): 153-8.

274 ---, "On-line mapmaking for the Dictionary of American Regional English", in Putschke 1977: 107-19.

275 ---, "What's new about DARE?", in Shores/Hines 1977: 13-17.

276 ---, "Computer-aided usage 'labeling' in a dictionary", Computers and the Humanities 11 (1977): 89-99.

277 ---, "Use of computers in one lexicographical project: DARE", in Raymond/Russell 1977: 133-42.

278 ---, "Gullah and Jamaican Creole: the African connection", in Alatis 1978: 621-9.

279 ---, "Computer mapping of lexical variants for DARE", in Ladislav Zgusta, ed., Theory and Method in Lexicography. Columbia, S.C.: Hornbeam 1980: 147-60.

280 ---, "The place of Gullah", AS 55 (1980): 3-16.

281 ---, "Geographical variation of English in the United States", in Bailey/Görlach 1982: 177-209.

282 --- et al., The Dictionary of American Regional English. Cambridge, Mass.: Belknap Press (forthcoming).

283 **Castonguay, C.** and **J. Marion,** "L'anglicisation du Canada", La monda lingvo-problemo 5 (1975): 145-56.

284 **Cato, Carl A.,** "A case for Ghettoese", Journal of Negro Education 43 (1974): 348-52.

285 **Cavender, Anthony Patterson,** "A phonemic and phonetic analysis of the folk speech of Bedford County, Tennessee." Thesis, U. of Tennessee 1974.

286 **Cazden, Courtney B., Vera P. John** and **Dell Hymes,** eds., Functions of Language in the Classroom. New York: Teachers College Press 1972.

287 **Chambers, J.K.,** "Canadian raising", Canadian Journal of Linguistics 18 (1973): 113-35.

288 ---, ed., Canadian English: Origins and Structures. Toronto: Methuen 1975.

289 ---, "The Ottawa Valley 'twang'", in Chambers 1975: 55-59.

290 ---, ed., The Languages of Canada. Montreal: Didier 1979.

291 ---, "Canadian English", in Chambers 1979: 168-204.

292 ---, "The Americanization of Canadian raising", in Papers from the Parasession on Language and Behavior, Chicago Linguistic Society. Chicago: U. of Chicago 1981: 20-35.

293 **Chantefort, Pierre,** "Diglossie au Québec: limites et tendances actuelles", Les Cahiers de Linguistique de l'Université du Québec 6 (1976): 23-53.

294 **Chen, Donna Huei-Chuing,** "The English pronunciation of Chinatown, San Francisco: an exploratory study." Ph.D. Ohio U. 1982. DAI 43: 5, 1526A.

295 **Chennault, Stephen D.,** "Black dialect: a cultural shock", in Fisher 1977: 71-79.

296 **Chisholm, William S.,** "The phonemicization of intervocalic 't, d'", AS 41 (1966): 114-8.

297 **Christian, Donna Marie,** "Aspects of verb usage in Appalachian speech." Ph.D. Georgetown U. 1978. DAI 39: 12, 7317A.

298 --- and **Walt Wolfram,** eds., Dialects and Educational Equity. Washington, D.C.: Center for Applied Linguistics 1979.

299 **Clapin, Sylvia,** A New Dictionary of Americanisms. Being a Glossary of Words Supposed to Be Peculiar to the United States and the Dominion of Canada. Detroit: Gale Research Co. 1968 / Repr. of 1903 ed., New York /.

300 **Clark, Jo Ann Richardson,** "A comparative analysis of selected writing errors of Oklahoma State University students learning English as a second language." Ed.D. Oklahoma State U. 1979. DAI 40: 12, 6256A.

301 **Clark, Thomas L.,** "Marietta, Ohio: the continuing erosion of a speech island", PADS 57 (1972).

302 ---, "Linguistic atlases: archival data for language study in the Western United States", JEngL 16 (1983): 13-17.

303 **Cofer, Thomas Michael,** "Linguistic variability in a Philadelphia speech community." Ph.D. U. of Pennsylvania 1972. DAI 33: 12, 6892A.

304 **Cohen, Andrew D.,** A Sociolinguistic Approach to Bilingual Education: Experiments in the American Southwest. Rowley, Mass.: Newbury House 1975.

305 **Cohen, Paul,** "The tensing and raising of short a in the metropolitan area of New York City." Master's thesis, Columbia U. 1970.

306 **Colbourne, B. Wade,** "A sociolinguistic study of Long Island, Notre Dame Bay, Newfoundland." M.A. Thesis, Memorial U. of Newfoundland 1982.

307 **Cole, Lorraine Theresa,** "A developmental analysis of social dialect features in the spontaneous language of preschool black children." Ph.D. Northwestern U. 1980. DAI 41: 6, 2132B.

308 **Coleman, William L.,** "Multiple modals in Southern States English." Ph.D. Indiana U. 1975. DAI 36: 4, 2174A.

309 **Collins** Gem Dictionary of American English. London: Collins 1968.

310 **Coltharp, Lurline H.,** "Pachuco, tirilón and chicano", AS 50 (1975): 25-29.

311 **Conley, John Martin,** "Judicial treatment of language variation in American law." Ph.D. Duke U. 1980. DAI 41: 12, 5156A.

312 **Conway, William David,** "A transformational analysis of the written and oral syntax of fourth, sixth, and eighth grade Omaha Indian children." Ph.D. U. of Nebraska 1971. DAI 32: 7, 3975A.

313 **Cook, Albert B. III,** "Perspectives for a Linguistic Atlas of Kansas", AS 53 (1978): 199-209.

314 **Cook, Mary Jane,** "Problems of Southwestern Indian speakers in learning English", in Turner 1973: 241-9.

315 **Cook, Stanley Joseph,** "Language change and the emergence of an urban dialect in Utah." Ph.D. U. of Utah 1969. DAI 30: 5, 2001A.

316 **Cooley, Ralph E.,** "Final devoicing, phonetically similar but phonologically different in blacks and whites", in Ingemann 1977: 63-67.

317 ---, **Mervin R. Barnes** and **John A. Dunn,** eds., Papers of the 1978 Mid-America Linguistics Conference at Oklahoma. Norman: Department of Communication, U. of Oklahoma 1979.

318 **Cooper, Deanna, Karin Matusek** and **Dianne Wood,** "Short 'o' vowels in Eastern Massachusetts speech", Speech Monographs 34 (1967): 93-94.

319 **Copperud, Roy H.,** American Usage: the Consensus. New York, London: Van Nostrand-Reinhold 1970.

320 **Courtney, Maureen Rosemary,** "Lexical choice as an index of acculturation: fifteen case studies." M.A. Thesis, Victoria, B.C. 1972.

321 **Covington, Ann,** "Black people and Black English: attitudes and deeducation in a biased macroculture", in Harrison/Trabasso 1976: 255-64.

322 **Cox, Adrienne Flore,** "The receptiveness of black students to dialects sometimes different from their own." Ed.D. Wayne State U. 1971. DAI 32: 12, 6739A.

323 **Coye, Dale Fincher,** "A linguistic guide to the pronunciation of English for actors: Standard American and selected dialects." Ph.D. Princeton U. 1979. DAI 40: 3, 1441A.

324 **Crane, Lindsay Ben,** "Social stratification of English among white speakers in Tuscaloosa, Alabama." Ph.D. U. of Massachusetts 1973. DAI 34: 10, 6615A.

325 ---, "The death of a prestige form, or the social stratification of /R/ in Tuscaloosa, Alabama." ERIC 1973.

326 ---, "The social stratification of /aɪ/ among white speakers in Tuscaloosa, Alabama", in Shores/Hines 1977: 189-200.

327 **Crisp, Raymond Dwight,** "Changes in attitudes toward English usage." Ph.D. Urbana-Champaign, Illinois 1971. DAI 32: 10, 5761A.

328 **Cullen, Constance,** "Dialect research on Prince Edward Island", The English Quarterly 4,3 (1971): 51-53.

329 **Cullinan, Bernice E., Angela M. Jaggar** and **Dorothy Strickland,** "Language expansion for black children in the primary grades: a research report", Young Children 29 (1974): 98-112.

330 **Cummins, Sarah,** "The low vowels", in Léon/Martin 1979: 15-18.

331 **Cunningham, Irma A.E.,** "A syntactic analysis of Sea Island Creole ("Gullah")." Ph.D. U. of Michigan 1970. DAI 32: 8, 4141A.

332 **Cunningham, Rodger,** "Appalachian /paɪt'naɪ/ 'almost': a notice and various etymologies", AS 46 (1971): 304.

333 **Dahl, Hartwig,** Word Frequencies of Spoken American English. Essex, Conn.: Verbatim 1979.

334 **Dakin, Robert F.,** "The dialect vocabulary of the Ohio river valley. A survey of the distribution of selected vocabulary forms in an area of complex settlement history." Ph.D. U. of Michigan 1966. DAI 27: 7, 2139A.

335 ---, "South Midland speech in the old northwest", JEngL 5 (1971): 31-48.

336 **Dalby, David,** "Black through white: patterns of communication in Africa and the New World", in Wolfram/Clarke 1971: 99-138.

337 ---, "The African element in American English", in Kochman 1972: 170-86.

338 **Daniel, Jack L.** and **Geneva Smitherman,** "How I got over: communication dynamics in the black community", The Quarterly Journal of Speech 62 (1976): 26-39.

339 **Darbelnet, Jean,** "Aspects of Canadian French-English bilingualism", in Keller/Teschner/Vierra 1976: 3-16.

340 **Darnell, Regna,** ed., Linguistic Diversity in Canadian Society. Edmonton: Linguistic Research 1971.

341 ---, ed., Canadian Languages in Their Social Context. Edmonton: Linguistic Research 1973.

342 ---, "Language use in Canada", Papers in Linguistics 9,3/4 (1976): 1-198.

343 **Dauphinais, Louise,** "Integration of alternative speaking patterns in bicultural classroom situations", in Barkin/Brandt 1980: 85-91.

344 **Davies, David L.,** Glossary and Handbook of Canadian-British Words. Vancouver: n.p. 1967.

345 **Davis, Alva Leroy,** "Developing and testing the checklist", AS 46 (1971): 34-37.

346 ---, ed., Culture, Class, and Language Variety: A Resource Book for Teachers. Urbana, Ill.: National Council of Teachers of English 1972.

347 ---, **Raven I. McDavid, Jr.,** and **Virginia G. McDavid,** eds., A Compilation of the Worksheets of the Linguistic Atlas of the United States and Canada and Associated Projects, 2nd ed. Chicago: UP 1969.

348 **Davis, Lawrence M.,** "The phonology of Yiddish-American speech." Ph.D. U. of Chicago 1967.

349 ---, "The stressed vowels of Yiddish-American English", PADS 48 (1967): 51-59.

350 ---, "Dialect research: mythology vs. reality", Orbis 18 (1969): 332-7.

351 ---, "Social dialectology in America: a critical survey", JEngL 4 (1970): 46-56.

352 ---, "Some social aspects of the speech of blue-grass Kentucky", Orbis 19 (1970): 337-41.

353 ---, "Worksheets and their variants", AS 46 (1971): 27-33.

354 ---, "A study of Appalachian speech in a northern urban setting", ERIC 1971.

355 ---, ed., Studies in Linguistics in Honor of Raven I. McDavid, Jr. University: Alabama UP 1972.

356 ---, "The diafeature: an approach to structural dialectology", JEngL 7 (1973): 1-20.

357 ---, "American social dialectology: a statistical appraisal", AS 57 (1982): 83-94.

358 ---, English Dialectology. An Introduction. University, Ala.: Alabama UP 1983.

359 **Davis, Margaret B.,** "A study of East Tennessee regional phonology: its influence on reading performance." Ph.D. U. of Tennessee 1975. DAI 36: 11, 7183A.

360 **Day, Richard R.,** ed., Issues in English Creoles. Papers from the 1975 Hawaii Conference. Heidelberg: Groos 1980.

361 **Deak, Etienne** and **Simone Deak,** Grand dictionnaire d'américanismes contenant les principaux termes américains avec leur équivalent exact en francais. 5e éd. augm. Montréal: Presses Sélect 1977.

362 **Dean, Florine,** "Names viewed through the racial looking glass", in Fred Tarpley and Ann Moseley, eds., Of Edsels and Marauders. Commerce, Texas: Names Institute Press 1971: 40-42.

363 **Dean, Patricia Kay Elder,** "A word atlas of north central Texas." Ph.D. East Texas State U. 1980. DAI 41: 2, 655A.

364 **de Belaval, Domitila Domeneck,** "An investigation of isochronism in the rhythm of American English speech." Ph.D. Louisiana State U. 1966. DAI 27: 5, 1355A.

365 **DeCamp, David** and **Ian F. Hancock,** eds., Pidgins and Creoles: Current Trends and Prospects. Washington, D.C.: Georgetown UP 1974.

366 **de Camp, L. Sprague,** "American English from Eastern Massachusetts", Journal of the International Phonetic Association 3 (1973): 40-41.

367 ---, "American English from central Texas", Journal of the International Phonetic Association 8 (1978): 81-82.

368 **De Frantz, Anita Page,** "A critique of the literature on Black English." Ph.D. Pittsburgh 1975. DAI 36: 10, 6647A.

369 **Deighton, Lee C.,** Handbook of American English Spelling. New York: Van Nostrand-Reinhold 1973.

370 **De La Zerda, Nancy** and **Robert Hopper,** "Employment interviewers' reactions to Mexican American speech", Communication Monographs 46 (1979): 126-34.

371 **D'Eloia, Sarah G.,** "Issues in the analysis of Nonstandard Negro English: a review of J.L. Dillard's Black English: Its History and Usage in the United States", JEngL 7 (1973): 87-106.

372 **Desberg, Peter, Dale E. Elliott** and **George Marsh,** "American Black English and spelling", in Uta Frith, Cognitive Processes in Spelling. New York: Academic 1980: 69-82.

373 **De Stefano, Johanna S.,** ed., Language, Society, and Education: A Profile of Black English. Worthington, Ohio: Charles A. Jones Publ. Co. 1973.

374 ---, "Black English", in De Stefano 1973: 4-9.

375 **DeVere, Louise H.,** "Non-Standard English in Norfolk city schools." M.A. Thesis, Old Dominion U., Norfolk, Va., 1971. ERIC ED 082 554.

376 ---, "Black English: problematic but systematic", South Atlantic Bulletin 36 (1971): 38-46.

377 **de Wolf, Gaelan,** "Transcription, coding, and data analysis of the SVEN survey", in Warkentyne 1981: 62-65.

378 **Dial, Wylene P.,** "The dialect of the Appalachian people", in David N. Mielke, ed., Teaching Mountain Children. Boone, N.C.: Appalachian Consortium 1978: 49-58.

379 **Dietrich, Julia C.,** "The Gaelic roots of a-prefixing in Appalachian English", AS 56 (1981): 314.

380 **Di Giulio, Robert C.,** "Measuring teacher attitudes toward Black English: a pilot project", FFLR 11 (1973): 25-26, 49.

381 **Dillard, Joey Lee,** "Negro children's dialect in the inner city", FFLR 5,3 (1967): 7-8, 10.

382 ---, "Nonstandard negro dialects: convergence or divergence?", FFLR 6,2 (1968): 9-12.

383 ---, "The creolist and the study of negro non-standard dialects in the continental United States", in Dell Hymes, ed., Pidginization and Creolization of Languages. Proceedings of a Conference Held at the University of the West Indies, Mona, Jamaica, April 1968. Cambridge: UP 1971: 393-408.

384 ---, "Black English in New York", English Record 21,4 (1971): 114-20.

385 ---, Black English. Its History and Usage in the United States. New York: Random House 1972.

386 ---, "On the beginnings of Black English in the New World", Orbis 21 (1972): 523-36.

387 ---, "The history of Black English in Nova Scotia: a first step", African Language Review 9 (1970-71 [1973]): 263-79.

388 ---, "Lay my isogloss bundle down: the contribution of Black English to American dialectology", Linguistics 119 (1974): 5-14.

389 ---, All-American English. New York: Random House 1975.

390 ---, ed., Perspectives on Black English. The Hague, Paris: Mouton 1975.

391 ---, "Perspectives on Black English", in Dillard 1975: 9-32.

392 ---, "Black English dialectology: theory, method", in Dillard 1975: 33-36.

393 ---, "The history of Black English: introduction", in Dillard 1975: 91-101.

394 ---, "Black English and the acculturation process: introduction", in Dillard 1975: 273-9.

395 ---, "The writings of Herskovits and the study of the language of the negro in the New World", in Dillard 1975: 288-95.

396 ---, American Talk: Where Our Words Came From. New York: Random House 1976.

397 ---, Lexicon of Black English: The Words the Slaves Made. New York: Continuum-Seabury 1977.

398 ---, "Bidialectal education: Black English and Standard English in the United States", in Spolsky/Cooper 1978: 293-311.

399 ---, "Creole English and Creole Portuguese: the early record", in Ian F. Hancock et al., eds., Readings in Creole Studies. Ghent: Story-Scientia 1979: 261-8.

400 ---, ed., Perspectives on American English. The Hague, Paris, New York: Mouton 1980.

401 ---, **James Sledd, Eric P. Hamp** and **Archibald A. Hill,** "Joinder and rejoinder", AS 54 (1979): 114-9.

402 **Dillon, V.M.,** "The Anglo-Irish element in the speech of the southern shore of Newfoundland." M.A. Thesis, Memorial U. of Newfoundland 1968.

403 **Di Pietro, Robert J.,** "Three case studies in Italian American ethnicity and language use", in Ornstein-Galicia/St. Clair 1980: 239-47.

404 --- and **Edward L. Blansitt, Jr.,** eds., The Third LACUS Forum 1976. Columbia, S.C.: Hornbeam 1977.

405 **Disenhouse, David S.,** "Phonological manifestations of ethnic identification: the Jewish community of New York City." Ph.D. New York U. 1974. DAI 35: 2, 1076A.

406 **Dohan, Mary Helen,** Our Own Words. New York: Knopf 1974.

407 **Domingue, Nicole,** "L'usage bilingue dans le centre de Montreal", in Michel Paradis, ed., The Fourth LACUS Forum 1977. Columbia, S.C.: Hornbeam 1978: 278-85.

408 **Donahue, Thomas S.,** "The nature of the Early American Black English lingua franca", in Derry L. Malsch, James E. Hoard and Clarence Sloat, eds., Proceedings of the Eighth Annual Meeting of the Western Conference on Linguistics, October 20 - 21, 1978. Edmonton: Linguistic Research 1979: 23-30.

409 **Dorrill, George Townsend,** "A comparison of negro and white speech in central South Carolina." M.A. Thesis, U. of South Carolina 1975.

410 ---, "Black and white speech in the South: Evidence from the Linguistic Atlas of the Middle and South Atlantic States." Ph.D. U. of South Carolina 1982. DAI 43: 7, 2335A.

411 **Doviak, Martin J.** and **Alison Hudson-Edwards,** "Phonological variation in Chicano English: word-final (z)-devoicing", in Blansitt/Teschner 1980: 82-96.

412 **Drechsel, Emanuel J.,** "'Ha, now me stomany that!' A summary of pidginization and creolization of North American Indian languages", Linguistics 173 (1976): 63-81.

413 **Dreyfuss, Gail Raimi,** "Pidgin and creole languages in the United States", in Lourie/Conklin 1978: 61-77.

414 **Drohomirecki, Yuri,** "Voiced t", in Léon/Martin 1979: 71-87.

415 **Drysdale, Patrick,** "Aspects of Canadian lexicography", in J.E. Congleton, J. Edward Gates and Donald Hobar, eds., Papers on Lexicography in Honor of Warren N. Cordell. Terre Haute: Dictionary Society of North America, Indiana State U. 1979: 37-45.

416 **Dubin, Fraida,** "Language and attitudes among Navajo adolescents." Ph.D. Los Angeles 1971. DAI 32: 8, 4590A.

417 **Dubois, Betty Lou,** "A plan to study the written English of Chicanos", in Harvey/Heiser 1975.

418 ---, "Further studies in Southwest English", in Dubois/Hoffer 1975.

419 ---, "A case study of Native American child bidialectalism in English: phonological, morphological, and syntactic evidence", Anthropological Linguistics 20 (1978): 1-13.

420 ---, "A close study of verb usage in context: Anglos and Chicanos", in Michel Paradis, ed., The Fourth LACUS Forum 1977. Columbia, S.C.: Hornbeam 1978: 604-14.

421 ---, "Societal and linguistic correlates in an investigation of the English writing of a selected group of university-level Chicanos", in Mackey/Ornstein 1979: 347-61.

422 --- and **Isabel Crouch,** eds., The Sociology of the Languages of American Women. San Antonio, Tex.: Trinity U. 1976, 2nd ed. 1979.

423 --- and **Bates Hoffer,** eds., Papers in Southwest English I: Research Techniques and Prospects. San Antonio: Trinity U. 1975.

424 --- and **Guadalupe Valdés,** "Mexican-American child bilingualism: double deficit?", The Bilingual Review 7 (1980): 1-7.

425 **Duckert, Audrey R.,** "The second time around: methods in dialect revisiting", AS 46 (1971): 66-72.

426 ---, "The winds of change", in Raymond/Russell 1977: 21-28.

427 **Dumas, Bethany K.,** "A study of the dialect of Newton County, Arkansas." Ph.D. U. of Arkansas 1971. DAI 32: 5, 2664A.

428 ---, "Suggestions for investigating Tennessee English: a sociolinguistic approach to dialect study." ERIC 1974.

429 ---, "The morphology of Newton County, Arkansas: an exercise in studying Ozark dialect", Mid-South Folklore 3 (1975): 115-25.

430 ---, "The Arkansas language survey: progress, problems, and prognostications", Orbis 25 (1976): 249-57.

431 ---, "Research needs in Tennessee English", in Shores/Hines 1977: 201-8.

432 **Dunbar, Ronald W.,** "The presence of German in the jargon of the American skier: a sociological look at the past, present, and future", in Steven M. Benjamin, ed., Papers from the Conference on German-Americana in the Eastern United States. Morgantown: Department of Foreign Languages, West Virginia U. 1980: 182-96.

433 **Dundes, Alan,** "The Henny-Penny phenomenon: a study of folk phonological esthetics in American Speech", Southern Folklore Quarterly 38 (1974): 1-9.

434 **Dunlap, Howard G.,** "Social aspects of a verb form: native Atlanta fifth-grade speech - The present tense of be." Ph.D. Emory U. 1973. DAI 34: 9, 4230A. Published: PADS 61-62 (1974).

435 ---, "Some methodological problems in recent investigations of the Ø copula and invariant be", in Shores/Hines 1977: 151-9.

436 **Dunn, Ernest F.,** ed., African Linguistic Structures in Black English. Proceedings of the Conference on the Black Pluriverse. Englewood, N.J.: Emerson 1974.

437 ---, "The black-southern white dialect controversy: who did what to whom?", in Harrison/Trabasso 1976: 105-22.

438 **Dunn, Marcia Louise,** "Language sampling: exploration of an alternative means of oral language assessment with black fifth and sixth grade males." Ph.D. Berkeley, California 1978. DAI 40, 184B.

439 **Dürmüller, Urs,** "American sociolinguistics 1980", Sociolinguistics Newsletter 11,2 (1980): 1-6.

440 ---, Towards a Variety Grammar of English. Bern: Peter Lang 1982.

441 **Dusková, Libuse,** "On some differences in the use of the perfect and the preterite between British and American English", Prague Studies in Mathematical Linguistics 5 (1976): 53-68.

442 **Dweik, Bader Saed,** "Factors determining language maintenance and language shift in Arabic-American communities." Ph.D. Buffalo, New York 1980. DAI 41: 8, 3557A.

443 **Dyhr, Niels,** "A pilot investigation of the Fo pattern in American English", Annual Report of the Institute of Phonetics, University of Copenhagen 14 (1980): 95-98.

444 **Eames, Edwin** and **Howard Robboy,** "The submarine sandwich: lexical variations in a cultural context", AS 42 (1967): 279-88.

445 **Eble, Connie C.,** "Slang, productivity, and semantic theory", in William C. McCormack and Herbert J. Izzo, eds., The Sixth LACUS Forum 1979. Columbia, S.C.: Hornbeam 1980: 215-27.

446 ---, "Scenes from slang", Review: The Southeastern Conference for Linguistics SECOL 5 (1981): 74-78.

447 **Edwards, Thomas Oliver,** "Communication skills in the inner city: effects of race and dialect on decoding." Ph.D. City U. of New York 1981. DAI 42: 4, 1546A.

448 **Edwards, Walter F.,** "Varieties of English in Guyana: some comparisons with BE", Linguistics 18 [229/230] (1980): 289-309.

449 **Eglin, Peter Anthony,** "Terms for Canadian doctors: language and sociology, ethnosemantics and ethnomethodology." Ph.D. U. of British Columbia 1975. DAI 36: 12, 8309A.

450 ---, Talk and Taxonomy: A Methodological Comparison of Ethnosemantics and Ethnomethodology with Reference to Terms for Canadian Doctors. Amsterdam: Benjamins 1980.

451 **Ehrlich, Eugene, Stuart Berg Flexner, Gorton Carruth** and **Joyce M. Hawkins,** *Oxford American Dictionary*. New York: Oxford UP 1980.

452 **Eisenstein, Miriam Rita,** "The development of dialect discrimination and stereotyping in adult learners of English as a second language." Ph.D. City U. of New York 1979. DAI 40: 9, 5032A.

453 **Eisiminger, Sterling,** "A glossary of ethnic slurs in American English", *Maledicta* 3 (1979): 153-74.

454 **Elgin, Suzette Haden,** "The crossover constraint and Ozark English", in John P. Kimball, ed., *Syntax and Semantics*. Vol. I. New York, London: Seminar Press 1972: 267-75.

455 ---, "What on earth is *that*?", *Georgetown University Papers on Languages and Linguistics* 16 (1979), 33-44.

456 **Elías-Olivares, Lucia Ernestina,** "Ways of speaking in a Chicano speech community: a sociolinguistic approach." Ph.D. Austin 1976. DAI 37: 5, 2829A.

457 ---, *Language Use in a Chicano Community: A Sociolinguistic Approach*. Austin: Southwest Education Development Laboratory 1976.

458 **Ellis, Stanley J.,** ed., *Studies in Honour of Harold Orton on the Occasion of His Seventieth Birthday*. Leeds: U. of Leeds 1968.

459 **Ellsworth, Jennifer Kathleen,** "The effect of kindergarten classrooms where standard English is spoken on the speech of Black English speaking children." Ph.D. U. of Wisconsin-Madison 1979.

460 **Emery, George,** "Negro English in Amber Valley, Alberta", in Darnell 1971: 45-59.

461 **Engler, Leo F.** and **Roger G. Hilyer,** "Once again: American and British intonation systems", *Acta Linguistica Hafniensia* 13 (1971): 99-108.

462 **English, L.E.F.,** *Historic Newfoundland*. St. John's, Nfld.: Newfoundland and Labrador Tourist Development Office 1968 (1st ed. 1955).

463 **Eschholz, Paul A.,** "Dialectology: a summing up and portent of things to come", in Shores/Hines 1977: 1-10.

464 **Evensen, Lars S., Arne Kjell Foldvik, Christopher W. Hammonds, Anders M. Kvam** and **F.J.J. Peters,** "Black English in the American TV programme: implications for dialect, EFL and sociolinguistic researcher in Scandinavia", in Stig Johansson and Bjørn Tysdahl, eds., *Papers from the First Nordic Conference on English Studies, Oslo,*

17 - 19 September, 1980. Oslo: Institute of English Studies, U. of Oslo 1981: 304-17.

465 **Faries, Rachel B.,** "A word geography of Missouri." Ph.D. U. of Missouri 1967. DAI 28: 10, 4156A.

466 **Faris, James C.,** "The dynamics of verbal exchange: a Newfoundland example", Anthropologica N.S. 8 (1966): 235-48.

467 ---, Cat Harbour: A Newfoundland Fishing Settlement. St. John's, Nfld.: Memorial U. of Newfoundland 1967.

468 **Farrison, W. Edward,** "Dialectology versus negro dialect", CLA Journal 13 (1969): 21-26.

469 **Fasold, Ralph W.,** "Tense and the form be in Black English", Language 45 (1969): 763-76.

470 ---, "Distinctive linguistic characteristics of Black English", in Alatis 1970: 233-8.

471 ---, "Minding your z's and d's: distinguishing syntactic and phonological variable rules", in: Papers from the Seventh Regional Meeting, Chicago Linguistic Society. Chicago: Dept. of Linguistics, U. of Chicago 1971: 360-7.

472 ---, Tense Marking in Black English. A Linguistic and Social Analysis. Washington, D.C.: Center for Applied Linguistics 1972.

473 ---, "One hundred years from syntax to phonology", in Sanford B. Steever, Carol A. Walker and Salikoko S. Mufwene, eds., Papers from the Parasession on Diachronic Syntax, April 22, 1976. Chicago: Chicago Linguistic Society 1976: 79-87.

474 ---, "The amazing replicability of a sociolinguistic pattern", Papers in Linguistics 13 (1980): 515-28.

475 ---, "The relation between black and white speech in the South", AS 56 (1981): 163-89.

476 --- and **Roger W. Shuy,** eds., Teaching Standard English in the Inner City. Washington, D.C.: Center for Applied Linguistics 1970.

477 ---, ---, eds., Analyzing Variation in Language. Papers from the Second Colloquium on New Ways of Analyzing Variation. Washington, D.C.: Georgetown UP 1975.

478 ---, ---, eds., Studies in Language Variation: Semantics, Syntax, Phonology, Pragmatics, Social Situations, Ethnographic Approaches. Papers from the Third Annual Colloquium on New Ways of Analyzing Variation, Georgetown U., 1974. Washington, D.C.: Georgetown UP 1977.

479 --- and **Walt Wolfram,** "Some linguistic features of negro dialect", in Fasold/Shuy 1970: 41-86.

480 **Feagin, Louise Crawford,** "A sociolinguistic study of Alabama White English: the verb phrase in Anniston. (Vol. I and II)." Ph.D. Georgetown U. 1976. DAI 38: 6, 3445A. Published under the title: Variation and Change in Alabama English. A Sociolinguistic Study of the White Community. Washington, D.C.: Georgetown UP 1979.

481 ---, "Woman's place in nonstandard southern white English: not so simple", in Roger W. Shuy and Anna Shnukal, eds., Languages and the Uses of Language. Washington, D.C.: Georgetown UP 1980: 88-97.

482 **Feinstein, Mark H.,** "Ethnicity and topicalization in New York City English", International Journal of the Sociology of Language 26 (1980): 15-24.

483 **Ferguson, Charles A.,** "'Short a' in Philadelphia English", in M.E. Smith 1972: 259-74.

484 --- and **Shirley Brice Heath,** eds., Language in the USA. Cambridge: Cambridge UP 1981.

485 **Ferris, M. Roger** and **Robert L. Politzer,** "Effects of early and delayed second language acquisition: English composition skills of Spanish-speaking Junior High School students", TESOL Quarterly 15 (1981): 263-74.

486 **Fetscher, Margaret Elizabeth,** "The speech of Atlanta schoolchildren: A phonological study." Ed.D. U. of Georgia 1971. DAI 32: 10, 5762A.

487 **Fickett, Joan Gleason,** "Aspects of morphemics, syntax and semology of an inner-city dialect (Merican)." Ph.D. Buffalo, New York 1970. Published: Taos: Deckerloft 1975.

488 ---, "Tense and aspect in Black English", JEngL 6 (1972): 17-19.

489 ---, "Ain't, not and don't in Black English", in Dillard 1975: 86-90.

490 ---, "He wasn't stuttering", Forum Linguisticum (Lake Bluff, Ill.) 2 (1977): 177-8.

491 **Finder, Morris,** "'Totalled' in Northwest English", AS 40 (1965): 158-9.

492 **Fine, Marlene G., Carolyn Anderson** and **Gary Eckles,** "Black English on black situation comedies", Journal of Communication 29,3 (1979): 21-29.

493 **Finegan, Edward Joseph,** "A study of the development of attitudes toward English usage in America." Ph.D. Ohio U. 1968. DAI 29: 4, 1220A.

494 ---, Attitudes toward English Usage. The History of a War of Words. New York, London: Teachers College Press 1980.

495 **Fink, Paul M.,** Bits of Mountain Speech Gathered between 1910 and 1965 along the Mountains Bordering North Carolina and Tennessee. Boone, N.C.: Appalachian Consortium 1974.

496 **Fisher, Dexter,** ed., Minority Language and Literature: Retrospective and Perspective. New York: MLA 1977.

497 **Fisher, Lawrence E.** and **Raven I. McDavid, Jr.,** "Aphaeresis in New England", AS 48 (1973): 246-9.

498 **Fishman, Joshua A.,** ed., Advances in the Sociology of Language. The Hague, Paris: Mouton 1971, 2nd ed. 1976.

499 ---, **Robert L. Cooper, Roxana Ma,** et al., Bilingualism in the Barrio. Bloomington: Indiana UP 1971.

500 --- and **Eleanor Herasimchuk,** "The multiple prediction of phonological variables in a bilingual speech community", in Fishman/Cooper/Ma 1971: 465-79.

501 --- and **Gary L. Keller,** eds., Bilingual Education for Hispanic Students in the United States. New York: Teachers College Press, Columbia U. 1982.

502 **Fitzgerald, Mary Carol,** "Double subjects in conversational English." Thesis, U. of South Carolina 1977.

503 **Flanigan, Beverly Olson,** "American Indian English in history and literature: the evolution of a pidgin from reality to stereotype." Ph.D. Indiana 1981. DAI 42: 8, 3582A.

504 **Flesch, Rudolf,** Look Up: A Deskbook of American Spelling and Style. New York: Harper and Row / London: Routledge and Kegan Paul 1977.

505 **Flexner, Stuart Berg,** I Hear America Talking: An Illustrated Treasury of American Words and Phrases. New York: Van Nostrand Reinhold 1976.

506 **Folb, Edith A.,** A Comparative Study of Urban Black Argot. San Francisco: Office of Education 1972.

507 ---, Runnin' Down Some Lines: The Language and Culture of Black Teenagers. Cambridge, Mass.: Harvard UP 1980.

508 **Foley, Lawrence M.,** "A phonological and lexical study of the speech of Tuscaloosa County, Alabama", PADS 58 (1972).

509 **Follett, Wilson,** Modern American Usage: A Guide. Ed. and completed by Jacques Barcum, in collaboration with Carlos Baker, Frederick W. Dupee, Dudley Fitts, James D. Hart, Phyllis McGinley, and Lionel Trilling. New York: Hill and Wang 1966.

510 **Fong, William,** "Canadian English spelling", English Language Teaching 22 (1968): 266-71.

511 **Ford, John Carnell,** "Polydialectism, Black English and the issue of Standard English." Ph.D. United States International U. 1975. DAI 36: 1, 549A.

512 **Forgue, Guy Jean,** "American English at the time of the revolution", Revue des langues vivantes 43 (1977): 255-68.

513 ---, Les Mots américains. Paris: Presses Universitaires de France 1976.

514 --- and **Raven I. McDavid, Jr.,** La Langue des Américains. Paris: Aubier Montaigne 1972.

515 **Foscue, Virginia O.,** "Background and preliminary survey of the linguistic geography of Alabama." Ph.D. U. of Wisconsin 1967. DAI 28: 1, 214A.

516 ---, "A preliminary survey of the vocabulary of white Alabamians", PADS 56 (1971).

517 **Foster, David W.** and **Robert J. Hoffman,** "Some observations on the vowels of Pacific Northwest English (Seattle Area)", AS 41 (1966): 119-22.

518 **Fox, Robert A.** and **Dale Terbeek,** "Dental flaps, vowel duration and rule ordering in American English", Journal of Phonetics 5 (1977): 27-34.

519 **Franchini, Angelino,** Il Rendenglese: Dialetto trentino-anglo-americano. Rendenese + English in U.S.A. and G.B. over a Century. Trento: Tipografia Editrice TEMI 1981.

520 **Francis, W. Nelson,** Dialectology. An Introduction. London: Longman 1983.

521 **Fraser, Bruce,** "Some 'unexpected' reactions to various American-English dialects", in Shuy/Fasold 1973: 28-35.

522 **Frazer, Shirley,** "Dialect preterites and past participles in the North Central States and Upper Midwest." Master's thesis, North Texas State U. 1973.

523 **Frazer, Timothy C.,** "Combining Atlas, DARE, and checklist materials", AS 46 (1971): 58-65.

524 ---, "Midland dialect areas in Illinois." Ph.D. U. of Chicago 1973.

525 ---, "Ohio and the 'North Midland' dialect area", Midwestern Journal of Language and Folklore 4 (1978): 45-52.

526 ---, "South Midland pronunciation in the North Central States", AS 53 (1978): 40-48.

527 ---, "Cultural geography in Illinois: regional speech and place name sources", Great Lakes Review 4,2 (1978): 19-30.

528 ---, "The speech islands of the American Bottoms: a problem in social history", AS 54 (1979): 185-93.

529 **Friebel, Isolde** and **Heinrich Händel,** Britain - USA: A Survey in Key-Words. Frankfurt a.M.: Diesterweg 1968.

530 **Freiman, Howard A.,** "Speech rate as a function of dialectal geography", in St. Clair 1979: 128-36.

531 **Frentz, Thomas Stanley,** "Children's comprehension of Standard and Black English sentences." Ph.D. U. of Wisconsin 1970. DAI 31: 11, 6032A.

532 **Friederich, Wolf,** "Amerikanischer Sprachgebrauch", Lebende Sprachen 16,1 (1971): 7-11; 17,2 (1972): 33-35; 18,2 (1973): 37-39; 18,4 (1973): 126-8; 18,6 (1973): 163-6; 19,2 (1974): 37-39; 20,1 (1975): 1-3.

533 **Fujii, Kenzo,** "A study of New England dialects. Its phonetic simplicity", Onsei no Kenkyu (Tokio) 14 (1969): 351-67.

534 ---, "Amerika no LAGS keikaku no genkyo to igi" (Progress and significance of LAGS), The Bulletin, The Phonetic Society of Japan 160 (1979): 16-18.

535 **Funkhouser, James L.,** "A various standard", College English 34 (1973): 806-10, 819-27.

536 ---, "Black English: from speech to writing." Ph.D. Saint Louis 1976. DAI 37: 4, 2156A.

537 **Galinsky, Hans,** Amerika und Europa. Sprachliche und sprachkünstlerische Wechselbeziehungen in amerikanistischer Sicht. Berlin: Langenscheidt 1968.

538 ---, Regionalismus und Einheitsstreben in den Vereinigten Staaten. Ein sprachwissenschaftlicher Forschungsbericht. Heidelberg: Carl Winter 1972.

539 ---, Das Amerikanische Englisch. Seine innere Entwicklung und internationale Ausstrahlung: Ein kritischer Forschungsbericht als Einführung in die Grundlegungsphase der sprachwissenschaftlichen Amerikanistik. Darmstadt: Wissenschaftliche Buchgesellschaft 1979.

540 **Gallagher, Brian,** "About us, for us, near us: the Irish and Harlem renaissances", Eire 16,4 (1981): 14-26.

541 **Gallardo, Andres,** "The standardization of American English." Ph.D. Buffalo, New York 1980. DAI 41: 8, 3557A.

542 **Gantt, Walter N.** and **Wilson M. Robert,** "Syntactical speech patterns of black children from a depressed urban area: educators look at linguistic findings." ERIC ED 070 079, 1972.

543 **Garcia, Juliet Villareal,** "The regional vocabulary of Brownsville, Texas." Ph.D. Austin 1976. DAI 37: 8, 4698A.

544 **Garcia, Ricardo L.,** "Identification and comparison of oral English syntactic patterns of Spanish-English speaking adolescent Hispanos." Ed.D. Denver 1973. DAI 34: 6, 3372A.

545 ---, "Toward a grammar of Chicano English", English Journal 63 (1974): 34-38.

546 ---, "Mexican American bilingualism and English language development", Journal of Reading 17 (1974): 467-73.

547 **Gatbonton-Segalowitz, Elizabeth,** "Systematic variations in second language speech: a sociolinguistic study." Ph.D. McGill U. (Canada) 1976. DAI 37: 5, 2829A.

548 **Gawthrop, Betty,** "The speech of the Calumet region." Ph.D. Purdue U. 1973. DAI 37: 5, 2829A.

549 **Gay, Judy** and **Ryan D. Tweney,** "Comprehension and production of

Standard and Black English by lower-class black children", Developmental Psychology 12 (1976): 262-8.

550 **Gay, Thomas John,** "A perceptual study of American English diphthongs." Ph.D. City U. of New York 1967. DAI 28: 4, 1548A.

551 **Genishi, Celia Shinobu,** "Rules for code-switching in young Spanish-English speakers: an exploratory study of language socialization." Ph.D. Berkeley, California 1976. DAI 37: 9, 5656A.

552 **Gester, Friedrich Wilhelm,** "Negro, Afro-American oder black? Zu einer aktuellen sprachlichen Auseinandersetzung in den Vereinigten Staaten", Die Neueren Sprachen N.F. 20 (1971): 53-63.

553 ---, "Linguistic aspects of the Vietnam War", Amerikastudien 20 (1975): 307-19.

554 **Gibbons, V.E.,** "A progress report on a word geography of Indiana", Midwest Folklore 11 (1966): 151-4.

555 **Gibson, Deborah Jean,** "A thesis on eh." M.A. Thesis, U. of British Columbia 1976.

556 ---, "Eight types of 'eh'", Sociolinguistics Newsletter 8,1 (1977): 30-31.

557 **Gilbert, Glenn G.,** ed., Texas Studies in Bilingualism. Spanish, French, German, Czech, Polish, Sorbian, and Norwegian in the Southwest. Berlin: de Gruyter 1970.

558 --- and **Jacob Ornstein,** Problems in Applied Educational Sociolinguistics: Readings on Language and Cultural Problems of United States Ethnic Groups. The Hague: Mouton 1978.

559 **Giles, Howard, Donald M. Taylor** and **Richard Bourhis,** "Towards a theory of interpersonal accommodation through language: some Canadian data", Language in Society 2 (1973): 177-92.

560 **Gilliland, C. Herbert,** "U.S. naval slang: shitcan", AS 55 (1980): 153-4.

561 **Gilman, Robert A.,** "A selective annotated bibliography of bibliographies and other sources of information potentially useful in Mexican American bilingual/bicultural education", in Keller/Teschner/Vierra 1976: 171-212.

562 **Ginn, Doris O.,** "Aspects of bidialectalism among Afro-Americans of the United States." Ph.D. Buffalo, New York 1980. DAI 41: 6, 2585A.

563 **Ginther, Dean Webster,** "Black dialectal-linguistic interference, cul

tural interference, and reading performance." Ph.D. Urbana-Champaign, Illinois 1976. DAI 37: 5, 2829A.

564 **Gläser, Rosemarie,** "Zur Soziolinguistik und Sprachsoziologie in den USA", Zeitschrift für Anglistik und Amerikanistik 19 (1971): 341-63.

565 **Goddard, Ives,** "Some early examples of American Indian Pidgin English from New England", International Journal of American Linguistics 43 (1977): 37-41.

566 ---, "A further note on Pidgin English", International Journal of American Linguistics 44 (1978): 73.

567 **Godfrey, William H., Jr.,** "Some features of an idiolect of a James Island, South Carolina Gullah speaker." Thesis Atlanta U. 1974.

568 **Gold, David L.,** "The pronunciation of ng as taught in a New York City High School about 1962", AS 49 (1974): 159-60.

569 ---, "Three New-York-cityisms: sliding pond, potsy, and akey", AS 56 (1981): 17-32.

570 **Golub, Lester S.,** "English syntax of black, white, Indian, and Spanish-American children", Elementary School Journal 75,5 (1975): 323-34.

571 **Goossens, Maria M.,** "Degree of bilingualism among Dutch immigrants in Calgary", in Darnell 1973: 151-6.

572 **Gordon, Barbara** and **Anita Stevens,** "A comparison of New Brunswick and Saskatchewan English", Calgary Working Papers in Linguistics 1,1 (1975): 8-16.

573 **Gordon, David Paul,** "Hospital slang for patients: crocks, gomers, gorks, and others", Language in Society 12 (1983): 173-85.

574 **Gräf, Gerhard** and **Harry Spitzbardt,** Amerikanisches Englisch. Leipzig: Enzyklopädie 1965, 2nd ed. 1974.

575 **Gramley, Stephan E.,** "American and British English: recent introductory literature", Zeitschrift für Anglistik und Amerikanistik 25 (1977): 233-43.

576 **Graves, Richard Layton,** "Language differences between upper and lower class negro and white eighth graders in east central Alabama." Ph.D. Florida State U. 1967. DAI 28: 9, 3657A.

577 **Gray, Barbara Quint,** "Auxiliary structure and syntactic maturity in the naturalistic speech of 3-to-5 year old lower-class urban black children." Ph.D. New York U. 1976. DAI 38: 2, 761A.

578 **Greatman, Bonnie M.,** "A dialect atlas of Maryland." Ph.D. New York U. 1970. DAI 31: 12, 6580A.

579 **Greenberg, S. Robert,** *An Experimental Study of Certain Intonation Contrasts in American English.* Los Angeles: UCLA Phonetics Laboratory 1969.

580 **Greene, Susan Lutters,** "A comparison of black and white speech in a rural Georgia county." Thesis, U. of Georgia 1972.

581 **Gregg, Robert J.,** "The Linguistic Survey of British Columbia: the Kootenay Region", in Darnell 1973: 105-16.

582 ---, "The Diphthongs əɪ and aɪ in Scottish, Scotch-Irish, and Canadian English", *Canadian Journal of Linguistics* 18 (1973): 136-45.

583 ---, "General background to the Survey of Vancouver English (SVEN)", in Warkentyne 1981: 41-47.

584 **Gregory, Omar Dean,** "A comparative description of the intonation of British and American English for teachers of English as a foreign language." Ed.D. Columbia U. 1966. DAI 27: 4, 1045A.

585 **Greibesland, Solveig C.,** "A comparison of uncultivated black and white speech in the upper South." Thesis, U. of Chicago 1970.

586 **Griffin, Hazel,** "Some folk expressions from northeastern North Carolina", *North Carolina Folklore* 15 (1967): 56-57.

587 **Griffith, Jerry** and **L.E. Miner,** eds., *The First Lincolnland Conference on Dialectology.* University, Ala.: Alabama UP 1970.

588 **Grobsmith, Elizabeth S.,** "Aspects of Lakota bilingualism", in Schach 1980: 119-28.

589 **Gross, Reuben E.,** "Dialect pronunciation, auditory discrimination, and reading." Ph.D. Yeshiva U. 1967. DAI 28, 2124B.

590 **Grubbs, Sam,** "The opposite of white: names for black Americans", in Fred Tarpley and Ann Moseley, eds., *Of Edsels and Marauders.* Commerce, Texas: Names Inst. Press 1971: 25-32.

591 **Gullon, Patricia,** "A comparison of M. Bloomfield's 'Western (Saskatchewan)' dialect and a dialect from the Regina area", *Calgary Working Papers in Linguistics* 1,1 (1975): 17-21.

592 **Gumperz, John J.,** "Dialect and conversational inference in urban communication", *Language in Society* 7 (1978): 393-409.

593 **Guthrie, Charles S.,** "Corn: the mainstay of the Cumberland Valley", Kentucky Folklore Record 12 (1966): 87-91.

594 ---, "Tobacco: cash crop of the Cumberland Valley", Kentucky Folklore Record 14 (1968): 38-43.

595 **Guy, Gregory R.,** "A new look at -t, -d deletion", in Fasold/Shuy 1977: 1-11.

596 ---, "Variation in the group and the individual: the case of final stop deletion", in Labov 1980: 1-36.

597 **Habick, Timothy,** "Sound change in Farmer City: a sociolinguistic study based on acoustic data." Ph.D. Urbana-Champaign, Illinois 1980. DAI 41: 2, 655A.

598 **Hackenberg, Robert Gregory,** "Appalachian English: a sociolinguistic study." Ph.D. Georgetown U. 1972. DAI 33: 12, 6893A.

599 **Hagemann, E.R.,** "A 1926 glossary of criminal argot", AS 57 (1982): 260-3.

600 **Hair, P.E.H.,** "Sierra Leone items in the Gullah dialect of American English", Sierra Leone Language Review 4 (1965): 79-84.

601 **Hall, Joan Houston,** "Rural southeast Georgia speech: a phonological analysis." Ph.D. Emory U. 1976. DAI 37: 5, 2830A.

602 ---, "DARE: the view from the letter F", Dictionaries 1 (1979): 25-46.

603 **Hall, Mary Pat Farber,** "A description of the linguistic characteristics of the careful speech of recent high school graduates in entry-level positions of job categories of large employment in selected counties of Southwest Virginia." Ed.D. Virginia Polytechnic Institute and State U. 1977. DAI 37: 9, 5656A.

604 **Hall, Richard W.,** "A muddle of models: the radicalizing of American English", English Journal 61 (1972): 705-10.

605 **Hall, William S.,** "Black and white children's responses to Black English Vernacular and Standard English sentences: evidence for code-switching", in Harrison/Trabasso 1976: 201-8.

606 ---, **Michael Cole, Stephen Reder** and **Gillian Dowley,** "Variations on young children's use of language: some effects of setting and dialect", in Roy O. Freedle, ed., Discourse Production and Comprehension. Norwood, N.J.: Ablex 1977: 161-73.

607 — and **Roy Freedle,** "A developmental investigation of Standard and non-Standard English among black and white children", Human Development 16 (1973): 440-64.

608 —, —, Culture and Language. The Black American Experience. Washington, D.C.: Hemisphere Publ. Co. 1975.

609 **Haller, Robert S.,** ed., Papers from the 1979 Mid-America Linguistics Conference, November 2 - 3, 1980, University of Nebraska-Lincoln. Lincoln: Area Studies Committee in Linguistics, U. of Nebraska-Lincoln 1980.

610 **Hamers, Josiane F.** and **Denise Deshaies,** "Effects des contacts intergroupes sur les attitudes envers la langue seconde et les membres de ce groupe culturel chez les élèves anglophones et francophones du Québec", in Jean-Guy Savard and Lorne Laforge, eds., Actes du 5e Congrès de L'Association Internationale de Linguistique Appliquée, Montreal août 1978. Québec: Les Presses de l'Université Laval 1981: 141-9.

611 **Hampson, Eloise Lemire,** "The dialect stereotypes of schoolchildren and teachers in the Bay Roberts area of Newfoundland." M.A. Thesis Memorial U. of Newfoundland 1982.

612 **Hancock, Ian F.,** "The acquisition of English by American Romani children", Word 27 (1971): 353-62.

613 —, "Creole features in the Afro-seminole speech of Brackettville, Texas." Caribbean Linguistics Society Occasional Paper No. 3, 1975.

614 —, "Patterns of English lexical adoption in an American dialect of Romanes", Orbis 25 (1976): 83-104.

615 —, The Relationship of Black Vernacular English to the Atlantic Creoles. Occasional paper. Austin: U. of Texas Afro-American Studies Center 1979.

615a —, English in St. Helena: Creole Features in an Island Speech. Society for Caribbean Linguistics, Occasional Paper 11 (1979).

616 —, The Texas Seminoles and Their Language. Austin: U. of Texas 1980.

617 —, "Texan Gullah: the creole English of the Brackettville Afro-Seminoles", in Dillard 1980: 305-35.

618 —, "Gullah and Barbadian - origins and relationships", AS 55 (1980): 17-35.

619 **Hand, Wayland D.,** "From idea to word - folk beliefs and customs underlying folk speech", *AS* 48 (1973): 67-76.

620 **Hankey, Clyde T.,** "'Tiger', 'tagger', and /aɪ/ in Western Pennsylvania" and "Diphthongal variants of /ɛ/ and /æ/ in Western Pennsylvania", *AS* 40 (1965): 226-29.

621 ---, "Notes on west Penn-Ohio phonology", in Davis 1972: 49-61.

622 **Hanley, T.D.** and **Moya Landsberg Andrews,** "Some acoustic differences between educated Australian and general American dialects", *Phonetica* 17 (1967): 241-9.

623 **Hanners, La Verne,** "The written and spoken dialect of the southeast Arkansas black college student." Ed.D. Ball State U. 1979. DAI 41: 9, 4016A.

624 **Hansell, Mark,** "Language in the workplace: the tobacco farm", in Kenneth Whistler *et al.*, eds., *Proceedings of the 3rd Annual Meeting of the Berkeley Linguistics Society*. Berkeley: Berkeley Linguistics Society, U. of California 1977: 488-97.

625 --- and **Cheryl Seabrook,** "Some conversational conventions of Black English", in Jeri J. Jaeger *et al.*, eds., *Proceedings of the Fourth Annual Meeting of the Berkeley Linguistics Society*. Berkeley, Calif.: Berkeley Linguistics Society, U. of California 1978: 576-87.

626 **Hansen, Chadwick,** "Jenny's toe: negro shaking dances in America", *American Quarterly* 19 (1967): 554-63.

627 **Harder, Kelsie B.,** "Hay-making terms in Perry County", *Tennessee Folklore Society Bulletin* 33 (1967): 41-48.

628 **Harpole, Charles,** "ERIC report: nonstandard speech", *Speech Teacher* 24 (1975): 226-31.

629 **Harris, Barbara Pritchard,** "Selected political, cultural and socio-economic areas of Canadian history as contributors to the vocabulary of Canadian English." Ph.D. Victoria, B.C. 1975. DAI 37: 6, 3589A.

630 --- and **Joseph F. Kess,** "Salmon fishing terms in British Columbia", *Names* 23 (1975): 61-66.

631 **Harris, Maverick M.,** "The retroflection of postvocalic /r/ in Austin", *AS* 44 (1969): 263-71.

632 **Harrison, Deborah Sears,** "Techniques for eliciting casual speech samples for the study of the Black English Vernacular", in Harrison/Trabasso 1976: 191-9.

633 --- and **Tom Trabasso,** eds., Black English: A Seminar. Hillsdale, N.J.: Erlbaum 1976.

634 **Hartford, Beverly Ann S.,** "The English of Mexican American adolescents in Gary, Indiana: a sociolinguistic description." Ph.D. Austin 1975. DAI 36: 5, 2778A.

635 ---, "Phonological differences in the English of adolescent Chicanas and Chicanos", in Dubois/Crouch 1976: 73-80.

636 ---, "Phonological differences in the English of adolescent female and male Mexican-Americans", International Journal of the Sociology of Language 17 (1978): 55-64.

637 **Hartman, Erika,** "The front vowels before r of the North-Central States." Ph.D. Illinois Institute of Technology 1981. DAI 42: 7, 3137A.

638 **Hartman, James W.,** "Pressures for dialect change in Hocking County, Ohio." Ph.D. U. of Michigan 1966. DAI 27: 7, 2140A.

639 ---, "Some preliminary findings from DARE", AS 44 (1969): 191-9.

640 ---, "DARE in 1970", JEngL 5 (1971): 87-93.

641 **Hartmann, Maryann,** "A descriptive study of the language of men and women born in Maine around 1900 as it reflects the Lakoff hypothesis in 'Language and women's place'", in Dubois/Crouch 1976: 81-90.

642 **Harvey, Gina C.** and **M.F. Heiser,** eds., Southwest Languages and Linguistics in Educational Perspective. San Diego, Calif.: Institute for Cultural Pluralism 1975.

643 **Hasebe-Ludt, Erika,** "Aspects of spontaneous speech in the urban dialect study of Vancouver English", in Warkentyne 1981: 57-61.

644 **Haskins, Jim** and **Hugh F. Butts,** The Psychology of Black Language. New York: Barnes and Noble 1973.

645 ---, ---, "The genesis of black American dialects", in Haskins/Butts 1973: 28-37.

646 **Hasselmo, Nils,** "Spanish-English bilingualism in the U.S.: comments on research during the 1970s", in Even Hovdhaugen, ed., The Nordic Languages and Modern Linguistics. Proceedings of the 4th International Conference of Nordic and General Linguistics in Oslo 1980. Oslo: U.-forl. 1980: 157-69.

647 **Haugen, Einar,** The Ecology of Language. Essays. Selected and introduced by Anwar S. Dil. Stanford, Calif.: UP 1972.

648 ---, "Bilingualism, language contact, and immigrant languages in the United States: a research report 1956-1970", in Sebeok 1973: 505-91.

649 **Hawkins, Opal Winchester,** "Southern linguistic variation as revealed through overseers letters, 1829-1858." Ph.D. Chapel Hill, North Carolina 1982. DAI 43: 6, 1957A.

650 **Haynes, Charles Smith,** "A grammar of modal and catenative auxiliaries in contemporary informal spoken American English." Ph.D. New York U. 1967. DAI 29: 1, 246A.

651 **Heald, Ann R.B.,** "A partial black word list from East Texas", in Mohammad Ali Jazayery, Edgar C. Polomé and Werner Winter, eds., Linguistic and Literary Studies in Honor of Archibald A. Hill. IV: Linguistics and Literature; Sociolinguistics and Applied Linguistics. The Hague: Mouton 1979: 259-63.

652 **Heap, Norman A.,** "A burley tobacco word list from Lexington, Kentucky", PADS 45 (1966): 1-27.

653 **Heard, Betty Ruth,** "A phonological analysis of the speech of Hays County, Texas." Ph.D. Louisiana State U. 1969. DAI 30: 4, 1546A.

654 **Heath, Shirley Brice,** "Language and politics in the United States", in Muriel Savill-Troike, ed., Linguistics and Anthropology. Washington, D.C.: Georgetown UP 1977: 267-96.

655 ---, "A national language academy? Debate in the new nation", Linguistics 189 (1977): 9-43.

656 **Hedberg, Johannes,** "The rise of Black English in the United States", Moderna Språk 74 (1980): 215-8.

657 **Hedges, James S.,** "Nouns with stressed final syllables in Midwestern folk speech", in Ingemann 1977: 115-20.

658 **Heller, Monica S.,** "'Bonjour, hello?': negotiations of language choice in Montreal", in Jeri J. Jaeger et al., eds., Proceedings of the Fourth Annual Meeting of the Berkeley Linguistics Society. Berkeley, Calif.: Berkeley Linguistics Society, U. of California 1978: 588-97.

659 **Heller, Murray,** "Black names in America: history and meaning." (Volumes I and II). Ph.D. Ohio State U. 1974. DAI 38: 5, 3446A.

660 **Hellerstein, Kathryn,** "Yiddish voices in American English", in Michaels/Ricks 1980: 182-201.

661 **Hellstrom, Robert Wilhelm,** "Finglish", AS 51 (1976): 85-93.

662 ---, "Finglish." Ph.D. U. of Oregon 1979. DAI 40: 9, 5033A.

663 **Henderson, Michael M.T.,** "Of matters lexicographical: Processing data for DARE - current practices", AS 49 (1974): 119-22.

664 ---, "Use of an interactive program in analyzing data for a dialect dictionary", Computers and the Humanities 9 (1975): 105-13.

665 **Henrie, Jr., Samuel Nyal,** "A study of verb phrases used by five year old Nonstandard Negro English speaking children." Ph.D. Berkeley, California 1969. DAI 31: 2, 743A.

666 **Hensey, Fritz,** "Recent developments in U.S. sociolinguistics", in Ornstein 1975: 71-74.

667 **Hernández-Chávez, Eduardo,** "The acquisition of grammatical structures by a Mexican-American child learning English." Ph.D. Berkeley, California 1977. DAI 38: 11, 6689A.

668 **Herndobler, Robin,** "White working-class speech: the East Side of Chicago." Ph.D. U. of Chicago 1977.

669 --- and **Andrew Sledd,** "Black English - notes on the auxiliary", AS 51 (1976): 185-200.

670 **Hess, Karen Matison,** "The language attitudes and beliefs of Minnesota elementary and high school English teachers." Ph.D. U. of Minnesota 1968. DAI 30: 1, 304A.

671 **Hewitt, Helen-Jo** and **Winfried P. Lehmann,** Selected Vowel Measurements of American English Speech. Austin: Dept. of Ling. 1965.

672 **Higgins, Cleo S.,** "The spoken English of black and white high school students of Palatka, Florida, implications for teaching and curriculum development." Ph.D. U. of Wisconsin 1973. DAI 34: 6, 3341A.

673 **Hilaire, Paul,** "A study of variations in the pronunciation of English among ninth-grade students in New Jersey." Ph.D. Rutgers U. 1975. DAI 36: 10, 6649A.

674 **Hill, Archibald A.,** "The tainted 'ain't' once more", College English 26 (1965): 298-303.

675 ---, "The habituative aspect of verbs in Black English, Irish English, and Standard English", AS 50 (1975): 323-4.

676 **Hindle, Donald Morris,** "Approaches to vowel normalization in the study of natural speech", in David Sankoff, ed., Linguistic Variation: Models and Methods. New York: Academic Press 1978: 161-72.

677 ---, "The social and situational conditioning of phonetic variation." Ph.D. U. of Pennsylvania 1980. DAI 40: 10, 5424A.

678 **Hines, Donald M.,** "Painter jargon of the Pacific northwest", AS 44 (1969): 5-32.

679 **Hinton, Norman D.,** "Let's go /fə'nark/ at the birds: a St. Louis term", AS 43 (1968): 78-79.

680 **Hirshberg, Jeffrey,** "Regional morphology in American English: evidence from DARE", AS 56 (1981): 33-52.

681 —, "Towards a Dictionary of Black American English on Historical Principles", AS 57 (1982): 163-82.

682 **Hobson, Charles David,** "Language and black children: the effects of dialects in selected passages on black third graders' reading strategies as revealed by oral reading miscues." Ph.D. Georgia State U. 1981. DAI 42: 3, 1075A.

683 **Hoff, Patricia J.,** "A dialect study of Faulkner County, Arkansas." Ph.D. Louisiana State U. 1968. DAI 29: 1, 247A.

684 **Hoffer, Bates L.,**"Towards implicational scales for use in Chicano English composition", in Dubois/Hoffer 1975: 59-74.

685 ---, "Acquisition of English syntax by Mexican Americans: grades 1 - 6", in Gilbert/Ornstein 1978: 63-71.

686 --- and **Jacob Ornstein,** eds., Sociolinguistics in the Southwest. San Antonio, Texas: Trinity U. 1974.

687 **Hoffman, Gerard,** "Puerto Ricans in New York: a language-related ethnographic summary", in Fishman/Cooper/Ma 1971: 13-42.

688 **Hoffman, Melvin J.,** "The segmental and suprasegmental phones, phonemes, and morphophones of an Afro-American dialect." Ph.D. Buffalo, New York 1970. DAI 31: 11, 6034A.

689 ---, "Second dialect pedagogy: hydra and hybrid", in L. Davis 1972: 63-79.

690 **Holmberg, Börje,** "Noah Webster and American pronunciation", English Studies 46 (1965): 118-29.

691 **Holt, Grace Sims,** "'Inversion' in black communication", in Kochman 1972: 152-9.

692 **Hooper, Joan B.,** "Constraints on schwa-deletion in American English", in Jacek Fisiak, ed., Recent Developments in Historical Phonology. The Hague: Mouton 1978: 183-207.

693 **Hoover, Mary Eleanor Rhodes,** "Appropriate use of Black English by black children as rated by parents." Ph.D. Stanford U. 1975. DAI 36: 4, 2079A.

694 ---, "Community attitudes toward Black English", Language in Society 7 (1978): 65-87.

695 **Hopkins, John Rathbone,** "The white middle class speech of Savannah, Georgia: a phonological analysis." Ph.D. U. of South Carolina 1975. DAI 37: 1, 265A.

696 **Horváth, Janda Izabella,** "English Hungarian and Hungarian English language interference phenomena in Chicago", in Peter A. Reich, ed., The Second LACUS Forum 1975. Columbia, S.C.: Hornbeam 1976: 590-5.

697 **Horvath, Joyce Knight,** "A study of selected vocalic phoneme discriminations in the speech of North Idaho school children: the implications for language arts teaching." Ed.D. U. of Idaho 1969. DAI 31: 5, 2367A.

698 **Houck, Charles L.,** "A computerized statistical methodology for linguistic geography: a pilot study", Folia Linguistica 1 (1967): 80-95.

699 ---, "A statistical and computerized methodology for analyzing dialect materials." Ph.D. U. of Iowa 1970. DAI 30: 8, 3429A.

700 **Hough, George Anthony III,** "Structures of modification in contemporary American English." Ph.D. Michigan State U. 1965. DAI 26: 8, 4647A. Published: The Hague: Mouton 1971.

701 **Houston, Susan H.,** "A sociolinguistic consideration of the Black English of children in northern Florida", Language 45 (1969): 599-607.

702 ---, "Child Black English: the school register", Linguistics 90 (1972): 20-34.

703 ---, "Competence and performance in Child Black English", in Luelsdorff 1975: 13-27.

704 **Howard, Eunice Laniece,** "Standard syntactic structures and dialect variations in the speech and writing of selected black college freshmen." Ph.D. Wayne State U. 1974. DAI 35: 12, 7891A.

705 **Howell, Ralph Daniel,** "Morphological features of the speech of white and negro students in a southern (Mississippi) community." Ph.D. Florida State U. 1971. DAI 32: 9, 5212A.

706 ---, "Dominicker: a regional racial term", AS 47 (1972): 305-6.

707 **Hrubi, Roger,** "Aspiration of initial voiceless stops", in Léon/Martin 1979: 61-69.

708 **Huber, Robin H.,** "The syntax of the written language of urban (Tallahassee) black and white fourth graders." Ph.D. Florida State U. 1973. DAI 34: 9, 5945A.

709 **Huckleberry, Alan W.,** "The disappearing post-vocalic /r/ of 'General American' English speech", in Bohuslav Hála, Milan Romportl and Premysl Janota, eds., Proceedings of the Sixth International Congress of Phonetic Sciences, held at Prague, 7 - 13 September 1967. Prague: Academia 1970: 449-52.

710 **Hudson, Randolph H.,** A Modern Handbook of American English: A Concise Guide to Grammar, Usage, and Rhetoric. Chicago: Science Research Associates 1966.

711 **Hudson-Edwards, Alan** and **Garland D. Bills,** "Intergenerational language shift in an Albuquerque barrio", in Blansitt/Teschner 1980: 139-58.

712 **Huerta, Ana Graciela,** "Code-switching among Spanish-English bilinguals: a sociolinguistic perspective." Ph.D. Austin 1978. DAI 39: 11, 6596A.

713 ---, "Code switching among Spanish-English bilinguals: a descriptive study", in Rose Nash and Domtila Belaval, eds., Readings in Spanish-English Contrastive Linguistics. Vol. II. San Juan: Inter American UP 1980: 206-31.

714 **Huffines, Marion Lois,** "English in contact with Pennsylvania German", German Quarterly 54 (1980): 352-66.

715 **Hughes, Anne E.,** "An investigation of certain socio-linguistic phenomena in the vocabulary, pronunciation and grammar of disadvantaged pre-school children, their parents and their teachers in the Detroit public schools." Ph.D. Michigan State U. 1967. DAI 28: 12, 5037A.

716 **Hultin, Neil C.,** "Dakota speech in 1894", AS 41 (1966): 65-67.

717 ---, "Canadian views of American English", AS 42 (1967): 243-60.

718 ---, "'Bushed' in Canadian English", AS 44 (1969): 150-1.

719 **Hunt, Donald Lewis,** "Characteristics of the black dialect as compared to standard and nonstandard English in southeast Missouri." Ed.D. U. of Mississippi 1976. DAI 37: 3, 1440A.

720 **Hunter, Alfred C.,** Glossary of Unfamiliar and Other Interesting Words in the Newfoundland Journal of Aaron Thomas. St. John's, Nfld.: Memorial U. of Newfoundland 1970.

721 **Hurlbut, Marilyn,** "Folk synonyms from Argyle, Texas", AS 51 (1976): 63-75.

722 **Hymes, Dell,** Language in Education: Ethnolinguistic Essays. Washington, D.C.: Center for Applied Linguistics 1980.

723 **Iarovici, Edith,** Engleza americana. Bucuresti: Editura stiintifica 1971.

724 **Ingemann, Frances,** ed., 1975 Mid-America Linguistics Conference Papers. Lawrence: Linguistics Department, U. of Kansas 1976.

725 —, ed., Papers from the 1975 Mid-America Linguistics Conference. Lawrence: Linguistics Department, U. of Kansas 1977.

726 **Ireland, Robert John,** "Canadian spelling: an empirical and historical survey of selected words." Ph.D. York U. (Canada) 1979. DAI 40: 5, 2636A.

727 **Irwin, Ruth Beckey,** "Judgements of vocal quality, speech fluency, and confidence of southern black and white speakers", Language and Speech 20 (1977): 261-6.

728 **Jackson, Patricia Ann Jones,** "The status of Gullah: an investigation of convergent processes." Ph.D. U. of Michigan 1978. DAI 39: 2, 851A.

729 **Jackson, Sarah E.,** "Unusual words, expressions, and pronunciations in a North Carolina mountain community", Appalachian Journal 2 (1975): 148-60.

730 **Jacobs, Noah Jonathan,** Amerika im Spiegel der Sprache. Bern, München: Francke 1968.

731 **Jacobsen, Betty Joan,** "LANE recordings: history and comparison of verb forms with fieldwork." Ph.D. Illinois Institute of Technology 1978. DAI 39: 8, 4920A.

732 **Jacobson, Rodolfo,** "An inquiry into the relevancy of current English instruction", Language Learning 22 (1972): 79-98.

733 ---, "Research in Southwestern English and the sociolinguistic perspective", in Dubois/Hoffer 1975: 59-74.

734 **Jaffe, Hilda,** "The speech of the central coast of North Carolina: the Carteret County version of the Banks 'Brogue'." Ph.D. Michigan State U. 1966. DAI 27: 5, 1355A. PADS 60 (1973).

735 **James, Eric,** "Vocalic oppositions", in Léon/Martin 1979: 19-34.

736 **James, Linda B.,** "Black children's perception of Black English", Journal of Psycholinguistic Research 5 (1976): 377-87.

737 **Janicki, Karol,** Elements of British and American English. Warszawa: Państwowe Wydawnictwo Naukowe 1977.

738 **Jasper, Susan Dale Penfield,** "Selected grammatical characteristics of Mohave English." Ph.D. U. of Arizona 1980. DAI 41: 2, 656A.

739 **Jeremiah, Milford Astor,** "The linguistic relatedness of Black English and Antiguan Creole: evidence from the eighteenth and nineteenth centuries." Ph.D. Brown U. 1977. DAI 38: 8, 4788A.

740 **Jochnowitz, George,** "Bilingualism and dialect mixture among Lubavitcher Hasidic children", AS 43 (1968): 182-200.

741 **Johansson, Stig,** "American and British English grammar: an elicitation experiment", English Studies 60 (1979): 195-215.

742 **Johnson, Ann, Roland Axelson, Lorene Lugo** and **Perry Zirkel,** "Native language and black dialect interference in the oral reproduction of Standard English by Puerto Rican pupils", in John F. Fanselow and Ruth H. Crymes, eds., On TESOL '76. Selections Based on Teaching Done at the 10th Annual TESOL Convention, New York, March 2 - 7, 1976. Washington, D.C.: Teachers of English to Speakers of Other Languages 1976: 129-35.

743 **Johnson, Bruce Lee,** "The Western Pennsylvania dialect of American English", Journal of the International Phonetic Association 1 (1971): 69-73.

744 **Johnson, Edith Trager,** "Black-on-black: an interview analyzed", in Ingemann 1976: 271-89.

745 --- and **Frank Abraham,** "Basic English and Spanish syntax of Spanish-speaking Americans: Some interactions and implications", in Rose Nash, ed., Readings in Spanish-English Contrastive Linguistics. Hato Rey, Puerto Rico: Inter American UP 1973: 72-122.

746 **Johnson, Guy B.,** "The Gullah dialect revisited: a note on linguistic acculturation", Journal of Black Studies 10 (1980): 417-24.

747 **Johnson, Kenneth R.,** "The influence of nonstandard negro dialect on reading achievement", English Record 21,4 (1971): 148-55.

748 ---, "The vocabulary of race", in Kochman 1972: 140-51.

749 ---, "Words used for skin color in the black culture", FFLR 11 (1973): 15-16, 44.

750 ---, "A comparison of black dialect-speaking children and Standard English-speaking children and their ability to hear final consonant stops", TESOL Quarterly 8 (1974): 375-87.

751 **Johnson, Lawrence A.,** "A sociolinguistic study of selected vowel changes in Los Angeles English." Ph.D. U. of Southern California 1974. DAI 35: 5, 2969A.

752 ---, "Sound change and mobility in Los Angeles", Linguistics 143 (1975): 33-48.

753 ---, "Voiced t in post-voiceless contexts", Lingua 44 (1978): 379-87.

754 **Johnson, Mae Coleman,** "An investigation of the extent of Standard English and Black English used by children from schools of varying racial compositions." Ph.D. U. of Maryland 1971. DAI 32: 6, 3283A.

755 **Johnson, Marion R.,** "Canadian eh", Working Papers in Linguistics, Ohio State U. 21 (1976): 153-60.

756 **Jones, Brenda,** "Rule ordering in Canadian English", Calgary Working Papers in Linguistics 1,1 (1975): 29-34.

757 **Jones, Mabel Jean,** "The regional English of the former inhabitants of Cades Cove in the Great Smoky Mountains." Ph.D. U. of Tennessee 1973. DAI 34: 8, 5146A.

758 **Jones, Nancy Nell Alsobrook,** "'Be in Dallas Black English." Ph.D. North Texas State U. 1972. DAI 33: 8, 4386A.

759 ---, "Black English in Dallas", in Hoffer/Ornstein 1974: 13-18.

760 **Jones-Jackson, Patricia A.,** "Gullah: on the question of Afro-American language", Anthropological Linguistics 20 (1978): 422-9.

761 **Jonz, Jon G.,** "Situated address in the United States marine corps", Anthropological Linguistics 17 (1975): 68-77.

762 **Joy, Richard J.,** Languages in Conflict: The Canadian Experience. Montreal 1967; repr. Toronto: McClelland and Stewart 1972.

763 **Jutronic, Dunja,** "Serbo-Croatian and American English in contact: A sociolinguistic study of the Serbo-Croatian community in Steelton, Pennsylvania." Ph.D. Pennsylvania State U. 1971. DAI 33: 1, 297A.

764 ---, "Language maintenance and language shift of the Serbo-Croatian language in Steelton, Pennsylvania", *General Linguistics* 16 (1976): 166-86.

765 **Jutte, F.,** *Het Engelse taaleigen van Amerika*. Zwolle: Tjeenk Willink 1966.

766 **Kahane, Henry** and **Renée Kahane,** "Virtues and vices in the American language: a history of attitudes", *TESOL Quarterly* 11 (1977): 185-202.

767 **Kannerstein, Gregory,** "Slang at a negro college: 'home boy'", *AS* 42 (1967): 238-9.

768 **Kay, Donald,** "*Tea-hounds* in Carolina: British fops and American hair", *AS* 47 (1972): 155-7.

769 **Keen, Ruth,** "A word study of *Musical Americana*", *AS* 40 (1965): 127-33.

770 **Keipe, Ashtoreth Marcia,** "The effects of instruction upon children's attitudes toward regional dialects." Ph.D. Madison, Wisconsin 1976. DAI 38: 1, 231A.

771 **Kell, Katharine T.,** "Folk names for tobacco", *Journal of American Folklore* 79 (1966): 590-9.

772 **Keller, Gary D., Richard V. Teschner** and **Silvia Vierra,** eds., *Bilingualism in the Bicentennial and Beyond*. Jamaica, N.Y.: Bilingual Press 1976.

773 **Kelly, L.G.,** "Language maintenance in Canada: research problems", in Migus 1975: 23-28.

774 **Kenwood, Christopher Michael,** "A study of slang and informal usage in the newspaper." M.A. Thesis, U. of British Columbia 1969.

775 **Kerr, Elizabeth M.** and **Ralph M. Aderman,** *Aspects of American English*. New York: Harcourt 1963, repr. 1971.

776 **Kessler, Carolyn,** "Noun plural absence", [annex] in Fasold 1972: 223-37.

777 **Kettemann, Bernhard,** "Der Vokalismus des Dialektes von Montgom-ery County, Ind.", Phonetica 24 (1971): 162-74.

778 ---, Aspekte der natürlichen generativen Phonologie eines amerika-nisch-englischen Dialekts. Frankfurt a.M.: Lang 1978.

779 **Key, Mary Ritchie, L. Fiege-Kollman** and **E. Smith,** "Features of chil black English", in William F. Mackey and Theodore Andersson, eds. Bilingualism in Early Childhood. Rowley, Mass.: Newbury 1977 185-98.

780 **Kilbury, James,** "Phonemic /aɪ/ ≠ /əɪ/, /aʊ/ ≠ /əʊ/ in America English?" Arbeiten aus Anglistik und Amerikanistik 1 (1976): 106-16.

781 **Kinloch, A. Murray,** "The Survey of Canadian English: possible evi-dence for pronunciation", English Quarterly 4,4 (1971): 59-65.

782 ---, "The use of pictures in elicitation", AS 46 (1971): 38-46.

783 ---, "The Survey of Canadian English: a first look at New Brunswic results", English Quarterly 5,4 (1972/73): 41-51.

784 ---, "The study of Canadian English", English Teacher 4,2 (1975): 4-7.

785 ---, "The phonology of Central/Prairie Canadian English", AS 5 (1983): 31-35.

786 --- and **Anthony B. House,** "The English language in New Brunswic and Prince Edward Island: research published, in progress, an required", Journal of the Atlantic Provinces Linguistic Associatio (Fredericton) 1 (1978): 34-45.

787 ---, **H. Rex Wilson** and **I.J. O'Neil,** "Classroom use of the survey o Canadian English", English Quarterly 6 (1973): 369-72.

788 **Kirchner, Gustav,** "Detached observations on prepositional use i modern, especially American English", Brno Studies in English (1969): 105-10.

789 ---, Die syntaktischen Eigentümlichkeiten des Amerikanischen Eng-lisch. 2 vols. München: Hueber / Leipzig: Enzyklopädie 1970, 1972.

790 **Kirwin, William J.,** "The present state of language studies in New-foundland", RLS 1 (1968): 1-3.

791 ---, "Bibliography of writings on Newfoundland English", RLS (1968): 4-7.

792 ---, "Either for any in Newfoundland", RLS 1 (1968): 8-10.

793 —, "Linguistic research materials in the Folklore Archive at Memorial University", RLS 1 (1968): 11-13.

794 —, "Linguistic research in Newfoundland", RLS 3 (1971): 13-15.

795 —, "A collection of popular etymologies in Newfoundland vocabulary", RLS 3 (1971): 16-18.

796 —, "Additions to previous bibliographies", RLS 3 (1971): 23.

797 —, "Ingressive speech reported in Newfoundland 'mummer-talk'", RLS 3 (1971): 24.

798 —, "Linguistic research in Newfoundland", RLS 4 (1972): 31-33.

799 —, "'Black English' in Newfoundland?", RLS 4 (1972): 33.

800 —, "Newfoundland usage in the Survey of Canadian English", RLS 5 (1974): 9-14.

801 —, "Linguistic research in Newfoundland", RLS 5 (1974): 30-34.

802 —, "Selecting and presenting the lexicon", RLS 6 (1975): 5-17.

803 **Kleederman, Frances,** "Black English: two viewpoints." ERIC ED 080 011, 1973.

804 **Klejnenberg, T.B.,** "Osobennosti upotreblenija soslagatel'nogo naklonenija v razlicnyx stiljax anglijskogo jazyka SSA" / Use of subjunctive in AmE /, in L.I. Apaeva, G.P. Boguslavskaja and T.V. Suldesova, eds., Voprosy germanskoy filologii. Yaroslav: Yaroslavskij orden T.K.Z. GPI im. K.D. Usinskogo 1971: 23-29.

805 **Kligman, Donna** and **Bruce Cronnell,** Black English and Spelling. Los Alamitos, Calif.: Southwest Regional Laboratories for Educational Research and Development 1974.

806 **Knapp, Margaret O.,** "Awareness of black dialects by first- and fifth-graders as related to race, socioeconomic status, and sex." Ed.D. Rutgers U. 1974. DAI 35: 6, 3525A.

807 **Knight, Margaret Bennett,** "Scottish Gaelic, English, and French: some aspects of the macaronic tradition of the Codroy Valley, Newfoundland", RLS 4 (1972): 25-30.

808 **Kochman, Thomas,** "Towards an ethnography of black American speech behavior", in Norman E. Whitten, Jr., and John F. Szwed, eds., Afro-American Anthropology. Contemporary Perspectives. New York: Free Press / London: Collier-Macmillan 1970: 145-62.

809 ---, ed., Rappin' and Stylin' Out: Communication in Urban Black America. Urbana, Ill.: Illinois UP 1972.

810 ---, "The kinetic element in black idiom", in Kochman 1972: 160-9.

811 ---, "Orality and literacy as factors of 'black' and 'white' communicative behavior", Linguistics 136 (1974): 91-115.

812 ---, "Grammar and discourse in vernacular Black English", Foundations of Language 13 (1975): 95-118.

813 ---, Boasting and Bragging: "Black and "White". Austin, Texas: Southwest Educational Development Laboratory 1979.

814 ---, Black and White Styles in Conflict. Chicago: UP 1981.

815 **Koessler, Maxime,** Les faux amis des vocabulaires anglais et américain. Nouv. ed. refondue et augm. Paris: Vuibert 1975.

816 **Kohn, Kurt,** "Schulische Aspekte des kanadischen Bilingualismus", Linguistische Berichte 78 (1982): 48-68.

817 **Kovac, Ceil,** "Children's acquisition of variable features." Ph.D. Georgetown U. 1980. DAI 42: 2, 687A.

818 **Krueger, John R.,** "Indiana limestone industry terms", AS 42 (1967): 289-96.

819 **Kruse, Vernon D.,** "The pronunciation of English in Kentucky, based on the records of the Linguistic Atlas of the North-Central States." Ph.D. Illinois Institute of Technology 1972. DAI 33: 8, 4388A.

820 **Krzeszowski, Tomasz P.,** An Outline of American English Phonetics. Warsaw: Państwowe Wydawnictwo Naukowe 1968.

821 **Kučera, Henry** and **W. Nelson Francis,** Computational Analysis of Present-Day American English. Providence: Brown UP 1967.

822 **Kulick, Susan Lynn,** "Does non-standard language dominance make a difference? Shibboleths and skirmishes: a study of the receptive competence of non-standard speakers of English in understanding the standard." Ph.D. New York U. 1981. DAI 42: 7, 3138A.

823 **Kurath, Hans,** "Some aspects of Atlantic seaboard English considered in their connection with British English", in Communications et Rapports du Premier Congrès International de Dialectologie Générale, Troisième Partie. Louvain: Centre International de Dialectologie Générale 1965: 236-40.

824 ---, A Word Geography of the Eastern United States. Ann Arbor: Michigan UP 1949, repr. 1966, 1970.

825 ---, "Contributions of British folk speech to American pronunciation", in Ellis 1968: 129-34.

826 ---, "The investigation of urban speech and some other problems confronting the student of American English", PADS 49 (1968): 1-7.

827 ---, "English sources of some American regional words and verb forms", AS 45 (1970): 60-68.

828 ---, "The sociocultural interpretation of dialect areas", in Roman Jakobson and Shigeo Kawamoto, eds., Studies in General and Oriental Linguistics, Presented to Shirô Hattori on the occasion of his sixtieth birthday. Tokyo: TEC Co. 1970: 374-7.

829 ---, Studies in Area Linguistics. Bloomington, London: Indiana UP 1972.

830 ---, "Relics of English folk speech in American English", in L. Davis 1972: 367-75.

831 ---, Handbook of the Linguistic Geography of New England, 2nd ed., with a new introduction, word-index, and inventory of LANE maps and commentary by Audrey R. Duckert, and a reverse index of LANE maps to worksheets by Raven I. McDavid, Jr. New York: AMS 1973.

832 --- et al., eds., Linguistic Atlas of New England. 1939, repr. New York: AMS 1972.

833 --- and **Raven I. McDavid, Jr.,** The Pronunciation of English in the Atlantic States. Based Upon the Collections of the Linguistic Atlas of the Eastern United States. Ann Arbor: Michigan UP 1961, repr. 1982.

834 ---, **Raven I. McDavid, Jr., Raymond K. O'Cain, George T. Dorrill** and **Sara L. Sanders,** "Preview: the Linguistic Atlas of the Middle and South Atlantic States", JEngL 13 (1979): 37-47.

835 **Kypriotaki, Lyn,** "A study in dialect: individual variation and dialect rules", in Bailey/Shuy 1973: 198-210.

836 **La Ban, Frank K.,** "A phonological study of the speech of the Conchs, early inhabitants of the Florida Keys, at three age levels." Ph.D. Louisiana State U. 1965. DAI 26: 6, 3318A.

837 ---, "From Cockney to Conch", in Williamson/Burke 1971: 301-8.

838 **Labov, Teresa,** "Social structure and peer terminology in a black adolescent gang", Language in Society 11 (1982): 391-411.

839 **Labov, William,** "Stages in the acquisition of Standard English", in Shuy 1965: 77-103.

840 ---, The Social Stratification of English in New York City. Washington, D.C.: Center for Applied Linguistics 1966, 3rd pr. 1982.

841 ---, "Hypercorrection by the lower middle class as a factor in linguistic change", in Bright 1966: 84-113.

842 ---, "Contraction, deletion and inherent variability of the English copula", Language 45 (1969): 715-62.

843 ---, The Study of Non-standard English. Champaign, Ill.: National Council of Teachers of English 1970.

844 ---, "The logic of Nonstandard English", in Alatis 1970: 1-43.

845 ---, "The reading of the -ed suffix", in Harry Levin and Joanna P. Williams, eds., Basic Studies on Reading, New York, London: Basic Books 1970: 222-45.

846 ---, "The study of language in its social context", in Fishman 1971: 152-216.

847 ---, "Variation in language", in Carroll E. Reed, ed., The Learning of Language. New York: Appleton-Century-Crofts 1971: 187-221.

848 ---, Language in the Inner City. Studies in the Black English Vernacular. Philadelphia: Pennsylvania UP 1972 / Oxford: Blackwell 1972.

849 ---, "Negative attraction and negative concord in English grammar", Language 48 (1972): 773-818.

850 ---, "The recent history of some dialect markers on the island of Martha's Vineyard", in L. Davis 1972: 81-122.

851 ---, "Rules for ritual insults", in Kochman 1972: 265-314.

852 ---, Sociolinguistic Patterns. Philadelphia: Pennsylvania UP 1972 / Oxford: Blackwell 1978.

853 ---, "Language characteristics: blacks", in Bentley/Crawford 1973: 96-116.

854 ---, "The linguistic consequences of being a lame", Language in Society 2 (1973): 81-115.

855 ---, "The place of linguistic research in American society", in Eric P. Hamp, ed., *Themes in Linguistics: The 1970s*. The Hague: Mouton 1973: 97-129.

856 ---, "Where do grammars stop?" in Shuy 1973: 43-88.

857 ---, "The quantitative study of linguistic structure", in K.-H. Dahlstedt, ed., *The Nordic Languages and Modern Linguistics*. Stockholm: Almqvist and Wiksell 1975: 188-244.

858 ---, *Sprache im sozialen Kontext*. 2 Bände. Kronberg/Ts.: Scriptor 1976.

859 ---, ed., *Locating Language in Time and Space*. New York *et al.*: Academic Press 1980.

860 ---, "The social origins of sound change", in Labov 1980: 251-65.

861 ---, "Is there a creole speech community?", in Albert Valdman and Arnold Highfield, eds., *Theoretical Orientations in Creole Studies*. New York: Academic Press 1980: 369-88.

862 ---, "Objectivity and commitment in linguistic science: the case of the Black English trial in Ann Arbor", *Language in Society* 11 (1982): 165-201.

863 ---, **Anne Bower, Donald Hindle, Elizabeth Dayton, Anthony Kroch, Matthew Lennig** and **Deborah Schiffrin,** *Social Determinants of Sound Change*. (Final Report to NSF on SOC75-00245). Philadelphia: U.S. Regional Survey 1980.

864 --- and **Paul Cohen,** "Systematic relations of standard and non-standard rules in the grammar of negro speakers", in DeStefano 1973: 149-60.

865 ---, ---, "Some suggestions for teaching Standard English to speakers of nonstandard urban dialects", in DeStefano 1973: 218-37.

866 ---, ---, **Clarence Robins** and **John Lewis,** *A Study of the Non-Standard English of Negro and Puerto Rican Speakers in New York City*. Cooperative Research Project No. 3288. Vol. I: *Phonological and Grammatical Analysis*. Vol. II: *The Use of Language in the Speech Community*. New York: Columbia U. 1968.

867 ---, **Clarence Robins, Paul Cohen** and **John Lewis,** "Classroom correction tests", in Dillard 1975: 313-30.

868 ---, **Malcah Yaeger** and **Richard Steiner,** *A Quantitative Study of Sound Change in Progress*. 2 vols. Philadelphia: U. of Pennsylvania 1972.

869 **Lacey, Pamela** and **Glenn Gilbert,** "The stratification of the diphthong /aɪ/ by social address in Jackson County, Ill.", in Cooley/Barnes/Dunn 1979: 453-61.

870 **Laferriere, Martha,** "A note on alternate rule ordering", Linguistic Inquiry 5 (1974): 628-31.

871 ---, "Boston short a: social variation as historical residue", in Fasold/Shuy 1977: 100-7.

872 ---, "Ethnicity in phonological variation and change", Language 55 (1979): 603-17.

873 ---, "Pragmatic features and phonological change", in Elizabeth Closs Traugott, Rebecca Labrum and Susan Shepherd, eds., Papers from the 4th International Conference on Historical Linguistics. Amsterdam: Benjamins 1980: 363-9.

874 **Laird, Charlton,** Language in America. New York: World Publishing Co. 1970 / Englewood Cliffs: Prentice Hall 1972.

875 **Lambert, Wallace E., Howard Giles** and **Gilbert J. Albert,** "Language attitudes in a rural community in Northern Maine", La monda lingvo-problemo 5 (1976): 129-44.

876 --- and **G. Richard Tucker,** "White and negro listeners' reactions to various American English dialects", Social Forces 47 (1969): 463-8.

877 **Lampe, Phil,** "Mexican American or Chicano", in Martha Cotera and Larry Hufford, eds., Bridging Two Cultures: Multidisciplinary Readings in Bilingual Bicultural Education. Austin: National Educational Laboratory 1980: 287-93.

878 **Lamy, Paul,** "Language and ethnicity: a study of bilingualism, ethnic identity, and ethnic attitudes." Ph.D. McMaster U. (Canada) 1976. DAI 38: 2, 1056A.

879 ---, "Bilingualism in Montreal: linguistic interference and communicational effectiveness", Papers in Linguistics 9 (1976): 1-14.

880 **Lance, Donald M.,** "Determining dialect boundaries in the United States by means of automatic cartography", in Putschke 1977: 289-303.

881 ---, "Spanish-English bilingualism in the American Southwest", in Mackey/Ornstein 1979: 247-64.

882 --- and **Daniel E. Gulstad,** eds., Papers from the 1976 Mid-America Linguistics Conference. Columbia: Linguistics Program, U. of Missouri 1978.

883 --- and **Stephen V. Slemons,** "The use of the computer in plotting the geographical distribution of dialect items", Computers and the Humanities 10 (1976): 221-9.

884 **Lane, Lea Bussey,** "Automotive terms in British and American English", AS 51 (1976): 285-91.

885 **Lanier, Dorothy Copeland,** "Black dialect: selected studies since 1865." Ed.D. East Texas State U. 1974. DAI 35: 5, 2945A.

886 ---, "Black dialect: grammar in fact and fiction", Publications of the Arkansas Philological Association 2,3 (1976): 50-55.

887 **Lanzinger, Klaus,** "Slave und Negro im amerikanischen Englisch vor dem Bürgerkrieg", Americana-Austriaca 1 (1966): 280-301.

888 **Lawendowski, Boguslaw** and **James Pankhurst,** British and American English. A Comparison of the Grammar and the Vocabulary. Warszawa: Panstwowe Wydawnictwo Naukowe 1975.

889 **Lawrence, Teleté Zorayda,** "Certain phonetic tendencies perceived in the idiolects of selected native Texans", in Bohuslav Hála, Milan Romportl and Premysl Janota, eds., Proceedings of the Sixth International Congress of Phonetic Sciences, Held at Prague, 7 - 13 September 1967. Prague: Academia 1970: 527-30.

890 ---, "Regional speech of Texas: A description of certain paralinguistic features", in Actes du Xe Congrès International des Linguistes, Bucarest, 28 août - 2 septembre 1967. Bucarest: Editions de l'Acad. de la République Socialiste de Roumanie 1970: 125-30.

891 **Lawson, Sarah,** "Immigrant in British and American usage", AS 45 (1970): 304-5.

892 **Leap, William L.,** "Language pluralism in a Southwestern pueblo: some comments on Isletan English", in Turner 1973: 275-93.

893 ---, "On grammaticality in native American English: the evidence from Isleta", Linguistics 128 (1974): 79-89.

894 ---, ed., Studies in Southwestern Indian English. San Antonio: Trinity U. 1977.

895 ---, "American Indian English and its implications for bilingual education", in Alatis 1978: 657-69.

896 ---, "Cleft and pseudo-cleft in Tewa English", in Barkin/Brandt 1980: 179-91.

897 ---, American Indian Language Education. Los Alamitos, Calif.: National Center for Bilingual Research 1981.

898 **Lebofsky, Dennis Stanley,** "The lexicon of the Philadelphia metropolitan area." Ph.D. Princeton U. 1970. DAI 31: 6, 2901A.

899 **Lecerf, Bernard,** "The nasalization of oral vowels followed by nasal consonants", in Léon/Martin 1979: 49-59.

900 **LeCompte, Nolan P., Jr.,** "A word atlas of LaFourche Parish and Grand Isle, Louisiana." Ph.D. Louisiana State U. 1967. DAI 28: 5, 1808A.

901 ---, "Certain points of dialectal usage in South Louisiana", Louisiana Studies 7 (1968): 149-58.

902 **Lee, Ann Morton,** "An annotated bibliography of Southern mountain speech." Thesis, East Tennessee State U. 1980.

903 **Lee, Lavance,** "The problem of Aframerican voice." Ph.D. Berkeley, California 1981. DAI 42: 10, 4438A.

904 **Lefebvre, Gilles-R.,** "Les aspects sociaux de la dualité linguistique au Canada", in O Simpósio de Sao Paulo, Janeiro de 1969: Atas. Sao Paulo: U. de Sao Paulo 1979: 153-71.

905 **Legum, Stanley E., Carol Pfaff, Gene Tinnie** and **Michael Nicholas,** The Speech of Young Black Children in Los Angeles. Inglewood, Ca.: Southwest Regional Laboratory 1971.

906 **Lehnert, Martin,** Die Sprache Shakespeares und das amerikanische Englisch. Berlin: Akademie-Verlag 1976.

907 **Lehtinen, Meri Kaisu Tuulikki,** "An analysis of a Finnish-English bilingual corpus." Ph.D. Indiana U. 1966. DAI 27: 12, 4224A.

908 **Leich, John Foster,** "Minority languages in contemporary Louisiana", La monda lingvo-problemo 6 (1977): 113-22.

909 **Leidner, David Raphael,** "An electromyographic and acoustic study of American English liquids." Ph.D. Connecticut 1974. DAI 34: 7, 4233A.

910 ---, "The articulation of American English /l/: a study of gestural synergy and antagonism", Journal of Phonetics 4 (1976): 327-35.

911 **Lencek, Rado L.,** "Linguistic research on language interference problems in the speech of Slavic communities in the United States", General Linguistics 16 (1976): 72-77.

912 **Léon, Pierre R.,** "Canadian English pronunciation: from the British to the American model", in Léon/Martin 1979: 1-7.

913 --- and **Philippe J. Martin,** eds., Toronto English: Studies in Phonetics. To Honour C.D. Rouillard. Ottawa: Didier 1979.

914 **Levin, Patricia Oppenheim,** "A psycholinguistic analysis of the miscues of learning disabled Black English speaking students and their relationship to readability." Ph.D. U. of Michigan 1981. DAI 42: 9, 3930A.

915 **Levine, Lewis** and **Harry J. Crockett, Jr.,** "Speech variation in a Piedmont community: postvocalic r", Sociological Inquiry 36 (1966): 204-26.

916 **Levitt, Jesse,** "Language conflict in Canada: the historical background and current developments", Geolinguistics 5 (1979): 33-46.

917 ---, "Thoughts and comments by the editor on Dr. Ashley's paper 'Bilingualism and the clash of cultures in the United States'", Geolinguistics 7 (1981): 49-58.

918 **Lewis, Brian A.,** "The phonology of the Glarus dialect in Green County, Wisconsin." Ph.D. U. of Wisconsin 1968. DAI 29: 12, 4474A.

919 **Lewis, J. Windsor,** A Concise Pronouncing Dictionary of British and American English. London: Oxford UP 1972.

920 **Li, Wen Lang,** "The language shift of Chinese Americans", International Journal of the Sociology of Language 38 (1982): 109-24.

921 **Liebe-Harkort, M.L.,** "Bilingualism and language mixing among the White Mountain Apaches", Folia Linguistica 13 (1979): 345-56.

922 ---, "A note on the English spoken by Apaches", International Journal of American Linguistics 49 (1983): 207-8.

923 **Lieberson, Stanley,** Language and Ethnic Relations in Canada. New York: Wiley 1970.

924 ---, "Bilingualism in Montreal: a demographic analysis", in S.L., Language Diversity and Language Contact. Essays. Selected and introduced by Anwar S. Dil. Stanford, Calif.: UP 1981: 131-57.

925 --- with **Timothy J. Curry,** "Language shift in the United States: some demographic clues", in S.L., Language Diversity and Language Contact. Essays. Selected and introduced by Anwar S. Dil. Stanford, Calif.: UP 1981: 158-72.

926 **Light, Richard L.,** "Syntactic structures in a corpus of nonstandard English." Ph.D. Georgetown U. 1969. DAI 30: 10, 4438A.

927 ---, "Social factors and speech variation: some observations in Albany, N.Y.", English Record 26 (1974): 15-25.

928 **Lighter, Jonathan Evan,** "The slang of the American Expeditionary Forces in Europe, 1917-1919: an historical glossary", AS 47 (1972): 5-142.

929 ---, "A historical dictionary of American slang. Vol. I. A." Ph.D. U. of Tennessee 1980. DAI 41: 10, 4400A.

930 ---, Historical Dictionary of American Slang. New York: Random House (forthcoming).

931 **Lindenfeld, Jacqueline,** "Pratiques langagières et bilinguisme des Chicanos de Californie", Etudes de Linguistique Appliquée 37 (1980): 118-24.

932 **Linn, Michael D.,** "Semantic change through dialect fusion", AS 58 (1983): 3-12.

933 **Lipski, John M.,** "Orthographic variation and linguistic nationalism", La mondo lingvo-problemo 6 (1976): 37-48.

934 **Little, Bert,** "Prison lingo: a style of American English slang", Anthropological Linguistics 24 (1982): 206-44.

935 **Lodge, David,** "Where it's at: California language", in Ricks 1980: 503-13.

936 **Loflin, Marvin D.,** "A note on the deep structure of nonstandard English in Washington, D.C.", Glossa 1 (1967): 26-32.

937 ---, "Negro Nonstandard and Standard English: same or different deep structure?", Orbis 18 (1969): 74-91.

938 ---, "On the passive in Nonstandard Negro English", Journal of English as a Second Language 4 (1969): 19-23.

939 ---, "On the structure of the verb in a dialect of American negro English", Linguistics 59 (1970): 14-28.

940 ---, "Black American English: independent motivation for the auxiliary hypothesis", in Luelsdorff 1975: 45-62.

941 ---, "Black American English and syntactic dialectology", in Dillard 1975: 65-73.

942 ---, "Black English deep structure", in Jessica R. Wirth, ed., Assessing Linguistic Arguments. Washington, D.C.: Hemisphere Publishing Corporation 1976: 249-73.

943 --- and **Thomas Guyette,** "The impact of education on dialect change", Linguistics 173 (1976): 49-62.

944 ---, **Nicholas J. Sobin** and **Joey L. Dillard,** "Auxiliary structures and time adverbs in Black American English", AS 48 (1973): 22-28.

945 **Loman, Bengt,** Conversations in a Negro American Dialect. Washington, D.C.: Center for Applied Linguistics 1967.

946 ---, "Prosodic patterns in a negro American dialect", in Hakan Ringbom et al., eds., Style and Text: Studies Presented to Nils Erik Enkvist. Stockholm: Sprakförlaget Skriptor 1975: 219-42.

947 **Lourie, Margaret A.,** "Black English Vernacular: a comparative description", in Lourie/Conklin 1978: 78-93.

948 --- and **Nancy Fares Conklin,** eds., A Pluralistic Nation: The Language Issue in the United States. Rowley, Mass.: Newbury House 1978.

949 **Love, Tracey,** "An examination of eh as question particle." B.A. Thesis, U. of Alberta 1973.

950 **Lubbers, Klaus,** "The development of '-ster' in modern British and American English", English Studies 46 (1965): 449-70.

951 **Luelsdorff, Philip A.,** "A segmental phonology of Black English." Ph.D. Georgetown U. 1971. DAI 33: 2, 742A. Published: The Hague, Paris: Mouton 1975.

952 ---, ed., Linguistic Perspectives on Black English. Regensburg: Carl 1975.

953 ---, "Some principal rules of Black English phonology", in Luelsdorff 1975: 63-82.

954 **Lusk, Melanie M.,** "Phonological variation in Kansas City: A sociolinguistic analysis of three-generation families." Ph.D. U. of Kansas 1976. DAI 38: 2, 764A.

955 ---, "Phonological variation in Kansas City: further evidence of interurban diffusion", in Ingemann 1977: 205-13.

956 **Lytal, Billy Dewayne,** "An analysis of the language of selected University students in Mississippi using cloze and other measures." Ph.D. U. of Southern Mississippi 1980. DAI 41: 11, 4628A.

957 **Ma, Roxana** and **Eleanor Herasimchuk,** "The linguistic dimensions of a bilingual neighbourhood", in Fishman/Cooper/Ma 1971: 347-464.

958 **Macias, Reynaldo Flores,** "Mexicano/Chicano sociolinguistic behavior and language policy in the United States." Ph.D. Georgetown U. 1979. DAI 40: 8, 4573A.

959 **Mackey, William Francis** and **Jacob Ornstein,** eds., Sociolinguistic Studies in Language Contact. Methods and Cases. The Hague: Mouton 1979.

960 **Mader, Diane C.,** "Black power and ego-defensiveness: a study in the rhetoric of despair", ETC 38 (1981): 167-80.

961 **Major, Clarence,** ed., Black Slang. A Dictionary of Afro-American Talk. New York: Intern. Publishers 1970 / London, Henley: Routledge and Kegan Paul 1971.

962 **Malécot, André,** "The force of articulation of American stops and fricatives as a function of position", Phonetica 18 (1968): 95-102.

963 --- and **Paul Lloyd,** "The /t/:/d/ distinction in American alveolar flaps", Lingua 19 (1968): 264-72.

964 **Malmstrom, Jean,** "Dialects - updated", in Bentley/Crawford 1973: 13-22.

965 **Marckwardt, Albert H.,** "General educational aims of native language teaching and learning", in Sebeok 1973: 206-27.

966 ---, American English (1958), revised by J.L. Dillard. New York: Oxford UP 1980.

967 **Markel, Norman N.** and **Clair Ann Sharpless,** "Socio-economic and ethnic correlates of dialect differences", in M.E. Smith 1972: 313-23.

968 **Marlos, Litsa** and **Ana Celia Zentella,** "A quantified analysis of code switching by four Philadelphia Puerto Rican adolescents", Pennsylvania Review of Linguistics 3 (1978): 46-57.

969 **Marshall, Helaine Weiss,** "The colloquial preterit versus the present perfect: a sociolinguistic analysis." Ph.D. Columbia U. 1979. DAI 40: 5, 2638A.

970 **Marshall, Howard W.** and **John M. Vlach,** "Toward a folklife approach to American Dialects", AS 48 (1973): 163-91.

971 **Marshall, Margaret M.,** "Bilingualism in southern Louisiana: a sociolinguistic analysis", Anthropological Linguistics 24 (1982): 308-24.

972 **Martin, Elizabeth Kathryn,** "Lexicon of the Texas oil fields." Ph.D. East Texas State U. 1969. DAI 30: 3, 2514A.

973 **Martin, Philippe,** "Toronto English - intonation of the declarative sentence", in Léon/Martin 1979: 143-57.

974 **Marwit, Samuel J., Elaine F. Walker** and **Karen L. Marwit,** "Reliability of standard English differences among black and white children at second, fourth, and seventh grades", Child Development 48 (1977): 1739-42.

975 **Mathews, Mitford M.,** Americanisms. A Dictionary of Selected Americanisms on Historical Principles. Chicago: UP 1966.

976 **Mathiot, Madeleine,** "The current state of sociolinguistics in the United States", in Samir K. Ghosh, ed., Man, Language and Society: Contributions to the Sociology of Language. The Hague: Mouton 1972: 169-78.

977 **Matluck, Joseph H.,** "Bilingualism of Mexican-American children: language characteristics", in Blansitt/Teschner 1980: 211-28.

978 **Matthews, Horace,** "Attitudes and classroom behaviors of Virginia middle school English teachers regarding Black English and certain other usages." Ed.D. U. of Virginia 1980. DAI 41: 9, 3861A.

979 **Matzkó, László,** "Some thoughts on dialect mapping in the United States", Hungarian Studies in English 10 (1976): 95-97.

980 **Maurer, David W.,** "The argot of narcotics addicts", in David W. Maurer and Victor H. Vogel, Narcotics and Narcotic Addiction. Springfield, Ill.: Charles C. Thomas 1967: 318-46.

981 —, Kentucky Moonshine. Lexington: Kentucky UP 1974.

982 —, The American Confidence Man. Springfield, Ill.: Charles C. Thomas 1974.

983 —, The Language of the Underworld. Ed. Allan W. Futrell and Charles B. Wordell. Lexington: Kentucky UP 1981.

984 — and **Allan W. Futrell,** "Criminal monickers", AS 57 (1982): 243-55.

985 **Maurer, Jay Kerlee,** "A comparison of language performance by English monolinguals and English-Spanish bilinguals in northern New Mexico." Ph.D. Columbia U. 1979. DAI 42: 9, 3984A.

986 **Maynor, Natalie,** "Grammatical judgements in LANE", AS 57 (1982): 228-31.

987 ---, "Changing speech habits in Mississippi", Mississippi Folklore Register 16,2 (1982): 17-23.

988 **Mays, Luberta,** "A case for Black English", in Charlotte B. Windsor, ed., Dimensions of Language Experience. New York: Agathon 1975: 65-67.

989 **McAlonan, John P.,** "The influence of French on Louisiana legal jargon", Southern Studies 19 (1980): 291-309.

990 **McCardle, Peggy Diana,** "Spelling ability as a reflection of underlying phonological representation in child speakers of Black English vernacular." Ph.D. Pennsylvania State U. 1980. DAI 41: 9, 4018A.

991 ---, "The deep structure of indirect questions in Vernacular Black English: its relation to language acquisition", The SECOL Review 6,1 (1981): 25-34.

992 **McCauley, Rebecca Joan,** "The discrimination of American English vowels." Ph.D. U. of Chicago 1981. DAI 42: 6, 2580B.

993 **McClure, Erica,** "Aspects of code-switching in the discourse of bilingual Mexican-American children", in Muriel Saville-Troike, ed., Linguistics and Anthropology. Washington, D.C.: Georgetown UP 1977: 93-115.

994 --- and **Jim Wentz,** "Code-switching in children's narratives", in Ingemann 1976: 338-50.

995 **McConnell, R.E.,** Our Own Voice: Canadian English and How It Is Studied. Toronto: Gage 1979.

996 **McCormack, William** and **Stephen A. Wurm,** eds., Language and Society. Anthropological Issues. The Hague: Mouton 1979.

997 **McCready, Michael Andrew,** "The effects of phonemic-graphemic correspondence problems upon reading comprehension of black nonstandard speakers of English." Ph.D. U. of Alabama 1972. DAI 33: 10, 5604A.

998 **McCullough, Michele Page,** "Teachers' knowledge of and attitudes towards Black English and correction of dialect-related reading miscues." Ph.D. U. of Michigan 1981. DAI 42: 9, 3984A.

999 **McDavid, Raven I., Jr.,** "American social dialects", College English 26 (1965): 254-60.

1000 ---, "The cultural matrix of American English", Elementary English 43 (1965): 13-21, 41.

1001 ---, "The cultural matrix of our language", in Wallace Stegner, Edwin Sauer and Clarence Hach, eds., Modern Composition: Book Six. New York: Holt, Rinehart and Winston 1965: 3-38.

1002 ---, "Sense and nonsense about American dialects", Publications of the Modern Language Association 81 (1966): 7-17.

1003 ---, "Dialect differences and social differences in an urban society", in Bright 1966: 72-83.

1004 ---, "The talk of the Middle West", Inland 52 (1966): 12-17.

1005 ---, "Dialect study and English education", in David Stryker, ed., New Trends in English Education. Champaign, Ill.: NCTE 1966: 43-52.

1006 ---, "A checklist of significant features for discriminating social dialects", in Eldonna L. Evertts, ed., Dimensions of Dialect. Champaign, Ill.: National Council of Teachers of English 1967: 7-10.

1007 ---, "Needed research in southern dialects", in Edgar T. Thompson, ed., Perspectives on the South: Agenda for Research. Durham, N.C.: Duke UP 1967: 113-24.

1008 ---, "System and variety in American English", in Alexander Frazier, ed., New Directions in American English. Champaign, Ill.: NCTE 1967: 125-39.

1009 ---, "Historical, regional, and social variation", JEngL 1 (1967): 25-40.

1010 ---, "Each in his own idiom", Indiana English 1,2 (1967): 1-8.

1011 ---, "Variations in Standard American English", Elementary English 45 (1968): 561-4, 608.

1012 ---, "Two studies of dialects of English", in Ellis 1968: 23-45.

1013 ---, "Social dialects and professional responsibility", College English 30 (1968-69): 381-5.

1014 ---, "Dialects: British and American Standard and Nonstandard", in Archibald A. Hill, ed., Linguistics Today. New York, London: Basic Books 1969: 79-88.

1015 ---, "Systematic features with social significance in North American English", in Actes du Xe Congrès International des Linguistes, Bucarest 28 août - 2 septembre 1967. I. Bucarest: Éditions de l'Acad. de la République Socialiste de Roumanie 1969: 635-8.

1016 ---, "The uniformity of American English", in Wallace Stegner, Edwin

Sauer and Clarence Hach, Modern Composition: Book Six. Revised ed. New York: Holt, Rinehart and Winston 1969: 397-405.

1017 ---, "The language of the city", Midcontinent American Studies Journal 10 (1969): 48-59.

1018 ---, "Social variety in American English", English Record 19 (1969): 32-47.

1019 ---, "Changing patterns of southern dialect", in Arthur Bronstein et al., eds., Essays in Honor of Claude M. Wise. Hannibal, Mo.: Standard Printing Co. 1970: 206-28.

1020 ---, "The sociology of language", in Albert H. Marckwardt, ed., Linguistics in School Programs. Chicago: National Society for the Study of Education Yearbook 1970: 65-108.

1021 ---, "Native whites", in Thomas D. Worn, ed., Reading for the Disadvantaged: Problems of Linguistically Different Learners. New York: Harcourt, Brace and World 1970: 135-9.

1022 ---, "A theory of dialect", in Alatis 1970: 45-62.

1023 ---, "The urbanization of American English", Jahrbuch für Amerikastudien 16 (1971): 47-59.

1024 ---, "Planning the grid", AS 46 (1971): 9-26.

1025 ---, "What happens in Tennessee", in Burghardt 1971: 119-29.

1026 ---, "English language: American dialects", in Lee C. Deighton et al., eds., The Encyclopedia of Education. Vol. 3. New York: Macmillan 1971: 373-81.

1027 ---, "Some notes on Acadian English", in A.L. Davis 1972: 184-7.

1028 ---, "Carry you home once more", Neuphilologische Mitteilungen 73 (1972): 192-5.

1029 ---, "The English language in the United States", in Sebeok 1973: 5-39.

1030 ---, "American social dialects", Indiana English Journal 7,4 (1973): 1-8.

1031 ---, "Go slow in ethnic attributions: geographic mobility and dialect prejudices", in Bailey/Robinson 1973: 258-70.

1032 ---, "The folk vocabulary of Eastern Kentucky", in Scholler/Reidy 1973: 147-64.

1033 ---, "New Directions in American Dialectology", Studia Anglica Posnaniensia 5 (1974 [for 1973]): 9-25.

1034 ---, "The urbanization of American English", Philologica Pragensia 18 (1975): 228-38.

1035 ---, "Notes on the pronunciation of Ohio", Names 23 (1975): 147-52.

1036 ---, "Linguistic Atlas of the North-Central States. Basic materials (Unaltered field records)", Orbis 25 (1976): 20-21.

1037 ---, "In memoriam: Albert H. Marckwardt (1903-1975) and the Linguistic Atlas of the North-Central States. A memorial", Orbis 25 (1976): 176-86.

1038 ---, "Notes on the pronunciation of American", AS 52 (1977): 98-104.

1039 ---, "The gathering and presentation of data", JEngL 12 (1978): 29-37.

1040 ---, Dialects in Culture. Essays in General Dialectology by Raven I. McDavid, Jr. Ed. by W. Kretzschmar. University, Ala.: Alabama UP 1979.

1041 ---, "American English: a bibliographic essay", American Studies International 17,2 (1979): 3-45.

1042 ---, "Social differences in white speech", in McCormack/Wurm 1979: 249-61.

1043 ---, "Linguistic and cultural pluralism: an American tradition", in Marta Sienicka, ed., Proceedings of a Symposium on American Literature. Poznan: Adam Mickiewicz U. 1979: 225-40.

1044 ---, "The Linguistic Atlas of the North-Central States - a work of salvage dialectology", Philologica Pragensia 22 (1979): 98-101.

1045 ---, Varieties of American English. Essays. Selected and introduced by Anwar Dil. Stanford: Stanford UP 1980.

1046 ---, "Linguistic geography", CEA Critic 42,3 (1980): 17-23.

1047 ---, "H.L. Mencken and the Linguistic Atlas project", Menckeniana 73 (1980): 7-9.

1048 ---, "Low-back vowels in Providence: a note in structural dialectology", JEngL 15 (1981): 21-29.

1049 ---, "Webster, Mencken, and Avis: spokesmen for linguistic autonomy", Canadian Journal of Linguistics 26 (1981): 118-25.

1050 ---, "The study of folk speech: opportunities in the Gulf States", Mississippi Folklore Register 16,2 (1982): 3-16.

1051 ---, "Retrospect", JEngL 16 (1983): 47-54.

1052 ---, "Sociolinguistics and historical linguistics", in Michael Davenport, Erik Hansen and Hans Frede Nielsen, eds., Current Topics in English Historical Linguistics. Proceedings of the Second International Conference on English Historical Linguistics Held at Odense University, 13 -15 April 1981. Odense: UP 1983: 55-66.

1053 --- and **William M. Austin,** Communication Barriers to the Culturally Deprived. Cooperative Research Project 2107. Office of Education, U.S. Department of Health, Education, and Welfare 1966.

1054 --- and **Alva L. Davis,** "The Linguistic Atlas of the Middle and South Atlantic States: an editorial comment", Orbis 22 (1973): 331-4.

1055 --- and **Lawrence M. Davis,** "The dialects of negro Americans", in M.E. Smith 1972: 303-12.

1056 --- and **Audrey R. Duckert,** eds., Lexicography in English. New York: New York Academy of Sciences 1973.

1057 --- and **Lawrence E. Fisher,** "Aphaeresis in New England", AS 48 (1973): 246-9.

1058 --- and **Virginia McDavid,** "The late unpleasantness: folk names for the Civil War", Southern Speech Journal 34 (1969): 194-204.

1059 ---, ---, "The folk vocabulary of Eastern Kentucky", in Scholler/Reidy 1973: 147-64.

1060 ---, ---, "Intuitive rules and factual evidence: /-sp, -st, -sk/- plus {z}", in Mohammad Ali Jazayery, Edgar C. Polomé and Werner Winter, eds., Linguistics and Literary Studies In Honor of Archibald A. Hill. II: Descriptive Linguistics. The Hague, Paris, New York: Mouton 1978: 73-90.

1061 --- and **Raymond K. O'Cain,** "Sociolinguistics and linguistic geography", Kansas Journal of Sociology 9 (1973): 137-56.

1062 ---, ---, "Southern standards revisited", in Shores/Hines 1977: 229-32.

1063 ---, ---, "From fieldworker to data retrieval: some questions", in Putschke 1977: 11-24.

1064 ---, ---, "Prejudice and pride: linguistic acceptability in South Carolina", in Sidney Greenbaum, ed., Acceptability in Language. The Hague: Mouton 1977: 103-32.

1065 ---, ---, "'Existential' *there* and *it*: an essay on method and interpretation of data", in Raymond/Russell 1977: 29-40.

1066 ---, ---, "*Louisiana* and *New Orleans*: notes on the pronunciation of proper names", *Mississippi Folklore Register* 11 (1977): 76-92.

1067 ---, ---, "Some notes on *Maryland* and *Baltimore*", *AS* 55 (1980): 278-87.

1068 ---, ---, and **Linda L. Barnes,** "Subjective appraisal of phonological variants", in Sidney Greenbaum, Geoffrey Leech and Jan Svartvik, eds., *Studies in English Linguistics: For Randolph Quirk*. New York: Longman 1980: 264-70.

1069 ---, ---, and **George T. Dorrill,** "The Linguistic Atlas of the Middle and South Atlantic States", *Special Library Association Geography and Map Division. Bulletin* 113 (1978): 17-23.

1070 ---, ---, *et al.*, *Linguistic Atlas of the Middle and South Atlantic States*. 2 fascicles. Chicago, London: Chicago UP 1980.

1071 --- and **Richard C. Payne,** eds., with the assistance of Duane Taylor and Evan Thomas, *Linguistic Atlas of the North-Central States. Basic Materials (Unaltered Field Records)*. (Microfilm) Chicago: U. of Chicago 1976.

1072 --- and **Sarah Ann Witham,** "Poor whites and rustics", *Names* 22 (1974): 93-103.

1073 **McDavid, Virginia Glenn,** "More on *ain't*", *College English* 26 (1965): 104-5.

1074 ---, "The social distribution of selected verb forms in the Linguistic Atlas of the North Central States", in Raymond/Russel 1977: 41-50.

1075 ---, "Some observations on the pronunciation of *Chicago* and *Illinois*", *Mississippi Folklore Register* 11 (1977): 93-100.

1076 **McDonald, Richard R.** and **Walburga von Raffler-Engel,** "A semantic analysis of some religious terms of a snake-handling sect in Appalachia", in Reza Ordoubadian and Walburga von Raffler-Engel, eds., *Views on Language*. Murfreesboro, Tenn.: Inter-U. Pub. 1975: 182-91.

1077 **McDowell, John** and **Susan McRae,** "Differential response of the class and ethnic components of the Austin speech community to marked phonological variables", *Anthropological Linguistics* 14 (1972): 228-39.

1078 **McGreevey, John,** "Breathitt County, Kentucky, grammar." Ph.D. Illinois Institute of Technology 1977. DAI 38: 9, 5437A.

1079 **McIntyre, Terry L.,** "The language of railroading", AS 44 (1969): 243-62.

1080 **McKay, Jane Rumery,** "A partial analysis of a variety of Nonstandard Negro English." Ph.D. Berkeley, California 1969. DAI 30: 10, 4967A.

1081 **McMenamin, Jerry,** "Rapid code switching among Chicano bilinguals", Orbis 22 (1973): 373-87.

1082 **McMillan, James B.,** "Southern speech", in Louis D. Rubin, ed., A Bibliographical Guide to the Study of Southern Literature. Baton Rouge, La.: Louisiana State U. 1969: 128-34.

1083 ---, "The study of regional and social variety in American English", in Virginia McDavid, ed., Language and Teaching: Essays in Honor of Wilbur W. Hatfield. Chicago: Chicago State College 1969: 47-54.

1084 ---, Annotated Bibliography of Southern American English. Coral Gables, Florida: Miami UP 1971.

1085 ---, "The naming of American dialects", in Shores/Hines 1977: 119-24.

1086 ---, "American lexicology, 1942 - 1973", AS 53 (1978): 141-63.

1087 **McRae, Kenneth,** "Political dynamics of bilingualism and biculturalism: lessons from the Royal Commission Reports", in Ornstein-Galicia/St. Clair 1980: 215-38.

1088 **Meierhoffer-Longoria, Lynn Vaulx,** "A sociolinguistic study of language use and language proficiency in South Texas." Ed.D. Texas A & I U. 1978. DAI 40: 8, 4574A.

1089 **Meisel, Jürgen,** "Political styles and language-use in Canada", in Les états multilingues: problèmes et solutions / Multilingual political systems: problems and solutions. Presentation: Jean-Guy Savard and Richard Vigneault. Québec: Presses de l'Univ. Laval 1975: 317-65.

1090 **Melendez, Mildred Gonzales,** "Phonological variation in the English speech of northern New Mexico bilinguals." Ph.D. Indiana U. of Pennsylvania 1982. DAI 43: 10, 3308A.

1091 **Melmed, Paul Jay,** Black English Phonology: The Question of Reading Interference. Berkeley: U. of California 1971.

1092 **Metcalf, Allan A.,** Riverside English. The Spoken Language of a Southern California Community. Riverside: U. of California 1971.

1093 ---, "Directions of change in southern California English", JEngL 6 (1972): 28-34.

1094 ---, "Mexican-American English in Southern California", Western Review 9 (1972): 13-21.

1095 ---, "The study of California Chicano English", Linguistics 128 (1974): 53-58.

1096 ---, "The study (or, nonstudy) of California Chicano English", in Bills 1974.

1097 ---, Chicano English. Arlington, Va.: Center for Applied Linguistics 1979.

1098 **Meyers, Walter E.,** "Can (and should) Standard American English be defined?" in Shores/Hines 1977: 219-24.

1099 **Meyerstein, Goldie Piroch,** "Bilingualism among American Slovaks: analysis of loans", PADS 46 (1966): 1-19.

1100 **Michaelis, William Jackson,** "Black American vernacular vocabulary: cultural insights and educational application." Ph.D. Berkeley, California 1980. DAI 41: 7, 2985A.

1101 **Michaels, Leonard** and **Christopher Ricks,** eds., The State of the Language. Berkeley: California UP 1980.

1102 **Migus, Paul M.,** ed., Sounds Canadian. Languages and Cultures in Multi-Ethnic Society. Toronto: Martin 1975.

1103 **Miles, Celia Hooper,** "Selected verb features in Haywood County, North Carolina: a generational study." Ph.D. Indiana U. 1980. DAI 41: 5, 2089A.

1104 **Miller, Joy L.,** "Be. Finite and absence. Features of speech - black and white?" Orbis 21 (1972): 22-27.

1105 **Miller, Mary Rita,** "Attestations of American Indian Pidgin English in fiction and nonfiction", AS 42 (1967): 142-7.

1106 ---, "Comptence in English-language learning by American Indian monolinguals and bilinguals", in William C. McCormack and Stephen A. Wurm, eds., Language and Man. Anthropological Issues. The Hague: Mouton 1976: 165-76.

1107 ---, Children of the Salt River: First and Second Language Acquisition among Pima Children. Bloomington: Indiana U. Research Center for Language and Semiotic Studies 1977.

1108 **Miller, Michael I.,** "Inflectional morphology in Augusta, Georgia: A sociolinguistic description." Ph.D. U. of Chicago 1978.

1109 **Miller, Patricia D.,** "On the writer/rider distinction: a brief experimental study", Ohio State University Working Papers in Linguistics 17 (1974): 180-97.

1110 **Miller, Peggy J.,** Amy, Wendy, and Beth: Learning Language in South Baltimore. Austin: Texas UP 1982.

1111 **Miller, Tracey R.,** "An investigation of the regional English of Unicoi County, Tennessee." Ph.D. U. of Tennessee 1973. DAI 34: 8, 5147A.

1112 **Miller, Wick R.,** "Multilingualism in its social context in aboriginal North America", in Jeri J. Jaeger et al., eds., Proceedings of the Fourth Annual Meeting of the Berkeley Linguistics Society. Berkeley, Calif.: Berkeley Linguistics Society, U. of California 1978: 610-6.

1113 **Mills, Carl,** "The sociolinguistics of the [a] - [ɒ] merger in Pacific Northwest English: a subjective reaction test", Papers in Linguistics 13 (1980): 345-88.

1114 **Minderhout, David,** "Final consonant cluster reduction", Georgetown University Working Papers on Languages and Linguistics 5 (1975): 8-15.

1115 **Minderhout, Mary Alice W.** and **David J. Minderhout,** The Speech of Fourth Graders in Fifteen Central Pennsylvania Schools: Phonological and Grammatical Variables. Bloomsburg, Pa.: Central Columbia School District 1973.

1116 **Miranda, Thomas Z.,** "The case for bilingual education: a response to the critics", Geolinguistics 7 (1981): 15-22.

1117 **Mitchell, Henry H.,** "Black English", in A.L. Smith 1972: 87-97.

1118 **Mitchell, Jacquelyn,** "Strategies for achieving one-upsmanship: a descriptive analysis of Afro-American siblings in two speech events." Ed.D. Harvard U. 1973. DAI 40: 12, 6258A.

1119 **Mitchell [-Kernan], Claudia I.,** "Language behavior in a black urban community." Ph.D. Berkeley, California 1969.

1120 ---, "Signifying, loud-talking, and marking", in Kochman 1972: 315-35.

1121 ---, "Signifying and marking: two Afro-American speech acts", in John J. Gumperz and Dell Hymes, eds., Directions in Sociolinguistics. The Ethnography of Communication. New York: Holt, Rinehart and Winston 1972: 161-79.

1122 ---, "On the status of Black English for native speakers: an assessment of attitudes and values", in Cazden/John/Hymes 1972: 195-210.

1123 **Mohan, Bernard A.,** "Sociolinguistics and context-dependence", in Luelsdorff 1975: 91-106.

1124 **Moll, Dianne-Lynn,** "A comparative study of the English language proficiency of monolingual and bilingual children." Ph.D. Pittsburgh 1978. DAI 40: 2, 829A.

1125 **Monshi-Tousi, Mohammad, Azar Hosseine-Fatemi** and **John W. Oller, Jr.,** "English proficiency and factors in its attainment: a case study of Iranians in the United States", TESOL Quarterly 14 (1980): 365-72.

1126 **Montgomery, Michael Bryant,** "Left dislocation: its nature in Appalachian English", The SECOL Bulletin: Southeastern Conference on Linguistics 2,2 (1978): 55-61.

1127 ---, "A discourse analysis of expository Appalachian English." Ph.D. U. of Florida 1979. DAI 40: 9, 5036A.

1128 ---, "The discourse organization of explanatory Appalachian speech", in Cooley/Barnes/ Dunn 1979: 293-302.

1129 ---, "Inchoative verbs in East Tennessee English", The SECOL Bulletin: Southeastern Conference on Linguistics 4 (1980): 77-85.

1130 **Moore, Barbara Joan Reeves,** "A sociolinguistic longitudinal study (1969-1979) of a Texas German community, including curricular recommendations." Ph.D. Austin 1980. DAI 41: 4, 1571A.

1131 **Moore, Mary Jo,** "A preliminary bibliography of American English dialects", ERIC 1969.

1132 **Morell, Richard Charles,** "The ability to match Black English and Standard English sentences with the appropriate social situation among good and poor readers who are Black English speakers at grades four, six, and eight." Ed.D. Columbia U. Teachers College 1982. DAI 43: 2, 437A.

1133 **Morgan, Lucia C.,** "North Carolina accents", Southern Speech Journal 34 (1969): 223-9.

1134 ---, "The status of /r/ among North Carolina speakers", in Arthur J. Bronstein, Claude L. Shaver and C. Stevens, eds., Essays in Honor of Claude M. Wise. New York: Speech Association of America 1970: 167-86.

1135 **Morse, J. Mitchell,** "The shuffling speech of slavery: Black English", College English 34 (1973): 834-43.

1136 **Moseley, Ann,** "The opposite of black: names for white Americans", in

Fred Tarpley and Ann Moseley, eds., Of Edsels and Marauders. Commerce, Texas: Names Institute Press 1971: 33-39.

1137 **Moses, Rae A., Harvey A. Daniels** and **Robert A. Gundlach,** "Teachers' language attitudes and bidialectalism", Linguistics 175 (1976): 77-91.

1138 **Moss, Norman,** What's the Difference? An American-British, British-American Dictionary. New York: Harper and Row 1973.

1139 **Mougeon, Raymond,** "Malbay: a sociolinguistic community study." Ph.D. McGill U. (Canada) 1973. DAI 34: 9, 5947A.

1140 ---, "Bilingualism and language maintenance in the Gaspe Peninsula, Quebec, Canada", Anthropological Linguistics 18 (1976): 53-70.

1141 **Moulton, William G.,** "The sounds of Black English", in Harrison/ Trabasso 1976: 149-70.

1142 ---, "Unity and diversity in the phonology of Standard American English", in Henriette Walter, ed., Phonologie et société. Montreal: Didier 1977: 113-27.

1143 **Muehl, Siegmar** and **Lois B. Muehl,** "Comparison of differences in dialect speech among black college students grouped by Standard English test performance", Language and Speech 19 (1976): 28-40.

1144 **Mufwene, Salikoko S.,** Some Observations on the Verb in Black English Vernacular. Austin: U. of Texas, Center for African and Afro-American Studies and Research 1983.

1145 **Mundell, Gordon H.,** "A history of American dialectology." Ph.D. Rochester 1973. DAI 34: 5, 2598A.

1146 **Murdoch, Margaret M.,** "Visual-aural prompting in the Vancouver Survey questionnaire", in Warkentyne 1981: 48-56.

1147 **Murray, Brenda,** "G-deletion in Canadian dialects of English", Calgary Working Papers in Linguistics 1,1 (1975): 39-43.

1148 **Murray, Thomas Edward,** "Speaking with style: language variation in graduate students." Ph.D. Indiana U. 1982. DAI 43: 8, 2653A.

1149 **Myers, Muriel,** "Phonological innovations of bilingual Samoans in San Francisco", Anthropological Linguistics 23 (1981): 113-34.

1150 **Nakatani, Lloyd H., Kathleen D. O'Connor** and **Carletta H. Aston,** "Prosodic aspects of an American English speech rhythm", Phonetica 38 (1981): 84-105.

1151 **Natalicio, Eleanor Diana Siedhoff,** "Formation of the plural in English: a study of native speakers of English and native speakers of Spanish." Ph.D. Austin 1969. DAI 30: 7, 2993A.

1152 **Naughton, Jane,** "Final stop consonant release", in Léon/Martin 1979: 89-95.

1153 **Needler, Geoffrey D.,** "On the origin of New York City's pathognomic diphthong: a new hypothesis", Speech Monographs 35 (1968): 462-9.

1154 ---, "Kings English: facts and folklore of Brooklyn speech", in Rita Seiden Miller, ed., Brooklyn USA: The Fourth Largest City in America. New York: Brooklyn Coll. P. 1979: 173-85.

1155 **Nekrassoff, Vladimir,** "The trickcyclist: Ein Glossar der Sprache der amerikanischen und kanadischen Rauschgiftsüchtigen", Lebende Sprachen 19 (1974): 161-70.

1156 **Neu, Helene,** "Ranking of constraints on /t,d/ deletion in American English: a statistical analysis", in Labov 1980: 37-54.

1157 **Nicholas, Karl,** "Standard American English: written or spoken", in Reza Ordoubadian and Walburga von Raffler-Engel, eds., Views on Language. Murfreesboro, Tenn.: Inter-U. Pub. 1975: 122-6.

1158 **Nichols, Patricia Causey,** "Linguistic change in Gullah: sex, age, and mobility", Ph.D. Stanford U. 1976. DAI 37: 5, 2834A.

1159 ---, "Black women in the rural South: conservative and innovative", International Journal of the Sociology of Language 17 (1978): 45-54.

1160 ---, "Women in their speech communities", in Sally McConnell-Ginet, Ruth Borker and Nelly Furman, eds., Women and Language in Literature and Society. New York: Praeger 1980: 140-9.

1161 ---, "Variation among Gullah speakers in rural South Carolina: implications for education", in Roger W. Shuy and Anna Shnukal, eds., Languages and the Uses of Language. Washington, D.C.: Georgetown UP 1980: 205-13.

1162 **Nishihara, Tadayoshi,** "A phonemic study of the obscure weak vowel in General American made on statistical level", Studies in English Literature and Language 25 (1975): 19-27.

1163 **Nist, John,** Handicapped English. The Language of the Socially Disadvantaged. Springfield, Ill.: Charles C. Thomas 1974.

1164 **Nix, Ruth Aleman,** "Linguistic variation in the speech of Wilmington, North Carolina." Ph.D. Duke U. 1980. DAI 42: 1, 277A.

1165 **Nobbelin, Kent G.,** "The low-back vowels of the North-Central states." Ph.D. Illinois Institute of Technology 1980. DAI 41: 5, 2089A.

1166 **Nober, E. Harris** and **Harry N. Seymour,** "Speaker intelligibility of black and white school children for black and white adult listeners under varying listening conditions", Language and Speech 22 (1979): 237-42.

1167 **Nodal, R.,** A Bibliography, with some Annotations, on the Creole Languages of the Caribbean, Including a Special Supplement on Gullah. Milwaukee: U. of Wisconsin 1972.

1168 **Norton, Darryl E.** and **William R. Hodgson,** "Intelligibility of black and white speakers for black and white listeners", Language and Speech 16 (1973): 207-10.

1169 **Noseworthy, R.G.,** "A dialect survey of Grandbank, Newfoundland." M.A. Thesis, Memorial U. of Newfoundland 1971.

1170 ---, "Verb usage in Grand Bank", RLS 4 (1972): 19-24.

1171 ---, "Fishing supplement: Linguistic Atlas of Newfoundland dialect questionnaire", RLS 5 (1974): 18-21.

1172 **Nunberg, Geoffrey,** "The speech of the New York City upper class", in Shopen/Williams 1980: 150-73.

1173 **Nunez-Wormack, Elsa Maria,** "The acquisition of English and Spanish grammatical morphemes by bilingual Puerto Rican children." Ed.D. Rutgers U. 1979. DAI 40: 7, 4007A.

1174 **O'Brien, Francis Joseph, Jr.,** "Reading comprehension among Black American English speakers in Black American English and Standard American English." Ph.D. Columbia U. 1980. DAI 41: 2, 640A.

1175 **O'Cain, Raymond K.,** "A sociolinguistic study of Charleston (S.C.) speech." Ph.D. U. of Chicago 1972.

1176 ---, "A diachronic view of the speech of Charleston, South Carolina", in Shores/Hines 1977: 135-50.

1177 ---, "Linguistic Atlas of New England", AS 54 (1979): 243-78.

1178 --- and **John R. Hopkins,** "The southern mountain vocabulary in the Low Country of South Carolina and Georgia", in J.W. Williamson, ed., An Appalachian Symposium. Boone, N.C.: Appalachian State UP 1977: 215-23.

1179 **Ohannessian, Sirarpi,** "The language problems of American Indian children", in Spolsky 1975: 13-24.

1180 **O'Hern, Edna M.,** "A phonological analysis of the language of five black pre-school children of low socio-economic status in Washington, D.C." ERIC 1975.

1181 **Olesen, Virginia** and **Elvi Whittacker,** "Conditions under which college students borrow, use, and alter slang", AS 43 (1968): 222-8.

1182 **Oliver, Raymond,** "More carnie talk from the west coast", AS 41 (1966): 278-83.

1183 **Oller, John W., Lori Baca** and **Fred Vigil,** "Attitudes and attained proficiency in ESL: a sociolinguistic study of Mexican Americans in the Southwest", TESOL Quarterly 11 (1977): 173-83.

1184 ---, **Alan J. Hudson** and **Phyllis Fei Liu,** "Attitudes and attained proficiency in ESL: a sociolinguistic study of native speakers of Chinese in the United States", Language Learning 27 (1977): 1-27.

1185 **O'Neal, Verley** and **Tom Trabasso,** "Is there a correspondence between sound and spelling? Some implications for Black English speakers", in Harrison/Trabasso 1976: 171-90.

1186 **O'Neill, George Joseph, Jr.,** "NNE grammatical items in the speech of negro elementary school children as correlates of age, grade, and social status", Ph.D. U. of Southern California 1972. DAI 32: 12, 6957A.

1187 **Oomen, Ursula,** Die englische Sprache in den USA: Variation und Struktur. Teil I. Tübingen: Niemeyer 1982.

1188 **Orkin, Mark M.,** Speaking Canadian English. An Informal Account of the English Language in Canada. Toronto: General Publishing Co. 1970 / London: Routledge and Kegan Paul 1971.

1189 ---, Canajan, Eh? Don Mills, Ont.: General Publishing 1973.

1190 **Ornstein [-Galicia], Jacob,** "Sociolinguistic research on language diversity in the American Southwest and its educational implications", Modern Language Journal 55 (1971): 223-9.

1191 ---, ed., Three Essays on Linguistic Diversity in the Spanish-Speaking World: The U.S. Southwest and the River Plate Area. The Hague: Mouton 1975.

1192 ---, "Sociolinguistics and the study of Spanish and English language varieties and their use in the U.S. Southwest (with a proposed plan of research)", in Ornstein 1975: 9-45.

1193 ---, "A cross-disciplinary sociolinguistic investigation of Mexican-American bilinguals/biculturals at a U.S. border university: language and social parameters", La linguistique 12 (1976): 131-45.

1194 ---, "A sociolinguistic investigation of Mexican-American students at a Southwest border university", La monda lingvo-problemo 6 (1977): 65-84.

1195 ---, "A broad-gauge sociolinguistic study of Mexican-American college-age bilinguals and Anglo peers at the University of Texas, El Paso: some findings", Orbis 27 (1978): 114-35.

1196 ---, "Relational bilingualism: a new approach to linguistic cultural diversity and a Mexican-American case study", Ethnicity 5 (1978): 148-66.

1197 ---, "Relational bilingualism: a socioeducational approach to studying multilingualism among Mexican-Americans", in McCormack/Wurm 1979: 285-305.

1198 ---, "Report on a project to apply sociolinguistic research findings to educational needs of Mexican American bilingual/biculturals", ITL: Review of Applied Linguistics 44 (1979): 25-50.

1199 --- and **Betty Lou Dubois,** "Mexican-American English: prolegomena to a neglected regional variety", in DiPietro/Blansitt 1977: 95-107.

1200 --- and **Paul W. Goodman,** "Socio-educational correlates of Mexican-American bilingualism", in Mackey/Ornstein 1979: 393-421.

1201 --- and **Robert St. Clair,** eds., Bilingualism and Bilingual Education: New Readings and Insights. San Antonio: Trinity U. 1980.

1202 ---, **Guadalupe Valdes-Fallis** and **Betty Lou Dubois,** "Bilingual child language acquisition along the United States-Mexico border: the El Paso-Ciudad Juárez-Las Cruces triangle", Word 27 (1971): 386-404.

1203 **Ortego, Philip Darraugh,** "Some cultural implications of a Mexican American border dialect of American English", Studies in Linguistics 21 (1969): 77-84.

1204 **Ortiz, Leroy I.,** "A sociolinguistic study of language maintenance in the Northern New Mexico community of Arroyo Seco." Ph.D. U. of New Mexico 1975. DAI 37: 4, 2159A.

1205 **Orton, Harold** and **Nathalia Wright,** Questionnaire for the Investigation of American Regional English: Based on the Work Sheets of the Linguistic Atlas of the United States and Canada. Knoxville: U. of Tennessee 1972.

1206 **Pace, George B.,** "On the eastern affiliations of Missouri speech", *AS* 40 (1965): 47-52.

1207 **Paddock, Harold,** "A dialect survey of Carbonear, Newfoundland." M.A. Thesis, Memorial U. of Newfoundland 1966. Published: *PADS* 68 (1982).

1208 ---, "Keep up the fince", *RLS* 5 (1974): 22-29.

1209 ---, "The folk grammar of Carbonear, Newfoundland", in Chambers 1975: 25-32.

1210 ---, "On roachness in English", *Phonetica* 34 (1977): 318.

1211 ---, ed., *Languages in Newfoundland and Labrador*. St. John's: Linguistics Dept., Memorial U. of Newfoundland 1982.

1212 **Paikeday, Thomas E.,** *The Winston Dictionary of Canadian English*. Indermediate edition. Toronto: Holt, Rinehart and Winston of Canada 1969. Repr. 1970.

1213 ---, ed., *The Compact Dictionary of Canadian English*. Toronto: Holt, Rinehart and Winston of Canada 1970. Repr. 1976.

1214 ---, ed., *The Winston Dictionary of Canadian English*. Elementary Edition. Toronto: Holt, Rinehart and Winston of Canada 1975.

1215 **Pampell, John R.,** "More on double modals", *Texas Linguistic Forum* 2 (1975): 110-21.

1216 **Paradis, Carole,** "La règle de Canadian raising et l'analyse en structure syllabique", *Canadian Journal of Linguistics* 25 (1980): 35-45.

1217 **Parker, Frank,** "There, their, and they", *The USF Language Quarterly* (Tampa, Fla.) 19 (1981): 46-48.

1218 **Parks, Thomas Ilon,** "A profile of the sociolinguistic attitudes of students, teachers, and home adults in four South Carolina school communities." Ph.D. George Peabody College for Teachers 1976. DAI 37: 4, 2159A.

1219 **Parslow, Robert L.,** "The pronunciation of English in Boston, Massachusetts: vowels and consonants." Ph.D. U. of Michigan 1967. DAI 28: 12, 5039A.

1220 **Parsons, Jeanette,** "A study of the relationship of noun pluralization skills and reading achievement with third-grade Black-English-speaking students." Ed.D. Columbia U. Teachers College 1980. DAI 41: 1, 182A.

1221 **Partridge, Eric,** A Dictionary of the Underworld, British and American, Being the Vocabulary of Crooks, Criminals, Racketeers, Beggars, and Tramps, Convicts, the Commercial Underworld, the Drug Traffic, the White Slave Traffic, spivs. 3rd ed., much enlarged. London: Routledge and Kegan Paul 1968.

1222 ---, Slang To-day and Yesterday, with a Short Historical Sketch and Vocabularies of English, American and Australian Slang. 4th ed., revised and brought up to date. London: Routledge and Kegan Paul 1970.

1223 ---, A Dictionary of Catch Phrases: British and America, from the Sixteenth Century to the Present Day. London: Routledge and Kegan Paul 1977 / New York: Stein and Day 1979.

1224 **Paternost, Joseph,** "Slovenian language on Minnesota's Iron Range: some sociolinguistic aspects of language maintenance and language shift", General Linguistics 16 (1976): 95-150.

1225 **Patterson, Kent,** "Checkschmuck! The slang of the chess player", AS 46 (1971): 231-6.

1226 **Payne, Arvilla C.,** "The acquisition of the phonological system of a second dialect." Ph.D. U. of Pennsylvania 1976. DAI 37: 11, 7115A.

1227 ---, "Factors controlling the acquisition of the Philadelphia dialect by out-of-state children", in Labov 1980: 143-78.

1228 **Pederson, Lee A.,** "The pronunciation of English in metropolitan Chicago", PADS 44 (1965).

1229 ---, "Some structural differences in the speech of Chicago negroes", in Shuy 1965: 28-51.

1230 ---, "The Mencken legacy", Orbis 14 (1965): 63-74.

1231 ---, "Middleclass negro speech in Minneapolis", Orbis 16 (1967): 347-53.

1232 ---, "Mark Twain's Missouri Dialects: Marion County phonemics", AS 42 (1967): 261-78.

1233 ---, An Annotated Bibliography of Southern Speech. Atlanta: Southern Educational Laboratory 1968.

1234 ---, "The Linguistic Atlas of the Gulf States: an interim report", AS 44 (1969): 279-86.

1235 ---, "Southern speech and the LAGS project", Orbis 20 (1971): 79-89.

1236 ---, "An approach to urban word geography", AS 46 (1971): 73-86.

1237 ---, "Chicago words: the regional vocabulary", AS 46 (1971): 163-92.

1238 ---, "Black speech, white speech, and the Al Smith syndrome", in L. Davis 1972: 123-34.

1239 ---, "Dialect patterns in rural northern Georgia", in Scholler/Reidy 1973: 195-207.

1240 ---, "The Linguistic Atlas of the Gulf States: interim report two", AS 49 (1974): 216-23.

1241 ---, "Tape, text and analogues", AS 49 (1974): 5-23.

1242 ---, "The plan for a dialect survey of rural Georgia", Orbis 24 (1975): 38-44.

1243 ---, "The Urban Language Series", AS 50 (1975): 98-110.

1244 ---, "The Linguistic Atlas of the Gulf States: interim report three", AS 51 (1976): 201-7.

1245 ---, "Aims and methods in a Chicago dialect survey", in Wolfgang Viereck, ed., Sprachliches Handeln - soziales Verhalten: ein Reader zur Pragmalinguistik und Soziolinguistik. München: Fink 1976: 193-202.

1246 ---, "Grassroots grammar in the gulf states", in Raymond/Russell 1977: 91-112.

1247 ---, "Structural description of linguistic geography", in Shores/Hines 1977: 19-24.

1248 ---, Toward a description of southern speech", in Shores/Hines 1977: 25-31.

1249 ---, "A compositional guide to the LAGS project." Atlanta: Emory U. Photo copy 1977.

1250 ---, "The randy sons of Nancy Whisky", AS 52 (1977): 112-21.

1251 ---, "Studies of American pronunciation since 1945", AS 52 (Issue for 1977; 1981): 262-327.

1252 ---, "Sociolinguistic aspects of American mobility", Amerikastudien 23 (1978): 299-319.

1253 ---, "Lexical data from the Gulf States", AS 55 (1980): 195-203.

1254 ---, "The Linguistic Atlas of the Gulf States: interim report four", AS 56 (1981): 243-59.

1255 ---, East Tennessee Folk Speech: A Synopsis. Frankfurt a.M., Bern: Lang 1983.

1256 --- and **Charles E. Billiard,** "The urban work sheets for the LAGS project", Orbis 28 (1979): 45-62.

1257 ---, **Howard G. Dunlap** and **Grace S. Rueter,** "Questionnaire for a dialect survey of rural Georgia", Orbis 24 (1975): 45-71.

1258 ---, **Raven I. McDavid, Jr., Charles W. Foster** and **Charles E. Billiard,** A Manual for Dialect Research in the Southern States. University, Ala.: Alabama UP 1972, 2nd ed. 1974.

1259 ---, **Grace S. Rueter** and **Joan H. Hall,** "Biracial dialectology: six years into the Georgia survey", JEngL 9 (1975): 18-25.

1260 --- et al., Linguistic Atlas of the Gulf States: The Basic Materials. Microform Collection. Ann Arbor, Mich.: University Microfilms International /1981/.

1261 --- et al., Concordance to the LAGS Microform Collection. Ann Arbor, Mich.: University Microfilms International (forthcoming).

1262 **Peñalosa, Fernando,** Chicano Sociolinguistics: A Brief Introduction. Rowley, Mass.: Newbury 1980.

1263 **Penfield, Joyce** and **Jack Ornstein-Galicia,** Chicano English. Amsterdam: Benjamins (forthcoming).

1264 **Pennington, Dorothy,** "Guilt-provocation: a strategy in black rhetoric", in Molefi Kete Asante and Abdulai S. Vandi, eds., Contemporary Black Thought: Alternative Analyses in Social and Behavioral Science. Beverly Hills: Sage 1980: 111-25.

1265 **Peters, F.J.J.,** "To INFINITIVE and -ING form divergence in British and American English", IRAL 18 (1980): 343-4.

1266 --- and **Toril Swan,** American English: A Handbook and Sociolinguistic Perspective. Oslo: Novus 1983.

1267 **Peters, Robert D.,** "The social and economic effects of the transition from a system of woods camps to a system of commuting in the Newfoundland pulpwood industry." /Incl. a glossary of 63 items used by lumbermen/ M.A. Thesis, Memorial U. of Newfoundland 1965.

1268 **Peterson, Joseph** and **Zacharias Thundyil,** "A computerized questionnaire for the dialect survey of the Upper Peninsula of Michigan", Annual Meeting Papers: Michigan Linguistic Society 1,3 (1971): 1-32.

1269 **Pfaff, Carol W.,** Historical and Structural Aspects of Sociolinguistic Variation: The Copula in Black English. Inglewood, Calif.: Southwest Regional Laboratory 1971.

1270 ---, "Hypercorrection and grammar change", Language in Society 5 (1976): 105-7.

1271 ---, "Functional and structural constraints on syntactic variation in code-switching", in Sanford B. Steever, Carol A. Walker and Salikoko S. Mufwene, eds., Papers from the Parasession on Diachronic Syntax, April 22, 1976. Chicago: Chicago Linguistic Society 1976: 248-59.

1272 ---, "Lexicalization in Black English", in Day 1980: 163-79.

1273 **Phillips, Betty S.,** "Lexical diffusion and Southern tune, duke, news", AS 56 (1981): 72-79.

1274 **Picard, M.,** "Canadian raising: the case against reordering", Canadian Journal of Linguistics 22 (1971): 144-55.

1275 **Pickens, William Garfield,** "Non-standard morphology in the writing of seventh-graders in the public schools of Hartford, Connecticut." Ph.D. Connecticut 1969. DAI 30: 7, 2994A.

1276 **Pietras, Thomas** and **Pose Lamb,** "Attitudes of selected elementary teachers toward non-standard black dialects", Journal of Educational Research 71 (1978): 292-7.

1277 **Pilati, Leona L.,** "The Fox dialect: the influence of Finnish on a local American English dialect", Neuphilologische Mitteilungen 70 (1969): 145-58.

1278 **Pitts, Walter,** "Beyond hypercorrection: the use of emphatic -s in BEV", in Roberta A. Hendrick, Carrie S. Masek and Mary Frances Miller, eds., Papers from the Seventeenth Regional Meeting, Chicago Linguistic Society. Chicago: Chicago Linguistic Society 1981: 303-10.

1279 **Pluto, Joseph A.,** "Black English and education in the United States", in Raymond O. Silverstein, eds., Proceedings of the Third International Conference on Frontiers in Language Proficiency and Dominance Testing, Held at Southern Illinois University at Carbondale, September 26 - 28, 1979. Carbondale: Department of Linguistics, Southern Illinois U. 1980: 218-27.

1280 **Pole, J.R.,** "The language of American presidents", in Michaels/Ricks 1980: 421-31.

1281 **Politzer, Robert L.** and **Arnulfo G. Ramirez,** "An error analysis of the spoken English of Mexican-American pupils in a bilingual school and a monolingual school", *Language Learning* 23 (1973): 39-62.

1282 --- and **Dwight Brown,** "A production test in black standard and nonstandard speech", *FFLR* 11 (1973): 21-24, 46.

1283 **Polson, James,** "A linguistic questionnaire for British Columbia: a plan for a postal survey of dialectal variation in B.C., with an account of recent research." M.A. Thesis, U. of British Columbia 1969.

1284 **Pope, Mike,** "The syntax of the speech of urban (Tallahassee) negro and white fourth graders." Ph.D. Florida State U. 1969. DAI 31: 3, 1252A.

1285 **Poplack, Shana,** "Dialect acquisition among Puerto Rican bilinguals", *Language in Society* 7 (1978): 89-103.

1286 ---, "Sometimes I'll start a sentence in Spanish *y termino en Espanol*: toward a typology of code-switching", *Linguistics* 18 (1980): 581-618.

1287 **Popova, L.G.,** *Leksika anglyskogo jazyka v Kanade* (The lexis of Canadian English). Moscow: Vyssaja skola 1978.

1288 **Porter, Bernard H.,** "Some Newfoundland phrases, sayings, and figures of speech", *AS* 41 (1966): 294-7.

1289 **Porter, Ruth Schell,** "A dialect study in Dartmouth, Massachusetts", *PADS* 43 (1965): 1-43.

1290 **Postman, Neil, Charles Weingartner** and **Terence P. Moran,** eds., *Language in America*. New York: Pegasus 1969.

1291 **Poston, Lawrence, III,** and **Francis J. Stillman,** "Notes on campus vocabulary, 1964", *AS* 40 (1965): 193-5.

1292 **Poulsen, Richard C.,** "The mountain man vernacular: its historical roots, its linguistic nature, and its literary uses." Ph.D. U. of Utah 1976. DAI 37: 5, 2878A.

1293 **Poulter, Virgil L.,** "A comparison of voiceless stops in the English and Spanish of bilingual natives of Fort Worth-Dallas", in Gilbert 1970: 42-49.

1294 ---, "A phonological study of the speech of Mexican-American college students native to Fort Worth-Dallas." Ph.D. Louisiana State U. 1973. DAI 35: 2, 1082A.

1295 **Powell, David R.,** "American vs. British English", Language Learning 16 (1966): 31-40.

1296 **Pratt, T.K.,** "The survey of Prince Edward Island English: a progress report", in Moshé Starets, ed., Papers from the Third Annual Meeting of the Atlantic Provinces Linguistic Association. Church Point, Nova Scotia: Université Ste Anne 1979: 33-47.

1297 ---, "The use of dialect words on Prince Edward Island", The English Quarterly 12,4 (1980/81): 60-69.

1298 ---, "I dwell in possibility: variable (ay) in Prince Edward Island", Journal of the Atlantic Provinces Linguistic Association 4 (1982): 27-35.

1299 ---, "A case for direct questioning in traditional fieldwork", AS 58 (1983): 150-5.

1300 **Preston, Dennis Richard,** "Bituminous coal mining vocabulary of the eastern United States: a pilot study in the collecting of geographically distributed occupational vocabulary." Ph.D. U. of Wisconsin 1969. Published: PADS 59 (1973). DAI 30: 9, 3929A.

1301 ---, "Proverbial comparisons from Southern Indiana", Orbis 24 (1975): 72-114.

1302 **Preston, Donald,** "Canadian slang." M.A. Thesis Victoria, B.C., 1973.

1303 **Pride, John B.,** ed., Sociolinguistic Aspects of Language Learning and Teaching. Oxford: UP 1979.

1304 **Pringle, Ian,** "The Gaelic substratum in the English of Glengarry County and its reflection in the novels of Ralph Connor", Canadian Journal of Linguistics 26 (1981): 126-40.

1305 ---, "The concept of 'dialect' and the study of Canadian English", Queen's Quarterly 90 (1983): 100-21.

1306 ---, English Dialects in the Ottawa Valley. Amsterdam: Benjamins (forthcoming).

1307 ---, "Attitudes to English in Canada", in Sydney Greenbaum, ed., Attitudes to English (forthcoming).

1308 ---, **C. Stanley Jones** and **Enoch Padolsky,** "The misapprehension of Ottawa standards in an adjacent rural area", English World-Wide 2 (1981): 165-80.

1309 --- and **Enoch Padolsky,** "The Irish heritage in the English of the Ottawa valley", English Studies in Canada 7 (1981): 338-52.

1310 ---, ---, "The Linguistic Survey of the Ottawa Valley", AS (forthcoming).

1311 **Pulliam, Cynthia Anne,** "The effect of using a contrastive linguistic instructional model on the code-switching ability of sixth grade black students." Ph.D. Kansas City 1978. DAI 39: 6, 3554A.

1312 **Putschke, Wolfgang,** ed., Automatische Sprachkartographie. Vorträge des Internationalen Kolloquiums zur Automatischen Sprachkartographie in Marburg vom 11. - 16. September 1977. Germanistische Linguistik 3-4 (1977).

1313 **Qazilbash, A. Husain,** "A dialect survey of the Appalachian region." Ph.D. Florida State U. 1971. DAI 32: 11, 6085A.

1314 **Quay, Lorene C.,** "Negro dialect and Binet performance in severely disadvantaged black four-year-olds", Child Development 43 (1972): 245-50.

1315 **Radden, Günter,** Ein Profil soziolinguistischer Variation in einer amerikanischen Kleinstadt. Frankfurt a.M., Bern, Cirencester: Lang 1979.

1316 **Raffler-Engel, Walburga von,** "Some phono-stylistic features of Black English", Phonetica 25 (1972): 53-64.

1317 ---, "Intonational and vowel correlates in contrasting dialects: a suggestion for further research", in André Rigault and René Charbonneau, eds., Proceedings of the Seventh International Congress of Phonetic Sciences, Held at the University of Montreal and McGill University, 22 - 28 August 1971. The Hague: Mouton 1972: 768-72.

1318 ---, "The language of immigrant children", in Chambers 1979: 226-59.

1319 **Rafky, David M.,** "The semantics of negritude", AS 45 (1970): 30-44.

1320 **Raith, Joachim,** "Pennsylvania German-American English bilingualism - a case study", in Carol Molony, Helmut Zobl and Wilfried Stölting, eds., Deutsch im Kontakt mit anderen Sprachen / German in Contact with Other Languages. Kronberg/Ts.: Scriptor 1977: 104-28.

1321 **Rawles, Myrtle Read,** "'Boontling': esoteric speech of Boonville, California", Western Folklore 25 (1966): 93-103.

1322 **Raybern, Judith Ann,** "An investigation of selected syntactic differences present in the oral and written language of lower socioeconomic status black third and fifth grade students." Ed.D. Indiana U. 1974. DAI 35: 9, 6122A.

1323 **Raymond, James C.** and **I. Willis Russell,** eds., James B. McMillan. Essays in Linguistics by his Friends and Colleagues. University, Ala.: Alabama UP 1977.

1324 **Read, Allen Walker,** "Is American English deteriorating?" Word Study 41 (1965): 1-3.

1325 ---, Classic American Graffiti-Lexical Evidence from Folk Epigraphy in Western North America: A Glossarial Study of the Low Element in the English Vocabulary. Waukesha, Wisc.: Maledicta 1977.

1326 **Reagan, Patty Sue,** "A word atlas of Central Texas." Ph.D. East Texas State U. 1980. DAI 40: 11, 5841A.

1327 **Redlinger, Wendy,** "Mothers' speech to children in bilingual Mexican-American homes", International Journal of the Sociology of Language 17 (1978): 73-82.

1328 **Reed, Carroll E.,** Dialects of American English. Cleveland: World 1967. Revised ed.: Amherst: Massachusetts UP 1977.

1329 ---, "The pronunciation of English in the Pacific Northwest", Language 37 (1966): 559-64.

1330 ---, "Linguistic backpacking in the Pacific Northwest", JEngL 16 (1983): 78-80.

1331 --- and **David W. Reed,** "Problems of English speech mixture in California and Nevada", in L. Davis 1972: 135-44.

1332 **Reeds, James A.,** "Front vowel aperture and diffuseness in Midwestern American English." Ph.D. U. of Michigan 1966. DAI 28: 1, 202A.

1333 **Reese, James Robert,** "Variation in Appalachian English: a study of the speech of elderly, rural natives of East Tennessee." Ph.D. U. of Tennessee 1977. DAI 38: 12, 7304A.

1334 ---, "Randomly distributed dialects in Appalachian English: syntactic and phonological variation in East Tennessee", The SECOL Bulletin: Southeastern Conference on Linguistics 2,2 (1978): 67-76.

1335 ---, "Goals for the collection and use of Appalachian oral materials in the 1980s", in Wilson Somerville, ed., Appalachia/America: Proceedings of the 1980 Appalachian Studies Conference. Johnson City, Tenn.: Appalachian Consortium 1981: 230-5.

1336 Regional Language Studies 6: The Growth of the Dictionary of Newfoundland English. St. John's, Nfdld.: Memorial U. of Newfoundland 1975.

1337 **Register, Norma,** "Some sound patterns of Chicano English", Journal of the Linguistic Association of the Southwest 2 (1977): 111-22.

1338 **Rempel, Rosemary,** "An introduction to trisyllabic laxing, vowel shift, and Canadian raising", Calgary Working Papers in Linguistics 1,1 (1975): 3-7.

1339 **Rey, Alberto,** "A study of the attitudinal effect of a Spanish accent on blacks and whites in South Florida." Ph.D. Georgetown U. 1974. DAI 35: 6, 3717A.

1340 ---, "Accents and acceptance: attitudinal reactions toward varying degrees of Spanish accented speech", in Ingemann 1976: 407-22.

1341 ---, "Accent and employability: language attitudes", Language Sciences 47 (1977): 7-12.

1342 **Reyes, Rogelio,** "Language mixing in Chicano bilingual speech", in J. Donald Bowen and Jacob Ornstein, eds., Studies in Southwest Spanish. Rowley, Mass.: Newbury 1976: 183-8.

1343 **Rickford, John R.,** "BIN (been) in black English." Thesis, U. of Pennsylvania 1973.

1344 ---, "The insights of the mesolect", in DeCamp/Hancock 1974: 92-117.

1345 ---, "Carrying the new wave into syntax: The case of Black English BIN", in Fasold/Shuy 1975: 162-83.

1346 ---, "The question of prior creolization in Black English", in Albert Valdman, ed., Pidgin and Creole Linguistics. Bloomington: Indiana UP 1977: 190-221.

1347 **Ridge, Martin,** ed., The New Bilingualism: An American Dilemma. Los Angeles: California UP / New Brunswick: Transaction 1981.

1348 **Riegel, Klaus F.** and **Roy Freedle,** "What does it take to be bilingual or bidialectal?", in Harrison/Trabasso 1976: 25-44.

1349 **Riley, Roberta D.,** "Should we teach urban black students Standard English?" in St. Clair 1979: 63-99.

1350 **Rink, Bernd,** Amerikanisch compact: die wichtigsten Abweichungen vom britischen Englisch in Wortschatz und Grammatik. München: Hueber 1977.

1351 **Roach, Polly Sue,** "A lexical study of the speech of Lauderdale County, Alabama." Thesis, U. of Alabama 1975.

1352 **Roberts, Elsa Ann,** "Five year old black children and Standard English: A study of cross-dialectal comprehension." Ph.D., Northwestern U. 1972. DAI 33: 6, 2917A.

1353 **Roberts, Margaret M.,** "The pronunciation of vowels in negro speech." Ph.D. Ohio State U. 1966. DAI 27: 10, 3328B.

1354 **Robertson, Barbara Mae,** "The socio-cultural determiners of French language maintenance: the case of Niagara Falls, Ontario." Ph.D. Buffalo, New York 1980. DAI 41: 8, 3559A.

1355 **Rockey, Randall Earl,** "Contrastive analysis of the language structures of three ethnic groups of children enrolled in head start programs." Ph.D. Cornell U. 1970. DAI 31: 12, 6585A.

1356 **Rodman, Lilita,** "Characteristics of B.[ritish] C.[olumbia] English", English Quarterly 7,4 (1974): 49-82.

1357 **Rodney, Ruby Veronica,** "Analysis: Guyanese Creole and American Black English with special emphasis on tense and aspect." Ed.D. Rutgers U. 1981. DAI 42: 4, 1520A.

1358 **Rogers, P.W.,** "Unlocking the Canadian word hoard", Queen's Quarterly 77 (1970): 111-23.

1359 **Rogge, Heinz,** "Das Erbe Afrikas in Sprache und Kultur der nordamerikanischen Gullahs", Zeitschrift für Volkskunde 61 (1965): 30-37.

1360 **Romero, Olga,** "Aspects of code-switching in bilingual children." Ph.D. City U. of New York 1982. DAI 43: 5, 1529A.

1361 **Ronson, Irwin,** "The effect of Labov's five phonological variables on perceived listener judgement", in Harry Hollien and Patricia Hollien, eds., Current Issues in the Phonetic Science. Proceedings of the IPS-77 Congress, Miami Beach, Florida, 17 - 19th Dec. 1977. Amsterdam: Benjamins 1979: 743-54.

1362 **Roper, Birdie Alexander,** "School desegregation and teacher attitudes toward the nonstandard dialect." Ph.D. Claremont Graduate School 1980. DAI 41: 1, 140A.

1363 **Ross, Stephen Bradford,** "A syntactic analysis of the written language of selected black elementary school children with reference to sociological variables." Ph.D. U. of Southern California 1973. DAI 33: 10, 5710A.

1364 **Rot, Sándor,** "On semasiological peculiarities of British and American slang", in Erzsébet Perényi and Tibor Frank, eds., Studies in English and American. Vol. II. Budapest: Department of English, L. Eötvös U. 1975: 379-98.

1365 **Roth, Ruth S.,** "The relevance of morpheme boundaries to nasal assimilation in Canadian English", Calgary Working Papers in Linguistics 1,1 (1975): 37-38.

1366 **Rowe, Nora Alice,** "A linguistic study of the Lake Ainslie area of Inverness County, Nova Scotia." M.A. Thesis, New Orleans 1968.

1367 **Royal Commission on Bilingualism and Biculturalism,** A Preliminary Report of the Royal Commission on Bilingualism and Biculturalism. New York: Arno 1978.

1368 **Rubrecht, August W.,** "Regional phonological variants in Louisiana speech." Ph.D. U. of Florida 1971. DAI 32: 11, 6958A.

1369 ---, "DARE in Louisiana", in Shores/Hines 1977: 45-59.

1370 **Ruch, William Vaughn,** "Communicating in their terms." Ph.D. Rensselaer Polytechnic Institute 1980. DAI 41: 3, 1043A.

1371 **Rudd, Mary Jo,** "The use of third person reference in multi-party conversations in an Appalachian community", Anthropological Linguistics 18 (1976): 38-59.

1372 **Rudnyćkyj, J.B.,** "Immigrant languages, language contact, and bilingualism in Canada", in Sebeok 1973: 592-652.

1373 ---, "Communicating in a multicultural society", in Darnell 1973: 117-28.

1374 **Rueter, Grace S.,** "Vowel nasality in the speech of rural middle Georgia." Ph.D. Emory U. 1975. DAI 36: 12, 8027A.

1375 ---, "A dialect survey of rural Georgia: the progress", in Shores/Hines 1977: 33-43.

1376 **Runcie, John F.,** "Truck drivers' jargon", AS 44 (1969): 200-9.

1377 **Russell, Lorraine Hansen,** "An acoustic description of selected phonetic types comprising /r/ in the general American dialect." Ph.D. City U. of New York 1977. DAI 37: 11, 6840A.

1378 **Ryan, Ellen Bouchard,** "Subjective reactions toward accented speech", in Shuy/Fasold 1973: 60-73.

1379 --- and **M.A. Carranza,** "Ingroup and outgroup reactions to Mexican American language varieties", in Howard Giles, ed., Language, Ethnicity and Intergroup Relations. London: Academic Press 1977: 59-82.

1380 ---, ---, and **Robert W. Moffie,** "Reactions toward varying degrees of accentedness in the speech of Spanish-English bilinguals", Language and Speech 20 (1977): 267-73.

1381 **Saint-Jacques, Bernard,** "The languages of immigrants: sociolinguistic aspects of immigration in Canada", in Chambers 1979: 207-25.

1382 **Saint-Pierre, Madeleine,** "Bilinguisme et diglossie dans la région montréalaise", Les Cahiers de Linguistique de l'Université du Québec 6 (1976): 179-98.

1383 **Samarin, William J.** and **Ivan Kalmar,** "Evaluational reactions to foreign accent among immigrants in Toronto", in Mackey/Ornstein 1979: 181-96.

1384 **Sanders, Sara L.,** "The speech of Fairfax, South Carolina, in its subregional context: selected phonological features." Thesis, U. of South Carolina 1978.

1385 **Sanders, Willease Story,** "Selected grammatical features of the speech of blacks in Columbia, S.C." Ph.D. U. of South Carolina 1978. DAI 39: 3, 1521A.

1386 /̄ **Sandilands, John** _/ Western Canadian Dictionary and Phrase Book. Edmonton: Alberta UP 1977. /̄ Facsim. of 1913 ed. _/

1387 **Sasiki, Midori,** "Southern Appalachian English: the language of Faulkner's country people", Chu-Shikoku Studies in American Literature 15 (1979): 37-46.

1388 **Saville-Troike, Muriel,** "Bilingual education and the native American", in Alatis 1978: 125-32.

1389 **Sawyer, Janet B.,** "Spanish-English bilingualism in San Antonio, Texas", in Gilbert 1970: 18-41.

1390 **Scargill, M.H.,** "The growth of Canadian English", in Carl F. Klinck, et al., eds., Literary History of Canada. Toronto: U. of Toronto 1965: 251-9; 2nd ed., vol. I, 1976: 265-73.

1391 ---, "Canadianisms from western Canada with special reference to British Columbia", Proceedings and Transactions of the Royal Society of Canada, 4th series, vol. 6, sec. II (1968): 181-5.

1392 ---, "Survey of Canadian English", Canadian Council of Teachers of English Newsletter 3,3 (1970): 1, 6.

1393 ---, "Is riz, some hot, clumb and other Canadianisms", English Quarterly 6,2 (1973): 115-21.

1394 ---, Modern Canadian English Usage: Linguistic Change and Reconstruction. Toronto: McClelland and Stewart 1974.

1395 ---, A Short History of Canadian English. Victoria, B.C.: Sono Nis Press 1977.

1396 --- and **H. Warkentyne,** "The Survey of Canadian English: a report", English Quarterly 5,3 (1972): 47-104.

1397 **Schach, Paul,** ed., Languages in Conflict: Linguistic Acculturation on the Great Plains. Lincoln: Nebraska UP 1980.

1398 **Scheer, Herfried,** "Bilingualism in Quebec", in Peter Hans Nelde, ed., Sprachkontakt und Sprachkonflikt. Wiesbaden: Steiner 1980: 209-16.

1399 **Schneidemesser, Luanne von,** "Purse and its synonyms", AS 55 (1980): 74-76.

1400 ---, "Report on the Dictionary of American Regional English", The Linguistic Reporter 23 (1981): 10-11.

1401 **Schneider, Edgar Werner,** Morphologische und syntaktische Variablen im amerikanischen Early Black English. Frankfurt a.M., Bern: Lang 1981.

1402 ---, "On the history of Black English in the USA: some new evidence", English World-Wide 3,1 (1982): 18-46.

1403 ---, "Writings on regional and social variation in American and Canadian English: a selective bibliography 1965-1981", English World-Wide 3,2 (1982): 161-205.

1404 ---, "The diachronic development of the Black English perfective auxiliary phrase", JEngL 16 (1983): 55-64.

1405 ---, "The origin of the verbal -s in Black English", AS 58 (1983): 99-113.

1406 ---, "Englisch in Nordamerika", in Englisch - Formen und Funktionen einer Weltsprache. Bamberg: Universitätsbibliothek 1983: 51-71.

1407 --- and **Wolfgang Viereck,** "The use of the computer in American, Canadian and British English dialectology and sociolinguistics", in

Hans Goebl, ed., Quantitative Dialektologie. Bochum: Brockmeyer (forthcoming).

1408 **Schnitzer, Marc L.,** "The 'Baltimore /o/' and generative phonology", General Linguistics 12 (1972): 86-93.

1409 **Scholler, Harald** and **John Reidy,** eds., Lexicography and Dialect Geography: Festgabe für Hans Kurath. Wiesbaden: Franz Steiner 1973.

1410 **Schrock, Earl Franklin, Jr.,** "A study of the dialect of the blacks in Pope County, Arkansas." Ph.D. U. of Arkansas 1980. DAI 41: 5, 2091A.

1411 **Schweda, Nancy Lee,** "Goal-oriented interaction in the French-speaking St. John River valley of Northern Maine: a sociolinguistic and ethnomethodological study of the use of verbal strategies by professional community members living in a bilingual society with French-English speech continuum." Ph.D. Georgetown U. 1979. DAI 40: 4, 2040A.

1412 **Scott, Jerrie,** "The need for semantic considerations in accounting for the variable usage of verb forms in black dialects of English (BDE)", University of Michigan Papers in Linguistics 1,2 (1973): 140-5.

1413 **Ščur, Georgij S.** and **Tat'jana I. Kasatkina,** "Some notes on Canadian English", Kwartalnik Neofilologiczny (Warsaw) 24 (1977): 403-8.

1414 --- and **N.V. Svavolya,** "On one peculiarity of the verb of the English language in the U.S.A. (with special reference to Black English)", Studia Anglica Posnaniensia 7 (1975): 21-28.

1415 **Seary, E.R., G.M. Story** and **W.J. Kirwin,** The Avalon Peninsula of Newfoundland: An Ethno-linguistic Study. Ottawa: Queen's Printer 1968.

1416 **Sebeok, Thomas A.,** ed., Current Trends in Linguistics. Vol. 10: Linguistics in North America. The Hague: Mouton 1973.

1417 **Séguinot, Candace,** "The intonation of yes-no-questions", in Léon/Martin 1979: 129-41.

1418 **Sen, Ann Louise F.,** "The linguistic geography of eighteenth-century New Jersey speech: phonology." Ph.D. Princeton U. 1973. DAI 34: 8, 5149A.

1419 ---, "Dialect variation in early American English", JEngL 8 (1974): 41-47.

1420 ---, "Reconstructing early American dialects", JEngL 12 (1978): 50-62.

1421 ---, "English in the big apple: historical backgrounds of New York City speech", The English Journal 68 (1979): 52-55.

1422 ---, "Some social implications of /r/ loss in American English", Orbis 29 (1980 /1982/): 55-59.

1423 **Sencer, Robert A.,** "An investigation of the effects of incorrect grammar on attitude and comprehension in written English messages." Ph.D. Michigan State U. 1965. DAI 26: 8, 4649.

1424 **Serapiglia, Theresa,** "Comparison of the syntax and vocabulary of bilingual Spanish, Indian, and monolingual Anglo-American children", Working Papers on Bilingualism (1978): 75-91.

1425 **Seymour, Harry N.** and **Charlena M. Seymour,** "Black English and Standard American English contrasts in consonantal development of four and five-year-old children", Journal of Speech and Hearing Disorders 46 (1981): 274-80.

1426 **Shafer, Robert E.,** "A cross-national study of teacher language attitudes in England and the United States", in Robin N. Campbell and Philip T. Smith, eds., Recent Advances in the Psychology of Language. Conference Held at the University of Stirling, Scotland, June 21 - 26, 1976. New York: Plenum 1978: 427-48.

1427 **Shaffer, Douglas,** "The spread of English over immigrant languages in the U.S.", in Mohammad Ali Jazayery, Edgar C. Polomé, and Werner Winter, eds., Linguistic and Literary Studies in Honor of Archibald A. Hill. IV: Linguistics and Literature/Sociolinguistics and Applied Linguistics. The Hague: Mouton 1979: 371-7.

1428 **Sharpless, Clair A.,** "Pronunciation characteristics of negro and white sixth-grade children from different socioeconomic levels." M.A. Thesis, U. of Florida 1966.

1429 **Shayer, Howard B.,** "The stressed vowels of negro and white speech of the southern states: a comparison", ERIC 1972.

1430 **Sheldon, D.R.,** "A short experimental investigation of the phonological view of the writer-rider contrast in U.S. English", Journal of Phonetics 1 (1973): 339-46.

1431 **Shell, Marc,** "The forked tongue: bilingual advertisement in Quebec", Semiotica 20 (1977): 259-69.

1432 **Shields, Kenneth, Jr.,** "Language attitudes in the Mid-South", The University of South Florida Language Quarterly 18 (1979): 2-6.

1433 **Shields, Portia H.,** "The language of poor black children and reading performance", The Journal of Negro Education 48 (1979): 196-208.

1434 **Shiels, Marie Eileen,** "Dialects in contact: A sociolinguistic analysis of four phonological variables of Puerto Rican English and Black English in Harlem." Ph.D. Georgetown U. 1972. DAI 32: 12, 6959A.

1435 **Shopen, Timothy,** "Selections from Bengt Lowman's 'Conversations in a negro American dialect'", in Shopen/Williams 1980: 139-49.

1436 --- and **Joseph M. Williams,** eds., Standards and Dialects in English. Cambridge, Mass.: Winthrop Publishers 1980.

1437 **Shores, David L.,** ed., Contemporary English. Change and Variation. Philadelphia, New York, Toronto: J.B. Lippincott 1972.

1438 ---, "Black English and black attitudes", in Shores/Hines 1977: 177-87.

1439 --- and **Carole P. Hines,** eds., Papers in Language Variation. SAMLA-ADS Collection. University, Ala.: Alabama UP 1977.

1440 **Shuy, Roger W.,** ed., Social Dialects and Language Learning. Champaign, Ill.: National Council of Teachers of English 1965.

1441 ---, "Sauce", AS 41 (1966): 74-75.

1442 ---, "An automatic retrieval program for the linguistic atlas of the United States and Canada", in Paul L. Garvin and Bernard Spolsky, eds., Computation in Linguistics. A Case Book. Bloomington, London: Indiana UP 1966: 60-75.

1443 ---, Discovering American Dialects. Urbana, Ill.: National Council of Teachers of English 1967.

1444 ---, "A selective bibliography on social dialects", Linguistic Reporter 10 (1968): 1-5.

1445 ---, "Detroit speech: careless, awkward, and inconsistent, or systematic, graceful, and regular?", Elementary English 45 (1968): 565-9.

1446 ---, "Subjective judgements in sociolinguistic analysis", in Alatis 1970: 175-88.

1447 ---, "Social dialect and employability: Some pitfalls of good intentions", in L. Davis 1972: 145-56.

1448 ---, "Sociolinguistics and teacher attitudes in a Southern school system", in Smith/Shuy 1972: 67-81.

1449 ---, "The study of vernacular Black English as a factor in educational change", Research in the Teaching of English 7 (1973): 297-311.

1450 ---, ed., Report of the Twenty-Third Annual Round Table Meeting on Linguistics and Language Studies: Sociolinguistics: Current Trends and Prospects. Washington, D.C.: Georgetown UP 1973.

1451 ---, "Dialectology", in Ronald Wardhaugh and H. Douglas Brown, eds., A Survey of Applied Linguistics. Ann Arbor: Michigan UP 1976: 182-206.

1452 ---, "Variability and the public image of language", TESOL Quarterly 15 (1981): 315-26.

1453 --- and **Ralph W. Fasold,** eds., Language Attitudes: Current Trends and Prospects. Washington, D.C.: Georgetown UP 1973.

1454 ---, **Lynn McCreedy** and **John Firsching,** "Toward the description of areal norms of syntax: some methodological suggestions", in Putschke 1977: 367-89.

1455 --- and **Frederick Williams,** "Stereotyped attitudes of selected English dialect communities", in Shuy/Fasold 1973: 85-96.

1456 ---, **Walter A. Wolfram** and **William K. Riley,** Linguistic Correlates of Social Stratification in Detroit Speech. Cooperative Research Project No. 6-1347. Final Report. East Lansing, Mich.: Michigan State U. 1967.

1457 ---, ---, ---, Field Techniques in an Urban Language Study. Washington, D.C.: Center for Applied Linguistics 1968.

1458 **Sigelman, Carol Kimball,** "Giving and taking directions: Subcultural communication barriers and evaluative reactions to speech." Ph.D. George Peabody College for Teachers 1972. DAI 33: 7, 3623A.

1459 **Silverman, Stuart,** "The learning of Black English by Puerto Ricans in New York City", in Dillard 1975: 331-57.

1460 **Simmons, Donald C.,** "Some special terms used in a University of Connecticut men's dormitory", AS 42 (1967): 227-30.

1461 **Simpson, Dagna,** "Constant variation in central Illinois: microanalysis of four LANCS records." Ph.D. Illinois Institute of Technology 1977. DAI 39: 2, 856A.

1462 **Singh, Rajendra,** "A note on multiple negatives", AS 45 (1970): 247-51.

1463 **Skillman, Billy G.,** "A Cleburne County, Arkansas, word list", PADS 46 (1966): 24-30.

1464 **Sledd, James H.,** "Breaking, umlaut, and the southern drawl", Language 42 (1966): 18-41.

1465 ---, "Bi-dialectalism: the linguistics of white supremacy", English Journal 58 (1969): 1307-15, 1329.

1466 ---, "Doublespeak: dialectology in the service of Big Brother", College English 33 (1972): 439-56.

1467 ---, "A note on buckra philology", AS 48 (1973): 144-6.

1468 ---, "After bidialectalism, what?", English Journal 62 (1973): 770-3.

1469 **Slotkin, Alan Robert,** "A survey of verb forms in the midlands of South Carolina." Ph.D. U. of South Carolina 1969. DAI 31: 10, 5426A.

1470 **Smith, Arthur L.,** ed., Language, Communication and Rhetoric in Black America. New York: Harper and Row 1972.

1471 **Smith, David M.** and **Roger W. Shuy,** eds., Sociolinguistics in Cross-Cultural Analysis. Washington, D.C.: Georgetown UP 1972.

1472 **Smith, Ernie Adolphus,** "The evolution and continuing presence of the African oral tradition in black America." Ph.D. Irvine, California 1975. DAI 35: 11, 7290A.

1473 **Smith, Henry Lee, Jr.,** "The morphophone and English dialects", in L. Davis 1972: 157-76.

1474 **Smith, Jack,** "Some notes on the dialect of Key West", Mississippi Folklore Record 2 (1968): 55-64.

1475 **Smith, Lawrence R.,** "Some subjective reactions to expletive use in Newfoundland", Papers in Linguistics 11 (1978): 321-41.

1476 **Smith, Max D.,** "The dragonfly: Linguistic Atlas underdifferentiation", AS 43 (1968): 51-57.

1477 **Smith, M. Estellie,** ed., Studies in Linguistics in Honor of George L. Trager. The Hague, Paris: Mouton 1972.

1478 **Smith, Michael D.,** "Assessing the verbal behavior of nonstandard speakers: some observations and proposals", The Journal of Negro Education 42 (1973): 473-88.

1479 **Smith, Riley B.,** "Interrelatedness of certain deviant grammatical structures in negro nonstandard dialects", JEngL 3 (1969): 82-88.

1480 ---, "Some phonological rules in the negro speech of East Texas." Ph.D. Austin 1973. DAI 34: 9, 5949A.

1481 ---, "Research perspectives on American Black English: a brief historical sketch", AS 49 (1974): 24-39.

1482 ---, "Hyperformation and basilect reconstruction", JEngL 8 (1974): 48-56.

1483 ---, "Sociological aspects of Black English dialects in the United States", in McCormack/Wurm 1979: 137-43.

1484 --- and **Donald M. Lance,** "Standard and disparate varieties of English in the United States: educational and sociopolitical implications", International Journal of the Sociology of Language 21 (1979): 127-40.

1485 **Smith, William H.,** "Low-country Black English", AS 54 (1979): 64-67.

1486 **Smitherman, Geneva,** "A comparison of the oral and written styles of a group of inner-city black students." Ph.D. U. of Michigan 1969. DAI 31: 2, 747A.

1487 ---, "English teacher, why you be doing the things you don't do?" English Journal 61 (1972): 59-65.

1488 ---, "Grammar and goodness", English Journal 62 (1973): 774-8.

1489 ---, "'God don't never change': Black English from a black perspective", College English 34 (1973): 828-33.

1490 ---, Talkin and Testifyin: The Language of Black America. Boston: Houghton Mifflin 1977.

1491 ---, "White English in blackface or who do I be?", in Michaels/Ricks 1980: 158-68.

1492 ---, ed., Black English and the Education of Black Children and Youth. Proceedings of the National Invitational Symposium on the King Decision. Detroit: Wayne State U., Center for Black Studies 1981.

1493 --- and **James McGinnis,** "Black language and black liberation", Black Books Bulletin 5,2 (1977): 8-14.

1494 **Sobin, Linda L.,** Noun Plural Marker Deletion in the Speech of Black Children. Austin: U. of Texas 1971.

1495 **Solé, Carlos A.,** "Language usage patterns among a young generation of Cuban-Americans", in Blansitt/Teschner 1980: 274-81.

1496 **Solé, Yolanda Russinovich,** "The Spanish/English contact situation in the Southwest", in Blansitt/Teschner 1980: 282-91.

497 **Somervill, Mary Ann,** "Language of the disadvantaged: toward resolution of conflict", Journal of Negro Education 43 (1974): 284-301.

498 **Sommer, Elisabeth,** "The course of black language in the United States", in Peter Hans Nelde, ed., Sprachkontakt und Sprachkonflikt. Wiesbaden: Steiner 1980: 287-96.

499 ---, "Methodology and data generizability in dialect research: the study of Black American English", in Steve Lander and Ken Reah, eds., Aspects of Linguistic Variation. Proceedings of the Conference on Language Varieties, July 1980. Sheffield: CECTAL 1981: 11-19.

500 **SoRelle, Zell Rodgers,** "Segmental phonology of Texas panhandle speech." Ph.D. U. of Denver 1965. DAI 26: 12, 7307A.

501 ---, "Segmental phonology of Texas panhandle speech", in The Study of Sounds. Vol. 12. Papers delivered at the Second World Congress of Phoneticians, Tokyo, 26 - 31 August 1965. Tokyo: Phonetic Society of Japan 1966: 463-76.

502 **Sorrells, Mary Suzanne Kirkman,** "Black dialect: Current linguistic studies and Black American novels." Ph.D. East Texas State U. 1971. DAI 33: 2, 742A.

503 **Sosa, Francisco,** "The phonic constituency of Barrio English: a case of phonological adoption", in DiPietro/Blansitt 1977: 120-7.

504 **Soudek, Lev,** Structure of Substandard Words in British and American English. Bratislava: Vyd. SAV 1967.

505 ---, "Conversions in British and American substandard English", Recueil Linguistique de Bratislava 2 (1968): 64-72.

506 ---, "The development and use of the morpheme burger in American English", Linguistics 68 (1971): 61-89.

507 **Southard, Bruce,** "Will Rogers and the language of the Southwest: a centennial perspective", in Arrell Morgan Gibson, ed., Will Rogers: A Centennial Tribute. Oklahoma City: Oklahoma Historical Society 1979: 113-23.

508 ---, "The Linguistic Atlas of Oklahoma and computer cartography", JEngL 16 (1983): 65-77.

509 **Southerland, R.H.,** ed., Readings on Language in Canada. Calgary 1973.

510 **Spears, Arthur K.,** The Other Come in Black English. Austin, Texas: Southwest Educational Development Laboratory 1980.

1511 ---, "The Black English semi-auxiliary come", Language 58 (1982) 850-72.

1512 **Spears, James E.,** "Notes on negro folk speech", North Carolina Folklore 18 (1970): 154-7.

1513 **Spears, Monroe K.,** "Black English", in Michaels/Ricks 1980: 169-79.

1514 **Spears, Richard A.,** Slang and Euphemism: A Dictionary of Oaths Curses, Insults, Sexual Slang and Metaphor, Racial Slurs, Drug Talk Homosexual Lingo, and Related Matters. Middle Village, N.Y.: Jonathan David Publ. 1981.

1515 **Spencer, Nancy J.,** "Singular y'all", AS 50 (1975): 315-7.

1516 **Spitzbardt, Harry,** "Some peculiarities of American English", CIEFL Bulletin 15,1 (1979): 77-87.

1517 **Spolsky, Bernard,** ed., The Language Education of Minority Children Rowley, Mass.: Newbury House 1972.

1518 ---, "American Indian bilingual education", Linguistics 198 (1977) 57-72.

1519 ---, "Bilingual education in the United States", in Alatis 1978: 268-84.

1520 --- and **Robert Cooper,** eds., Frontiers in Bilingual Education. Rowley Mass.: Newbury House 1977.

1521 ---, ---, eds., Case Studies in Bilingual Education. Rowley, Mass. Newbury House 1978.

1522 --- and **Wayne Holm,** "Bilingualism in the six-year-old child", in William F. Mackey and Theodore Andersson, eds., Bilingualism in Early Childhood. Rowley, Mass.: Newbury 1977: 167-73.

1523 --- and **James Kari,** "Trends in the study of Athapaskan language maintenance and bilingualism", in Joshua A. Fishman, ed., Advances in the Study of Societal Multilingualism. The Hague: Mouton 1978 90-104.

1524 **Sprauve, Gilbert A.,** "Toward the parameters of Black English", in Harrison/Trabasso 1976: 45-54.

1525 **Stanley, George Edward,** "Phonoaesthetics and West Texas dialect" Linguistics 71 (1971): 95-102.

1526 **St. Clair, Robert N.,** ed., Perspectives on Applied Sociolinguistics From the Language Medium of Education to the Semiotic Language of the Media. Lawrence, Kansas: Coronado 1979.

1527 ---, **Guadalupe Valdes** and **Jacob Ornstein-Galicia,** *Social and Educational Issues in Bilingualism and Biculturalism*. Washington, D.C.: UP of America 1982.

1528 **Steffensen, Margaret Siebrecht,** "The acquisition of Black English", Ph.D. Urbana-Champaign, Illinois 1974. DAI 35: 7, 4489A.

1529 **Steinmetz, Sol,** "Jewish English in the United States", *AS* 56 (1981): 3-16.

1530 **Stephens, M. Irene,** "Elicited imitation of selected features of two American English dialects in head start children", *Journal of Speech and Hearing Research* 19 (1976): 493-508.

1531 **Stephenson, Edward A.,** "Is 'totalled' spreading?", *AS* 41 (1966): 160.

1532 ---, "Some Newfoundland phrases, sayings, and figures of speech", *AS* 41 (1966): 294-7.

1533 ---, "The beginnings of the loss of postvocalic /r/ in North Carolina", *JEngL* 2 (1968): 57-77.

1534 ---, "Linguistic predictions and the waning of southern [ju] in *tune*, *duke*, *news*", *AS* 45 (1970): 297-300.

1535 ---, "On defining Standard American English", in Shores/Hines 1977: 211-8.

1536 **Stern, H.H.,** "Unity and diversity in L2 teaching: English in non-native settings from a Canadian perspective", in Larry E. Smith, ed., *English for Cross-Cultural Communication*. New York: St. Martin's Press /London: Macmillan 1981: 57-73.

1537 **Stern, Henry R.,** "The changing language of American catholicism", *AS* 54 (1979): 83-89.

1538 **Sternglass, Marilyn S.,** "Dialect features in the compositions of black and white college students: the same or different?", *College Composition and Communication* 25 (1974): 259-63.

1539 **Stevens, James H., Kenneth F. Ruder** and **Roy Tew,** "Speech discrimination in black and white children", *Language and Speech* 16 (1973): 123-9.

1540 **Stevenson, Roberta,** "The pronunciation of English in British Columbia: an analysis." M.A. Thesis, U. of British Columbia 1978.

1541 **Stewart, Penny Helen,** "Linguistic signals to ethnic group and socioeconomic class among eighty ten-year-olds in Hattiesburg, Mississippi." Ph.D. U. of Southern Mississippi 1976. DAI 37: 9, 5796A.

1542 **Stewart, William A.,** "Nonstandard speech patterns", Baltimore Bulletin of Education 43 (1966): 52-65.

1543 ---, "Sociolinguistic factors in the history of American negro dialects", FFLR 5,2 (1967): 11, 22, 24, 26, 30.

1544 ---, "Continuity and change in American negro dialects", FFLR 6,1 (1968): 3-4, 14-16, 18.

1545 ---, "Sociopolitical issues in the linguistic treatment of negro dialect", in Alatis 1970: 215-23.

1546 ---, "Historical and structural bases for the recognition of negro dialect", in Alatis 1970: 239-47.

1547 ---, "Toward a history of American negro dialect", in Frederick Williams, ed., Language and Poverty. Perspectives on a Theme. Chicago: Markham 1970: 351-97.

1548 ---, "Observations (1966) on the problems of defining negro dialect", FFLR 9, 1/2 (1971): 47-49, 57.

1549 ---, "Facts and issues concerning black dialect", The English Record 21,4 (1971): 121-35.

1550 **Stobie, Margaret,** "A bluff is a grove of trees", English Language Notes 5 (1967): 49-51.

1551 **Story, George M.,** "Newfoundland dialect: an historical view", Canadian Geographical Journal 70 (1965): 126-31.

1552 ---, "The dialects of Newfoundland", in Joseph R. Smallwood, ed., The Book of Newfoundland. Vol. III. St. Johns, Nfld.: Newfoundland Book Publishers 1967: 559-63.

1553 ---, "Newfoundland English usage", Encyclopedia Canadiana, vol. 7. Ottawa 1968: 321-2.

1554 ---, "A critical history of dialect collecting in Newfoundland", RLS 6 (1975): 1-4.

1555 ---, "The dialects of Newfoundland", Canadian Antiques Collector 10,2 (1975): 22-23.

1556 --- and **William Kirwin,** "National dictionaries and regional homework", RLS 3 (1971): 19-22.

1557 ---, ---, "The dictionary of Newfoundland English: progress and promise", RLS 5 (1974): 15-17.

1558 ---, ---, and **John D.A. Widdowson,** "Collecting for 'The Dictionary of Newfoundland English'", in McDavid/Duckert 1973: 104-8.

1559 ---, ---, ---, "Selected sample entries", RLS 6 (1975): 10-17.

1560 ---, ---, ---, Dictionary of Newfoundland English. Toronto: UP 1982.

1561 **Straker, Dolores Yvonne,** "Situational variables in language use." Ph.D. Yeshiva U. 1978. DAI 40, 3374B.

1562 ---, "Situational variables in language use", International Journal of the Sociology of Language 26 (1980): 101-22.

1563 **Strevens, Peter,** British and American English. London: Collier and Macmillan 1972.

1564 **Strickland, Arney L.,** "A study of geographical and social distribution of some folk words in Indiana." Ph.D. Ball State U. 1970. DAI 31: 9, 4750A.

1565 **Strite, Victor L.,** "Black English: the progressive dialect", in Lance/Gulstadt 1978: 505-12.

1566 ---, "Focusing and control in Black English pronouns", in Cooley/Barnes/Dunn 1979: 436-43.

1567 **Stuart, Jesse,** "New wine in old bottles: Part II", Kentucky Folklore Record 13 (1967): 20-24.

1568 **Summerlin, Nan Jo Corbitt,** "A dialect study: affective parameters in the deletion and substitution of consonants in the Deep South." Ph.D. Florida State U. 1972. DAI 33: 8, 4394A.

1569 ---, Some Systematic Phonological Variations from the Regional Standard in the Oral Language of Lower Socio-Economic White and Negro Students in a Rural Deep South County. Final Report. Tallahassee: Florida State U. 1973.

1570 **Švejcer, Aleksandr D.,** Standard English in the United States and England. The Hague: Mouton 1978.

1571 **Swacker, Marjorie Elizabeth,** "Attitudes of native and nonnative speakers toward varieties of American English." Ph.D. Texas A & M U. 1977. DAI 38: 11, 6692A.

1572 **Syeed, Sayyid Mohammad,** "Psychology of dialect differentiation: the emergence of Muslim English in America", Islamic Culture: An English Quarterly 51 (1977): 241-51.

1573 **Szwed, John Francis,** Private Cultures and Public Imagery: Interpersonal Relations in a Newfoundland Peasant Society. St. John's, Nfld.: Memorial U. of Newfoundland 1966.

1574 **Tabbert, Russell,** "Alaskan data in the Dictionary of Canadianisms", AS 58 (1983): 191-2.

1575 **Tally, Justine,** "Roots: a case for Black English", Revista Canaria de Estudios Ingleses 3 (1981): 46-56.

1576 **Tamony, Peter,** "Western words", Western Folklore 24 (1965): 115-8, 202-5; 25 (1966): 41-45; 26 (1967): 124-7, 192-5; 27 (1968): 117-24.

1577 **Tannen, Deborah,** "New York Jewish conversational style", International Journal of the Sociology of Language 30 (1981): 133-49.

1578 **Tarone, Elaine Elisabeth,** "Aspects of intonation in vernacular white and black English speech." Ph.D. U. of Washington 1972. DAI 33: 12, 7068A.

1579 ---, "Aspects of intonation in Black English", AS 48 (1973): 29-36.

1580 **Tarpley, Fred A.,** From Blinky to Blue-John: A Word Atlas of Northeast Texas. Wolfe City, Tex.: UP 1970.

1581 ---, "Language development programs for Southern American negroes", in George E. Perren and John L.M. Trim, eds., Applications of Linguistics. Selected Papers of the Second International Congress of Applied Linguistics, Cambridge 1969. London: Cambridge UP 1971: 407-15.

1582 **Taubitz, Ronald,** "British and American English: some differences and their implications for the EFL teacher", Die Neueren Sprachen 77 (1978): 159-64.

1583 **Taylor, Danille,** "Black English in black folklore", in Harrison/Trabasso 1976: 209-25.

1584 **Taylor, John Morgan, III,** "A preliminary analysis of certain phonological characteristics of South Florida, urban, black speech." Ph.D. Miami 1973. DAI 34: 1, 301A.

1585 **Taylor, Orlando L.,** "An introduction to the historical development of Black English: some implications for American education." ERIC ED 035 863, 1969.

1586 ---, "Teachers' attitudes toward black and nonstandard English as measured by the language attitude scale", in Shuy/Fasold 1973: 174-201.

1587 --- and **Dianna Ferguson,** "A study of cross-cultural communication between blacks and whites in the U.S. army", Linguistic Reporter 17,3 (1975): 8-11.

1588 **Tchalekian, Chavarche,** "A bird's eye view of bilingualism in Canada", Proceedings of the Pacific Northwest Council on Foreign Languages 29,2 (1978): 22-24.

1589 **Teller, Joan W.,** "The treatment of foreign terms in Chicago restaurant menus", AS 44 (1969): 91-105.

1590 **Terrebonne, Nancy Goppert,** "The Black English vernacular in the writing of young adults from Dayton, Ohio." Ph.D. Louisiana State U. 1975. DAI 36: 4, 2180A.

1591 **Terrell, Francis,** "Dialectal differences between middle-class black and white children who do and do not associate with lower-class black children", Language and Speech 18 (1975): 65-73.

1592 ---, **Sandra L. Terrell** and **Sanford Golin,** "Language productivity of black and white children in black versus white situations", Language and Speech 20 (1977): 377-83.

1593 **Terrell, Tracy D.,** "Some theoretical considerations on the merger of the low vowel phonemes in American English", in Henry Thompson et al., eds., Proceedings of the Second Annual Meeting of the Berkeley Linguistics Society, February 14 - 16, 1976. Berkeley, California: Berkeley Linguistics Society, U. of California 1976: 350-9.

1594 ---, "A quantitative study of the merger of /a/ and /ɔ/ in southern California", in Harold H. Key, Gloria G. McCullough and Janet B. Sawyer, eds., The Bilingual in a Pluralistic Society: Proceedings of the Sixth Southwest Areal Language and Linguistics Workshop. SWALLOW VI. Long Beach: California State U. 1978: 224-39.

1595 **Teschner, Richard V.,** "Historical-psychological investigations as complements to sociolinguistic studies in relational bilingualism: two Mexican-American cases", The Bilingual Review 8 (1981): 42-55.

1596 ---, **Garland D. Bills** and **Jerry R. Craddock,** Spanish and English of United States Hispanos: A Critical, Annotated, Linguistic Bibliography. Arlington, Va.: Center for Applied Linguistics 1975.

1597 **Thomas, Alain,** "The pronunciation of /h/", in Léon/Martin 1979: 111-27.

1598 **Thomas, Charles K.,** "Florida pronunciation", *Southern Speech Journal* 33 (1968): 223-9.

1599 **Thomas, William J.,** "Black language in America", *Wichita State University Bulletin* 49,1 (1973): 3-14.

1600 **Thompson, Carolyn McLendon,** "A comparative study of standard and nonstandard English syntactic features in the language of lower socioeconomic children." Ph.D. Ohio State U. 1981. DAI 42: 5, 2005A.

1601 **Thompson, Roger Mark,** "Language loyalty in Austin, Texas: A study of a bilingual neighborhood." Ph.D. Austin 1971. DAI 32: 11, 6408A.

1602 ---, "Mexican American language loyalty and the validity of the 1970 census", *Linguistics* 128 (1974): 7-18.

1603 ---, "Mexican-American English: social correlates of regional pronunciation", *AS* 50 (1975): 18-24.

1604 **Tibbetts, Arn** and **Charlene Tibbetts,** *What's Happening to American English?* New York: Scribner's 1978.

1605 **Timm, L.A.,** "Spanish-English code switching: el porque and how not to", *Romance Philology* 28 (1975): 473-82.

1606 **Tixier y Vigil, Yvonne** and **Nan Elsasser,** "The effects of the ethnicity of the interviewer on conversation: a study of Chicana women", *International Journal of the Sociology of Language* 17 (1976): 161-70.

1607 **Tobin, Terence,** "An approach to black slang", *AS* 47 (1972): 151-5.

1608 **Todd, Julia McAmis,** "A phonological analysis of the speech of aged citizens of Claiborne County, Mississippi." Ph.D. Louisiana State U. 1965. DAI 26: 8, 4894A.

1609 **Tomaszczyk, Jerzy,** "Some thoughts on accented speech: the English of Polish Americans", *Studia Anglica Posnaniensia* 13 (1981): 131-47.

1610 **Toon, Thomas E.,** "Riding point on the lexicon of the North American West", *Dictionaries* 1 (1979): 57-68.

1611 ---, "Making a North American dictionary after Avis", *Canadian Journal of Linguistics* 26 (1981): 142-9.

1612 ---, "Variation in contemporary American English", in Bailey/Görlach 1982: 210-50.

1613 **Torrey, Jane W.,** "Teaching standard English to speakers of other dialects", in G.E. Perren and J.L.M. Trim, eds., *Applications of Linguistics. Selected Papers of the Second International Congress of*

Applied Linguistics, Cambridge 1969. London: Cambridge UP 1971: 423-8.

1614 **Traugott, Elizabeth Closs,** "Postscript on 'Black English'", in E.C.T., A History of English Syntax. A Transformational Approach to the History of English Sentence Structures. New York: Holt, Rinehart and Winston 1972: 187-94.

1615 ---, "Pidgins, creoles and the origins of vernacular Black English", in Harrison/Trabasso 1976: 57-93.

1616 ---, "Why Black English retains so many creole forms", in Ian F. Hancock, ed., Readings in Creole Studies. Ghent: Story-Scientia 1979: 339-46.

1617 **Troike, Rudolph C.,** "On social, regional, and age variation in Black English", FFLR 11 (1973): 7-8.

1618 **Trudgill, Peter** and **Jean Hannah,** International English. A Guide to Varieties of Standard English. London: Edward Arnold 1982.

1619 **Tucker, C. Allen,** "The Chinese immigrant's language handicap: its extent and its effects", FFLR 7,1 (1969): 44-45, 170.

1620 **Tucker, Carlene,** "Perception of students' characteristics as a function of Standard English and variants of Black English speech." Ph.D. Chapel Hill, North Carolina 1981. DAI 42: 12, 5110A.

1621 **Tucker, G. Richard,** "Language issues for the 1980's: examples from the United States", Canadian Modern Language Review 37 (1981): 441-6.

1622 **Tucker, R. Whitney,** "Contraction of 'was'", AS 41 (1966): 76-78.

1623 **Turner, Paul R.,** ed., Bilingualism in the Southwest. Tucson: Arizona UP 1973. 2nd ed., revised and updated, 1982.

1624 **Tway, Patricia V.,** "An ethnography of communication in a china factory: a case study of an occupational jargon." Ph.D. Syracuse U. 1974. DAI 36: 1, 383A.

1625 ---, "Workplace isoglosses: lexical variation and change in a factory setting", Language in Society 4 (1975): 171-83.

1626 ---, "Speech differences of factory worker age groups", Studies in Linguistics 18 (1975): 65-73.

1627 ---, "Verbal and nonverbal communication of factory workers", Semiotica 16 (1976): 29-44.

1628 ---, "Cognitive processes and linguistic forms of factory workers", Semiotica 17 (1976): 13-20.

1629 ---, "The careful and casual speech of factory workers", Studia Linguistica 30 (1976): 68-76.

1630 **Tyson, Adele,** "Pleonastic pronouns in Black English", JEngL 10 (1976): 54-59.

1631 **Udell, Gerald,** "The speech of Akron, Ohio: the segmental phonology: a study of the effects of rapid industrialization on the speech of a community." Ph.D. U. of Chicago 1967.

1632 **Udelson, Teresa Ann McAllister,** "The syntactic patterns of a group of Chicago school children: hesitations and spontaneous speech." Ph.D. Northwestern U. 1975. DAI 36: 7, 4458A.

1633 **Umeda, Noriko,** "Vowel duration in American English", Journal of the Acoustical Society 58 (1975): 434-45.

1634 ---, "Consonant duration in American English", Journal of the Acoustical Society 61 (1977): 846-58.

1635 --- and **C.H. Coker,** "Allophonic variation in American English", Journal of Phonetics 2 (1974): 1-5.

1636 ---, ---, "Subphonemic details in American English", in G. Fant, ed., Auditory Analysis and Perception of Speech. London: Academic Press 1975: 539-64.

1637 **Underwood, Gary N.,** "Semantic confusion: evidence from the Linguistic Atlas of the Upper Midwest", JEngL 2 (1968): 86-95.

1638 ---, "Slop pail: an example of dialectal blending", AS 43 (1968): 268-76.

1639 ---, "Vocabulary change in the Upper Midwest", PADS 49 (1968): 8-28.

1640 ---, "Cobweb and spiderweb", Word Watching 45 (1970): 4-6.

1641 ---, "The dialect of the Mesabi Iron Range in its historical and social context." Ph.D. U. of Minnesota 1970. DAI 31: 10, 5384A. Published: PADS 67 [1982].

1642 ---, "Midwestern terms for the grounds squirrel", Western Folklore 29: 167-74.

1643 ---, "Some rules for the pronunciation of English in northwest Arkansas." ERIC ED 057 652, 1971.

1644 ---, "The research methods of the Arkansas Language Survey", AS 47 (1972): 211-20.

1645 ---, "Problems in the study of Arkansas dialects", Orbis 22 (1973): 64-71.

1646 ---, "American English dialectology: alternatives for the Southwest", Linguistics 128 (1974): 19-40.

1647 ---, "How you sound to an Arkansawyer", AS 49 (1974): 208-15.

1648 ---, "Razorback slang", AS 50 (1975): 50-69.

1649 ---, "The orthoepy of Jim Everhart, or how to talk like the proverbial good old boy from Texas", in Barkin/Brandt 1980: 205-14.

1650 ---, "Arkansawyer postvocalic /r/", AS 57 (1982): 32-43.

1651 **Underwood, Lawrence Eugene,** "Overland stages: a sociolinguistic study of place names along a portion of Arkansas' southwest trail." Ed.D. East Texas State U. 1980. DAI 41: 10, 4387A.

1652 **Urion, Carl,** "Canadian English and Canadian French: a review", in Darnell 1971: 33-44.

1653 ---, "A German-English interlingual 'key'", in Darnell 1971: 223-30.

1654 **Uskup, Frances,** "Social markers of urban speech: a study of elites in Chicago." Ph.D. Illinois Institute of Technology 1974. DAI 35: 5, 2973A.

1655 **Valdés-Fallis, Guadalupe,** "Code-switching and language dominance: some initial findings", General Linguistics 18 (1978): 90-104.

1656 **Vallee, F.G.** and **J. de Vries,** "Trends in bilingualism in Canada", in Joshua A. Fishman, ed., Advances in the Study of Societal Multilingualism. The Hague: Mouton 1978: 761-92.

1657 **Vandergriff, James,** "An Eskimo-English dialect: a discussion of some major features", The University of South Florida Language Quarterly 18 (1980): 36-38.

1658 **Van Horn, Lawrence Franklin,** "Differential language use at Burnt Church, a bilingual Micmac Indian Community of Eastern Canada." Ph.D. City U. New York 1977. DAI 38: 5, 2889A.

1659 **Van Riper, William R.,** "Shortening the long conversational dialect interview", in L. Davis 1972: 177-83.

1660 ---, "General American: an ambiguity", in Scholler/Reidy 1973: 232-42.

1661 **Van Riper, Mrs. William R.,** "The speech of the American heartland: Oklahoma", JEngL 13 (1979): 65-71.

1662 **Van Sertima, Ivan,** "My Gullah brother and I: exploration into a community's language and myth through its oral tradition", in Harrison/Trabasso 1976: 123-46.

1663 **Vass, Winifred Kellersberger,** The Bantu Speaking Heritage of the United States. Los Angeles: Center for Afro-American Studies, U. of California 1979.

1664 **Vaughn-Cooke, Anna Fay,** "The implementation of a phonological change: the case of resyllabification in Black English (Parts 1 and 2)." Ph.D. Georgetown U. 1976. DAI 38: 1, 234A.

1665 --- and **Ida Stockman,** "A new thrust in developmental research on Black English", Linguistic Reporter 24,1 (1981): 1, 3-5.

1666 **Veltman, Calvin J.,** "New opportunities for the study of language shift: the anglicization of New England language minorities", Language Problems and Language Planning / Lingvaj Problemoj kaj Lingvo-Planado 3 (1979): 65-75.

1667 **Vickers, Carol,** " 'Meddlin' and other words in Black English", Mississippi Folklore Register 16,2 (1982): 55-59.

1668 **Viereck, Wolfgang,** "Zur Negersprache in den Vereinigten Staaten", Idioma 6 (1969): 55-60.

1669 ---, "Britische und amerikanische Sprachatlanten", Zeitschrift für Dialektologie und Linguistik 38 (1971): 167-205.

1670 ---, "The growth of dialectology", JEngL 7 (1973): 69-86.

1671 ---, "Die Erforschung des Black English in den USA - Sinn und Unsinn", Grazer linguistische Studien 2 (1975): 102-18.

1672 ---, Regionale und soziale Erscheinungsformen des britischen und amerikanischen Englisch. Tübingen: Niemeyer 1975.

1673 ---, "Arbeiten zur regionalen und sozialen Variation des amerikanischen Englisch: Anmerkungen zur Bedeutung der 'American Dialect Society'", Arbeiten aus Anglistik und Amerikanistik 2 (1977): 153-5.

1674 ---, "Afro-amerikanische Aspekte der Mobilität: 'Black English' - eine kritische Auseinandersetzung", Amerikastudien 23 (1978): 330-40.

1675 ---, "Sprachliche Variation im Englischen und ihre Erforschung", Zeitschrift für Dialektologie und Linguistik 45 (1978): 161-74.

1676 ---, "Social dialectology: a plea for more data", Studia Anglica Posnaniensia 11 (1979): 15-25.

1677 ---, "Das amerikanische Englisch in Forschung und Lehre", Zeitschrift für Dialektologie und Linguistik 49 (1982): 351-65.

1678 ---, "On the history of American English: sense and nonsense", Eigoseinen. The Rising Generation (Tokyo) 129,7 (1983): 329-31.

1679 **Viney, Jean-Paul,** "Problèmes de bilinguisme au Canada", in L.G. Kelly, ed., Description and Measurement of Bilingualism. An International Seminar, University of Moncton, June 6 - 14, 1967. Toronto: UP 1967: 367-401.

1680 **Vogel, Phyllis Palmer,** "A comparative survey of the morphology of lower class rural kindergarten students in Alachua County, Florida." Ed.D. U. of Florida 1970. DAI 31: 11, 6040A.

1681 **Wächtler, Kurt,** "Zur substantivischen Wortbildung mittels Lehnsuffix im amerikanischen Englisch", in Herbert E. Brekle and Leonhard Lipka, eds., Wortbildung, Syntax und Morphologie: Festschrift zum 60. Geburtstag von Hans Marchand am 1. Oktober 1967. The Hague: Mouton 1968: 230-41.

1682 ---, Geographie und Stratifikation der englischen Sprache. Düsseldorf: Bagel / Bern: Francke 1977.

1683 ---, "Vom Regionaldialekt zur Konsensusvarietät: sozialdialektologische und sozialpsychologische Aspekte der Mobilität in den USA", Amerikastudien 23 (1978): 341-6.

1684 **Wagner, Marilyn Diane,** "Receptive and expressive language differences between lower and middle-income black children and their relationship to performance on tasks requiring spatial and conceptual inferences." Ph.D. Emory U. 1980. DAI 41: 4, 1573B.

1685 **Wald, Benji,** "English in Los Angeles: searching for a speech community", in Timothy Shopen and Joseph M. Williams, eds., Style and Variables in English. Cambridge, Mass.: Winthrop 1981: 250-72.

1686 **Walker, D.C.,** "Another Edmonton idiolect: comments on an article by Professor Avis", in Chambers 1975: 129-32.

1687 **Walker, Sheila,** "Black English: expression of the Afro-American experience", Black World 20,7 (1971): 4-16.

1688 **Walker, Ursula G.,** "Structural features of negro English in Natchitoches Parish." M.A. Thesis, Northwestern State College of Louisiana 1968.

1689 **Walsh, Harry** and **Victor L. Mote,** "A Texas dialect feature: origins and distribution", AS 49 (1974): 40-53.

1690 **Walters, Joel,** "Variation in the requesting behavior of bilingual children", International Journal of the Sociology of Language 27 (1981): 77-92.

1691 **Wanamaker, Murray G.,** "The language of Kings County, Nova Scotia." Ed.D. U. of Michigan 1965. DAI 26: 5, 2740A.

1692 ---, "The language of Kings County, Nova Scotia", Journal of the Atlantic Provinces Linguistic Association 2 (1980): 48-55.

1693 **Wang, William S-Y.,** "Assessing language incompetence", The Linguistic Reporter 22 (1980): 2.

1694 **Ward, Charles A.,** "The Serbian and Croatian communities in Milwaukee", General Linguistics 16 (1976): 151-65.

1695 **Ward, Mabel,** "Logging terms from Coos County, Oregon", Northwest Folklore 1 (1965): 29-30.

1696 **Ward, Norman,** "Talk Canadian!" Quarterly of Canadian Studies 1 (1972): 164-7.

1697 **Warden, Michael,** "The phonetic realization of diphthongs", in Léon/Martin 1979: 35-47.

1698 **Warkentyne, H.J.,** "Contemporary Canadian English: a report of the Survey of Canadian English", AS 46 (1971): 193-9.

1699 ---, ed., Papers from the Fourth International Conference on Methods in Dialectology (Methods IV). Victoria, B.C.: Dept. of Linguistics, U. of Victoria 1981.

1700 --- and **A.C. Brett,** "Changing norms in Canadian English usage", Journal of the Atlantic Provinces Linguistic Association 3 (1981): 3-18.

1701 **Watson, D.R.,** "Analysing readings of Black American speech: some general observations on description in ordinary language", Journal of Pragmatics 2 (1978): 71-76.

702 **Weber, Debby,** "Canadian raising in a Windsor, Ontario, dialect", Calgary Working Papers in Linguistics 1,1 (1975): 22-25.

703 **Welch, Kay,** "Australian lowering: a study of one dialect difference between Canadian and Australian spoken English", Calgary Working Papers in Linguistics 1,1 (1975): 44-46.

704 **Wells, John C.,** Accents of English. Vol. 3: Beyond the British Isles. Cambridge: UP 1982.

705 **Welna, Jerzy,** "On the rise of the New English central vowel phoneme /ə:/", Leuvense Bijdragen 67 (1978), 163-7.

706 **Welsh, James M.,** "Addenda to the vocabulary of railroading", AS 43 (1968): 282-90.

707 **Wentworth, Harold** and **Stuart Berg Flexner,** Dictionary of American Slang, with a Supplement by Stuart Berg Flexner. New York: Crowell 1967. 2nd Suppl. Ed. 1975.

708 **Wentz, Jim** and **Erica McClure,** "Aspects of the syntax of the code-switched discourse of bilingual children", in Ingemann 1976: 351-70.

709 **Wescott, Roger W.,** "The phonology and morphology of American English slang", in DiPietro/Blansitt 1977: 108-19.

710 ---, "'Zazzification in American English slang", Forum Linguisticum (Lake Bluff, Ill.) 3 (1978): 185-7.

711 **West, John Foster,** "Dialect of the southern mountains", North Carolina Folklore 14 (1966): 31-34.

712 **West, Michael** and **William F. Mackey,** Canadian Reader's Dictionary. Don Mills, Ontario: Longmans, Canada / Montreal: Centre Educatif et Culturel 1968.

713 **White, William,** "Teen-gang talk in Philadelphia", AS 41 (1966): 72.

714 **Whiteman, Marcia Farr,** "Dialect influence and the writing of black and white working class Americans." Ph.D. Georgetown U. 1976. DAI 37: 6, 3595A.

715 ---, ed., Reactions to Ann Arbor: Vernacular Black English and Education. Washington, D.C.: Center for Applied Linguistics 1981.

716 **Whitley, M. Stanley,** "Dialectal syntax: plurals and modals in Southern American", Linguistics 161 (1975): 89-108.

717 **Whittaker, Della Silverman,** "A content analysis of Black English

markers in compositions of community college freshmen." Ph.D. U. o Maryland 1972. DAI 34: 2, 756A.

1718 **Widdowson, John David A.,** "The dialect of Fortune Harbour, New foundland: A pronouncing glossary", Folia Linguistica 2 (1968) 316-26.

1719 ---, "Aspects of traditional verbal control: threats and threatenin figures in Newfoundland folklore." Ph.D. Memorial U. of Newfound land 1973. DAI 40: 12, 6255A.

1720 ---, "Speech, sounds and tape recorded evidence in the Dictionary o Newfoundland English", RLS 6 (1974): 18-20.

1721 ---, "A checklist of Newfoundland expressions", Lore and Language (1979): 33-40.

1722 **Wiggins, Antoinette Violet,** "A study of dialect differences in th speech of first grade negro children in the inner city schools o Cleveland, Ohio." Ed.D. Thesis, Indiana U. 1970. DAI 31: 10, 5682A.

1723 **Wiggins, M. Eugene,** "The cognitive deficit - difference controversy: black sociopolitical perspective", in Harrison/Trabasso 1976: 241-54.

1724 **Wiggins, Rudolph Valentino,** "A comparison of children's interest in a attitude towards reading material written in Standard and Blac English forms." Ph.D. Ohio State U. 1971. DAI 32: 7, 3808A.

1725 **Wilbur, Verna Martin,** "Language attitudes of teachers at selecte historically black colleges as measured by the language attitud scale." Ph.D. Texas Women's U. 1981. DAI 42: 8, 3487A.

1726 **Willcott, Paul** and **Jacob Ornstein,** eds., College English and th Mexican American. San Antonio, Texas: Trinity U. 1977.

1727 **Williams, Cratis,** "Appalachian speech", North Carolina Historica Review 55 (1978): 174-9.

1728 **Williams, Darlene Faye,** "Black English and the Stanford-Binet test o intelligence." Ph.D. Stanford U. 1981. DAI 42: 5, 2005A.

1729 **Williams, Darrell,** "An investigation of possible Gullah survivals in th speech and cultural patterns of black Mississippians." Ph.D. Ohi State U. 1973.

1730 **Williams, Frederick G.,** "Portuguese bilingualism among Azoreans i California", Hispania 63 (1980): 724-30.

1731 **Williams, Robert L.,** ed., Ebonics: The True Language of Black Folks St. Louis, Mo.: Robert L. Williams and Associates 1975.

732 **Williamson, Juanita V.,** "A phonological and morphological study of the speech of the negro of Memphis, Tennessee." PADS 50 (1968).

733 ---, The Speech of Negro High School Students in Memphis, Tennessee. Final report, project no. 5-0592-12-1. United States Department of Health, Education, and Welfare, 1968.

734 ---, "A note on it is / there is", Word Study 45 (1969): 5-6.

735 ---, "Selected features of speech: black and white", CLA Journal 13 (1970): 420-3.

736 ---, "A look at Black English", Crisis 78 (1971): 169-73, 185.

737 ---, "A look at the direct question", in L. Davis 1972: 207-14.

738 ---, "On the embedded question", in Scholler/Reidy 1973: 260-7.

739 --- and **Virginia M. Burke,** eds., A Various Language. Perspectives on American Dialects. New York et al.: Holt, Rinehart and Winston 1971.

740 **Willis, Clodius,** "Synthetic vowel categorization and dialectology", Language and Speech 14 (1971): 213-28.

741 ---, "Perception of vowel phonemes in Fort Erie, Ontario, Canada, and Buffalo, New York: an application of synthetic vowel categorization tests to dialectology", Journal of Speech and Hearing Research 15 (1972): 246-55.

742 **Wilson, Gordon,** "Mammoth Cave words. I - VIII", Kentucky Folklore Record 11 (1965): 5-8, 28-31, 52-55, 78-81; 12 (1966): 15-20, 67-71, 93-98, 119-22.

743 ---, "Similes from the Mammoth Cave region with a farm flavor", Kentucky Folklore Record 14 (1968): 44-50, 69-75.

744 **Wilson, H. Rex,** "The geography of language", in Albert H. Marckwardt, ed., Linguistics in School Programs. Part II. Chicago, Ill.: U. of Chicago Press 1970: 64-84.

745 ---, "Canadian English", in Sidney I. Landon and Ronald J. Bogus, eds., The Doubleday Dictionary for Home, School, and Office. New York: Doubleday 1975: xxv-xxvii.

746 **Wilson, Joseph B.,** "The English spoken by German Americans in central Texas", in Schach 1980: 157-73.

747 **Winther, Kris,** Amerikanskt slanglexicon. Stockholm: Prisma 1970.

1748 **Wiseman, Dennis,** "Non-Standard negro dialect: myth or reality", English Record 25,3 (1974): 9-12.

1749 **Wofford, Jean Elizabeth,** "Code-switching in black third grade low-socioeconomic status children in formal and informal situations." Ph.D. Berkeley, California 1978. DAI 39: 9, 5485A.

1750 ---, "Ebonics: a legitimate system of oral communication", Journal of Black Studies 9 (1979): 367-82.

1751 **Wölck, Wolfgang** and **Paul L. Garvin,** eds., The Fifth LACUS Forum 1978. Columbia, S.C.: Hornbeam 1979.

1752 **Wolfe, Virginia Smith,** "The social significance of negro speech." Ph.D. Ohio State U. 1968. DAI 29, 1870B.

1753 **Wolfram, Walter A.,** "Linguistic correlates of social stratification in the speech of Detroit negroes." Ph.D. Hartford Seminary Foundation 1969. Published as A Sociolinguistic Description of Detroit Negro Speech. Washington, D.C.: Center for Applied Linguistics 1969.

1754 ---, "Linguistic correlates of social differences in the negro community", in Alatis 1970: 249-57.

1755 ---, "Black-white speech differences revisited", in Wolfram/Clarke 1971: 139-61.

1756 ---, "Overlapping influence and linguistic assimilation in second generation Puerto Rican English", in Smith/Shuy 1972: 15-46.

1757 ---, "Objective and subjective parameters of language assimilation among second-generation Puerto Ricans in East Harlem", in Shuy/Fasold 1973: 148-73.

1758 ---, "A note on fluctuating variants and the status of Vernacular Black English." ERIC ED 093 174, 1973.

1759 ---, "The relationship of white southern speech to vernacular Black English", Language 50 (1974): 498-527.

1760 ---, Sociolinguistic Aspects of Assimilation. Puerto Rican English in New York City. Arlington, Va.: Center for Applied Linguistics 1974.

1761 ---, "Language assessment in Appalachia: a sociolinguistic perspective", Appalachian Journal: A Regional Studies Review 4 (1977): 224-34.

1762 ---, "On the linguistic study of Appalachian speech", Appalachian Journal: A Regional Studies Review 5 (1977): 92-102.

1763 ---, "Toward a description of a-prefixing in Appalachian English", AS 51 (Issue for 1976; 1979): 45-56.

1764 ---, "Landmark decision affects Black English speakers", The Linguistic Reporter 22,2 (1979): 1, 6-7.

1765 ---, "a-prefixing in Appalachian English", in Labov 1980: 107-42.

1766 ---, "Language knowledge and other dialects", AS 57 (1982): 3-18.

1767 --- and **Donna Christian,** Appalachian Speech. Arlington, Va.: Center for Applied Linguistics 1976.

1768 ---, ---, "The language frontier in Appalachia", Appalachian Notes 5,3 (1977): 33-41.

1769 ---, ---, "On the application of sociolinguistic information: test evaluation and dialect differences in Appalachia", in Williams 1980: 177-218.

1770 ---, ---, **William Leap** and **Lance Potter,** Variability in the English of Two Indian Communities and Its Effect on Reading and Writing. Washington, D.C.: Center for Applied Linguistics 1979.

1771 --- and **Nona H. Clarke,** eds., Black-White Speech Relationships. Washington, D.C.: Center for Applied Linguistics 1971.

1772 --- and **Ralph W. Fasold,** The Study of Social Dialects in American English. Englewood Cliffs, New Jersey: Prentice-Hall 1974.

1773 --- and **Robert Johnson,** Phonological Analysis: Focus on American English. Washington, D.C.: Center for Applied Linguistics 1982.

1774 **Wood, Gordon** R., Sub-regional Speech Variations in Vocabulary, Grammar, and Pronunciation. USOE Cooperative Research Project 3046. Edwardsville: Southern Illinois U. 1967.

1775 ---, "On ways to examine the local language", Computer Studies 3,2 (1970): 100-10.

1776 ---, Vocabulary Change: A Study of Variation in Regional Words in Eight of the Southern States. Carbondale: Southern Illinois UP 1971.

1777 ---, "Refinements in tabular models of variation in regional American English", in Computational and Mathematical Linguistics. Proceedings of the International Conference on Computational Linguistics. Pisa 27.8. - 1.9.1973. Firenze 1977: 343-6.

1778 **Woods, Howard Bruce,** "A socio-dialectology survey of the English spoken in Ottawa: a study of sociological and stylistic variation in

Canadian English." Ph.D. U. of British Columbia 1979. DAI 40: 11, 5846A.

1779 ---, "A summary of a study of sociological and stylistic variation in Canadian English", Sociolinguistics Newsletter 11 (1980): 10-12.

1780 **Woolf, Henry Bosley,** "Mencken revisited", English Studies 47 (1966): 102-18.

1781 **Wright, Richard Louis,** "Language standards and communicative style in the black church." Ph.D. Austin 1976. DAI 37: 9, 5797A.

1782 **Wyatt, P.J.,** "Wichita dialect: A study in a Kansas urban community." Ph.D. Indiana U. 1976. DAI 37: 8, 5098A.

1783 **Yalden, Maxwell F.,** "The bilingual experience in Canada", in Ridge 1981: 71-87.

1784 **Yamasawa, Kayoko,** "A study of certain sound changes in present-day American speech: the Japanese learner's problem", in Collected Essays by the Members of the Faculty. No. 11. Kyoritsu, Japan: Kyoritsu Women's Junior College 1968: 90-113.

1785 **Yellin, David,** "The Black English controversy: implications for the Ann Arbor case", Journal of Reading 24 (1980): 150-4.

1786 **Yoshioka, Hirohide, Anders Löfqvist** and **Hajime Hirose,** "Laryngeal adjustments in the production of consonant clusters and geminates in American English", Journal of the Acoustical Society 70 (1981): 1615-23.

1787 **Young, Jean Skoronski,** "Cohesion in spoken discourse: a preliminary analysis of the speech of lower-income black drug abusers." Ph.D. Illinois Institute of Technology 1979. DAI 40: 10, 5428A.

1788 **Young, Robert W.,** "English as a second language for Navajos", in Lourie/Conklin 1978: 162-72.

1789 **Young, Rodney W.,** "The development of semantic categories in Spanish-English and Navajo-English bilingual children", in Turner 1973: 95-105.

1790 **Zandvoort, R.W.,** "American English", in A.N.J. den Hollander and Sigmund Skard, eds., American Civilisation: An Introduction. London: Longman 1968: 375-88.

1791 **Zawadzki, Paul A.** and **David P. Kuehn,** "A cineradiographic study of static and dynamic aspects of American English /r/", Phonetica 37 (1980): 253-66.

1792 **Zentella, Ana Celia,** "'Hablamos los dos. We speak both': Growing up bilingual in El Barrio." Ph.D. U. of Pennsylvania 1981. DAI 42: 7, 3142A.

1793 ---, "Spanish and English in contact in the United States: the Puerto Rican experience", Word 33 (1982): 41-57.

1794 **Zettersten, Arne,** A Statistical Study of the Graphic System of Present-day American English. Lund: Studentlitteratur 1969.

1795 **Zue, Victor W.** and **Martha Laferriere,** "Acoustic study of medial /t, d/in American English", Journal of the Acoustical Society of America 66 (1979): 1039-50.

1796 **Zviadadze, Givi,** A Dictionary of Modern American and British English on a Contrastive Basis: A Reference Book Giving Indispensable Information on How to Distinguish American English from British English in Words, Phrases, Meanings, Grammar, Orthography, and Pronunciation. Tbilisi, Georgia, USSR: Tbilisi State U. Publ. 1973.

1797 **Zwicky, Arnold M.,** "Across the channel and across the Atlantic", Linguistic Inquiry 9 (1978): 725-8.

1798 **Zwicky, Ann D.** and **Arnold M. Zwicky,** "America's national dish: the style of restaurant menus", AS 55 (1980): 83-92.

Index

This index groups the titles of the bibliography mainly by regional and ethnic categories. Thus, it is intended to facilitate the use of the bibliography considerably. It does not include counties or smaller localities as categories; these are subsumed under the respective state. Apart from this limitation, however, references are as specific as possible. Studies dealing with the English of some ethnic group in a specific area can usually be found under both headings, which often provides information not indicated in the title of the respective publication. Of course, a few categories overlap to a certain extent, e.g. 'Mexican Americans' and 'Southwest', 'Appalachia' and 'Tennessee' or 'North Carolina', etc. In such cases, my aim was to give the user as much information as possible, i.e. such items are entered under both headings if possible. American and Canadian English are treated as two separate main categories. Essay collections, which include several articles on American or Canadian English and are required mainly for internal reference within the bibliography, constitute a third separate group, as their inclusion in one of the other two classes would have been misleading. The category "American English (general)" includes studies on (standard) AmE without further specification, studies dealing with variation in AmE in the whole of the country, and theoretical or methodological studies which present data from a number of different communities. Sub-groups are ordered alphabetically.

1.0. United States of America

1.1. American English (general)

1.2. Regions

1.3. States

Alabama 72, 211-2, 508, 515-6, 576, 1351.

Alaska 1574, 1657.

Arizona 129, 921, 1106-7.

Arkansas 427, 429-30, 454-5, 623, 683, 1410, 1463, 1643-5, 1647-8, 1650-1.

California 7, 8, 10, 17, 18, 213, 693, 931, 935, 1092-6, 1321, 1331, 1594, 1730.

Connecticut 624, 1460.

Florida 57, 672, 701, 706, 836-7, 967, 1339-41, 1474, 1584, 1598, 1680.

Georgia 116, 154, 580, 601, 1178, 1238-9, 1242, 1250, 1257, 1259, 1374-5, 1531.

Idaho 49, 697.

Illinois 242, 244, 524, 527-8, 548, 597, 869, 994, 1461, 1708.

Indiana 255-6, 554, 634-6, 777-8, 818, 1148, 1301, 1315, 1564.

Iowa 217, 698-9.

Kansas 313, 880, 883.

Kentucky 178, 188, 352, 593-4, 597, 652, 819, 981, 1032, 1059, 1078, 1567, 1742-3.

Louisiana 193, 229, 239, 900-1, 908, 971, 989, 1368-9, 1688.

Maine 641, 875, 1411.

Maryland 578.

Massachusetts 318, 366, 850, 852, 858, 1289, 1740.

Michigan 704, 1268.

Minnesota 670, 1224, 1641.

Mississippi 189, 705, 956, 987, 1541, 1608, 1664, 1667, 1729, 1759.

Missouri 454-5, 465, 679, 719, 880, 883, 1206, 1232.

Nebraska 312.

1.4. Urban and metropolitan areas

1.5. Ethnic groups and bilingualism

1.6. Slang and argot

43, 67, 187, 236, 258, 432, 445-6, 560, 573, 599, 767, 771, 928-30, 934, 980-4 1155, 1181, 1221-2, 1225, 1291, 1364, 1370, 1376, 1460, 1504-5, 1514, 1707 1747.

2.0. Canada

2.1. Canadian English (general)

68, 74-77, 79-82, 84-90, 92-95, 113, 134, 215-6, 246, 287-8, 290-2, 299, 340-2 344, 415, 449-50, 510, 555-6, 582, 629, 717-8, 726, 755-6, 762, 781-2, 784-5 787, 912, 933, 949, 995, 1027, 1049, 1109, 1147, 1188-9, 1212-4, 1216, 1274 1287, 1305, 1307, 1312, 1338, 1358, 1365, 1386, 1390, 1392-6, 1403, 1406-7 1413, 1509, 1550, 1556, 1611, 1618, 1682, 1696, 1698, 1700, 1703-4, 1712 1745.

2.2 Provinces

Alberta 460.

British Columbia 320, 581, 630, 1283, 1356, 1391, 1540.

Labrador 155, 1211.

New Brunswick 141, 572, 783, 786, 1658.

Newfoundland 306, 402, 462, 466-7, 611, 720, 790-802, 807, 1169-71, 1207 11, 1267, 1288, 1336, 1415, 1475, 1532, 1551-5, 1557-60, 1573, 1718-21.

Nova Scotia 112, 1366, 1691-2.

Ontario 83, 265, 289, 1304, 1306, 1308-10, 1354, 1702, 1740-1.

Prince Edward Island 328, 786, 1296-9.

Quebec 238, 289, 293, 916, 1139-40, 1306, 1308-10, 1382, 1398, 1431.

Saskatchewan 227, 572, 591.

2.3 Urban and metropolitan areas

Calgary 571.

Edmonton 78, 1686.

2.4 Ethnic groups and bilingualism

2.5. Slang and argot

3.0. Essay Collections

A selective bibliography of English as a world language (1965 - 1983)

Manfred Görlach

he following list is an attempt to select bibliographical references to the ıost useful books and articles on the subject of varieties of English outside ireat Britain, Ireland, the United States and Canada. It is a by-product of :.W. Bailey/M. Görlach, eds., English as a World Language (1982). An earlier ersion of this bibliography has appeared in AAA (Görlach 1979).

he field of 'World English' is becoming more and more difficult to survey. I m sadly aware of omissions and, probably, errors in this list, which I was orced to compile in a most unsystematic way - mostly from other bibliog- aphies and lists of references, or from articles and lists of publications indly sent by friends and colleagues. Among them, it is a pleasure to thank ı particular: R.W. Bailey, D. Blair, W. Branford, R.D. Eagleson, I.F. ancock, M. Hellinger, B.B. Kachru, T. Kandiah, L.W. Lanham, D. Lawton, .B. LePage, R.R. Mehrotra, P. Mühlhäusler, J.T. Platt, J.B. Pride, J.E. einecke, L. Todd, P.J. Trudgill, S.K. Verma, and R.E. Wood.

he standard bibliographies have of course been used, but since these are ften a number of years behind schedule, lists such as those in Current ontents Linguistics (Frankfurt/M.: Universitätsbibliothek) and Carrier idgin have provided invaluable information on recent and current research.

number of decisions I had to take call for explanation:

. I have included Hawaii and the Caribbean, but not U.S. varieties proper.

. Tok Pisin and Sranan etc. cannot be regarded as varieties of English. They have been included for historical reasons as English-based, and for the reason that some pidgins may develop into a continuum with an English acrolect.

. Problems of English as an additional language and special teaching issues have in general been excluded. However, much of the varieties literature on the Caribbean, Africa and India is necessarily on teaching English, and so it would have been unwise to be too narrow. Creative writing and literary aspects have also been excluded except where they make a special contribution to the subject.

4. I have generally not included collections of texts, except where the introductions and other explanatory matter justified it. Also excluded are short notes, often on single words, essayistic and popular treatments, all articles from daily papers, etc. For more complete information on individual regions the specialized bibliographies (such as those compiled by Aggarval (1982), Blair (1979), Fishman (1977), Holm (1983), Reinecke et al. (1975), Sandefur (1983)) will have to be consulted.

5. The cut-off date 1965 is arbitrary and excludes much relevant research, which, however, will be easily accessible in other bibliographies. On the other hand, I have tried to be more complete for the period 1977 -summer 1983, including as much as was accessible to me. I have also (cautiously) given a number of references to forthcoming books, if they are likely to appear in the near future.

Abbreviations

conf.	conference
cong.	congress
proc.	proceedings
U.	University
AA	American Anthropologist
AAA	Arbeiten aus Anglistik und Amerikanistik
AfrLS	African Language Studies
AnL	Anthropological Linguistics
ArL	Archivum Linguisticum
AS	American Speech
AUMLA	Journal of the Australasian Universities Language and Literature Association
CIE(FL)	Central Institute of English, Hyderabad (Bulletin)
CJL	Canadian Journal of Linguistics
CP	The Carrier Pidgin
CQ	Caribbean Quarterly
CTL	Current Trends in Linguistics, ed. T. Sebeok
DAI	Dissertation Abstracts International
EAW	English Around the World
EinA	English in Africa

ETF	English Teaching Forum
ELTJ	English Language Teaching Journal
ES	English Studies
EUSA	English Usage in South Africa
EWW	English World-Wide
FoLi	Folia Linguistica
GL	General Linguistics
GURT	Georgetown University Round Table
IJSL	International Journal of the Sociology of Language
IncL	The Incorporated Linguist
IRAL	International Review of Applied Linguistics
ITL	Review of Applied Linguistics
JAL	Journal of African Languages
JCS	Journal of Creole Studies
JEL	Journal of English Linguistics
JIPA	Journal of the International Phonetic Association
JL	Journal of Linguistics
JMMD	Journal of Multilingual and Multicultural Development
Kivung	Journal of the Linguistic Society of the University of Papua and New Guinea
L&S	Language and Speech
LingC	Linguistic Communications
LingR	Linguistic Reporter
LL	Language Learning
LMLP	La Mondo Lingvo-Problemo
LPLP	Language Problems and Language Planning
LSoc	Language in Society
LSp	Lebende Sprachen
Meanjin	M. Quarterly
ML	Modern Languages
PacL	Pacific Linguistics
R(E)LC	Regional (English) Language Centre, Singapore (Journal)
RPh	Romance Philology
SCL	Society for Caribbean Linguistics, Occasional Papers

TeReo Proceedings of the Linguistic Society of New Zealand

TESOLQ Teachers of English to Speakers of Other Languages Quarterly

TPS Transactions of the Philological Society

VEAW Varieties of English Around the World

WAJML West African Journal of Modern Languages

WP(L) Working Papers (in Linguistics)

ZAA Zeitschrift für Anglistik und Amerikanistik

ZDL Zeitschrift für Dialektologie und Linguistik

ZPSK Zeitschrift für Phonetik, Sprachwissenschaft und Kommunikationsforschung

1 **Abdulaziz, M.M.H.,** "Triglossia and Swahili-English bilingualism in Tanzania", LSoc 1 (1972): 197-213.

2 **Abrahams, Roger D.,** The Man-of-Words in the West Indies. Performance and the Emergence of Creole Culture. Baltimore: The Johns Hopkins UP 1983.

3 --- and **R. Bauman,** "Sense and nonsense in St. Vincent: speech behaviour and decorum in a Caribbean community", AA 73 (1971): 762-72.

4 **Achebe, Chinua,** "The African writer and the English language", repr. in Morning Yet on Creation Day. London: Heinemann 1975: 55-62.

5 **Acheson, P.,** "The English language in Saudi-Arabia", EAW 11 (1974): 1-3, 7.

6 **Adams, C.M.,** "A survey of Australian English pronunciation", Phonetica 20 (1969): 81-130.

7 **Adekunle, M.A.,** "Toward a realistic approach to problems of English instruction in West Africa", ELTJ 24,3 (1970): 269-78.

8 ---, "Sociolinguistic problems in English language instruction in Nigeria", in David M. Smith and Roger W. Shuy, eds., Sociolinguistics in Cross-Cultural Analysis. Washington, D.C., 1972.

9 ---, "Oral English in Nigeria: the sociolinguistic realities", Lagos Review of English Studies 1,1 (1978): 11-21.

10 ---, "Non-random variation in the Nigerian English", in Ubahakwe 1979: 27-42.

11 **Adeniran, Adekunle,** "Personalities and policies in the establishment of English in Northern Nigeria (1900-1943)", IJSL 22 (1979): 57-77.

12 ---, "Nigerian elite English as a model of Nigerian English", in Ubahakwe 1979: 227-41.

13 **Adesanoye, F.A.,** "A study of varieties of written English in Nigeria." Ph.D. Ibadan 1973.

14 ---, "Formality as an aspect of unreadability in Nigerian English", in Ubahakwe 1979: 184-99.

15 **Adetugbo, A.,** "Appropriateness and Nigerian English", in Ubahakwe 1979: 137-66.

16 ---, "Nigerian English and communicative competence", in Ubahakwe 1979: 167-83.

17 **Adey, A.D.,** "South African 'Black' English: some indications", EUSA 8 (1977): 35-39.

18 **Adler, M.,** Pidgins, Creoles and Lingua Francas. Hamburg: Buske 1977.

19 **Afendras, Evangelos A.,** "Studies of the sociology of language in Singapore: an integrative report", RELC 9,2 (1978).

20 --- and **Eddie C.Y. Kuo,** eds., Language and Society in Singapore. Singapore: UP 1980.

21 **Afolayan, A.,** "The linguistic problem of Yoruba learners and users of English." Ph.D. London 1968.

22 ---, "Acceptability of English as a second language in Nigeria", in Greenbaum 1978: 13-25.

23 **Aggarval, Narindar K.,** English in South Asia: a Bibliographical Survey of Resources. Gurgaon: Indian Documentation Service 1982.

24 **Agheyisi, Rebecca M.,** "West African Pidgin English: simplification and simplicity." Ph.D. Stanford 1971. DAI 32: 8, 4558A.

25 **Ahmad, H.E.G.,** "The future of the English language in Pakistan", in Anwar S. Dil, ed., Pakistan Forum I. Abbottabad, W.P.: Bookservice 1966.

26 **Aitchison, Jean,** Language Change: Progress or Decay? London: Fontana 1981. (Tok Pisin 193-216 etc.)

27 **Akere, Funso,** "Grammatical competence and communictive competence in relation to the users of English as a second language", Lagos Review of English Studies 1,1 (1978): 22-32.

28 ---, "Socio-cultural constraints and the emergence of a Standard Nigerian English", AnL 20 (1978): 407-21; repr. in Pride 1982: 85-99.

29 **Akers, Glenn A.,** "Final consonant clusters in the Jamaican continuum", in DeCamp/Hancock 1974: 1-73.

30 ---, Phonological Variation in the Jamaican Continuum. Ph.D. Harvard 1977; pr. Ann Arbor: Karoma 1981.

31 **Alam, Q.Z.,** "A lexical feature of newspaper English in India", Indian Linguistics 36 (1975): 29-36.

32 **Alatis, James E.,** ed., International Dimensions of Bilingual Education. GURT 1978. Washington, D.C.: Georgetown UP 1979.

33 **Alleyne, Mervyn C.,** "The linguistic continuity of Africa in the Caribbean", Black Academy Review 4 (1970): 3-16; repr. in Henry Richards, ed., Topics in Afro-American Studies. Buffalo: Black Academic Press 1971: 3-16.

34 ---, "Acculturation and the cultural matrix of creolization", in Hymes 1971: 169-86.

35 ---, "Dimensions and varieties of West Indian English and the implications for teaching", TESL Talk 7,1 (Toronto 1976): 51-55.

36 ---, Comparative Afro-American. Ann Arbor: Karoma 1980.

37 **Allsopp, S.R.R.,** "British Honduras - 'The linguistic dilemma'", CQ 11 (1965): 54-61.

38 ---, "Some problems in the lexicography of Caribbean English", CQ 17 (1971): 10-24.

39 ---, "Why a dictionary of Caribbean English usage?" etc., Circulars A1-3, T4. Bridgetown, Barbados: UWI at Cave Hill 1972-77.

40 ---, "A proposed dictionary of Caribbean usage", ELT Documents 6 (1973): 12-15.

41 ---, Africanisms in the Idioms of Caribbean English. SCL, Occ. Paper 6 (1976).

42 ---, "The case for Afrogenesis", in Cave 1976.

43 ---, "Washing up our wares: towards a dictionary of our use in English", in Rickford 1976: 173-94.

44 ---, "The need for sociolinguistic determinants of status-labelling in a regional lexicography", paper 1977, rev. in SCL 1978.

45 ---, "Some methodological aspects in the preparation of the Dictionary of Caribbean English Usage (DCEU)", Studies in Lexicography 2,1 New York: Bantam 1978: 30-43.

46 ---, "How does the creole lexicon expand?" in Valdman/Highfield 1980: 89-107.

47 ---, "The Creole treatment of passivity", in Carrington 1983: 142-54.

48 ---, "Cross-referencing many standards: some sample entries for the Dictionary of Caribbean English Usage (DCEU)", in Görlach (forthcoming).

49 **Amastae, Jon,** "Dominican English Creole phonology: an initial sketch", AnL 21 (1978): 182-204.

50 ---, "Agentless constructions in Dominican Creole", Lingua 59,1 (1983): 47-76.

51 **Amayo, Airen,** "Tone in Nigerian English", Papers from the Regional Meeting Chicago Linguistic Society 16 (1980): 1-9.

52 **Anand, M.R.,** "A plea for English for higher education", in Language and Society in India, Transactions of the Indian Institute for Advanced Study, 8. Simla 1969.

53 **Andersen, R.,** ed., Pidginization and Creolization as Language Acquisition. Rowley, Mass.: Newbury House 1983.

54 **Angogo, Rachel,** "Language and politics in South Africa", Studies in African Linguistics 9 (1978): 211-21.

55 --- and **Ian F. Hancock,** "English in Africa: Emerging standards or diverging regionalism?" EWW 1 (1980): 67-96.

56 **Ansari, Iqbal A.,** Uses of English. Varieties of English and their Uses. New Delhi 1978.

57 **Ansre, Gilbert,** "Four rationalisations for maintaining European languages in education in Africa", African Languages 5,2 (1979): 10-17.

58 **Armstrong, R.,** "Language policies and language practices in West Africa", in Fishman et al. 1968.

59 **Atkinson, R.E.B.,** "RP and English as a world language", IRAL 13 (1975): 69-72.

60 **Augustin, John J.,** "Regional standards of English in peninsular Malaysia", in Pride 1982: 249-58.

61 **Awatefe, C.** et al., Nigerian Pidgin: Self Study Tables and Dialogs. Rowley, Mass.: Educ. Services 1966.

62 **Babu, B.A.P.,** "Prosodic features in Indian English - stress, rhythm and intonation", CIEFL Bulletin 8 (1970-71): 33-39.

63 **Bähr, Dieter,** Standard English und seine geographischen Varianten. UTB 160. München: Fink 1974.

64 **Bailey, Beryl L.,** Jamaican Creole Syntax: a Transformational Approach. Cambridge 1966.

65 ---, Jamaican Creole Language Course. Washington, D.C. 1968.

66 ---, "Jamaican Creole: can dialect boundaries be defined?" in Hymes 1971: 341-8.

67 **Bailey, Charles-James N.,** Variation and Linguistic Theory. Arlington: 1973.

68 ---, "The patterning of language variation", in Bailey/Robinson 1973: 156-86.

69 --- and **Roger W. Shuy,** eds., New Ways of Analyzing Variation in English. Washington, D.C.: Georgetown UP 1973.

70 **Bailey, Richard W.** and **J.L. Robinson,** eds., Varieties of Present-day English. New York: Macmillan 1973.

71 --- and **Manfred Görlach,** eds., English as a World Language. Ann Arbor: Michigan UP 1982.

72 **Baker, Sidney J.,** The Australian Language. Sydney: Currawong Press, 2nd ed. 1966.

73 **Balasubramian, T.,** "Stress and rhythm in English and Tamil: a study in contrast", CIEFL Bulletin 11 (1975): 1-13.

74 **Balint, A.,** "Towards an encyclopedic dictionary of Nuginian (Melanesian Pidgin)", Kivung 6 (1973): 1-31.

75 **Bamgboṣe, Ayọ,** "The English language in Nigeria", in Spencer 1971: 35-48.

76 ---, Language and Society in Nigeria. Stanford: UP 1973.

77 ---, "Standard Nigerian English: issues of identification", in Kachru 1982: 99-111.

78 **Banjo,** Ayọ, "A historical view of the English language in Nigeria", Ibadan 28 (1970): 63-68.

79 ---, "Towards a definition of standard Nigerian spoken English", Annales de l'Université d'Abidjan, Ser. H, vol. I, 1971: 165-75.

80 ---, "Standards of correctness in Nigerian English", West African Journal of Education 15,2 (1971): 123-7.

81 ---, "University and standardization of the English language", WAJML 1 (1976): 93-98.

82 --- and **Peter Young,** "On editing a second-language dictionary: the proposed Dictionary of West African English (DWAE)", EWW 3 (1982): 87-91.

83 **Bansal, R.K.,** "Spoken English in India, suggestions for improvement", CIEFL Bulletin 6 (1966-67): 95-116.

84 ---, "A study of the intonation patterns in educated Indian English", CIEFL Bulletin 6 (1966-67): 117-22.

85 ---, The Intelligibility of Indian English. Monograph 4. Hyderabad: CIEFL 1969.

86 ---, "A phonetic analysis of English spoken by a group of well educated speakers from Uttar Pradesh", CIEFL Bulletin 8 (1970-71): 1-9.

87 ---, "Indian English", Souvenir of the Sixth All-India Conference of Dravidian Linguists, Andhra U., Waltair (1976): 55-57.

88 ---, "The phonology of Indian English", in Mohan 1978: 101-14.

89 --- and **J.B. Harrison,** Spoken English for India: a manual of speech and phonetics. Madras: Orient Longman 1976.

90 **Barbag (-Stoll), Anna,** "Pidgins - their origin, function and extension", Africana Bulletin 20 (1974).

91 ---, "Some aspects of semantic shifts in English loanwords in West African Pidgin English", Africana Bulletin 22 (1975): 131-8.

92 ---, "The role of the English language in the development of African nationalism", Africana Bulletin 24 (1976): 35-42.

93 ---, "Sierra Leone and Liberia experiment: a historical and linguistic overview", Africana Bulletin 26 (1977): 103-12.

94 ---, "Nigerian Pidgin English as a medium of literary expression", Africana Bulletin 27 (1978): 55-63.

95 ---, "Nigerian Pidgin lexicon - a phonological, morphological and semantic analysis", Africana Bulletin 30 (1981).

96 ---, Social and Linguistic History of Nigerian Pidgin English. Tübingen: Stauffenberg 1983.

97 **Barbeau, D.,** "Le pidgin English comme moyen d'expression littéraire chez les romanciers du Nigéria", Annales de l'Université d'Abidjan, ser. D, 5 (1972): 5-30.

98 **Barnickel, Klaus-Dieter,** Sprachliche Varianten des Englischen. München: Hueber 1982.

99 **Bates, R.H.** and **R.G. Hay,** Understanding Australian Speech. A Programmed Introduction to Australian English. Randwich: NSW UP 1972.

100 **Baudet, Martha M.,** "Identifying the African grammatical base of the Caribbean creoles: a typological approach", in Highfield/Valdman 1981: 104-17.

101 **Bauer, Anton,** Das melanesische und chinesische Pidginenglisch. Regensburg: Carl 1974.

102 ---, Das neomelanesische Englisch: Soziokulturelle Funktion und Entwicklung einer lingua franca. Bern: Lang 1975.

103 ---, Das Kanton-Englisch. Ein Pidginidiom als Beispiel für ein soziolinguistisches Kulturkontaktphänomen. Bern: Lang 1975.

104 **Bautista, Maria Lourdes S.,** "The Filipino bilingual's competence: a model based on an analysis of Tagalog-English code switching." Ph.D. Manila, Ateneo U. 1974; pr. PacL C59, Canberra 1980.

105 ---, "The noun phrase in Tagalog-English code-switching", Studies in Philippine Linguistics 1,1 (1977): 1-16.

106 ---, "Yaya English: an idiosyncratic dialect of Philippine English", paper Singapore 1981.

107 **Bayer, Jennifer,** "Anglo-Indians and their mother tongue", Indian Linguistics 40,2 (1979): 78-84.

108 **Beau, Thomas William,** "An analysis of the oral reading miscues of Hawaiian Islands dialect speakers in grades four, five, and six." Ph.D. Arizona State U. 1976. DAI 37: 6, 3392A.

109 **Beeton, D.R.,** "Some aspects of English usage in South Africa", Taalfasette 6 (Pretoria, 1968): 7-16.

110 --- and **H. Dorner,** A Dictionary of English Usage in Southern Africa. Cape Town: Oxford UP 1975.

111 **Bell, Alan G.,** "The language of radio news in Auckland: a sociolinguistic study of style, audience and subediting variation." Ph.D. Auckland 1978. DAI 39: 11, 6735A.

112 ---, "This isn't the BBC: colonization in New Zealand English", Applied Linguistics 3,3 (1982): 246-58.

113 ---, "Broadcast news as a language standard", IJSL 40 (1983): 29-42. (NZE)

114 **Bernard, J.R.L.-B.,** "Some measurements of some sounds of Australian English." Ph.D. Sydney 1967.

115 ---, "On the uniformity of spoken Australian English", Orbis 18 (1969): 62-73.

116 **Bernhardt, Stephen,** "Dialect and style shifting in the fiction of Samuel Selvon", in Carrington 1983: 266-76.

117 **Berry, Jack,** A Dictionary of Sierra Leone Krio. Evanstown 1968.

118 ---, "Pidgins and creoles in Africa", CTL 7 (1971): 510-36.

119 ---, ed., "Language and Education in the Third World", IJSL 8 (1976).

120 ---, "Tone and intonation in Guyanese English", in A. Juilland, ed., Linguistic Studies Offered to Joseph Greenberg, II: Phonology. Saratoga, Ca.: Anma Libri 1976: 263-70.

121 **Bhargava, Prem Sagar,** "Linguistic interference from Hindi, Urdu and Punjabi and internal analogy in the grammar of Indian English." Ph.D. Cornell U. 1968.

122 **Bhatia, Sugan Chand,** "Comprehensibility of Educated Indian English and its implications in curriculum and pedagogy." Ph.D. Austin 1972.

123 ---, "The choice of an instrumental model in English language teaching in India", IRAL 13 (1975): 152-7.

124 **Bhatia, Tej K.,** "English and the vernaculars of India: contact and change", Applied Linguistics 3,3 (1982): 235-45.

125 **Bhatnagar, C.P.,** "To kill or not to kill: the role of English in India and the factors threatening to throttle it", Modern Review 141,4 (1977): 209-18.

126 **Bickerton, Derek,** "The nature of a creole continuum", Language 49 (1973): 640-69.

127 ---, "Creolization, linguistic universals, natural semantax and the brain", Hawaii WPL 6 (Honolulu, 1974): 125-41; repr. in Day 1980: 1-18.

128 ---, "The structure of polylectal grammars", in R. Shuy, ed., 23rd Round Table. Washington, D.C., 1975: 17-42.

129 ---, The Dynamics of a Creole System. London: Cambridge UP 1975.

130 ---, "Can English and Pidgin be kept apart?" in McElhanon 1975: 21-27.

131 ---, "Pidgin and creole studies", Annual Review of Anthropology 5 (1976): 169-93.

132 ---, "Creole tense-aspect systems and universal grammar", in Cave 1976.

133 ---, "Pidginization and creolization: language acquisition and language universals", in Valdman 1977: 49-69.

134 ---, "Putting back the clock in variation studies", Language 53 (1977): 353-62.

135 ---, "Some problems of acceptability and grammaticality in pidgins and creoles", in Greenbaum 1978: 27-37.

136 ---, "The status of BIN in the Atlantic creoles", in Hancock 1979: 309-14.

137 ---, "Decreolization and the creole continuum", in Valdman/Highfield 1980: 1091-27.

138 ---, Roots of Language. Ann Arbor: Karoma 1981.

139 ---, "Creole languages", Scientific American 249,1 (July 1983): 108-15.

140 --- and **Carol Odo,** Change and Variation in Hawaiian English, I, II. Honolulu: Social Sciences and Linguistics Institute, U. of Hawaii 1976-7.

141 **Bickley, Verner,** "The international uses of English: research in progress", in Brumfit 1982: 81-94.

142 **Bishop, Hezekiah Adolfo,** "Bidialectal traits of West Indians in the Panama Canal Zone." Ed.D. Columbia U. Teachers Coll. 1976. DAI 37: 9, 5790A.

143 **Blair, David,** "On the origins of Australian pronunciation", Macquarie WP 1,1 (North Ryde, 1975): 17-27.

144 ---, "Judging the varieties of Australian English", Macquarie WP 1,5 (1977): 109-11.

145 ---, "An Australian English bibliography", Macquarie WP 2,1 (1978): 1-46.

146 **Boadi, L.A.,** "Education and the role of English in Ghana", in Spencer 1971: 49-65.

147 **Boggs, Stephen T.,** "The development of verbal disputing in part-Hawaiian children", LSoc 7,3 (1978): 325-44.

148 **Bokamba, Eyamba G.,** ed., Language Policies in African Education. Washington, D.C.: UP of America 1979.

149 ---, "The Africanization of English", in Kachru 1982: 77-98.

150 **Boretzky, Norbert,** Kreolsprachen, Substrate und Sprachwandel. Wiesbaden: Harrassowitz 1983.

151 **Branford, Jean,** A Dictionary of South African English. Cape Town: Oxford UP 1978; 2nd ed. 1980.

152 **Branford, William,** "English in the South African Republic - an interim report", EAW 14 (1976): 1-2, 6.

153 ---, "A dictionary of South African English as a reflex of the English-speaking cultures of South Africa", in de Villiers 1976: 297-316.

154 ---, Voorloper. An Interim Presentation of Materials for a Dictionary of South African English on Historical Principles. Grahamstown: 1977.

155 **Brann, Conrad Max Benedict,** Mother Tongue, Other Tongue, and Further Tongue. Maiduguri, Nigeria: University 1979.

156 **Brash, Elton,** "Tok Pisin, Tok Piksa na Tok Bokis", Kivung 4 (1971): 12-20.

157 —, "Tok Pisin", Meanjin 34 (1975): 320-37.

158 **Brauner, S.,** "Ist der Begriff 'Nationalsprache' auch für Sprachen des subsaharischen Afrika anwendbar?" ZPSK 28 (1975): 263-70.

159 **Brennan, Paul W.,** "Issues of language and law in Papua New Guinea", Language Planning Newsletter 9,2 (1983): 1-7.

160 **Brink, A.P.,** "English and the Afrikaans writer", EinA 3 (1976): 35-46.

161 **Broadbridge, Claire,** Some Devices for Focus in Trinidadian. SCL Occ. Paper 14 (1980).

162 —, "A methodology for the analysis of language use in a post-creole community", in Carrington 1983: 130-41.

163 **Brockman, C.T.,** "Language, communication and ethnicity in British Honduras", in W.F. Mackey and J. Ornstein, eds., Studies in Language Contacts: Methods and Cases. The Hague: Mouton 1979: 161-80.

164 **Bruce, Donald E.** and **John Walsh,** "English in Guam and Micronesia", EAW 28 (1983): 1, 6-7.

165 **Brumfit, Christopher J.,** ed., English for International Communication. Oxford: Pergamon 1982.

166 **Bughwan, D.,** "An investigation into the use of English by Indians in South Africa with special reference to Natal." Ph.D. Pretoria 1970.

167 **Burgess, O.,** "Intonation patterns in Australian English", L&S 16 (1973): 314-26.

168 **Burrowes, Audrey** (in collaboration with Richard Allsopp), "Barbadian Creole: A note on its social history and structure", in Carrington 1983: 38-45.

169 **Camden, Bill,** A Descriptive Dictionary, Bislama to English. Vila, New Hebrides, 1977.

170 —, "Parallels in structure and lexicon and syntax between New Hebrides Bislama and the South Santo language spoken at Tangoa", Papers in Pidgin and Creole Linguistics 2, PacL A57, Canberra 1979: 51-118.

171 **Campbell, Donald** et al., "English in international settings: problems and their causes", EWW 3 (1982): 66-76; repr. in Smith 1983: 35-47.

172 **Candler, W.J.,** "Teaching English as a second dialect in Liberia", ELTJ 31 (1977): 321-5.

173 **Capell, Arthur,** "The changing status of Melanesian Pidgin", LMLP 1 (1969): 107-15.

174 **Cariappa, G.K.M.,** "The English language in India", in G.S. Reddy, ed., The Language Problem in India. New Delhi 1973.

175 **Carls, Uwe,** "Select bibliography of Indian English (up to 1978)", ZAA 27 (1979): 327-40.

176 ---, "The status of English in India", Linguistische Studien A 100. Berlin: Akad. Wiss. 1982: 80-87.

177 **Carr, Elizabeth Ball,** Da Kine Talk, From Pidgin to Standard English in Hawaii. Honolulu: Hawaii UP 1972.

178 **Carrington, Lawrence D.,** "Deviations from Standard English in the speech of primary school children in St. Lucia and Dominica: a preliminary survey", IRAL 7 (1969): 165-84, 259-81.

179 ---, "Determining language education policy in Caribbean socio-linguistic complexes", in Berry 1976: 27-43.

180 ---, "Basilect, mesolect and corrective pressure in the speech of some Trinidadian children", in Cave 1976.

181 ---, Literacy in the English-speaking Caribbean. Paris: UNESCO 1981.

182 ---, ed., Studies in Caribbean Language. St. Augustine: SCL 1983.

183 ---, "The substance of creole studies - a reappraisal", in Gilbert 1984.

184 **Carter, Hazel,** Evidence for the Survival of African Prosodies in West Indian Creoles. SCL, Occ. Paper 13 (1979).

185 ---, "Suprasegmentals in Jamaican and Guyanese: some African comparisons", in Gilbert 1984.

186 **Cassidy, Frederic G.,** "Multiple etymologies in Jamaican Creole", AS 32 (1966): 49-53.

187 ---, "Teaching Standard English to speakers of creole in Jamaica", in J.E. Alatis, ed., GURT 1969.

188 ---, "Tracing the pidgin element in Jamaican creole", in Hymes 1971: 203-22.

189 ---, "Revisions in the Dictionary of Jamaican English", in Cave 1976.

190 ---, "Gullah and Jamaican creole - the African connection", in Alatis 1979: 621-9.

191 ---, "The place of Gullah", AS 55 (1980): 3-16.

192 ---, "Interjections in Jamaican Creole", in Gilbert 1984.

193 --- and **R.B. LePage,** Dictionary of Jamaican English. London: 1967, 2nd ed. 1980.

194 **Castelo, C.M.,** "Filipino-English bilingualism", ZPSK 23 (1970): 129-37.

195 **Caudmont, Jean,** "La situation linguistique dans l'Archipel de San Andrés et Providencia (Colombie)", in R. Werner, ed., Sprachkontakte. Tübingen: Narr 1980: 129-50.

196 ---, Etude d'un parler créole anglais de Colombie. (forthcoming).

197 **Cave, G.N.,** "Some sociolinguistic factors in the production of standard language in Guyana and implications for the language teacher", LL 20 (1970): 249-63.

198 ---, ed., New Directions in Creole Studies. Georgetown: U. of Guyana 1976.

199 **Central Institute of English and Foreign Languages,** The Sound System of Indian English. Hyderabad: CIEFL 1972.

200 ---, A Bibliography of Indian English. Hyderabad: CIEFL 1972.

201 **Champion, E.A.,** "The contribution of English language and West African literature to the rise of national consciousness in West Africa." Ph.D. Bowling Green S. U. 1974.

202 **Chandler, L.,** "Language contact and interference in South Africa", EUSA 6,2 (1975): 13-19.

203 **Charpentier, Jean-Michel,** Le Pidgin Bislama(n) et le multilingisme aux Nouvelles-Hébrides. Paris: SELAF 1979.

204 --- and **Darrell T. Tryon,** "Functions of Bislama in the New Hebrides and in independent Vanuatu", EWW 3,2 (1982): 146-60.

205 **Chatterjee, K.K.,** *English Education in India: Issues and Opinions*. Delhi: Macmillan 1976.

206 **Chaudhuri, N.C.,** "The English language in India - past, present and future", in A. Niven, ed., *The Commonwealth Writer Overseas: Themes of Exile and Expatriation*. Bruxelles: RLV 1976: 89-105.

207 **Cheng, Chin-Chuan,** "Chinese varieties of English", in Kachru 1982: 125-40.

208 **Chinnakarn, Sanit,** "A linguistic analysis of English in Indian advertisements", M.A. U. of Baroda 1977.

209 **Chishimba, Maurice M.,** "Language teaching and literacy: East Africa", *Annual Review of Applied Linguistics* 3 (1982): 168-88.

210 ---, "African varieties of English: text in context." Ph.D. Urbana (forthcoming).

211 **Chong, H.K.,** "A study of language maintenance and language shift in Singapore as a multilingual society", *RELC* 8,2 (1977): 43-62.

212 **Christie, Pauline,** "A sociolinguistic study of some Dominican Creole speakers." Ph.D. York 1969 = Creole Language Studies Resources Kit, York U. 1976.

213 ---, "Assertive 'no' in Jamaican Creole", *SCL Occ. Paper* 10 (1979).

214 ---, "In search of the boundaries of Caribbean Creoles", in Carrington 1983: 13-22.

215 ---, "Grammatical evidence from discourse", in Gilbert 1984.

216 **Christophersen, P.,** "English in West Africa: review article", *ES* 54 (1973): 51-58.

217 **Clark, Ross,** *In Search of Beach-la-mar: Historical Relations Among Pacific Pidgins and Creoles*. U. of Auckland, Anthrop. WP 48, 1977.

218 ---, "Social contexts of early South Pacific pidgins", in Woolford/ Washabaugh 1983: 10-27.

219 **Clyne, Michael G.,** "Migrant English in Australia", in Ramson 1970: 123-36.

220 ---, ed., *Australia Talks: Essays on the Sociology of Australian Immigrant and Aboriginal Languages*. PacL D23, Canberra 1976.

221 ---, "Communicative competences in contact", *ITL* 43 (1979); repr. in Smith 1983: 147-61.

222 ---, "'Second generation' foreigner talk in Australia", IJSL 28 (1981): 69-80.

223 **Cobarrubias, Juan** and **Joshua A. Fishman,** eds., Progress in Language Planning. International Perspectives. Contributions to the Sociology of Language 31. Berlin: Mouton 1983.

224 **Cohen, Pedro I.** et al., Primera Tornadas Linguïstícas: el Criollo Inglés de Panamá. Panama: Editorial Universitaria 1976.

225 **Collins, H.E.,** "The sources of Australian pronunciation", Macquarie WP 1,1 (1975): 115-28.

226 **Collins, Harold Reeves,** The New English of the Onitsha Chapbooks. Athens, Ohio, 1973.

227 **Collins, Peter,** "'Dare' and 'need' in Australian English: a study of divided usage", ES 59 (1978): 434-42.

228 ---, "Investigating acceptability in Australian English", Word 32,1 (1981): 15-34.

229 **Collymore, F.A.,** Notes for a Glossary of Words and Phrases of Barbadian Dialect. Bridgetown, Barbados: Advocate, 4th ed. 1970.

230 **Conrad, Andrew W.** and **J.A. Fishman,** "English as a world language: the evidence", in Fishman et al. 1977: 3-76.

231 **Constable, D.,** "Bilingualism in the United Republic of Cameroon", ELTJ 31 (1977): 249-53.

232 **Coomber, M.E. Ajayi,** "Form, distribution and function/meaning of the Krio particle dɛn", African Research Bulletin 8,2-3 (1978): 45-54.

233 **Cooper, Robert L.,** ed., Language Spread: Studies in Diffusion and Social Change. Bloomington: Indiana UP (forthcoming).

234 ---, "Fantasti! Israeli attitudes towards English", in Greenberg 1984.

235 --- and **Joshua A. Fishman,** "A study of language attitudes", in Fishman et al. 1977: 239-76.

236 --- and **Fern Seckbach,** "Economic incentives for the learning of a language of wider communication: a case study", in Fishman et al. 1977: 212-9.

237 **Cooper, Vincent O'Mahony,** "Basilectal creole, decreolization, and autonomous language change in St. Kitts-Nevis." Ph.D. Princeton U. 1979. DAI 40: 7, 3999A.

238 ---, "On the notice of decreolization and St. Kitts personal pronouns", in Day 1980: 39-50.

239 **Craig, Dennis,** "Bidialectal education: creole and standard in the West Indies", IJSL 8 (1967); repr. in Pride 1979: 164-84.

240 ---, "Education and Creole English in the West Indies: some sociolinguistic factors", in Hymes 1971: 371-91.

241 ---, "Developmental and social class differences in language", Caribbean Journal of Education 1 (1974): 5-23.

242 ---, "Bidialectal education: creole and standard in the West Indies", in Berry 1976: 93-134.

243 ---, "Creole languages and primary education", in Valdman 1977: 313-22.

244 ---, "Language education in a post-creole society", in Spolsky/Cooper 1978: 407-26.

245 ---, "Creole and standard: partial learning, base grammar and the mesolect", in Alatis 1979: 602-20.

246 ---, "A creole English continuum and the theory of grammar", in Day 1980: 111-31.

247 ---, "Models for educational policy in creole-speaking communities", in Valdman/Highfield 1980: 245-65.

248 ---, "Toward a description of Caribbean English", in Kachru 1982: 198-209.

249 ---, "Social class and the use of language: a case study of Jamaican children", in Görlach (forthcoming).

250 **Crewe, William,** "The Singapore writer and the English language", RELC 9,1 (1976).

251 ---, ed., The English Language in Singapore. Singapore: Eastern UP 1977a.

252 ---, "Singapore English as a non-native dialect", in Crewe 1977a: 83-95.

253 ---, ed., Singapore English and Standard English: Exercises in Awareness. Singapore: Eastern UP 1977b.

254 **Criper, L.,** "A classification of types of English in Ghana", JAL 10 (1971): 6-17.

255 **Cripwell, K.R.,** "Governmental writers and African readers in Rhodesia", LSoc 4 (1975): 147-54.

256 **Crowley, Terry** and **Bruce Rigsby,** "Cape York Creole", in Timothy Shopen, ed., Languages and Their Status. Cambridge, Mass.: Winthrop 1979: 153-207.

257 **Dabke, Roswitha,** Morphology of Australian English. München: Fink 1976.

258 **Dakin, J.,** ed., Language in Education: the Problems of Commonwealth Africa and the Indo-Pakistan Sub-continent. London 1968.

259 **Dalby, David,** Black through White: Patterns of Communication. London 1970.

260 **Dalgish, G.M.,** A Dictionary of Africanisms. Contributions of Sub-Saharan Africa to the English Language. Westport, Conn. / London 1982.

261 **Das, Bikram K.,** "English for a developing country: a plea for linguistic relativism in teaching", CIEFL Bulletin 9 (1972-73): 18-26.

262 **Das, Sisir Kumar,** "Indian English", in Pride 1982: 141-9.

263 **d'Aste Surcouf, Alexandra A.,** "The impact of socio-economic and nationalistic factors on international uses of English: a case study of Birzeit University." Ph.D. Ann Arbor 1983.

264 **Daswani, C.J.,** "Indian English", Journal of the School of Languages. New Delhi: J. Nehru U. 1975.

265 ---, "Pidginization in a multilingual society: the case of Indian English", paper 1978, in Proceedings, 5th Int. Congress of Applied Linguistics, Montreal.

266 ---, "Some theoretical implications for investigating Indian English", in Mohan 1978: 115-28.

267 **Datta, Sunanda,** "The pronunciation of English by Bengali speakers", CIEFL Bulletin 9 (1972-73): 35-40.

268 **Day, Richard Roy,** "Patterns of variation in copula and tense in the Hawaiian post-creole continuum." Ph.D. Hawaii 1972. DAI 34: 1, 297A.

269 ---, "Patterns of variation in copula and tense in the Hawaiian post-creole continuum", Hawaii WPL 5, Honolulu 1973.

270 ---, "Tense neutralization in the Hawaiian post-creole gradatum", in Bailey/Shuy 1973: 306-12.

271 ---, "Decreolization: coexistent systems and the post-creole continuum", in DeCamp/Hancock 1974: 38-45.

272 ---, "The acquisition and maintenance of language by minority children", LL 29 (1979): 295-303.

273 ---, ed., Issues in English Creoles. Papers from the 1975 Hawaii Conference. Heidelberg: Groos 1980.

274 **Dayley, John,** Belizean Creole. Grammar Handbook and Glossary. Brattleboro, Vt.: Experiment in International Living for Peace Corps 1979.

275 **d'Azevedo, Warren L.,** Some Terms from Liberian Speech. Monrovia: U.S. Peace Corps in Liberia 1970.

276 **D'Costa, Jean,** "Language and dialect in Jamaica", Jamaica Journal 2 (1968).

277 ---, "The West Indian novelist and language: a search for a literary medium", in Carrington 1983: 252-65.

278 **DeBose, C.E.,** "Creole speech communities", Ohio WPL 19 (1975): 103-12.

279 ---, "The status of native speaker in a polylectal grammar", Berkeley Ling. Society 3 (1977): 465-74.

280 **DeCamp, David,** "Diasystem vs. overall pattern. The Jamaica syllabic nuclei", in E.B. Atwood and A.A. Hill, eds., Studies in Language, Literature and Culture of the Middle Ages and Later. Austin: Texas UP 1969.

281 ---, "The study of pidgin and creole languages", in Hymes 1971: 13-39.

282 ---, "Toward a generative analysis of a post-creole speech continuum", in Hymes 1971: 349-70.

283 ---, "Neutralizations, iteratives, and ideophones: the locus of language in Jamaica", in DeCamp/Hancock 1974: 46-60.

284 ---, "The development of pidgin and creole studies", in Valdman 1977: 3-20.

285 --- and **I.F. Hancock,** eds., Pidgins and Creoles: Current Trends and Prospects. Washington, D.C., 1974.

286 **de Féral, Carole,** "Le pidgin english au Cameroun: présentation sociolinguistique", Bulletin ALCAM 2 (Yaoundé: ONAREST, 1977): 107-28.

287 ---, "Le pidgin english au Cameroun: que décrire?" Bulletin ALCAM 4 (1977).

288 ---, "Le cas du pidgin Camérounais", WAJML 3 (1977): 144-53.

289 ---, "Le pidgin-english camerounais: essai de définition linguistique et sociolinguistique." U. de Nice, thèse de Doctorat de 3e cycle 1980.

290 **Delbridge, Arthur,** "The recent study of Australian English", in Ramson 1970: 15-31.

291 ---, "Good Australian speech", in Turner 1972: 195-208.

292 ---, "Making a dictionary of Australian English", LingC 11 (1973): 41-50.

293 **Denison, Norman,** "The use of English as a medium of communication in Europe", IncL 10,2 (1971).

294 **Denton, Johnnie Mae,** "Towards a model of ESL for Krio speakers in Sierra Leone." M.A. thesis, U. of Texas 1976.

295 **De Quincey, Paul,** "The pre-verbal tense and aspect markers in Nigerian Pidgin." M.A. thesis, U. of Leeds 1979.

296 **Desai, B.T.,** "A linguistic study of the English elements in Kannada-English codeswitching." Ph.D. Hyderabad: CIEFL 1982.

297 **Desai, S.K.,** ed., Experimentation with Language in Indian Writing in English (Fiction). Kolhapur: Dept. of English, Shivaji U. 1974.

298 **de Villiers, André,** ed., English-speaking South Africa Today. Cape Town: Oxford UP 1976.

299 **Devonish, Hubert St. Laurent,** "The selection and codification of a widely understood and publicly useable language variety in Guyana, to be used as a vehicle of national development." D.Phil. York 1978.

300 ---, "Towards the establishment of an Institute for Creole Language Standardization and Development in the Caribbean", in Carrington 1983: 300-16.

301 ---, "Language policy in the creole-speaking Commonwealth Caribbean", in Görlach (forthcoming).

302 Dictionary of Guyanese Folklore. Georgetown, Guyana: National History and Arts Council 1975.

303 **Dil, A.S.,** "The position and teaching of English in Pakistan", in Pakistani Linguistics, Shahidullah Presentation Volume (1966): 185-242.

304 **Dillard, Joe Lee,** "Standard Average Foreign in Puerto Rico", in Bailey/Robinson 1973: 77-90.

305 ---, ed., "Socio-historical factors in the formation of the creoles", IJSL 7 (1976).

306 ---, "Creole English and Creole Portuguese: the early records", in Hancock 1979: 261-8.

307 **DiPietro, R.,** "Role enactment and verbal strategies in the U.S. Virgin Islands", in Cave 1976.

308 **Dixon, Paul W., Nobuko K. Fukuda, Verner L. Gibson** and **Robert O.H. Petersen,** "Phoneme use and the perception of meaning by children in Hawaii", L&S 15 (1972): 317-27.

309 **Dorcas 'Wale, O.,** "Register in oral discourse", in Ubahakwe 1979: 107-26.

310 **Dreyfuss, Gail Raimi,** "Relative clause structure in four creole languages." Ph.D. Michigan 1978. DAI 38: 11, 6688A.

311 **Dungworth, David,** "The future of English as a world language", LSp 23 (1978): 1-3.

312 **Dutton, Thomas E.,** "The informal English speech of Palm Island Aboriginal children, North Queensland", JEL 3 (1969): 18-36.

313 ---, "Informal English in the Torres Straits", in Ramson 1970: 137-60.

314 ---, Conversational New Guinea Pidgin. PacL D12, Canberra 1973.

315 ---, Queensland Canefields English of the Late Nineteenth Century. PacL D29, Canberra 1980.

316 --- and **Peter Mühlhäusler,** "Queensland Kanaka English", EWW 4,2 (1983).

317 **Dwamina, Wingrove Charles,** English Literature and Language Planning in West Africa. Ph.D. SUNY Buffalo 1972; pr. Buffalo 1973.

318 **Dwivedi, R.K.,** "English in Indian administration", CIEFL Bulletin 8 (1970-71): 63-71.

319 **Dwyer, D.** and **D. Smith,** An Introduction to West African Pidgin-English. East Lansing 1966.

320 **Eagleson, Robert D.,** "The nature and study of Australian English", JEL 1 (1967): 11-24.

321 ---, "Prolegomena to a dictionary of Australian English", AULLA Proceedings 11 (1967): 362-72.

322 ---, "Some divergences in Australian English usage", Kivung 5 (1972): 103-14.

323 ---, "Aspects of Australian English usage", AULLA Proceedings 14 (1972): 204-16.

324 ---, "Sociolinguistic implications of some variations in Australian English usage", LingC 10 (1973): 2-10.

325 ---, "The evidence for the existence of social dialects in Australian English", in Clyne 1976: 7-27.

326 ---, "English and the urban Aboriginal", Meanjin 36 (1977): 535-44.

327 ---, "Disadvantaged English", English in Australia 39 (1977): 23-47.

328 ---, "Sociolinguistic reflections on acceptability", in Greenbaum 1978: 63-72.

329 ---, "Popular and professional attitudes to prestige dialects", Talanya 5 (1978): 15-22.

330 ---, "Urban Aboriginal English", AUMLA 49 (1978): 52-64.

331 ---, "English in Australia and New Zealand", in Bailey/Görlach 1982: 415-38.

332 ---, **S. Kaldor** and **I.G. Malcolm,** English and the Aboriginal Child. Canberra: Curriculum Development Centre 1982.

333 **Eckman, Fred** and **William Washabaugh,** "The acculturation model and the problem of variation in second language acquisition", in R. Anderson (forthcoming).

334 **Edwards, J.D.,** "Social linguistics on San Andres and Providence Islands", Louisiana SU 1968, mimeo.

335 ---, "Aspects of bilingual behavior on San Andres Island, Colombia", Louisiana SU 1970, mimeo.

336 ---, "African influences on the English of San Andres Island", in DeCamp/Hancock 1974: 1-26.

337 --- et al., "Conversation in a West Indian taxi - an ethnolinguistic analysis", LSoc 4 (1975): 295-321.

338 **Edwards, Viv K.,** "Effects of dialect on the comprehension of West Indian children", Educational Research 18 (1976): 83-95.

339 ---, "Dialect interference in West Indian children", L&S 21 (1978): 76-86.

340 **Edwards, Walter F.,** "Sociolinguistic behaviour in rural and urban circumstances in Guyana." Ph.D. York = Creole Language Studies Resources Kit, York U. 1976.

341 ---, "Some phonological differences between Standard English and basilectal Guyanese Creole", The Language Forum 1 (Georgetown, U. of Guyana 1973): 7-22.

342 ---, "A quantitative study of sociolinguistic behaviour in rural and urban circumstances in Guyana: 1", York PL 5 (1975): 67-86.

343 ---, Sociolinguistic Models and Phonological Variation in Guyana. SCL, Occ. Paper 8 (1977).

344 ---, "Varieties of English in Guyana: some comparisons with BEV", Linguistics 229/230 (1980): 289-310.

345 **Egbe, Daniel I.,** "Spoken and written English in Nigeria", in Ubahakwe 1979: 86-106.

346 ---, "Aspects of English grammar and usage", Papers in Linguistics 14,2 (Edmonton, 1981): 271-96.

347 **Ekong, P.A.,** "On describing the vowel system of a standard variety of Nigerian spoken English." M.A. U. of Ibadan 1978.

348 **Ekpenyong, J.O.,** "The use of English in Nigeria", in Press 1965: 144-50.

349 **Emanuel, Lezmore Evan,** "Surviving Africanisms in Virgin Islands English Creole." Ph.D. Harvard 1970. DAI 32: 11, 6315A.

350 **Eng, Oor Boo,** "Indian poets and the use of English", Journal of Commonwealth Literature 9 (1974).

351 Englisch - Formen und Funktionen einer Weltsprache. Ausstellung des Lehrstuhls für Englische Sprachwissenschaft und Mediävistik und der

Universitätsbibliothek. Katalog. Bamberg: Universitätsbibliothek Bamberg 1983.

352 English as an International Language. ELT Documents. London 1978.

353 English as an International Language: Discourse Patterns Across Cultures. Proceedings of the Hawaii Conference June 1983 (forthcoming).

354 **Escure, Geneviève J.,** "Vocalic change in the Belizean English-Creole continuum and markedness theory", Berkeley Linguistics Society 4 (1978): 283-92.

355 ---, "Linguistic variation and ethnic interaction in Belize: Creole/Carib", in Giles/Saint-Jacques 1979: 101-16.

356 ---, "Decreolization in a creole continuum: Belize", in Highfield/Valdman 1981: 27-39.

357 ---, "Belizean Creole", in Holm 1983: 29-70.

358 ---, "Contrastive patterns of intragroup and intergroup interaction in the creole continuum of Belize", LSoc 11,2 (1982): 239-64.

359 ---, "The Belizean copula: a case of semantactic shift", in Carrington 1983: 190-202.

360 ---, "Sex differentiation and copula variability in a creole continuum", in Gilbert 1984.

361 **Eze, Smart N.,** Nigerian Pidgin English Sentence Complexity. Wien: AFRO-PUB 1980.

362 **Fanaroff, D.,** South African English Dialect: a Literature Survey. Pretoria: HSRC 1972.

363 **Farquhar, Bernadette Brenda,** "A grammar of Antiguan Creole." Ph.D. Cornell U. 1974. DAI 35: 2, 1077A.

364 **Fasold, Ralph** and **Roger Shuy,** Analysing Variation in Language. Washington, D.C.: Georgetown UP 1975.

365 **Fayer, Joan H.,** "Written Pidgin English in Old Calabar in the 18th and 19th centuries." Ph.D. U. of Pennsylvania 1982. DAI 43: 3, 787A.

366 **Feitelson, Dina,** ed., Mother Tongue or Second Language? On the Teaching of Reading in Multilingual Societies. Newark, DE: Intern. Reading Assoc. 1979.

367 **Feldman, Carol Fleisher** et al., "Standard and non standard dialect competencies of Hawaiian Creole English speakers", TESOLQ 11 (1977): 41-50.

368 **Ferguson, Charles A.,** "Absence of copula and the notion of simplicity: a study in normal speech, baby talk, and pidgins", in Hymes 1971: 141-50.

369 ---, "Toward a characterization of foreigner talk", AnL 17 (1975): 1-14.

370 --- and **C.E. DeBose,** "Simplified registers, broken language, and pidginization", in Valdman 1977: 99-125.

371 **Fernando, Chitra,** "Between two worlds: an examination of attitudes and language in Ceylonese creative writing", New Ceylon Writing 3 (1973): 31-46.

372 ---, "English in Ceylon: a case study of a bilingual community", LSoc 6 (1977): 341-61; repr. in Pride 1982: 188-207.

373 **Fielding, J.** and **W.S. Ramson,** "Settlers and convicts: firste fynderes of our fair longage", AUMLA 36 (1973): 165-76.

374 **Fishman, Joshua A.,** ed., Readings in the Sociology of Language. The Hague: Mouton 1968.

375 ---, "Sociolinguistic perspective on the study of bilingualism", Linguistics 39 (1968): 21-50.

376 ---, "Sociolinguistics and the language problems of developing nations", Intern. Social Science Journal 30 (1968): 211-22.

377 ---, "National languages and languages of wider communication in the developing nations", AnL 11 (1969): 111-35.

378 ---, The Sociology of Language. Rowley, Mass.: Newbury 1972.

379 ---, "Bilingual education, language planning and English", EWW 1 (1980): 11-24.

380 ---, "Sociology of English as an additional language", in Kachru 1982: 15-22.

381 --- et al., Language Problems of Developing Nations. New York: 1968.

382 --- et al., eds., The Spread of English. The Sociology of English as an Additional Language. Rowley, Mass.: Newbury 1977.

383 --- et al., "English the world over: a factor in the creation of bilingualism today", in P.A. Hornby, ed., Bilingualism. Psychological, Social and Educational Implications. New York: Academic P. 1977: 108-39.

384 ---, "Knowing, using and liking English, as an additional language", TESOLQ 11 (1977).

385 ---, ed., Advances in the Study of Societal Multilingualism. The Hague: Mouton 1978.

386 **Flint, E.H.,** "Aboriginal English: linguistic description as an aid to teaching", English in Australia 6 (1968): 3-21.

387 ---, "The influence of prosodic patterns upon the mutual intelligibility of Aboriginal and general Australian English", Pacific Linguistic Studies in Honour of Arthur Capell, PacL C13, Canberra 1970: 717-40.

388 ---, "The sociology of language in Queensland-Aboriginal communities", Kivung 5,3 (1972): 150-63; LingC 10 (1973): 1-15.

389 ---, "Relexification in current Australian English", Talanya 3 (1976): 60-74.

390 ---, "Stable societal diglossia on Norfolk Island", in William Francis Mackey and Jacob Ornstein, eds., Sociolinguistic Studies in Language Contact. The Hague: Mouton 1979.

391 **Folarin, B.,** "Context, register and language varieties: a proposed model for the discussion of varieties of English in Nigeria", in Ubahakwe 1979: 77-85.

392 **Fonlon, Bernard,** "The language problem in Cameroon", Comparative Educational Review 5 (1969): 25-49.

393 **Fox, M.J.,** Language and Development: a Retrospective Survey of Ford Foundation Language Projects 1952-74. New York: Ford Found. 1975.

394 **Fox, Robert Paul,** "A transformational treatment of Indian English syntax." Ph.D. Urbana 1968.

395 **Franklin, K.J.,** "Some comparisons between Chinese Pidgin English and Melanesian Pidgin English", Talanya 6 (1979): 40-59.

396 **French, Robert A.,** "An ethnography of speaking of the Belize Creole speech community." Ph.D. Harvard U. 1975.

397 **Fresco, E.M.,** "Some problems in defining a standard Nigerian English", Journal of the Nigeria English Studies Association 2 (1967).

398 **Full, Susan F.,** "Dialect and its implications for education in the Bahama Islands." Dipl.Educ. London 1977.

399 **Fyle, Clifford N.,** "Krio ways of thought and expression", African Research Bulletin 3 (1974): 3-13.

400 --- and **Eldred D. Jones,** A Krio-English Dictionary. Oxford: UP / Freetown: Sierra Leone UP 1980.

401 **Gage, W.W.** and **S. Ohannessian,** "ESOL enrolments throughout the world", LingR 16 (1974): 13-16; repr. in ETF (July 1977): 19-21.

402 **Gair, James W.,** "Sinhala and English: the effects of a language act", LPLP 7,1 (1983): 43-59.

403 **Gebhard, J.G.,** "Thai adaptation of English language features: a study of Thai-English", in Papers in Pidgin and Creole Linguistics 2, PacL A57, Canberra 1979: 201-16.

404 **Geraghty, Paul,** "Fiji Pidgin and bilingual education", Fiji English Teachers' Journal 12 (1977): 2-8.

405 **Ghosh, N.,** "Standard and disparate varieties of English in Sri Lanka: education and sociopolitical implications. Eine Commonwealth Studie." Dr.phil. Salzburg 1982.

406 **Gibbons, John,** "U-gay-wa: a linguistic study of the campus language of students at the University of Hong Kong", in Robert Lord, ed., Hong Kong Language Papers. Hong Kong: UP 1979.

407 ---, "Attitudes towards languages and code-mixing in Hong Kong", JMMD 4 (1983): 129-47.

408 **Gilbert, Glenn G.,** ed., Pidgin and Creole Languages: Essays in Memory of John E. Reinecke. Ann Arbor: Karoma 1984.

409 ---, "The Negro English of West Africa: a newly discovered manuscript by Hugo Schuchardt", in Gilbert 1984.

410 ---, "Hugo Schuchardt and the Atlantic creoles", in Gilbert 1984.

411 **Giles, Howard** and **Bernard Saint Jacques,** eds., Language and Ethnic Relations. Oxford: Pergamon 1980.

412 **Gilman, Charles,** "The comparative structure in French, English and Cameroonian Pidgin English." Ph.D. Northwestern U. 1971. DAI 33: 6, 2916A.

413 ---, "Lexical loss in Cameroon Pidgin", Anthropos 74 (1979): 174-80.

414 ---, "Cameroonian Pidgin English, a neo-African language", in Hancock 1979: 269-80.

415 ---, "The origin of Cameroonian pidgin dialects", AnL 22,9 (1980): 363-72.

416 **Gimson, Alfred C.,** "The Twentyman lecture, 1981: The pronunciation of English: its intelligibility and acceptability in the world", ML 62,2 (1981): 61-68.

417 **Glissmeyer, Gloria,** "In-progress analysis of English idiolects, Keaukaha, Hilo, Hawaii", in Actes du Xe Congrès International des Linguistes, Bucarest, 28 août - 2 septembre 1967. Bucarest: Editions de l'Acad. de la République Socialiste de Roumanie 1970: 141-8.

418 ---, "Some characteristics of English in Hawaii", in Bailey/Robinson 1973: 190-222.

419 ---, A Tagmemic Analysis of Hawaii English Clauses. PacL B46, Canberra 1976 = Ph.D. Hawaii 1971. DAI 32: 2, 946A.

420 **Glock, N.,** "Clause and sentence in Saramaccan", JAL 11 (1972): 45-61.

421 --- and **J.E. Grimes,** "A Saramaccan narrative pattern", Language 46 (1970): 408-25.

422 **Görlach, Manfred,** "A selective bibliography of English as a World Language 1965-1979", AAA 2 (1979): 231-68.

423 ---, "The function of texts in the description of varieties of English", in Dieter Riemenschneider, ed., The History and Historiography of Commonwealth Literature. Tübingen: Narr 1983: 233-43.

424 ---, "Introduction", in M. Görlach, ed., Max and Moritz in English Dialects and Creoles. Hamburg: Buske 1984.

425 ---, ed., Focus on: The Caribbean. (VEAW) Amsterdam: Benjamins (forthcoming).

426 ---, "English in Africa - African English?" Revista Canaria de Estudios Ingleses 6 (La Laguna, Tenerife, 1984) (forthcoming).

427 ---, "Weltsprache Englisch - eine neue Disziplin?" Studium Linguistik (forthcoming).

428 --- and **Konrad Schröder,** "'Good usage' in an EFL context", in Greenberg 1984.

429 **Gold, David,** "An introduction to English in Israel", LPLP 5 (1981): 11-56.

430 **Gonzalez, Andrew B.,** "The future of English in the Philippines", Likha 1,2 (1977): 37-46.

431 ---, Language and Nationalism. The Philippine Experience So Far. Quezon City: Ateneo de Manila UP 1980.

432 ---, "English in the Philippines mass media", in Pride 1982: 211-26.

433 ---, "When does an error become a feature of Philippine English", in Noss 1983: 150-72.

434 --- and **Wilfredo Alberca,** Philippine English of the Mass Media. Manila: De la Salle U. 1978 (mimeo).

435 **Gorman, T.P.,** "Bilingualism in the educational system of Kenya", Comparative Education 4 (1968): 213-21.

436 ---, ed., Language and Education in Eastern Africa. Nairobi 1970.

437 ---, "Sociolinguistic implications of a choice of media of instruction", in Whiteley 1971: 198-220.

438 ---, "Language allocation and language planning in a developing nation", in J. Rubin and R. Shuy, eds., Language Planning: Current Issues and Research. Washington, D.C., 1973: 72-82.

439 ---, "Approaches to the study of educational language policy in developing nations", in Harrison 1975.

440 **Greenbaum, Sidney,** ed., Acceptability in Language. The Hague: Mouton 1978.

441 ---, ed., The English Language Today. Oxford: Pergamon 1984.

442 **Greenberg, J.R.,** "Urbanism, migration, and language", in H. Kuper, ed., Urbanization and Migration in West Africa. U. of California 1965: 50-59.

443 **Greenfield, L.** and **J.A. Fishman,** "Situational measures of normative language views in relation to person, place, and topic among Puerto

Rican bilinguals", in S.K. Ghosh, ed., Man, Language and Society. The Hague: Mouton 1972: 64-86.

444 **Greenfield, P.M.,** "Oral or written language: the consequences for cognitive development in Africa, the United States and England", L&S 15 (1972): 169-78.

445 **Gregory, M.,** "Aspects of varieties differentiation", JL 3 (1967): 177-98.

446 **Griard, D.,** "The special demands on English in Europe today", IncL 9,3 (1970).

447 **Grimes, J.E.,** ed., Languages of the Guianas. Norman, Okl.: SIL 1972.

448 **Grimshaw, A.,** "Some social factors and some social functions of pidgin and creole languages", in Hymes 1971: 427-46.

449 **Grosjean, François,** Life with Two Languages. Harvard UP 1982.

450 **Gumperz, J.J.** and **D. Hymes,** eds., Directions in Sociolinguistics: the Ethnography of Communication. New York 1972.

451 **Gunn, J.S.,** "Twentieth-century Australian idiom", in Ramson 1970: 49-68.

452 ---, "Change in Australian idiom", in Turner 1972: 47-63.

453 ---, "A possible source of some Australian sounds and their relationship with Received English", Linguistics 164 (1975): 5-15.

454 --- and **B. Levy,** A Word History of Bushranging. Occ. Papers 17. Sydney: The U. 1980.

455 **Gupta, R.S.,** "A sociolinguistic study of the use of mixed Hindi-English in metropolitan Delhi." D.Phil. York 1979. DAI-C 39: 3-4, 3105.

456 **Gupta, Sagar Mal,** "Vowel reduction in U.P. (Uttar Pradesh) English: an instrumental study", CIEFL Bulletin 16,1 (1979): 31-40.

457 **Guy, J.B.M.,** Handbook of Bichelamar/Manuel de Bichelamar. PacL C34, Canberra 1974.

458 ---, "Notes on Bichelamar: sound systems and spelling systems", Kivung 7 (1974): 23-46.

459 **Hall, Raymond,** ed., Ethnic Autonomy - Comparative Dynamics: The Americas, Europe and the Developing World. New York: Pergamon 1979.

460 **Hall, Robert A., Jr.,** Pidgin and Creole Languages. Ithaca 1966.

461 ---, "Creole linguistics", CTL 4 (1968): 361-71.

462 ---, "Relexification and regrammaticalization", in McElhanon 1975: 181-8.

463 **Halpé, A.,** "Creative writing in English", in K.M. de Silva, ed., Sri Lanka: a Survey. London: Hurst 1975.

464 **Halverson, J.,** "Prolegomena to a study of Ceylon English", U. of Ceylon Review 24 (1969): 61-75.

465 **Hammarström, Göran,** Australian English: Its Origin and Status. Hamburg: Buske 1980.

466 **Hancock, Ian F.,** "A provisional comparison of the English-based Atlantic creoles", African Language Review 8 (1969): 7-72.

467 ---, Dictionary of Sierra Leone Krio. London 1970.

468 ---, "A study of the sources and development of the lexicon of Sierra Leone Krio." Ph.D. London SOAS 1971.

469 ---, "West Africa and the Atlantic creoles", in Spencer 1971: 113-22.

470 ---, "Nautical sources of Krio vocabulary", IJSL 7 (1976): 23-36.

471 ---, "English in Liberia", AS 49 (1974 (1977)): 224-9.

472 ---, "Lexical expansion with a closed system", in B.G. Blount and M. Sanchez, eds., Sociocultural Dimensions of Language Change. New York 1977: 161-71.

473 ---, "Recovering pidgin genesis: approaches and problems", in Valdman 1977: 277-94.

474 ---, "Repertory of pidgin and creole languages", in Valdman 1977: 362-91 (earlier version in Hymes 1971).

475 --- and **P. Kobbah,** "Liberian English of Cape Palmas", in J. Dillard, ed., Perspectives on Black English. The Hague: Mouton 1975: 248-71.

476 ---, ed., Readings in Creole Studies. Gent: Story-Scientia 1979.

477 ---, "Gullah and Barbadian: origins and relationships", AS 55 (1980): 17-35.

478 ---, "Lexical expansion in creole languages", in Valdman/Highfield 1980: 63-88.

479 ---, ed., Diversity and Development in English-related Creoles. Ann Arbor: Karoma 1983.

480 ---, "A preliminary classification of the Anglophone Atlantic Creoles, with syntactic data from twenty-three representative dialects", in Gilbert 1984.

481 --- and **Rachel Angogo,** "English in East Africa", in Bailey/Görlach 1982: 306-23.

482 **Hansen, Klaus,** "Zur regionalen Differenzierung des Englischen", Linguistische Studien A100. Berlin: Akad. Wiss. 1982: 65-80.

483 **Harlech-Jones, Brian,** "Is there an African English?" ELTIC Reporter 4,1 (Johannesburg, 1979): 25-30.

484 **Harrison, Godfrey,** "Mandarin and the mandarins: language policy and the media in Singapore", JMMD 1,2 (1980): 175-80.

485 **Harrison, Shirley,** "A language history of Norfolk Island", Macquarie WP (July 1976): 1-172.

486 ---, "Variation in the speech of Norfolk Islanders." Ph.D. Macquarie U. (forthcoming).

487 **Harrison, William** et al., English-Language Policy Survey of Jordan: a Case Study of Language Planning. Arlington, Va.: Center for Applied Linguistics 1975.

488 **Hartford, Beverly** and **Albert Valdman,** eds., Issues in International Bilingual Education. New York / London: Plenum Press 1982.

489 **Hauptfleisch, T.,** Research into the Position of the Official Languages in the Educational System of Whites in South Africa: a Literature Survey. Pretoria: HSRC 1975.

490 ---, Language Loyalty in South Africa, 3 vols. Pretoria: HSRC 1977-79.

491 **Hawkins, P.R.,** "The sound-patterns of New Zealand English", Proc. of the 15th AULLA Congress. Sydney 1973: 1-8.

492 ---, "A phonemic transcription for New Zealand English", Te Reo 16 (1973).

493 ---, "The role of New Zealand English in a binary feature analysis of English short vowels", JIPA 6,2 (1976): 50-66.

494 **Haynes, Lilith M.,** "Language in Barbados and Guyana: attitudes, behaviour and comparisons." Ph.D. Stanford U. 1973. DAI 34: 7, 4230A.

495 ---, "Language choice and language change: all in a Guyanese family", Word 27 (1971 (1975)): 363-77.

496 ---, "A note on creolization and the continuum", in Hancock 1979: 335-8.

497 ---, "Caribbean English: form and function", in Kachru 1982: 210-26.

498 ---, "Rural and urban groups in Barbados and Guyana: language attitudes and behaviors", IJSL 34 (1982): 67-81.

499 ---, "Dialogue in Island Voices", in Görlach (forthcoming).

500 **Heine, Bernd,** Status and Use of African Lingua Francas. München: IFO 1970.

501 **Hellinger, Marlis,** "Aspects of Belizean Creole", FoLi (1973): 118-35.

502 ---, "How to write Belizean Creole", National Studies 2,4 (Belize, 1974); with commentaries by R. Hadel and C. Young.

503 ---, "The future of Belizean Creole", National Studies (Belize) 3,3 (1974): 11-15.

504 ---, "Creole as a literary language", National Studies 4,6 (1976): 19-31.

505 ---, "Across base language boundaries: the creole of Belize (British Honduras)", in Hancock 1979: 315-33.

506 ---, "Creole als Sprache der schwarzen Literatur", in E. Breitinger, ed., Black Literature. München: Fink 1979: 75-102.

507 ---, "On writing English-related creoles", in Görlach (forthcoming).

508 ---, Pidgin- und Kreolsprachen. Erträge der Forschung. Darmstadt: Wiss. Buchgesellschaft (forthcoming).

509 **Herbst, R.,** "English - a European language?" IncL 9 (1970).

510 **Herzfeld, Anita,** "Second language acrolect replacement in Limon Creole", Kansas WPL 2 (1977): 193-222.

511 ---, "Towards the description of a creole", Proc. of the 1976 Mid-America Linguistics Conf. Minneapolis: U. of Minn. 1977: 121-32.

512 ---, "Tense and aspect in Limon Creole: a sociolinguistic view towards a creole continuum." Ph.D. U. of Kansas 1978. DAI 39: 7, 4216A.

513 ---, "Bilingual instability as a result of government induced policies", ITL 48 (1980): 3-20.

514 ---, "Vida o muerte del criollo Limonense", Revista de Filología y Linguística de la Universidad de Costa Rica (1980?).

515 ---, "The creoles of Costa Rica and Panama", in Holm 1983: 131-56.

516 ---, "Limon Creole and Panamian Creole: comparison and contrast", in Carrington 1983: 23-37.

517 **Hesseling, Dirk Christiaan,** On the Origin and Formation of Creoles: A Miscellany of Articles. Edited and translated by T.L. Markey and Paul T. Roberge. Introduction by Pieter Muysken and Guus Meijer. Ann Arbor: Karoma 1979.

518 **Hill, K.C.,** ed., The Genesis of Language. The First Michigan Colloquium, 1979. Ann Arbor: Karoma 1979.

519 **Hill, Trevor,** "The pronunciation of English stressed vowels in Tanzania", Bulletin of the Lang. Assoc. of Tanzania 4,2 (1973): 4-13.

520 **Hocking, B.D.W.,** All What I Was Taught. Nairobi: OUP 1974.

521 **Hofman, J.E.,** "Language attitudes in Rhodesia", in Fishman et al. 1977: 277-302.

522 **Hollyman, K.J.,** "Les pidgins européens de la région calédonienne", Te Reo 19 (1976): 25-66.

523 **Holm, John A.,** "Copula variability on the Afro-American continuum", in Cave 1976.

524 ---, "Miskito words in Belize Creole", National Studies (Belize) 5,6 (1977): 1-17.

525 ---, "The Creole English of Nicaragua's Miskito Coast: its sociolinguistic history and a comparative study of its lexicon and syntax." Ph.D. London 1978. DAI 42: 11, 4816A.

526 ---, "The creole 'copula' that highlighted the world", in J. Dillard, ed., Perspectives on American English. The Hague: Mouton 1980: 367-75.

527 ---, "African features in White Bahamian English", EWW 1 (1980): 45-66.

528 ---, "Sociolinguistic history and the creolist", in Highfield/Valdman 1981: 40-51.

529 ---, "Central American English: Introduction", in Holm 1983: 7-27.

530 ---, "Nicaragua's Miskito Coast Creole English", in Holm 1983: 95-130.

531 ---, ed., Central American English. (VEAW T2) Heidelberg: Groos 1983.

532 ---, "On the relationship of Gullah and Bahamian", AS (1983).

533 ---, "Variability of the copula in Black English and its creole kin, with an afterword", in Gilbert 1984.

534 Creole Languages. Cambridge: UP (forthcoming).

535 --- and **Alison Shilling,** "Accountability and verification in regional lexicography", EWW 1 (1980): 229-35.

536 ---, ---, Dictionary of Bahamian English. Cold Spring, N.Y.: Lexik House 1982.

537 **Holmes, J.,** "Investigating subjective judgments of New Zealand English", ArL 9,2 (1979): 123-34.

538 **Hosali, Priya,** "Butler English: form and function." Ph.D. Hyderabad: CIEFL 1983.

539 **Hudson, Joyce,** "Grammatical and semantic aspects of Fitzroy Valley Kriol." M.A. Canberra 1982; pr. in Work Papers of SIL-AAB, Ser. A (1983).

540 **Huebner, Thom** et al., Solomon Islands Pijin. 4 vols. Peace Corps Language Handbook Series. Brattleboro: Experiment in International Living 1979.

541 **Hughes, A.,** "Non-standard English of Grenada", CQ 12 (1966): 47-54.

542 **Huttar, George L.,** "Sources of creole semantic structures", Language 51 (1975): 684-95.

543 ---, "SIL work in English-based creoles", EWW 2 (1981): 83-86.

544 ---, "On the study of Creole lexicons", in Carrington 1983: 82-89.

545 **Huygens, Ingrid,** "Sociolinguistic stereotyping in New Zealand." M.A. Auckland 1979.

546 --- and **G.M. Vaughan,** "Language attitudes, ethnicity and social class in New Zealand", JMMD 4 (1983): 207-23.

547 **Hymes, Dell,** ed., Pidginization and Creolization of Languages. Cambridge: UP 1971.

548 **Ikara, Bashir,** "Some linguistic and sociocultural variables in a Nigerian variety of English", paper RELC Singapore 1981.

549 **Imhoof, M.,** "The English language in Egypt", EAW 17 (1977): 1-3.

550 **Iyengar, K.R.S.,** "Indian writing in English: prospect and retrospect", in Mohan 1978: 1-10.

551 **Jain, M.P.,** "Error analysis of an Indian English corpus", Journal of the School of Languages 3,1 (New Delhi, 1975): 28-52.

552 **Jama, Virginia,** "The English language in Somalia", EAW 26 (1982): 1, 4-5; repr. in le lingue del mondo 48,1 (1983): 49-53.

553 **James, Gregory,** "Some aspects of interlanguage: an analysis of some features of a Tamil-speaker's English", Indian Journal of Applied Linguistics 5,1 (1979): 20-50.

554 **James, S.L.,** "Three basic functions of the English language in Nigeria", in Ubahakwe 1979: 257-67.

555 **Jeremiah, Milford Astor,** "The linguistic relatedness of Black English and Antiguan Creole: evidence from the eighteenth and nineteenth centuries." Ph.D. Brown U. 1977. DAI 38: 8, 4788A.

556 **Jernudd, B.H.,** "A listener experiment: variants of Australian English", LingC 10 (1973): 26-40.

557 **Jibril, Munzali,** "Regional variation in Nigerian spoken English", in Ubahakwe 1979: 43-53.

558 ---, "Nigerian English: an introduction", in Pride 1982: 73-84.

559 ---, "Phonological variation in Nigerian English." Ph.D. Lancaster 1982.

560 **Johnson, Alex C.,** "Language and society in West African literature: a stylistic investigation into the linguistic resources of West African drama in English." Ph.D. Ibadan 1981.

561 **Johnson, D.E.** et al., A Survey of Materials for the Study of Uncommonly Taught Languages, fasc. 2 "Pidgins and creoles (European based)". Arlington: Center for Applied Linguistics 1976.

562 **Johnston, G.K.W.,** "The language of Australian literature", in Ramson 1970: 188-202.

563 **Jones, David W.** and **Carlyle A. Glean,** "The English-speaking communities of Honduras and Nicaragua", CQ 17,2 (1971): 50-61.

564 **Jones, Eldred,** "Some tense, mode and aspect markers in Krio", African Language Review 7 (1968): 86-89.

565 ---, "Krio: an English-based language of Sierra Leone", in Spencer 1971: 66-94.

566 **Jones, Frederick C.V.,** "English words in Krio." Ph.D. Leeds 1983.

567 **Jones, J.A.,** ed., Language Teaching, Linguistics, and the Teaching of English in a Multilingual Society. Mona, Jamaica, 1965; 2nd ed. 1970.

568 **Jussawala, Feroza,** "Family quarrels: towards a criticism of Indian writing in English." Ph.D. Utah 1983.

569 **Justavino, Nilsa Esther,** "West Indian dialects: a historical, social and linguistic approach." B.A. U. of Panama 1975.

570 **Kachru, Braj B.,** "The Indianness of Indian English", Word 21 (1965): 391-410.

571 ---, "English in South Asia", CTL 5 (1969): 627-78; rev. version in Fishman 1978: 477-551; in Aggarval 1982: ix-lxx.

572 ---, "Some style features of South Asian English", in K. Goodwin, ed., National Identity. London: Heinemann 1971.

573 ---, "English in India, a pan-Indian and international link", EAW 4 (1971): 1-2, 4-7.

574 ---, "Toward a lexicon of Indian English", in Kahane festschrift. Urbana 1973: 352-76.

575 ---, "Lexical innovations in South Asian English", IJSL 4 (1975): 55-94; repr. in Mohan 1978: 80-100.

576 —, "Models of English for the third world: white man's linguistic burden or language pragmatics?" TESOLQ 10 (1976): 221-39.

577 —, "New Englishes and old models", ETF (July 1977).

578 —, "Linguistic schizophrenia and language census: a note on the Indian situation", Linguistics 186 (1977): 17-33.

579 —, "Indian English: a sociolinguistic profile of a transplanted language", in B. Krishnamurti, ed., Introduction to Indian Languages and Linguistics. New Delhi: NBT 1978.

580 —, "Code-mixing as a communicative strategy in India", in Alatis 1979: 107-24.

581 —, "The New Englishes and old lexicons: Directions in lexicographical research in non-native varieties of English", in L. Zgusta, ed., Theory and Method in Lexicography: Western and Non-western Perspectives. Columbia, S.C.: Hornbeam 1980: 71-101.

582 —, "The non-native literatures as a resource for language teaching", RELC Journal 11,2 (1980): 1-9.

583 —, "The pragmatics of non-native varieties of English", in Smith 1981: 15-39.

584 —, "American English and other Englishes", in Charles A. Ferguson and Shirley Brice Heath, eds., Language in the USA. Cambridge: UP 1981: 21-43.

585 Entry deleted.

586 —, "Language policy in South Asia", Annual Review of Applied Linguistics 3 (1982): 60-85.

587 —, "South Asian English", in Bailey/Görlach 1982: 353-83.

588 —, "Introduction: the other side of English", in Kachru 1982: 1-12.

589 —, "Models for Englishes", in Kachru 1982: 31-57; repr. in Smith 1983: 69-86.

590 —, "Meaning in deviation: toward understanding non-native English texts", in Kachru 1982: 325-50; Noss 1983: 20-49.

591 —, ed., The Other Tongue. English across Cultures. Urbana: Illinois UP 1982.

592 —, "Normes régionales de l'anglais", in Edith Bédard and Jacques

Maurais, eds., La Norme. Québec: Conseil de la langue française 1983: 707-30.

593 ---, "Models for new Englishes", in Cobarrubias/Fishman 1983: 145-70.

594 ---, "English as a second language", in Greenbaum 1984.

595 ---, "The alchemy of colonial Englishes: functional power of non-native varieties", in Cheris Kramarae and Muriel Schulz, eds., Language and Power (forthcoming).

596 **Källgard, Anders,** "Pitcairnese - a report 30 years after Moverley", Göteborgs U. 1981 (mimeo).

597 **Kaldor, Susan,** "Verb, tense and aspect distinctions in Aboriginal children's English", 15th Pacific Science Congress 1983; Proc. in PacL (forthcoming).

598 --- and **I.G. Malcolm,** "The language of the school and the language of the Western Australian Aboriginal school child: implications for education", in R.M. and C.H. Berndt, eds., Aborigines of the West. Nedlands: Western Australia UP 1979.

599 **Kandiah, Thiru,** "New Ceylon English", New Ceylon Writing (1971): 90ff.

600 ---, "Disinherited Englishes: the case of Lankan English", paper 1978, in Navasilu (Sri Lanka).

601 ---, "Linguistic self-expropriation in Sri Lankan creative writing in English", Journal of South Asian Literatures (1979).

602 ---, "Lankan English schizoglossia", EWW 2 (1981): 63-82.

603 **Kang-Kwong, Luke** and **Jack C. Richards,** "English in Hong Kong: functions and status", EWW 3 (1982): 47-64.

604 **Kashoki, Mubanga E.,** "What kind of English can the Zambian teacher of English realistically expect to teach?" Bulletin of the Zambia Language Group (1975).

605 ---, "Rural and urban multilingualism in Zambia: some trends", IJSL 34 (1982): 137-66.

606 **Kassulamemba, Frederick T.,** "Tanzanian spoken English: error analysis of the vowel system." M.A. Dar es Salaam 1977.

607 **Kay, P.** and **G. Sankoff,** "A language-universals approach to pidgins and creoles", in DeCamp/Hancock 1974: 61-72.

608 **Keane, Y.** and **M. Martineau,** "A proposal for a common phonemic script for Caribbean creoles", in Cave 1976.

609 **Kelley, Sr. F.,** "The English spoken colloquially by a group of adolescents in Suva", Fiji English Teachers' Journal 11 (1975): 19-43.

610 **Kelly, L.C.,** ed., The Description and Measurement of Bilingualism. Toronto 1969.

611 **Kelly, L.G.,** "English as a second language: a sociolinguistic perspective", Eng. Quart. 11,2 (1978): 39-49.

612 **Kernan, Keith T., John Sodergren** and **Robert French,** "Speech and social prestige in the Belizean speech community", in B.G. Blount and M. Sanches, eds., Sociocultural Dimensions of Language Change. New York: Academic Press 1977: 35-50.

613 **Khan, I.,** "Dialect in West Indian literature", in L. Brown, ed., The Black Writer in Africa and the Americas. Los Angeles 1973.

614 **Khubchandani, Lachman Mulchand,** "Functional importance of Hindi and English in India", in A. Poddar, ed., Language and Society in India. Simla: IIAS 1967.

615 ---, "Indian bilingualism and English: a demographic study", Demography, India (1973).

616 ---, "English in India: a sociolinguistic appraisal", Intern. Journal of Dravidian Linguistics 2 (1973): 199-211.

617 ---, "English as a contact language in South Asia", RELC 7 (1976): 21-30.

618 ---, "Language factor in census", in Verdoodt/Kjolseth 1976: 92-124.

619 ---, "Language ideology and language development: an appraisal of Indian education policy", Linguistics 193 (1977): 33-52.

620 ---, "Distribution of contact languages in India. A study of the 1961 bilingualism returns", in Fishman 1978: 553-85.

621 ---, "Multilingual education in India", in Spolsky/Cooper 1978: 88-125.

622 **Killingley, S.-Y.,** "Clauses and sentence types in Malayan English", Orbis 21 (1973): 537-48.

623 **King, A.H.,** "Intercomprehensibility - the humpty-dumpty problem of English as a world language", IncL 10 (1971).

624 **Kinney, L.,** "A psycholinguistic approach to pidgin and creole languages." Ph.D. Georgia 1976. DAI 37: 8, 5093A.

625 **Kloss, Heinz,** "Types of multilingual communities: a discussion of the variables", in S. Lieberson, ed., Explorations in Sociolinguistics. The Hague: Mouton 1967: 7-17.

626 ---, Die Entwicklung neuer germanischer Kultursprachen seit 1800. Düsseldorf: Schwann, 2nd ed. 1978.

627 ---, Problems of Language Policy in South Africa. Wien: Braunmüller 1979.

628 **Knappert, J.,** "The problem of national languages and education in Africa", LMLP 2,4 (1970): 21-37.

629 **Knowles, Roberta Quarles,** "The understanding and use of varieties of spoken English by selected Virgin Island adults." Ed.D. New York U. 1980. DAI 42: 2, 686A.

630 **Koenig, Edna,** "Ethnicity and language in Corozal District, Belize: an analysis of code switching." Ph.D. U. of Texas 1975. DAI 36: 2, 961A.

631 **Kohlman, Aarona M.,** "The dialect of Grand Cayman." M.A. Iowa State U. 1969.

632 ---, Wotcha Say: An Introduction to Colloquial Caymanian. Grand Cayman: Cayman Artventures 1979(?).

633 **Köppl, Sebastian,** "Englisch in Süd- und Südostasien", in Englisch - Formen und Funktionen einer Weltsprache 1983: 117-43.

634 ---, "Englisch in Australien und Neuseeland", in Englisch - Formen und Funktionen einer Weltsprache 1983: 145-54.

635 **Kosok, H.** and **H. Prießnitz,** Literaturen in englischer Sprache. Ein Überblick über englisch-sprachige Nationalliteraturen außerhalb Englands. Bonn: Bouvier 1977.

636 **Kotey, P.F.** and **H. Der-Houssikian,** eds., Language and Linguistic Problems in Africa. Proceedings of the VII Conference on African Linguistics. Columbia, S.C.: Hornbeam 1977.

637 **Krishnamurti, Bh.,** "Spelling pronunciation in Indian English", in Mohan 1978: 129-39.

638 **Krishnaswami, N.,** "Indian English: a descriptive study", Pakha Sanjam 3, 1-2 (1970): 94-100.

639 ---, "Indian English?" NIE Journal 6,2 (1971): 6-10.

640 --- and **Salim A. Aziz,** "Understanding values, TEIL, and the Third World", in Smith 1983: 95-101.

641 **Krušina, A.,** "Anglictina v Indii", Sbornik lingvistických prací (Praha, 1970): 96-118.

642 **Kuki, H.** and **M. Yoshioka,** "An introduction to the New Hebridean English pidgin or le bichelamar", Gengo Kenkyu 72 (1977): 47-86.

643 **Kuo, Eddie C.Y.,** "Language status and literacy trend in a multilingual society - Singapore", RELC 5 (1974): 1-15.

644 ---, "Language, nationhood and communication planning: the case of a multilingual society", Southeast Asian Journal of Social Science 4 (1976): 31-42.

645 ---, "Measuring communicativity in multilingual societies: the cases of Singapore and West Malaysia", AnL 21,7 (1979): 328-40.

646 ---, "The status of English in Singapore: a sociolinguistic analysis", in Crewe 1977a: 10-33.

647 ---, "Unity in diversity: the sociolinguistic situation in Singapore", in Teodoro A. Llamzon, ed., Papers in Southeast Asian Languages ... RELC Anthology Series 5. Singapore: RELC 1977.

648 ---, "Multilingualism and mass media communications in Singapore", Asian Survey 18,10 (1978): 1067-83.

649 ---, "A sociolinguistic profile of Singapore", in R. Hassan, ed., Singapore: A Society in Transition.

650 **Kwan-Terry, A.,** "The meaning and the source of the la and the what particles in Singapore English", RELC 9,2 (1978): 22-35.

651 **Kwok, H.** and **M. Chan,** "Where we twain do meet: a preliminary study of the language habits of university undergraduates in Hong Kong", GL 12 (1972): 63-82.

652 **Labov, William,** "On the notion of 'system' in creole languages", in Hymes 1971: 447-72.

653 ---, "Is there a creole speech community?" in Valdman/Highfield 1980: 369-88. (Belize)

654 **Labru, G.L.,** "Indian newspaper English." Diploma Leeds 1968.

655 **Langker, R.,** Flash in New South Wales 1788-1850. (Occ. Papers 18) Sydney: The U. 1980.

656 **Lanham, L.W.,** The Pronunciation of South African English. Cape Town 1967.

657 ---, "English as a second language in Southern Africa since 1820", in de Villiers 1976: 279-96.

658 ---, "English teaching in African schools", in Education in Southern Africa (1976?): 249-63.

659 ---, "An outline history of the languages of Southern Africa", in Lanham/Prinsloo 1978: 13-28.

660 ---, "South African English", in Lanham/Prinsloo 1978: 138-65.

661 ---, "English in South Africa", in Bailey/Görlach 1982: 353-83.

662 --- and **C.A. McDonald,** The Standard in South African English and its Social History. Heidelberg: Groos 1979.

663 --- and **K. Prinsloo,** eds., Language and Communication Studies in South Africa. Cape Town: Oxford UP 1978.

664 **Larimore, Nancy K.,** "A comparison of predicate complementation in Krio and English." Ph.D. Northwestern U. 1976. DAI 37: 7, 4328A.

665 **Lattey, Elsa,** "Beyond variable rules", Papers in Pidgin and Creole Linguistics 2, PacL A57, Canberra 1979: 21-36 (Tok Pisin).

666 **Laveau, P.,** Apprenons le bichlamar. Port Vila 1973.

667 **Laver, J.,** "Assimilation in educated Nigerian English", ELTJ 22 (1968): 156-60.

668 **Lawton, David L.,** "The implications of tone for Jamaican Creole", AnL 10 (1968): 22-26.

669 ---, "Linguistic developments in the Caribbean, 1950/1975", La revista interamericana 5 (1975).

670 ---, "Language attitude, utterance recognition, and the creole continuum in Jamaica: fact or fiction", Papers in Linguistics 2,2 (U. of Michigan, 1976): 48-57.

671 ---, "Code shifting in Jamaican Creole", in Cave 1976: 1-25.

672 ---, "Bilingual strategies of communication: evidence from the text", Fourth LACUS Forum. Washington, D.C., 1977: 218-25.

673 ---, "Code shifting in Puerto Rican Spanish/English", Linguistics 217-8 (1979): 257-66.

674 ---, "Code-shifting in Jamaican Creole: a Caribbean context", Orbis 29 (1980): 234-50.

675 ---, "Language attitude, discreteness, and code-shifting in Jamaican Creole", EWW 1 (1980): 211-26.

676 ---, "English in the Caribbean", in Bailey/Görlach 1982: 251-80.

677 **Laycock, Don,** "Pidgin's progress", New Guinea and Australia 4,2 (1969): 8-15.

678 ---, "Pidgin English in New Guinea", in Ramson 1970: 102-22.

679 ---, Materials in New Guinea Pidgin (Coastal and Lowlands). PacL D5, Canberra 1970.

680 ---, "Creative writing in New Guinea Pidgin", in Wurm 1977: 609-38.

681 **Lazar-Meyn, H.A.,** "Save and stap in Tok Pisin", Penn Review Ling 2,2 (1978).

682 **Lee, Ernest W.,** Pride and Prejudice. The Status of Solomon Island Pijin. Honiara: Pijin Literacy Project 1980.

683 **Lee, Mary Hope,** "Ethnographic statement in the Nigerian novel, with special reference to pidgin", in Hancock 1979: 295-302.

684 **Leith, Dick,** A Social History of English. London: Routledge 1983. (chapter 7, "English overseas", 184-212).

685 **Lennox-Short, A.,** "Trends in South Africa's English", in G. Roberts, ed., Seven Studies in English. Cape Town 1971: 106-21.

686 ---, ed., English and South Africa. Cape Town: Oxford UP 1973.

687 **LePage, Robert B.,** "Intercomprehensibility between West Indian English and other forms of English", in Remedial Education (Oxford, Pergamon 1967): 129-35.

688 ---, "Problems of description in multilingual communities", TPS (1968): 189-212.

689 ---, "Problems to be faced in the use of English as the medium of education in four West Indian territories", in Fishman 1968: 431-41.

690 ---, "Dialect in West Indian literature", Journal of Commonwealth Literature 7 (1969): 1-7.

691 ---, *Sample West Indian Texts*. York: U., Dept. of Lang. 1972; 2nd ed. 1981.

692 ---, "Preliminary report on the sociolinguistic survey of multilingual communities. Part I: survey of Cayo District, British Honduras", *LSoc* 1 (1972): 155-72.

693 ---, "The concept of competence in a creole/contact situation", *York PL* 3 (1973): 31-50.

694 --- *et al.*, "Further report on the sociolinguistic survey of multilingual communities. Part I: survey of Cayo District, B.H.", *LSoc* 3 (1974): 1-32.

695 ---, "Processes of pidginization and creolization", *York PL* 4 (1974): 41-69; rev. version in Valdman 1977: 222-55.

696 ---, "Polarizing factors: political, social, economic, operating on the individual's choice of identity through language use in British Honduras", in J.-G. Savard and R. Vigneault, eds., *Les états multilingues: problèmes et solutions*. Québec: U. Laval 1975.

697 ---, "Sociolinguistics and the problem of 'competence'", in *Language Teaching and Linguistics: Abstracts* 8 (1975): 137-56; rev. in V. Kinsella, ed., *Language Teaching and Linguistics: Surveys*. Cambridge: UP 1978: 39-59.

698 ---, "De-creolization and re-creolization: a preliminary report on the sociolinguistic survey of multilingual communities stage II: St. Lucia", *York PL* 7 (1977): 107-28.

699 ---, "Projection, focussing and diffusion, or steps towards a sociolinguistic theory of language", *SCL* 9 (1978).

700 ---, "Some preliminary comments on comparative lexicography in the Caribbean", *Proc. Conf. SCL*. Barbados: UWI 1978.

701 ---, "Theoretical aspects of sociolinguistic studies in pidgin and creole languages", in Valdman/Highfield 1980: 331-67. (Belize, St. Lucia).

702 --- and **A. Tabouret-Keller,** "Models and stereotypes of ethnicity and language", *JMMD* 3,3 (1982): 161-92.

703 **Lewis, Maureen Warner,** "The African impact on language and literature in the English-speaking Caribbean", in Margaret E. Crahan and Franklin W. Knight, eds., *Africa and the Caribbean: The Legacies of a Link*. Baltimore: Johns Hopkins UP 1979: 104-23.

704 **Lieberman, Dena,** "Language attitudes in St. Lucia", Journal of Cross Cultural Psychology 6 (1975): 471-81.

705 **Lieberson, Stanley J.** and **Edward J. McCabe,** "Domains of languag usage and mother-tongue shift in Nairobi", IJSL 34 (1982): 83-94.

706 **Liefrink, Frans** and **John Jones,** A Survey of the Languages Spoken b Students at U.P.N.G. U. Papua New Guinea 1974.

707 **Lim Kiat Boey,** "Language learning and language use among som Singapore students", RELC Journal 11,2 (1980): 10-28.

708 **Litteral, Robert,** "A proposal for the use of pidgin in Papua Ne Guinea's education system", in McElhanon 1975: 155-65; repr. in Prid 1979: 152-63.

709 **Llamzon, Teodoro A.,** Standard Filipino English. Manila: Ateneo U 1969.

710 ---, "Emerging patterns in the English language situation in Singapor today", in Crewe 1977a: 34-45.

711 ---, "A new approach to the teaching of English in the Philippines", i Richards 1979: 131-40.

712 ---, "Essential features of new varieties of English", in Noss 1983 92-112.

713 **Lowenberg, Peter H.,** "Language contact and change: English in th Malay Archipelago." Ph.D. Urbana (forthcoming).

714 **Lutze, L.,** "Linguistic prospects of the emergence of an interna contact language for India", South Asian Studies 4 (1968): 25-42.

715 **Lynch, J.,** "Bislama phonology and grammar: a review article", Kivun 8 (1977): 186-208.

716 **McElhanon, K.A.,** ed., Tok Pisin i go we. Kivung Special Publ. 1. Por Moresby 1975.

717 ---, "Appreciating the possibilities of Tok Pisin: evangelism and th use of Tok Pisin idioms", Catalyst 5,3 (1975): 21-37.

718 **McEntegart, Damian,** Final Report and Appraisal of the Collectio and Analysis of the Data in the Sociolinguistic Survey of Multilingua Communities, Stages I (Belize) and II (St. Lucia). London: SSRC 1980.

19 --- and **Robert B. LePage,** "An appraisal of the statistical techniques used in the Sociolinguistic Survey of Multilingual Communities", in Suzanne Romaine, ed., Sociolinguistic Variation in Speech Communities. London: Arnold 1982: 105-24.

20 **McGregor, G.P.,** English in Africa. London 1971.

21 **McKesey, George,** The Belizean Lingo. Belize City: National Printers 1974.

22 **Mackiewicz-Krassowska, H.,** "Nasality in Australian English", Macquarie WP 1,3 (1976): 27-40.

23 **McLean, Guillermo** and **Ray Past,** "Some characteristics of Bluefields English", in Robert J. DiPietro and Edward L. Blansitt, Jr., eds., The Third LACUS Forum 1976. Columbia, S.C.: Hornbeam 1977: 87-94.

24 **Mafeni, Bernard,** "Some aspects of the phonetics and phonology of Nigerian Pidgin." M.Litt. Edinburgh U. 1965.

25 ---, "Nigerian Pidgin", in Spencer 1971: 95-112.

26 **Maghway, Josephat B.,** "Spoken English in Tanzania: spelling and the pronunciation of vowels." M.A. Dar es Salaam 1980.

27 **Malcolm, Ian,** "Classroom communication and the Aboriginal child: a sociolinguistic investigation in Western Australian schools." Ph.D. Western Australia 1979.

28 **Malherbe, E.G.,** Demographic and Socio-Political Forces Determining the Position of English in the South African Republic: English as Mother-Tongue. Johannesburg: The English Academy 1966.

29 ---, "Bilingual education in the Republic of South Africa", in Spolsky/Cooper 1978: 167-202.

30 **Malla, Kamal Prakash,** English in Nepalese Education. Kathmandu: Ratna pustak bhandar 1977.

31 --- and **James J. Donnelly,** "Nationalism, multilingualism and English teaching as a factor in national development: a case study of Nepal", Edinburgh: The University (mimeo).

32 **Manuel, M.** and **K. Ayyappa Paniker,** eds., English and India. Essays presented to Professor Samuel Mathai. Madras 1978.

33 **Markey, T.L.,** "Diffusion, fusion and creolization: a field guide to developmental linguistics", Papiere zur Linguistik 24, Heft 1/81 (Tübingen, 1981): 3-38.

734 --- and **Peter Fodale,** "Lexical diathesis, focal shifts and passivization: the creole voice", EWW 4,1 (1983): 69-84.

735 **Martinez, Norma D.,** Standard Filipino English Pronunciation. Manila National Book Store 1975.

736 **Masica, Colin** and **P.B. Dave,** The Sound System of Indian English Hyderabad: CIEFL 1972.

737 **Mazrui, Ali,** "The English language and political consciousness in British Colonial Africa", Journal of Modern African Studies 4 (1966) 295-311.

738 ---, "Islam and the English language in East and West Africa", in Whiteley 1971: 179-97.

739 ---, "The English language and the origins of African nationalism", in Bailey/Robinson 1973: 56-76.

740 ---, "Language and Black destiny", in A. Mazrui, World Culture and Black Experience. Washington: UP 1974.

741 ---, The Political Sociology of the English Language: an African Perspective. The Hague: Mouton 1975.

742 ---, "The racial boundaries of the English language: an African perspective", in Savard/Vigneault 1975: 61-86.

743 **Mbassi-Manga, F.,** "English in Cameroon: a study in historical contacts, patterns of usage and current trends." Ph.D. Leeds 1973.

744 ---, "The state of contemporary English in Cameroon", Cameroon Studies in English and French 1 (1976): 49-63.

745 **Mehrotra, Raja Ram,** "Dimensions of language policy - the case for English", in S. Saberval, ed., Toward a Cultural Policy. New Delhi Vikas 1974: 112-25.

746 ---, "Some registral features of matrimonial advertisement in Indian English", ELTJ 30,1 (1975): 9-12.

747 ---, "Matrimonial advertisements: a study in correlation between linguistic and situational features", Indian Institute of Advanced Studies, Occ. Papers, Studies in Ling. (1976): 41-61.

748 ---, "English in India: the current scene", ELTJ 31 (1976-77): 163-70.

749 ---, "Indian English: a sociolinguistic profile", in Pride 1982: 150-73.

750 ---, "International communication through non-native varieties of English: the case of Indian English", in Brumfit 1982: 73-80.

751 ---, "Indian English: some myths and misconceptions", Perspectives on Indian English. Bihar U., Muzaffarpur (forthcoming).

752 ---, India. (VEAW) Amsterdam: Benjamins (forthcoming).

753 **Menon, Usha,** The Indianness of Indian English: an Examination of Features Specifically Indian in Indo-Anglian Fiction. Calicut 1975.

754 **Midgett, D.,** "Bilingualism and linguistic change in St. Lucia", AnL 12 (1970): 158-70.

755 **Mihalic, Francis,** The Jacaranda Dictionary and Grammar of Melanesian Pidgin. Milton, Qld., 1971.

756 ---, "Standardisation in Pidgin", in McElhanon 1975: 54-59.

757 **Minderhout, David J.,** "A sociolinguistic description of Tobagonian English." Ph.D. Georgetown U. 1973.

758 ---, "Language variation in Tobagonian English", AnL 19 (1977): 167-79.

759 **Mintz, S.W.,** "The socio-historical background to pidginization and creolization", in Hymes 1971: 481-96.

760 **Mitchell, A.G.,** "The Australian accent", in Ramson 1970: 1-14.

761 --- and **A. Delbridge,** The Speech of Australian Adolescents. Sydney: Angus and Robertson 1965.

762 **Mittelsdorf, S.,** "African retentions in Jamaican Creole: a reassessment." Ph.D. Northwestern U. 1978. DAI 39: 10, 6104A.

763 **Moag, Rodney F.,** "The life cycle of non-native Englishes: a case study", in Kachru 1982: 270-88.

764 ---, "On English as a foreign, second, native and basal language", in Pride 1982: 11-50.

765 --- and **L.B. Moag,** "English in Fiji, some perspectives and the need for language planning", Fiji English Teachers' Journal 13 (1977): 2-26; repr. in Richards 1979: 73-90.

766 **Mogi, Noboru,** ed., English Around the World. 2 vols. Tokyo: Kenkyusha 1983 (in Japanese).

767 **Mohan, Ramesh,** ed., Indian Writing in English. New Delhi: Orient Longman 1978.

768 ---, "Some aspects of style and language in Indian English fiction", in Mohan 1978: 192-202.

769 **Mosel, U.,** "Early language contact between Tolai, Pidgin and English in the light of its sociolinguistic background (1875-1914)", in Papers in Pidgin and Creole Linguistics 2, PacL A57, Canberra 1979: 163-82.

770 **Moss, W.R.,** "English in the Commonwealth: 7 - Pakistan", ELTJ 18,2 (1964): 63-69.

771 **Muecke, Stephen,** "Stereotyping and 'Strine'", in Clyne 1976: 29-41.

772 ---, "Australian Aboriginal narratives in English: a study in discourse analysis." Ph.D. U. of Western Australia 1981.

773 **Mühlhäusler, Peter,** Pidginization and Simplification of Language. PacL B26, Canberra 1974.

774 ---, "The influence of German administration on New Guinea Pidgin", Journal of Pacific History 10 (1975): 94-111.

775 ---, "Sociolects in New Guinea pidgin", in McElhanon 1975: 59-75.

776 ---, "Reduplication and repetition in New Guinea Pidgin", in McElhanon 1975: 198-214.

777 ---, "Samoan plantation pidgin English and the origin of New Guinea pidgin", Journal of Pacific History 11 (1976); rev. version in Papers in Pidgin and Creole Linguistics, PacL A58, Canberra 1979: 67-120.

778 ---, "Synonymy and communication across lectal boundaries in Tok Pisin", Papers in Pidgin and Creole Linguistics 2, PacL A57, Canberra 1979: 1-20.

779 ---, "On regional dialects in New Guinea Pidgin"; "The social role of pidgin in Papua New Guinea today"; "Sociolects in New Guinea Pidgin"; "Creolization of New Guinea Pidgin", in Wurm 1977: 533-7; 549-57; 559-66; 567-76.

780 ---, Growth and Structure of the Lexicon of New Guinea Pidgin. Ph.D. Canberra 1976 = PacL C52, 1979.

781 ---, "The functional possibilities of lexical bases in New Guinea Pidgin", Papers in Pidgin and Creole Linguistics, PacL A58, Canberra 1979: 121-73.

782 ---, "Papuan Pidgin English rediscovered", in Proc. Second Intern. Conf. on Austronesian Linguistics, PacL C61, Canberra 1978: 1377-1446.

783 ---, "Remarks on the pidgin and creole situation in Australia", Newsletter of the Australian Institute of Aboriginal Studies New Series 12 (1979): 41-53.

784 ---, "Structural expansion and the process of creolization", in Valdman/Highfield 1980: 19-55.

785 ---, "Foreigner talk, tok masta in New Guinea", IJSL 28 (1981): 93-113.

786 ---, "The development of the category of number in Tok Pisin", in Muysken 1981: 35-84.

787 ---, "Tok Pisin in Papua New Guinea", in Bailey/Görlach 1982: 439-66.

788 ---, "Etymology and pidgin and creole languages", TPS 1982: 99-118.

789 ---, "Language and communiction efficiency: the case of Tok Pisin", Language and Communication 2,2 (1982): 105-21.

790 ---, "Samoan plantation pidgin English and the origin of New Guinea Pidgin", in Woolford/Washabaugh 1983: 28-76.

791 ---, "The development of derivational morphology in Tok Pisin", Folia Linguistica (1983).

792 ---, "The number of pidgin Englishes in the Pacific", Proceedings of Pacific Science Conf. PacL, Canberra (forthcoming).

793 ---, "The history of research into Tok Pisin 1900-1975", in Gilbert 1984.

794 ---, **J.A.** Bennett and **D.T. Tryon,** "Some English-based pidgins in the southwestern Pacific", in Wurm 1979: 53-78.

795 --- and **Tom Dutton,** "Papuan Pidgin English and Hiri Motu", in Wurm 1979: 209-24.

796 --- and **S.A. Wurm,** "Registers in New Guinea Pidgin", in Register Range and Change. IJSL 35 (1982): 69-86.

797 **Mufwene, Salikoko S.,** "Observations on time reference in Jamaican and Guyanese creoles", EWW 4,2 (1983).

798 ---, "Notes on durative constructions in Jamaican and Guyanese Creoles", in Görlach (forthcoming).

799 **Mukherjee, Meenakshi,** "The language of the Indo-Anglian novelist", in Mohan 1978: 150-6.

800 **Murphy, R.P.** and **J. Ornstein,** "A survey of research on language diversity: a partial who's who in sociolinguistics", Second LACUS Forum, 1975. Columbia, S.C., 1976: 413-61.

801 **Murtagh, Edward Joseph,** "Creole and English used as languages of instruction with Aboriginal Australians." Ph.D. Stanford 1979.

802 ---, "Creole and English as used as languages of instruction in bilingual education with Aboriginal Australians: some research findings", IJSL 36 (1982): 15-33.

803 **Muthiah, S.,** "Is English India's vanishing language?" Indian Review 73,7 (1977): 39-42.

804 **Mutt, O.,** Social and Regional Varieties of Present-day English. Tartu SU, Dept. of English 1977.

805 **Muysken, Pieter,** ed., Generative Studies on Creole Languages. Dordrecht: Foris 1981.

806 **Nababan, P.W.J.,** "The non-native variety of English in Indonesia", in Noss 1983: 113-24.

807 **Nadel, E.** et al., "English in Israel: a sociolinguistic study", AnL 19 (1977): 26ff.; also in Fishman et al. 1977: 137-67.

808 **Nagara, Susumu,** "A bilingual description of some linguistic features of Pidgin English used by Japanese immigrants on the plantations of Hawaii: a case study in bilingualism." Ph.D. U. of Wisconsin 1969. DAI 30: 12, 5433A.

809 ---, Japanese Pidgin English in Hawaii. Honolulu: UP 1972.

810 **Nagarajan, Sankalapuram,** "The decline of English in India: some historical notes", in Manuel/Paniker 1978: 161-71.

811 **Nambiar, K.C.,** "Stylistic studies in Indian writing in English - a suggested framework", in Mohan 1978: 157-72.

812 **Narasimhan, Raji,** "Indo-English: new depth, new dimensions", Indian Literature. Annual Survey of the 22 Languages and Literatures of India 24,6 (1981): 24-33.

813 **Narayan, R.K.,** "English in India", in J. Press, ed., Commonwealth Literature. London 1965.

814 **Naro, A.J.,** "The origin of West African pidgin", CLS 9 (1973): 442-9.

815 ---, "A study on the origins of pidginization", Language 54 (1978): 314-47.

816 **Nash, E.A.,** Dictionary of Solomon Islands Pidgin. Honiara 1979.

817 **Nash, Rose,** "Spanglish: language contact in Puerto Rico", AS 45 (1970): 223-33; repr. in Dillard 1980: 265-75.

818 ---, "Englañol: more language contact in Puerto Rico", AS 46 (1971): 106-22.

819 ---, "Phantom cognates and other curiosities in Puerto Rican Englañol", LMLP 5 (1976): 157-67.

820 ---, "Aspects of Spanish-English bilingualism and language mixture in Puerto Rico", in A. Makkai et al., Linguistics at the Crossroads. Lake Bluff, Ill., 1977: 205-25.

821 ---, "Pringlish: still more language contact in Puerto Rico", in Kachru 1982: 250-69.

822 **Nelson, Cecil,** "Intelligibility and non-native varieties of English", in Kachru 1982: 58-73.

823 **Ngara, E.A.,** Bilingualism, Language Contact and Language Planning. Proposals for Language Use and Language Teaching in Zimbabwe. Gwelo: Mambo Press 1982.

824 ---, "Non-contrastive errors in African English: types and significance", IRAL 21,1 (1983): 35-45.

825 **Nichols, J.,** "Pidgins and creoles: synchronic and diachronic aspects of linguistic discontinuity", RPh 28 (1975).

826 **Nihalani, P.** et al., Indian and British English. A Handbook of Usage and Pronunciation. New Delhi: Oxford UP 1979.

827 **Niles, Norma Anita,** "Provincial English dialects and Barbadian English." Ph.D. Ann Arbor 1980. DAI 41: 9, 4018A.

828 **Nodal, R.,** A Bibliography, with some Annotations, on the Creole Languages of the Caribbean, Including a Special Supplement on Gullah. Milwaukee: U. of Wisconsin 1972.

829 **Noel, J.,** "Legitimacy of pidgin in the development of Papua New Guinea toward nationhood", in McElhanon 1975: 76-85.

830 **Northcote-Bade, J.,** "An introduction to New Zealand English", Englisch 11 (1976): 147-51.

831 **Noss, Richard B.,** ed., Language Teaching Issues in Multilingual Environments in Southeast Asia. Anthology Series 10. Singapore: RELC 1982 (P.W.J. Nababan, "Indonesia", 1-47; Anthony J. Rogers, "Malaysia", 48-77; Andrew B. Gonzalez, "The Philippines", 78-136; Goh Soo Tian, "Singapore", 137-76; Achara Wangsotorn, "Thailand", 177ff.)

832 —, ed., Varieties of English in Southeast Asia. RELC Anthology Series 11. Singapore: UP (for RELC) 1983.

833 **Obiechina, E.N.,** ed., Onitsha Market Literature. New York 1972.

834 —, "Variety differentiation in English usage", Journal of the Nigeria English Studies Assoc. 6 (1974): 77-94.

835 —, Culture Tradition and Society in the West African Novel. Cambridge: UP 1975.

836 **Obilade, Anthony O.,** "The nominal phrase in West African Pidgin English (Nigeria)." Ph.D. Northwestern U. 1976. DAI 37: 7, 4330A.

837 —, "On the inadequacy of the nativity/reduction theory in creole studies: evidence from West African Pidgin English", Africana Marburgensia 11,2 (1978): 3-14.

838 —, "Pidgin English as a medium of instruction: the Nigerian experience", Africana Marburgensia 13,1 (1978): 59-69.

839 **O'Callaghan, Evelyn,** "A study of creole in the West Indian novel." M.Litt. Oxford 1981.

840 **Odo, Carol,** "English patterns in Hawaii", AS 45 (1970): 234-8.

841 —, "Variation in Hawaiian English: underlying r", Hawaii WPL 3,2 (1971): 1-30.

842 —, "Focusing and defocusing in Hawaiian English", in Bailey/Shuy 1973: 297-305.

843 —, "Phonological representation in Hawaiian English", Hawaii WPL 9,3 (1977): 77-85.

844 **O'Donnell, W.R.** and **Loreto Todd,** Variety in Contemporary English. London: Allen & Unwin 1980.

845 **Odumuh, Adama Emmanuel,** "Aspects of the semantics and syntax of 'Educated Nigerian English'." Ph.D. Ahmadu Bello U. (Nigeria) 1981. DAI 43: 9, 2984A.

846 **Ofuani, Ogo A.,** "Future time expression in Nigerian Pidgin", Papers in Linguistics 14,3 (Edmonton, 1981): 309-26.

847 ---, "Pidgin in Nigerian journalism", Papers in Linguistics 14,3 (1981): 327-46.

848 **Ohannessian, Sirarpi,** ed., Reference List of Materials for English as a Second Language. Arlington: n.d.

849 --- et al., Language Surveys in Developing Nations. Arlington, Va.: Center for Applied Linguistics 1975.

850 **Ola Oke, D.,** "On the genesis of new world Black English", CQ 23 (1977): 63-79.

851 **Olewale, E.** et al., "General thoughts on teaching pidgin" etc., in Wurm 1977: 639-757.

852 **Olshtain, Elite,** "A theoretical model for developing the teaching of a language of wider communication (LWC) on a national scale." Ph.D. Los Angeles 1979. DAI 40: 6, 3273A.

853 **Oluikpe, B.O.,** "Noun phrase in legal English. A grammatical sketch", in Ubahakwe 1979: 200-26.

854 **Omar, Asmah Haji,** "The roles of English in Malaysia in the context of national language planning", in Noss 1983: 229-50.

855 **Omolewa, M.,** "The emergence of non-standard English in Nigeria 1842-1926", in Ubahakwe 1979: 14-26.

856 **Otley, C.R.,** Creole Talk (Trinibagianese) of Trinidad and Tobago. Port of Spain 1971.

857 **Owens, Jonathan,** "Monogenesis, the universal, and the particular in creole studies", AnL 22,3 (1980): 97-117.

858 **Pace, S.,** "A sociolinguistic consideration of the English spoken in Grenada, British West Indies", in W.F. Mackey and J. Ornstein, eds., Sociolinguistic Studies in Language Contact. The Hague: Mouton 1979: 265-76.

859 **Pai, A. Dada** and **T. Oderinde,** "An empirical study of the acceptability of four accents spoken in Nigeria", in Ubahakwe 1979: 242-56.

860 **Panchal, M.R.,** Teaching English in India: Old and New Approaches. New Delhi, 2nd ed. 1976.

861 **Pandit, P.B.,** "Calling names - some observations on the folk categories of language labels", in Mohan 1978: 173-83.

862 **Pandya, Indubala Hiren,** "Deviations in advertising in India", Indian Linguistics 37 (1976): 102-14.

863 ---, English Language in Advertising: A Linguistic Study of Indian Press Advertising. Delhi: Ajanta 1977.

864 **Parasher, S.V.,** "Certain aspects of the functions and form of Indian English: a sociolinguistic study." Ph.D. Hyderabad: CIEFL 1979.

865 ---, "Indian English: model, identity and use", Journal of Indian Education 5 (1979): 68-75.

866 ---, "A synchronic view of English bilingualism in India", CIEFL Bulletin 15,1 (1979): 65-76.

867 ---, "Mother tongue - English diglossia: a case study of educated Indian bilinguals' language use", AnL 22 (1980): 151-62.

868 ---, "Indian English. A sociolinguistic perspective", ITL 51 (1981): 59-70.

869 ---, "English in India: a sociolinguistic reappraisal", ZAA 29 (1981): 330-42.

870 ---, "Indian English: certain grammatical, lexical and stylistic features", EWW 4,1 (1983): 27-42.

871 **Pascasio, Emy M.,** "The language situation in the Philippines", Philippine Studies (Manila, 1975).

872 ---, ed., The Filipino Bilingual. Studies in Philippine Bilingualism and Bilingual Education. Quezon City: Ateneo de Manila UP 1977.

873 **Pattanayak, Devi Prasanna,** Aspects of Applied Linguistics. London: Asia Publishing 1969; ch.6 "English in India", 41-48.

874 ---, "Some observations on English in India: its form and function", in Mohan 1978: 184-91; repr. in his Multilingualism and Mother-Tongue Education. New Delhi: Oxford UP 1981: 160-79.

875 **Pattison, B.,** "English as a foreign language over the world today", ELTJ 20 (1975): 1-20.

876 **Peet, William, Jr.,** "Omission of subject relative pronouns in Hawaiian English restrictive relative clauses", in Roger W. Shuy and Charles-James N. Bailey, eds., *Towards Tomorrow's Linguistics*. Washington, D.C.: Georgetown UP 1974: 253-66.

877 ---, "Relativization in a creole continuum." Ph.D. Hawaii 1978. DAI 39: 12, 7323A.

878 ---, "The nominative shift in Hawaiian Creole pronominalisation", *Papers in Pidgin and Creole Linguistics* 2, PacL A57, Canberra 1979: 151-61.

879 **Perlman, Alan M.,** "Grammatical structure and style-shift in Hawaiian Pidgin and Creole." Ph.D. Chicago 1973.

880 ---, "Deep and surface aspects of Hawaiian English existentials", in Robin E. Grossman, L. James San and Timothy J. Vance, eds., *Papers from the Eleventh Regional Meeting, Chicago Linguistic Society, April 18 - 20, 1975*. Chicago: Chicago Linguistic Society 1975: 423-8.

881 ---, "Observations on creolization: the case of Hawaiian English *Da Kine*", in Frances Ingemann, ed., *1975 Mid-America Linguistics Conference Papers*. Lawrence, Kansas: Linguistics Department, U. of Kansas 1976: 371-87.

882 ---, "Neuter pronoun variation in Hawaiian English", in Salikoko S. Mufwene, Carol A. Walker and Sanford B. Steever, eds., *Papers from the Twelfth Regional Meeting, Chicago Linguistic Society, April 23 - 25, 1976*. Chicago: Chicago Linguistic Society 1976: 516-22.

883 **Pilch, Herbert,** "Some phonemic peculiarities of Australian English", *Zwirner festschrift*. Copenhagen 1971: 269-75.

884 **Platt, John T.,** "The Singapore English speech continuum and its basilect 'Singlish' as a 'creoloid'", *AnL* 17 (1975): 363-74.

885 ---, "English past tense acquisition by Singaporeans - implicational scaling versus group averages of marked forms", *ITL* 38 (1977): 63-83.

886 ---, "A model for polyglossia and multilingualism (with special reference to Singapore and Malaysia)", *LSoc* 6 (1977): 361-78.

887 ---, "The 'creoloid' as a special type of interlanguage", *Interlanguage Studies Bulletin* 2,3 (Utrecht, 1977): 22-38.

888 ---, "The sub-varieties of Singapore English: their sociolectal and functional status", in Crewe 1977a: 83-95.

889 ---, "Sociolects and their pedagogical implications", *RELC* 9,1 (1978): 28-38.

890 ---, "The concept of a 'creoloid' - exemplification: basilectal Singapore English", in Papers in Pidgin and Creole Linguistics, PacL A58, Canberra 1979: 53-65.

891 ---, "Variation and implicational relationships: copula realization in Singapore English", GL 19,1 (1979): 1-14.

892 ---, "Varieties and functions of English in Singapore and Malaysia", EWW 1 (1980): 97-122.

893 ---, "Multilingualism, polyglossia, and code selection in Singapore", in Afendras/Kuo 1980: 63-83.

894 --- "The lingue franche of Singapore - an investigation into strategies of interethnic communication", in Howard Giles et al., eds., Language: Social Psychological Perspectives. Oxford: Pergamon 1980: 171-7.

895 ---, "English in Singapore, Malaysia, and Hong Kong", in Bailey/Görlach 1982: 415-38.

896 ---, "The relationship between sociolects and styles in established and new varieties", in Noss 1983: 213-28.

897 --- and **Ho Mian Lian,** "A case of language indigenisation: some features of colloquial Singapore English", JMMD 3,4 (1982): 267-76.

898 --- and **Heidi Weber,** English in Singapore and Malaysia. Status - Features - Functions. Kuala Lumpur: Oxford UP 1980.

899 ---, ---, "The position of two ESL varieties in a tridimensional model", Language Learning and Communication 1,1 (1982): 73-88.

900 ---, --- and **Ho Mian Lian,** Singapore and Malaysia. (VEAW) Amsterdam: Benjamins 1983.

901 **Poddar, A.,** ed., Language and Society in India. Simla 1969.

902 **Pollard, Velma,** "Codeswitching in Jamaican Creole: some educational implications", Caribbean Journal of Education 5, 1-2 (1978): 16-31.

903 ---, "The social history of Dread Talk", in Carrington 1983: 46-62.

904 **Polomé, Edgar C.,** "Sociolinguistically oriented language surveys", LSoc 11 (1982): 265-83.

905 --- and **C.P. Hill,** Language in Tanzania. Ford Foundation Surveys. Oxford: UP 1980.

906 **Povey, J.,** "The English language of the contemporary African novel", Critique 11 (1969): 79-86.

907 ---, "The role of English in Africa: a survey", EinA 3,1 (1976): 13-22.

908 ---, "The role of English in Africa", Workpapers in Teaching English as a Second Language 10 (1976): 79-87.

909 **Prabhakar, Babu,** "Newspaper headlines: a study in registral features", CIEFL Bulletin 8 (1970-71): 41-48.

910 ---, A Phonological Study of English Spoken by Telugu Speakers. Hyderabad 1977.

911 **Prator, Clifford H.,** "The survey of language use and language teaching in Eastern Africa", LingR 9 (1967).

912 ---, "The British heresy in TESL", in Fishman et al. 1968: 459-76.

913 ---, "The survey of language use and language teaching in Eastern Africa in retrospect", in Ohannessian et al. 1975: 145-58.

914 Entry deleted.

915 **Press, John,** ed., Commonwealth Literature: Unity and Diversity in a Common Culture. London 1965.

916 **Preston, Dennis,** "Variation in language: its significance in English as a second language", Studia Anglica Posnaniensia 6 (1975): 135-46.

917 **Pride, John B.,** ed., Sociolinguistic Aspects of Language Learning and Teaching. Oxford: UP 1979.

918 ---, "Native competence and the bilingual/multilingual speaker", EWW 2 (1981): 141-53.

919 ---, "Communicative needs in the learning and use of English", in John Anderson, ed., Language Form and Linguistic Variation. Papers Dedicated to Angus McIntosh. Amsterdam: Benjamins 1982: 321-77.

920 ---, "The appeal of the new Englishes", in Pride 1982: 1-7.

921 ---, ed., New Englishes. Rowley, Mass.: Newbury House 1982.

922 ---, "Linguistic competence and the expression of cultural identity", in Noss 1983: 50-91.

923 --- and **J. Holmes,** eds., Sociolinguistics. Harmondsworth: Penguin 1972.

924 **Purcell, April,** "Research report on Hawaiian Pidgin/Creole English and second language acquisition in Hawaii", Second Language Acquisition. Notes and Topics 11 (1982): 1-7.

925 ---, "Variation in speech by children from Hawaii." Ph.D. Hawaii 1979. DAI 40, 4576A.

926 **Pyne-Timothy, H.,** "An analysis of negative in Trinidad creole", JCS 1 (1976): 110-21.

927 ---, "Relationships between the phonological systems of Trinidad Creole and Standard English", in G. Nickel, ed., Proc. 4th Intern. Cong. of Applied Ling. Stuttgart: Hochschulverlag 1976: 175-86.

928 ---, "Grammatical structure and system in Trinidad Creole", in Kotey/Der-Houssikian 1977: 443-51.

929 **Quirk, Randolph,** The English Language and Images of Matter. London: 1972.

930 ---, "International communication and the concept of nuclear English", in Smith 1981: 151-65.

931 ---, "Language variety: nature and art", in Noss 1983: 3-19.

932 **Rafat, T.,** "Towards a Pakistani idiom", Venture: A Bi-annual Review of English Language and Literature 6 (1969): 60-73.

933 **Ralston, L.D.,** "Stammering: one result of language interference in a bidialectal community, Nevis, West Indies", in Cave 1976.

934 **Ramchand, K.,** "The language of the master?" (1970), excerpt in Bailey/Robinson 1973: 115-49.

935 **Ramish, L.,** "An investigation of the phonological features of the English of Singapore and the relation to the linguistic substrata of Malay, Tamil and Chinese languages." Ph.D. Brown U. 1970. DAI 31: 12, 6584A.

936 **Ramson, W.S.,** Australian English: An Historical Study of the Vocabulary, 1788-1898. Canberra 1966.

937 ---, "Australian and New Zealand English: the present state of studies", Kivung 2 (1969): 42-56.

938 ---, English Transported: Essays on Australian English. New York 1970.

939 ---, "Nineteenth-century Australian English", in Ramson 1970: 32-48.

940 ---, "Distinctive features of Australian English", in Turner 1972: 33-45.

941 **Ramunny, Kavita,** "Acceptability and intelligibility of various forms of Indian English", CIEFL Bulletin (1975).

942 **Reddy, Guda A.,** Indian Writing in English and its Audience. Bareilly 1979.

943 **Reinecke, John E.,** Language and Dialect in Hawaii: A Sociolinguistic History to 1935. Honolulu: Hawaii UP 1969.

944 --- et al., A Bibliography of Pidgin and Creole Languages. Honolulu: UP 1975.

945 **Reisman, K.M.L.,** "The isle is full of noises: a study of creole in the speech patterns of Antigua, West Indies." Ph.D. Harvard U. 1965.

946 ---, "Cultural and linguistic ambiguity in a West Indian village", in N.E. Whitton and J.F. Szwed, eds., Afro-American Anthropology. New York 1970: 129-44.

947 ---, "Contrapuntal conversations in an Antiguan village", in R. Bauman and J. Sherzer, eds., Explorations in the Ethnography of Speaking. Cambridge: UP 1974.

948 **Reyburn, William D.,** "Assessing multilingualism: an abridgement of 'Problems and Procedures in Ethnolinguistic Surveys'", in S. Ohannessian et al., eds., Language Surveys in Developing Nations. Washington, D.C.: Center for Applied Linguistics 1975: 87-114. (Nicaragua)

949 **Richards, H.,** "Trinidadian folk usage and Standard English: a contrastive study", Word 26 (1970): 79-87.

950 **Richards, Jack C.,** "Variation in Singapore English", in Crewe 1977a: 68-82.

951 ---, "Rhetorical and communicative styles in the new varieties of English", LL 29,1 (1979): 1-26; repr. in Pride 1982: 227-48.

952 ---, "The dynamics of English as an international, foreign, second and auxiliary language", Paper Hawaii EIAL, revised as "Models of language use and language learning", in Richards, ed., Understanding Second and Foreign Language Learning. Rowley, Mass.: Newbury.

953 ---, "Form and function in second language learning: an example from Singapore", in Proc. TESOL Convention, Acquisition and Use of a Second Language ... 1979. Rowley, Mass.: Newbury.

954 ---, ed., New Varieties of English. Issues and Approaches. Occasional Papers 8. Singapore: RELC 1979.

955 ---, "Talking across cultures", Language Learning and Communication 1,1 (1982): 61-71.

956 ---, "Singapore English: rhetorical and communicative styles", in Kachru 1982: 154-67.

957 --- and **M.W. Tay,** "The la particle in Singapore English", in Crewe 1977a: 141-56.

958 ---, ---, "Norm and variability in language use and language learning", in Smith 1979: 40-56.

959 **Rickford, John R.,** "The insights of a mesolect", in DeCamp/Hancock 1974: 92-117.

960 ---, ed., A Festival of Guyanese Words. Georgetown: U. of Guyana 1976, 2nd. ed. 1978.

961 ---, "Cut eye and suck-teeth: African words and gestures in new world guise", Journal of African Folklore (July/Sept. 1976).

962 ---, "The field of pidgin-creole studies: a review article on Loreto Todd's Pidgins and Creoles ...", World Literature in English 16 (1977): 477-511.

963 ---, "Variation in a creole continuum: quantitative and implicational approaches." Ph.D. U. of Pennsylvania 1979. DAI 40: 6, 3273A. Book version New York: Academic Press (forthcoming).

964 ---, "How does doz disappear?" in Day 1980: 77-96.

965 ---, "Analyzing variation in creole languages", in Valdman/Highfield 1980: 165-84.

966 ---, "Decreolization paths for Guyanese singular pronouns", in Gilbert 1984.

967 ---, "What happens in decreolization", in Andersen 1983.

968 ---, ed., Guayana. VEAW Text Series. Amsterdam: Benjamins (forthcoming).

969 **Riemenschneider, Dieter,** Grundlagen zur Literatur in englischer Sprache: West- und Ostafrika. München: Fink 1983.

970 **Riley, G.A.,** "A sociolinguistic study of language in the Territory of Guam." Ph.D. New Mexico 1974. DAI 35: 9, 6122A.

971 **Roberts, Peter A.,** Speech of 6 Year Old Jamaican Children. SCL, Occ. Paper 1 (1973).

972 ---, "Hypercorrection as systematic variation", in Cave 1976.

973 ---, "Duont: a case for spontaneous development", JCS 1,1 (1977): 101-8.

974 ---, "The adequacy of certain theories in accounting for important grammatical relationships in a creole language", in Day 1980: 19-38.

975 **Rodney, Ruby Veronica,** "Analysis: Guyanese Creole and American Black English with special emphasis on tense and aspect." Ed.D. Rutgers U. 1981. DAI 42: 4, 1520A.

976 **Romanyuk, L.E.,** "Substantival and verbal set-phrases in Australian English." Candidate Thesis, Moscow 1979.

977 **Ross, Alan S.C.** and **A.W. Moverley,** The Pitcairnese Language. London: Deutsch 1964.

978 **Rotimi, Ola,** Dictionary of Nigerian Pidgin English. 1977 (mimeo).

979 **Rountree, S.C.,** "Saramaccan tone in relation to intonation and grammar", Lingua 29 (1972): 308-25.

980 **Rubdy, Rani Sumant,** "A phonological analysis of English spoken by Marathi speakers from Maharashtra", CIEFL Bulletin (1974/75).

981 **Ryan, J.S.,** "Isolation and generation within a conservative framework. A unique dialect situation for English", Orbis 15 (1966): 35-50.

982 ---, "Austral English and the native languages: problems confronting the researcher", Zeitschrift für Mundartforschung N.F. 4 (1968): 743-60.

983 ---, "Blayk is white on the Bay Islands", U. of Michigan WPL 1,2 (1973): 128-39.

984 **Sabbagha, N.G.,** "English, South African", in Standard Encyclopedia of Southern Africa, vol. 4. Cape Town: Nasou 1971: 323-8.

985 **Sabino, Robin,** "A preliminary examination of the + intermittent dichotomy as it relates to aspect marking in Virgin Islands English Creole", AnL 23,2 (1981): 88ff.

986 **Sadler, Wesley,** Tok Pisin, a Handbook for Writers. Port Moresby: U. of PNG 1974.

987 **Sadtono, Eugenius,** "Problems and progress in teaching English as a foreign language in Indonesia", in Feitelson 1979: 32-45.

988 **Salami, A.,** "Defining a 'Standard Nigerian English'", Journal of the Nigeria English Studies Association 2,2 (1968): 99-106.

989 **Samarin, William,** "Standardization and instrumentalization of creole languages", in Valdman/Highfield 1980: 213-36. (Tok Pisin)

990 **Samonte, A.L.,** "Teaching English for international and intranational purposes: the Philippine context", in Smith 1981: 74-82.

991 **Sandefur, John R.,** An Australian Creole in the Northern Territory: A Description of Ngukurr-Bamyili Dialects (Part 1). Berrimah, N.T., Aus.: SIL 1979.

992 --- and **J.L.,** Beginnings of a Ngukurr-Bamyili Creole Dictionary. Berrimah, N.T.: SIL 1979.

993 ---, "Kriol and the question of decreolization", IJSL 36 (1982): 5-13.

994 ---, "Modern Australian Aboriginal languages: the present state of knowledge", EWW 4,1 (1983): 43-68.

995 ---, "Dynamics of an Australian creole system", 15th Pacific Science Congress 1983; Proc. in PacL (forthcoming).

996 **Sandell, Liza,** English Language in Sudan: A History of its Teaching and Politics. London: Ithaca Press 1982.

997 **Sankoff, Gillian,** "Sampela nupela lo i kamap long Tok Pisin", in McElhanon 1975: 235-40.

998 ---, "Political power and linguistic inequality in Papua New Guinea", in W.M. O'Barr and J.F. O'Barr, eds., Language and Politics. The Hague: Mouton 1976; repr. in 1980: 5-27.

999 ---, "Multilingualism in Papua New Guinea", in Wurm 1977: 265-307; repr. in 1980: 95-132.

1000 ---, "Creolization and syntactic change in New Guinea Tok Pisin", in B.G. Blount and M. Sanchez, eds., Sociocultural Dimensions of Language Change. New York 1977: 117-30.

1001 ---, "Variability and explanation in language and culture: cliticization in New Guinea Tok Pisin", in M. Saville-Troike, ed., GURT 1977; repr. in 1980: 257-70.

1002 ---, The Social Life of Language. Pennsylvania UP 1980. (Tok Pisin)

1003 ---, "Variation, pidgins and creoles", in Valdman/Highfield 1980: 139-64.

1004 --- and **P. Brown,** "The origins of syntax in discourse: a case study of Tok Pisin relatives", Language 52 (1976): 631-66; repr. in 1980: 211-55.

1005 --- and **S. Laberge,** "On the acquisition of native speakers by a language", Kivung 6 (1973): 32-47; repr. in DeCamp/Hancock 1974: 73-84, and in 1980: 195-209.

1006 **Sato, C.J.,** "Variation in Hawaiian Pidgin and Creole English: go + verb constructions", M.A. Hawaii 1978.

1007 **Savard, J.-G.** and **R. Vigneault,** eds., Les états multilingues: problèmes et solutions. Québec: U. Laval 1975.

1008 **Schlemmer, Lawrence,** "English-speaking South Africans today: identity and integration into the broader national community", in de Villiers 1976: 91-135.

1009 **Schmied, Josef,** "Englisch in Afrika und Vorderasien", in Englisch - Formen und Funktionen einer Weltsprache 1983: 87-116.

1010 **Schneider, Edgar,** "Englisch in der Karibik", in Englisch - Formen und Funktionen einer Weltsprache 1983: 73-85.

1011 **Schneider, Gilbert D.,** Preliminary Glossary: English / Pidgin-English (WesKos). Athens, Ohio: Center for Int. Studies 1965.

1012 ---, West African Pidgin English: a Descriptive Linguistic Approach. Athens, Ohio, 1966.

1013 ---, "West African Pidgin English - an overview: phonology, morphology", JEL 1 (1967): 49-56.

1014 **Schuchardt, Hugo,** The Ethnography of Variation. Selected Writings on Pidgins and Creoles. Edited and translated by Tom L. Markey. Introduction by Derek Bickerton. Ann Arbor: Karoma 1979.

1015 ---, Pidgin and Creole Languages. Selected Essays... Edited and translated by Glenn G. Gilbert. London: Oxford UP 1980.

1016 **Schulz, R.,** "Warum das Englisch nicht Welthilfssprache sein kann", in Ingeborg Meyer, ed., Fünftes Werkstattgespräch Interlinguistik... Paderborn: FEoLL 1981: 66-78.

1017 **Schumann, J.H.** et al., New Frontiers in Second Language Teaching. Rowley, Mass.: Newbury 1974.

1018 ---, "The relationship of pidginization, creolization and decreolization to second language acquisition", LL 28,2 (1978): 367-79.

1019 **Schuring, G.K.,** A Multilingual Society: English and Afrikaans Amongst Blacks in the RSA. Pretoria: HSRC 1979.

1020 **Scotton, C. Myers,** Choosing a Lingua Franca in an African Capital. Edmonton 1972.

1021 ---, "Multilingualism in Lagos - What it means to the social scientist", Ohio WPL 19 (1975): 78-90.

1022 ---, "Strategies of neutrality: language choice in uncertain situations", Language 52 (1976): 919-41.

1023 ---, "The role of norms and other factors in language choice in work situations in three African cities (Lagos, Kampala, Nairobi)", in Verdoodt/Kjolseth 1976: 201-32.

1024 ---, "Language in East Africa. Linguistic patterns and political ideologies", in Fishman 1978: 719-59.

1025 --- and **W. Urey,** "Bilingual strategies: the social functions of code-switching", IJSL 13 (1977), and Linguistics 193 (1977): 5-20.

1026 ---, "The linguistic situation and language policy in Eastern Africa", Annual Review of Applied Linguistics 3 (1982): 8-20.

1027 **Sčur, G.S.** and **N.K. Erochina,** "Variativnost' v glagol'nyx slovosočetanijax v anglijskom jazyke Indii" (Variation in verb phrases in English of India), ZPSK 33 (1979): 439-44.

1028 **Searle, C.,** The Forsaken Lover: White Words and Black People. London 1972.

1029 **Senghor, Leopold S.,** "The essence of language: English and French", Cultures 2,2 (1975): 75-98.

1030 **Serpell, Robert,** "Learning to say it better: a challenge for Zambian education", Bulletin of the Zambia Language Group (1975); repr. in Pride 1982: 100-18.

1031 **Seshakri, C.K.,** "English in India - a historical perspective", Journal of the U. of Baroda, Hum. 25-26 (1976-77): 13-30.

1032 **Sethi, J.,** "Consonant clusters in educated Panjabi-speakers' English", CIEFL Bulletin 16,1 (1979): 7-29.

1033 ---, "The consonant system in educated Panjabi-speakers' English", CIEFL Bulletin 15,2 (1979): 21-36.

1034 ---, "The vowel system in educated Punjabi-speakers' English", JIPA 10 (1980): 64-73.

1035 **Sey, Kofi A.,** Ghanaian English. London: Macmillan 1973.

1036 **Sharp, D.,** Language in Bilingual Communities. London 1973.

1037 **Sharpe, Margaret C.,** "Notes on the 'pidgin English' creole of Roper River", Australian Institute of Aboriginal Studies Newsletter, n.s. 2 (1974): 2-12, LingC 13 (1975): 38-60, and PacL A36, Canberra 1975: 1-20.

1038 ---, "The English of Alice Springs Aboriginal children", in S.A. Wurm, ed., Australian Linguistic Studies, PacL C54, Canberra 1979.

1039 ---, "Kriol - an Australian language resource", 15th Pacific Science Congress 1983; Proc. in PacL (forthcoming).

1040 --- and **J. Sandefur,** "The creole language of the Katherine and Roper River areas, Northern Territory", in Clyne 1976: 63-77.

1041 **Sharwood, J.A.,** Vocabulary of the Australian Dried Vine Industry. (Occ. Papers 20) Sydney: The U. 1982.

1042 **Shaw, Willard D.,** "Asian student attitudes towards English", in L. Smith 1981: 108-22.

1043 **Sheory, Ravindra,** "A lexical and syntactic analysis of Indian journalese", CIEFL Bulletin (1971).

1044 **Shepherd, Susan Carol,** "Modals in Antiguan Creole, child language acquisition, and history." Ph.D. Stanford 1981. DAI 42: 8, 3586A.

1045 ---, "Creoles and language acquisition: parallels in the expression of modality", in Carrington 1983: 178-89.

1046 **Shields, A.F.,** "On the identification of Singapore English vocabulary", in Crewe 1977a: 120-40.

1047 **Shilling, Alison Watt,** "Negation in Bahamian English", in Cave 1976.

1048 ---, "Some non-standard features of Bahamian dialect syntax." Ph.D. Hawaii 1977. DAI 39: 8, 4923A.

1049 ---, "Bahamian English - a non-continuum?" in Day 1980: 133-46.

1050 **Shnukal, Anna,** "A sociolinguistic study of Australian English: phonological and syntactic variation in Cessnock, NSW." Ph.D. Georgetown U. 1978. DAI 39: 12, 7324A.

1051 --- and **Lynell Marchese,** "Creolization of Nigerian Pidgin English: a progress report", EWW 4,1 (1983): 17-26.

1052 **Shores, David L.** and **Carole P. Hines,** eds., Papers on Language Variation. SAMLA-ADS Collection. University, Ala.: Alabama UP 1977.

1053 **Sidavan, C.P.,** "Linguistic experimentation in contemporary Indian verse in English." Ph.D. Calicut 1977.

1054 **Siegel, Jeff,** "Developments in written Tok Pisin", AnL 23,1 (1981): 20-35.

1055 ---, "Tok Pisin in the media", in PacL (forthcoming).

1056 ---, "New Guinea Pidgin as a written language", 15th Pacific Science Congress 1983; Proc. in PacL (forthcoming).

1057 **Silva, Penny,** "The 1820 settlement: some aspects of its influence on the vocabulary of South African English", EinA 5,1 (1978): 61-70.

1058 **Simons, Linda,** Differences between the Pidgins of Papua New Guinea and the Solomon Islands. Honiara: SIL 1977.

1059 --- and **Hugh Young,** Pijin blong yumi: a Guide to Solomon Islands Pijin. Honiara: Solomon Islands Christian Assoc. 1978.

1060 **Singler, John V.,** "Language in Liberia in the nineteenth century: the settlers' perspective", Liberian Studies Journal 7,2 (1976-77): 73-85.

1061 ---, An Introduction to Liberian English. (Peace Corps) East Lansing: Michigan SU 1981.

1062 **Sinha, S.P.,** English in India. A Historical Study with Particular Reference to English Education in India. Patna: Janaki Prakashan 1978 (= Ph.D. Bhagalpur 1969).

1063 **Sisson, Ralph Richard,** "A comparative analysis of the speech sound system of Southern British English and Hindi." Ph.D. New York 1968.

1064 ---, "The description and comparison of stress in Southern British English and Hindi", Linguistics 68 (1971): 35-60.

1065 **Skinner, David** and **Barbara E. Harrell-Bond,** "Misunderstandings arising from the use of the term 'creole' in the literature on Sierra Leone", Journal of the International African Institute (London) 47 (1977): 305-20.

1066 **Smeall, C.,** "A quantitative analysis of variation: i in Tok Pisin", Berkeley Linguistics Society 1 (1975): 403-9.

1067 **Smith, Anne-Marie,** The Papua New Guinea Dialect of English. (ERU Research Report 15) University, Papua New Guinea, 1978.

1068 **Smith, Larry E.,** ed., English for Cross-Cultural Communication. London, New York: Macmillan 1981.

1069 ---, ed., Readings in English as an International Language. Oxford: Pergamon 1983.

1070 ---, "English as an international auxiliary language", RELCJ 7,2 (1976); repr. in Smith 1983: 1-5.

1071 ---, "English as an international language", Gaikokugo 3 (1981); repr. in Smith 1983: 7-11.

1072 --- and **Khalilullah Rafiqzad,** "English for cross-cultural communication: the question of intelligibility", TESOLQ 13 (1979): 371-80; repr. in Smith 1983: 49-58.

1073 --- and **John A. Bisazza,** "The comprehensibility of three varieties of English for college students in seven countries", LL 32,2 (1982): 259-70; repr. in Smith 1983: 59-67.

1074 **Smithies, M.,** "English as a university language: the case of the Papua New Guinea University of Technology", EAW 25 (1981): 6-8.

1075 **Söderlind, J.,** "Recording non-native English", Studia Neophilologica 53,1 (1981): 63-68.

1076 **Solomon, D.,** "Foreign language, native language, standard dialect: and examination of teaching theory", Caribbean Journal of Education (1976): 158-83.

1077 **Sommer, Bruce A.,** "Aboriginal non-standard English", English in Australia 26 (1974): 39-46.

1078 --- and **J. Marsh,** "Vernacular and English: language comprehension of some North Queensland Aborigines", AnL 11 (1970): 48-57.

1079 **Southers, Donna E.,** "A transformational analysis of Tobagonian Creole English." Ph.D. U. of N. Carolina 1975. DAI 36: 10, 6652A.

1080 **Spencer, John,** "The Anglo-Indians and their speech. A socio-linguistic essay", Lingua 16 (1966): 57-70.

1081 ---, "Language policies of the colonial powers and their legacies", CTL 7 (1971): 537-47.

1082 ---, ed., The English Language in West Africa. London: Longman 1971.

1083 **Spitzbardt, Harry,** "Zur Frage der Sprachplanung in den jungen Nationalstaaten", ZPSK 26 (1973): 533-54.

1084 ---, English in India. Halle/S.: Niemeyer 1976.

1085 **Spitzer, Leo,** "Creole attitudes toward Krio: an historical survey", Sierra Leone Language Review 5 (1966): 39-49.

1086 **Spolsky, Bernard** and **Robert L. Cooper,** eds., Case Studies in Bilingual Education. Rowley, Mass.: Newbury 1978.

1087 **Spragg, Myles Marva,** "Origin and nature of the English dialect of Colon and its implications for the teaching of Standard English." B.A. U. of Panama 1973.

1088 **Sprauve, Gilbert A.,** "Toward a reconstruction of Virgin Islands English phonology." Ph.D. Princeton U. 1974. DAI 36: 3, 1478A.

1089 **Sridhar, Kamal Keskar,** "The development of English as an elite language in the multilingual context of India: its educational implications." Ph.D. Illinois 1977. DAI 38: 6, 3390A.

1090 ---, "English in the socio-cultural context of India", Studies in Language Learning 2,2 (1979): 63-79.

1091 **Sridhar, S.N.,** "English as the language of wider communication in India", in R.N. Srivastava, ed., Visions of India. New Delhi 1978.

1092 ---, "Non-native literatures: context and relevance", in Kachru 1982: 291-306.

1093 **Stanlaw, James,** "English in Japanese communicative strategies", in Kachru 1982: 168-97.

1094 **Stauble, A.E.,** "Decreolization: a model for second language development", LL 28 (1978): 29-54.

1095 **Steffensen, Margaret S.,** "Reduplication in Bamyili Creole", Papers in Pidgin and Creole Linguistics, PacL A57, Canberra 1979: 119-33.

1096 **Stephenson, C.,** "Det indo-engelska språkets och litteraturens uppkomst", Bonniers literära magasin 42 (Stockholm, 1973): 251-61.

1097 **Stevens, Paul,** "A bibliography of Caribbean sociolinguistics", Sociolinguistics Newsletter 11,2 (1980): 32-37.

1098 **Stilz, Gerhard,** Grundlagen zur Literatur in englischer Sprache: Indien. München: Fink 1982.

1099 **Strevens, Peter,** "Pronunciation of English in West Africa", in his Papers in Language and Language Teaching. Oxford: UP 1965.

1100 ---, "English as an international language: when is a local form of English a suitable target for ELT purposes?" ELT Documents (1977).

1101 ---, "Forms of English: an analysis of the variables", in Smith 1981: 1-14.

1102 ---, "The localized forms of English", in Kachru 1982: 23-30.

1103 ---, "World English and the world's Englishes - or, whose language is it anyway?" Journal of the Royal Society of Arts 130 (June 1982): 418-31.

1104 ---, "The state of the English language in 1980: an essay in geolinguistics", Recherches et Echanges (Paris, 1983) (forthcoming).

1105 ---, "Teachers of - what? A global look at the 'E' of TESOL", TESOL Convention, May 1982, in Proceedings (forthcoming).

1106 **Strickert, Frederick,** Diksenari bilong Nupela Testeman. Madang: Kristen Pres 1978.

1107 **Subramanian, K.,** "Penchant for the florid", ETF 15 (1977); Mohan 1978: 203-6.

1108 **Sukwiwat, Mayuri,** "Crossing the cultural threshold: a challenge to users of EIL", in Smith 1981: 216-24.

1109 ---, "Interpreting the Thai variety of English: a functional approach", in Noss 1983: 190-212.

1110 **Sutton, P.,** "Cape Barren English", LingC 13 (1975): 61-97.

1111 **Tabouret-Keller, Andrée,** "Language use in relation to the growth of towns in West Africa: a survey", Intern. Migration Review 5 (1971): 180-203.

1112 ---, "'They don't fool around with the creole much, as with the Spanish': a family case in San Ignacio, Cayo District (Belize)", York PL 9 (1980): 241-60.

1113 --- and **Robert LePage,** "A longitudinal study of the expansion of the use of Creole in its relation to Belizean identity in Cayo district", in Carrington 1983: 277-99.

1114 **Tadadjeu, M.,** "Language planning on Cameroon: toward a trilingual education system", Ohio WPL 19 (1975): 53-75.

1115 **Taiwo, O.,** "Varieties of English in Nkem Nwankwo's novels", in Ubahakwe 1979: 54-76.

1116 **Tambiah, S.J.,** "The politics of language in India and Ceylon", Modern Asian Studies 1,3 (1967): 215-40.

1117 **Tavadia, A.M.,** "Erratic behaviour of nouns and verbs in Indian English: a study in generative semantics." Ph.D. Delhi 1971.

1118 **Tay, Mary W.J.,** "The uses, users and features of English in Singapore", in Richards 1979: 91-111, Pride 1982: 51-70.

1119 ---, "The phonology of Educated Singapore English", EWW 3 (1982): 135-45.

1120 --- and **Anthea Frazer Gupta,** "Towards a description of Standard Singapore English", in Noss 1983: 173-89.

1121 **Taylor, B.A.,** "Towards a structural and lexical analysis of 'swearing' and the language of abuse in Australian English", Linguistics 164 (1975): 17-43.

1122 **Taylor, Douglas,** "New languages for old in the West Indies", in Fishman 1968: 607-19.

1123 ---, Languages of the West Indies. Baltimore: J. Hopkins UP 1977.

1124 **Taylor, D.S.,** "Non-native speakers and the rhythm of English", IRAL 19,3 (1981): 219-26.

1125 **Taylor, Harvey M.** and **A.V. Knishna Rao,** "Indian English 'errors' and American English usage", IRAL 19,2 (1981): 137-47.

1126 **Taylor, Susan,** "A preliminary study of the stress system in Indian English." Ph.D. Urbana 1967.

1127 **Teck, Goh Yee,** "Students' perception and attitude towards the varieties of English spoken in Singapore", in Noss 1983: 251-77.

1128 **Thomas, J.,** "ESL, ELS, EFL ... Yes, but EIAL?" *RELC* 9,1 (1978).

1129 **Thundy, Zacharias,** "The origins of Indian English", *CIEFL Bulletin* 12 (Hyderabad, 1976): 29-40.

1130 **Tiffen, B.W.,** "The intelligibility of Nigerian English." Ph.D. London 1974.

1131 ---, "The intelligibility of African English", *ELT Documents* 2 (1974): 10-12.

1132 **Todd, Loreto,** "Pidgin English of West Cameroon." M.A. Belfast U. 1969.

1133 ---, "Pidgin English of West Cameroon", *Camelang* 1 (Cameroon, 1969): 35-57.

1134 ---, "'To be or not to be' - What would Hamlet have said in Cameroonian Pidgin. An analysis of Cameroon Pidgin's BE verb", *ArL* 4 (1973): 1-15.

1135 ---, *Pidgins and Creoles.* London: Routledge 1974.

1136 ---, "Base-form and substratum: two case studies of English in contact." Ph.D. Leeds 1975.

1137 ---, "Cameroon Pidgin in transition", in Cave 1976.

1138 ---, "Lexical patterning in Cameroon Pidgin and Tok Pisin", *JCS* 1 (1977): 59-72.

1139 ---, *Some Day Been Dey. West African Pidgin Folktales.* London: Routledge 1979.

1140 ---, "Cameroonian: a consideration of 'What's in a name?'", in Hancock 1979: 281-94.

1141 ---, "Language options for education in a multilingual society: Cameroon", *Polyglot* (1980).

1142 ---, "The English language in West Africa", in Bailey/Görlach 1982: 281-305.

1143 ---, *Cameroon.* (VEAW T1) Heidelberg: Groos 1982 (with cassette).

1144 ---, "Education in Cameroon: Education in a multilingual society", in Pride 1982: 119-37.

1145 ---, "The CM2 process: a selection of riddles in Cameroon Pidgin English", in Gilbert 1984.

1146 ---, Modern Englishes: Pidgins and Creoles. London: Deutsch (forthcoming).

1147 --- and **P. Mühlhäusler,** "Idiomatic expressions in Cameroon Pidgin English and Tok Pisin", Papers in Pidgin and Creole Linguistics, PacL A58, Canberra 1979: 1-35.

1148 **Tongue, R.K.,** The English of Singapore and Malaysia. Singapore: Eastern UP 1974.

1149 **Tonkin, J. Elizabeth,** "Some aspects of language from the viewpoint of social anthropology, with particular reference to multilingual situations in Nigeria." Ph.D. Oxford 1970.

1150 ---, "Some coastal pidgins of West Africa", in E. Ardener, ed., Social Anthropology and Language. Tavistock 1971: 129-55.

1151 ---, "Uses of pidgin in the early literate English of Nigeria", in Hancock 1979: 303-8.

1152 **Topping, Donald M.,** "Language planning issues in Vanuatu", Language Planning Newsletter 8,2 (1982): 1-3, 6.

1153 **Traugott, Elizabeth Closs,** "Pidgins, creoles and the origins of vernacular Black English", in D.S. Harrison and T. Trabasso, eds., Black English: A Seminar. Hillsdale, N.J.: Lawrence Erlbaum 1976: 57-93.

1154 ---, "Pidginization, creolization, and language change", in Valdman 1977: 70-98.

1155 ---, "Pidginization, creolization, and the 'naturalness' hypothesis", in W.C. McCormack and S.A. Wurm, eds., Approaches to Language. Anthropological Issues. The Hague: Mouton 1978: 135-50.

1156 --- and **John Rickford,** "Pidgins and creoles", in Greenbaum 1984.

1157 **Treffgarne, Carew,** The Role of English and French as Languages of Communication between Anglophone and Francophone West African States. London: Africa Educational Trust 1975.

1158 **Trifonovitch, G.,** "English as an international language: an attitudinal approach", in Smith 1981: 211-5.

1159 **Tryon, Darrell T.,** "The language situation in the New Hebrides", in Wurm 1979: 11-31.

1160 ---, "Remarks on the language situation in the Solomon Islands", in Wurm 1979: 33-51.

1161 **T'sou, Benjamin K.,** "Aspects of a Chinese-English creole: a study in semilingualism", paper RELC 1981.

1162 **Tsuzaki, Stanley M.,** "Problems in the study of Hawaiian English", Hawaii WPL 1,3 (1969): 117-33.

1163 ---, ed., The English Language in Hawaii: a Book of Readings. Honolulu: UP 1971.

1164 ---, "Coexistent systems in language variation: the case of Hawaiian English", in Hymes 1971: 327-40.

1165 **Tucker, G.R.,** "A survey of English use in Jordan", in Fishman 1978: 587-632.

1166 **Tunstall, Jeremy,** The Media are American. Anglo-American Media in the World. London: Constable 1977.

1167 **Turner, G.W.,** The English Language in Australia and New Zealand. London: Longman 1966, 2nd ed. 1972.

1168 ---, "New Zealand English today", in Ramson 1970: 84-101.

1169 ---, "Good English in Australia and New Zealand", in Turner 1972: 11-31.

1170 ---, ed., Good Australian English and Good New Zealand English. Sydney: Reed Educ. 1972.

1171 **Ubahakwe, Ebo,** "The dilemma in teaching English in Nigeria as a language of international communication", ELTJ 34 (1979): 156-63.

1172 ---, ed., Varieties and Functions of English in Nigeria. Ibadan: African UP 1979.

1173 **Ullrich, Helen E.,** "Rural and urban multilingualism: a south Indian case", IJSL 34 (1982): 25-50.

1174 **United Nations,** Toward a Language Policy for Namibia. English as the Official Language: Perspectives and Strategies. Lusaka: UN Institute for Namibia 1981.

1175 **Valdman, Albert,** ed., Pidgin and Creole Linguistics. Bloomington: Indiana UP 1977.

1176 ---, Le créole. Structure, statut, et origine. Paris: Klincksieck 1978.

1177 --- and **J.S. Phillips,** "Pidginization, creolization and the elaboration of learner systems", Colloque Theoretical Models in Applied Linguistics IV. U. de Neuchatel 1975.

1178 --- and **Arnold Highfield,** eds., Theoretical Orientations in Creole Studies. New York: Academic Press 1980.

1179 **Valentine, Elias,** "The phonology of Anglo-Indian English." Ph.D. CIEFL, Hyderabad 1969.

1180 ---, "Some non-segmental features of Anglo-Indian English", in Manuel/Paniker 1978: 190-212.

1181 **Vanderslice, Ralph** and **Laura S. Pierson,** "Prosodic features of Hawaiian English", The Quarterly Journal of Speech 53 (1967): 156-66.

1182 **Van Valkenburg, David,** "Some features of Belize Creole." B.A. Stanford U. 1977.

1183 **Van Wyk, E.B.,** "Language contact and bilingualism", in Lanham/ Prinsloo 1978: 29-52.

1184 "Varieties of English: a worldwide question", ETF (1977): 22-35.

1185 Varieties of English Around the World. Monograph series, ed. M. Görlach. Heidelberg: J. Groos 1979-83; Amsterdam: Benjamins 1983-

1186 **Varma, Manindra,** "A synchronic comparative study of the structure of the noun phrase in English and Hindi." Ph.D. Ann Arbor 1966.

1187 **Venter, J.A.,** "Twelve years of English teaching in Afrikaans schools", EUSA 6,2 (1975): 1-12.

1188 **Verdoodt, A.** and **R. Kjolseth,** eds., Language in Sociology. Louvain: Ed. Peeters 1976.

1189 **Verma, Shivendra Kishore,** "A linguist's view of English in India", Indian and Foreign Review 10 (1972).

1190 ---, "The systemicness of Indian English", ITL 22 (1973): 1-9.

1191 ---, "Code-switching between Hindi and English", Lingua 38 (1971): 153-65.

1192 ---, "Syntactic irregularities of Indian English", in Mohan 1978: 207-20.

1193 ---, "Swadeshi English: form and function", in Pride 1982: 174-87.

1194 **Verma, Y.P.,** "The role of English in Nepal, with particular reference to the English language press." Ph.D. Kathmandu 1973.

1195 **Vermeer, H.J.,** Das Indo-Englische. Situation und linguistische Bedeutung. Heidelberg: Groos 1969.

1196 **Viereck, Wolfgang,** "Englisch als Weltsprache", in Englisch - Formen und Funktionen einer Weltsprache 1983: 9-25.

1197 ---, "Englisch in Ozeanien", in Englisch - Formen und Funktionen einer Weltsprache 1983: 155-81.

1198 **Voorhoeve, Jan,** "The regularity of sound correspondences in a creole language (Sranan)", JAL 9 (1970): 51-69.

1199 ---, "Varieties of creole in Suriname: church creole and pagan cult languages", in Hymes 1971: 305-15.

1200 ---, "Historical and linguistic evidence in favour of the relexification theory in the formation of the creoles", LSoc 2 (1973): 133-45.

1201 ---, "De oorsprong van het Sranan Tongo", Forum der Letteren 18 (1977): 139-49.

1202 **Vorster, J.** and **L. Proctor,** "Black attitudes to 'white' languages in South Africa: a pilot study", Journal of Psychology 92 (1976): 103-8.

1203 **Wächtler, Kurt,** Geographie und Stratifikation der englischen Sprache. Düsseldorf: Bagel 1977.

1204 **Walsh, D.S.,** "Tok Pisin syntax - the Austronesian factor", Papers in Pidgin and Creole Linguistics, PacL A58, Canberra 1979: 185-98.

1205 **Walsh, N.G.,** "Distinguishing types and varieties of English in Nigeria", Journal of the Nigerian English Studies Association 2 (1967): 47-55.

1206 **Warantz, Elissa,** "The Bay Islands English of Honduras", in Holm 1983: 71-94.

1207 **Warner, K.,** "Creole languages and national identity in the Caribbean", CLA Journal 20,3 (1977).

1208 **Warner, M.P.,** "Language in Trinidad, with special reference to English." M.Phil. York 1967.

1209 **Washabaugh, William,** "Variability in decreolization on Providence Island, Columbia." Ph.D. Wayne SU. 1974. DAI 35: 12, 7895A.

1210 ---, "Constraining variation in decreolization", Language 53 (1977): 329-52.

1211 ---, "Decreolization and second-language acquisition", in F.R. Eckman, ed., Current Themes in Linguistics. New York: Wiley 1977: 71-97.

1212 ---, "Complexities in creole continua", Lingua 46 (1978): 245-62.

1213 ---, "From preposition to complementizer in Caribbean English Creole", in Day 1980: 97-110.

1214 ---, "Brainstorming creole languages", in Valdman/Highfield 1980: 129-38.

1215 ---, "Pursuing creole roots", in Muysken 1981: 85-102. (San Andres / Providencia)

1216 ---, "The creoles of the off-shore islands: Providencia, San Andrés and the Caymans", in Holm 1983: 157-79.

1217 ---, "Communicative action and the standardization of creole languages", in Gilbert 1984.

1218 --- and **Sidney M. Greenfield,** "The development of Atlantic creole languages", in Woolford/Washabaugh 1983: 106-19.

1219 **Watson, J.K.P.,** "Cultural pluralism, nation-building and educational policies in Peninsular Malaysia", JMMD 1,2 (1980): 155-74.

1220 **Watts, H.L.,** "A social and demographic portrait of English-speaking white South Africans", in de Villiers 1976: 41-90.

1221 **Weir, Ann Lowry,** "Style range in new English literatures", in Kachru 1982: 307-22.

1222 **Welch, F.,** "The danger of de-standardizing English", Lugha 4,1 (1974): 12-16.

1223 **Wells, John C.,** Accents of English. Vol. 3 Beyond the British Isles. Cambridge: UP 1982.

1224 ---, "The Irish element in Montserrat Creole", in Carrington 198

1225 **Whinnom, K.,** "Linguistic hybridization and the 'special' case of pidgins and creoles", in Hymes 1971: 91-116.

1226 **Whiteley, W.H.,** ed., Language Use and Social Change: Problems of Multilingualism with Special Reference to Eastern Africa. London: 1971a.

1227 ---, ed., Language in Kenya. Nairobi 1971b.

1228 ---, "Language policies of independent African states", CTL 7 (1971): 548-58.

1229 **Wickramasuriya, B.S.S.A.,** "The nominal phrase in Sinhalese and its bearing on Sinhalese English." M.A. London 1965.

1230 **Wilkes, G.A.,** Dictionary of Australian Colloquialisms. Sydney: UP 1978.

1231 **Willeford, Mary Jo,** "Africanisms in the Bajan dialect", Bim 12 (1968): 90-97.

1232 **Williams, Wayne R.,** "Serial verb constructions in Krio", Studies in African Linguistics, suppl. 2 (1971): 47-65.

1233 ---, "Variation in the Krio speech community", Ohio WPL 20 (1975): 279-93.

1234 ---, "Linguistic change in the syntax and semantics of Sierra Leone Krio." Ph.D. Indiana 1976. DAI 37: 8, 5097A.

1235 ---, "The so-called relativized and cleft predicates in Krio: one step closer to an understanding of creolization", in Kotey/Der-Houssikian 1977: 467-78.

1236 **Willmott, M.B.,** "Variety signifiers in Nigerian English", ELTJ 33,3 (1979): 227-33.

1237 **Winer, Lise,** Dictionary of Trinidadian English. (forthcoming).

1238 ---, "A classification of language continua", in Gilbert 1984.

1239 **Winford, D.,** "A sociolinguistic description of two communities in Trinidad." Ph.D. York 1972.

1240 ---, "Aspects of the social differentiation in Trinidad", Caribbean Issues 1 (1974).

1241 ---, "Teachers' attitudes toward language varieties in a creole community", in Berry 1976: 45-75.

1242 ---, "Phonological hypercorrection in the process of decreolization - the case of Trinidadian English", JL 14 (1978): 277-91.

1243 ---, Phonological Variation and Change in Trinidadian English - the Evolution of the Vowel System. SCL, Occ. Paper 12 (1979).

1244 ---, "The creole situation in the context of sociolinguistic studies", in Day 1980: 51-76.

1245 ---, "A sociolinguistic analysis of negation in Trinidad English", in Carrington 1983: 203-10.

1246 **Wolfe, Terry A.,** "An exploratory study of the morphology and syntax of the English of the Province of Limon, Costa Rica." Ph.D. U. de Costa Rica 1970.

1247 **Wolfers, E.P.,** "The vocabulary of New Guinea English as used by expatriates", Kivung 2 (1969): 52-64.

1248 **Wong, Irene F.H.,** "English in Malaysia", in Smith 1981: 94-107.

1249 ---, "Native-speaker English for the Third World today?" in Pride 1982: 259-86.

1250 ---, "Simplification features in the structure of colloquial Malaysian English", in Noss 1983: 125-49.

1251 **Wood, Richard E.,** "English in international broadcasting", EAW 15 (1976): 1-3, 6-7.

1252 ---, "Visible language policy - bilingualism and multilingualism on postage stamps", Visible Language 14 (1980): 30-51.

1253 **Woolford, Ellen,** "Variation and change in the i 'predicate marker' of New Guinea Tok Pisin", Papers in Pidgin and Creole Linguistics 2, PacL A57, Canberra 1979: 37-50.

1254 ---, "Aspects of Tok Pisin grammar." Ph.D. Duke U. 1977; DAI 38: 12, 7307A; pr. PacL B66, Canberra 1979.

1255 ---, "The developing complementiser system in Tok Pisin", in Muysken 1981: 125-40.

1256 --- and **William Washabaugh,** eds., The Social Context of Creolization. Ann Arbor: Karoma 1983.

1257 **Wright, M. Fernando,** "Limon Creole: a syntactic analysis." Ph.D. U. de Costa Rica 1974.

1258 **Wurm, Stephen A.,** "Papua New Guinea nationhood: the problem of a national language", Journal of the Papua New Guinea Society 1,1 (1967): 1-13.

1259 ---, New Guinea Highlands Pidgin: Course Materials. PacL D3, Canberra 1971.

1260 ---, "The question of language standardisation and pidgin", in McElhanon 1975: 108-20.

1261 ---, "Pidgins, creoles, lingue franche, and national development", in Valdman 1977: 333-57.

1262 ---, ed., New Guinea Area Languages and Language Study. 2 vols. PacL C40, Canberra 1977.

1263 ---, "Descriptive and prescriptive grammar in New Guinea Pidgin", in Papers in Pidgin and Creole Linguistics, PacL A58, Canberra 1979: 175-83.

1264 ---, "Language planning and New Guinea Pidgin", Papers in Pidgin and Creole Linguistics, PacL A58, Canberra 1979: 37-51.

1265 ---, "The language situation in the New Guinea area", in Wurm 1979: 3-10.

1266 ---, ed., New Guinea and Neighboring Areas: A Sociolinguistic Laboratory. The Hague: Mouton 1979.

1267 ---, "Standardisation and instrumentalisation in Tok Pisin", in Valdman/Highfield 1980: 237-44.

1268 **Yankson, Kofi,** "The use of pidgin in No Longer at Ease and A Man of the People", Asemka 1,2 (1974): 68-80.

1269 **Young, C.,** "A study of the creolized English spoken in the City of Belize, in its cultural and social setting." Ph.D. York 1973 = Creole L. Resources Kit, York U., 1976.

1270 **Young, D.,** "'English' and 'English language' in education", in Lanham/Prinsloo 1978: 187-214.

1271 **Young, Hugh,** A Directory of Solomon Pidgin Idioms. Honiara 1976 (mimeo).

1272 **Young, P.,** "The language of West African writing in English, with special reference to Nigerian prose fiction." Ph.D. Durham 1969/70.

1273 ---, "The language of West African literature in English", in Spencer 1971b: 165-84.

1274 **Zettersten, Arne,** "The mutineers of the Bounty and the languages of their descendants", Moderna Språk 60 (1966): 393-8.

1275 ---, "The linguistic situation on Tristan da Cunha", FoLi 1 (1967): 119-24.

1276 ---, The English of Tristan da Cunha. Lund Studies in English, 37 (Lund, 1969).

1277 ---, "Studies in the Norfolkese language", Copenhagen: Dept. of English, the U. 1981 (mimeo).

1278 **Zuengler, J.E.,** "Kenyan English", in Kachru 1982: 112-24.

Index

The following list comprises

1) regions (in upper case letters). The references here are as specific as possible: for 'AFRICA' also see EAST, SOUTH and WEST AFRICA; for 'WEST AFRICA' also see CAMEROON, GHANA, LIBERIA, NIGERIA, SIERRA LEONE, etc. Classification according to regions is primary so that names of languages such as Krio or Tok Pisin are found under SIERRA LEONE or PAPUA NEW GUINEA respectively.

2) topics (in lower case letters). The listing is intended to be of practical use, and the terms are, therefore, not based on a coherent theoretical framework. It must be stressed that the publications listed often employ terms in vague or non-technical senses, or with meanings differing from those in other works. It must also be pointed out that important books (such as 129 for creolistics) may well contain seminal definitions of terms - here for instance, postcreole continuum without having the term in the title; in most such cases, reference to the term will not be made in the list. Also, handbooks such as 71 contain treatments of most of the topics here listed, but again the reference is found only under the respective areas for the chapters, and under "International English" for the book itself.

3) cross-references. In both 2) and 3) I have tried to reduce the number of concepts as much as possible in order to keep the list short and manageable. Thus, e.g., acrolect, mesolect and basilect do not occur - they are represented by the more general entries continuum or sociolect etc., whatever may be the author's focus.

In the VARIETIES OF ENGLISH AROUND THE WORLD series the following volumes have been published thusfar:

Text Series

T1. TODD, Loreto: *Cameroon*. Heidelberg (Groos), 1982.
Spoken examples on tape (ca. 56 min.)

T2. HOLM, John: *Central American English*. Heidelberg (Groos), 1982.
Spoken examples on tape (ca. 90 min.)

T3. MACAFEE, Caroline: *Glasgow*. Amsterdam, 1983.
Spoken examples on tape (60 min.)

T4. PLATT, John, Heidi WEBER & Mian Lian HO: *Singapore and Malaysia*. Amsterdam, 1983.

General Series

G1. LANHAM, L.W. & C.A. MACDONALD: *The Standard in South African English and its Social History*. Heidelberg (Groos), 1979.

G2. DAY, R.R. (ed.): *ISSUES IN ENGLISH CREOLES: Papers from the 1975 Hawaii Conference*. Heidelberg (Groos), 1980.

G3. VIERECK, Wolfgang, Edgar SCHNEIDER & Manfred GÖRLACH (comps.): *A Bibliography of Writings on Varieties of English, 1965-1983*. Amsterdam, 1984.

Scheduled for 1984:

G4. GÖRLACH, Manfred (ed.): *FOCUS ON: SCOTLAND*.

G5. VIERECK, Wolfgang (ed.): *FOCUS ON: ENGLAND AND WALES*.

- -

VARIETIES OF ENGLISH AROUND THE WORLD is a companion series of books to the journal

ENGLISH WORLD-WIDE
A journal of Varieties of English
ISSN 0172-8865

EDITORS
Manfred Görlach (*University of Heidelberg*)
Braj B. Kachru (*University of Illinois, Urbana*)
Loreto Todd (*University of Leeds*)

From vol. 4, onwards published by John Benjamins Publ. Co.
2 x p/y. ca. 320 pages.
Vol.5. 1984.

Subscr. price	Hfl.	120,--/$ 48.00
Postage	Hfl.	14,--/$ 5.00

* Private subscriptions Hfl. 60,--/$ 24.00, postage included (Prepayment required).
Back vols. 1-4 available at current subscription price.